Max Weber

SOCIOLOGICAL WRITINGS

Max Weber

SOCIOLOGICAL WRITINGS

Edited by
Wolf Heydebrand

RAWAT PUBLICATIONS
Jaipur • New Delhi • Bangalore • Hyderabad • Guwahati

ISBN 978-81-316-0500-4

Indian Reprint, 2012

Published by arrangement with **The Continuum International Publishing Group.**

First published in 2006 by
Continuum International Publishing Group
The Tower Building, 11 York Road, London SE1 7NX
80 Maiden Lane, Suite 704, New York, NY 10038

Acknowledgments will be found on page 322, which constitutes an extension of the copyright page.

Published by
Prem Rawat for **Rawat Publications**
Satyam Apts., Sector 3, Jawahar Nagar, Jaipur 302 004 (India)
Phone: 0141 265 1748 / 7006 Fax: 0141 265 1748
E-mail : info@rawatbooks.com
Website: www.rawatbooks.com

New Delhi Office
4858/24, Ansari Road, Daryaganj, New Delhi 110 002
Phone: 011-23263290

Also at *Bangalore, Hyderabad* and *Guwahati*

Printed at Chaman Enterprises, New Delhi

Contents

Introduction

Max Weber was one of the most important social thinkers of this century. He wrote on bureaucracy and politics, law and economics, science and religion. His method came to be known as interpretive sociology and he developed the ideal type, a conceptual construct used to understand highly complex and multifaceted phenomena of comparative modern history. Writing in Germany from before the turn of the century until his death in 1920, Weber described the rise of rationalism throughout the Western World. In the United States, the Chicago economist Frank H. Knight introduced Weber in 1927 through a translation of his lectures on General Economic History, and in 1930 Talcott Parsons published his translation of *The Protestant Ethic and the Spirit of Capitalism.* But Weber's influence did not spread until after World War II, starting with such well-known translations as those by Hans Gerth and C. Wright Mills in 1946 *(From Max Weber: Essays in Sociology);* Talcott Parsons in 1947 *(The Theory of Social and Economic Organization);* Edward Shils and Henry Finch in 1949 *(Max Weber on the Methodology of the Social Sciences);* Hans Gerth and Don Martindale in 1952 *(Ancient Judaism);* and Max Rheinstein and Edward Shils in 1954 *(Max Weber on Law in Economy and Society).* Only relatively recently, however, has Weber's work been made fully available and critically articulated by the scholarly efforts of the sociologists Reinhard Bendix (*Max Weber: An Intellectual Portrait,* 1977) and Guenther Roth (*Max Weber, Economy and Society,* 3 vols., 1968), among others, and only now, more than 70 years after Weber's death, can we look back with adequate comprehension on the enormous scope of his work, not to mention the vast secondary literature that has grown up around this eminent figure.

Biographical Sketch

Max Weber was born in 1864 in Erfurt, Germany, the oldest son of a public official and politician and his wife, Helene Fallenstein, who came from a wealthy Anglo-German merchant family. When he was five, his family moved to Berlin, where the young Weber grew up and lived, with only brief interruptions, in his father's house and financially dependent on him until age twenty-nine. Here, he was exposed to a circle of liberal intellectuals, politicians, and academics.

After finishing high school in 1882 and studying law, philosophy, history, and economics in Heidelberg and Goettingen, he spent a year of military service in Strassbourg, then returned to Berlin to continue his legal training. In 1889 he submitted his doctoral dissertation on the legal and economic history of medieval trading companies, but continued his practical legal training as well as his preparation for teaching law. In the early 1890s, Weber had begun to embark on a career of teaching, research, and writing in law, legal history, and political economy, and in 1894 he accepted a professorship in Freiburg and two years later a similar position at the University of Heidelberg. In 1893, he had married Marianne Schnitger, who was also a descendant of the Weber family, a patrician family of linen merchants from Bielefeld. Marianne became his life-long intellectual companion and the posthumous editor of some of his works, but Max Weber was also influenced by other relationships, notably Else von Richthofen and Mina Tobler.

While Weber began to establish his own circle of friends and intellectuals in the university town of Heidelberg, a circle which included such notables as the legal scholar Georg Jellinek, the theologian Ernst Troeltsch and others too numerous to mention, his strained relationship with his authoritarian father was not resolved, but exploded on the occasion of a visit by the parents in the summer of 1897. Weber's father died about a month later, and Weber himself suffered a mental and emotional breakdown from which he never fully recovered. Manic and depressive episodes continued to punctuate his life and prevented him from returning to full-time teaching. In 1903 he agreed to join Werner Sombart and Edgar Jaffe as one of the editors of a prominent contemporary journal, the *Archives for Social Science and Social Policy*. In 1904, Weber visited the United States for a conference at the occasion of the World's Fair in St. Louis, and presented a paper on the social structure of Germany. Upon his return to Heidelberg, Weber finished and published, among other things, his famous *The Protestant Ethic and the Spirit of Capitalism*. He continued to work as a private scholar supported, in part, by sizeable inheritances by his mother and his wife. During the subsequent decade and a half, Weber wrote furiously and produced the immense corpus of sociological and historical work for which he is justly famous. He also became politically more active, was a founding member of the German Democratic Party after World War I, and wrote about politics and the need for charismatic leadership in a time of revolutionary turmoil. He returned to university teaching briefly in 1918 and 1919 at the Universities of Vienna and Munich, but died of pneumonia a year later when he was only fifty-six years old.

Marianne Weber's biography of her husband and countless other studies of Weber's life and work all emphasize the creative tension and dualism between his enduring normative commitments and his keen, realistic appreciation of political power. This brief biographical sketch must suffice in suggesting that there was, indeed, an intimate relationship between the contingencies of his own life and the nature of his intellectual perspective which he brought to bear so productively and fruitfully on the most significant sociological and historical issues of his time as well as ours.

The Dualistic Structure of Weber's Categorical Framework

Weber's work ranges across the social sciences, from ancient to modern history, and from detailed empirical and historical studies to painstaking conceptual analysis and broad theoretical generalization. A brief introduction such as this one cannot hope to do justice to the fine detail and deep insights of a thinker of Weber's stature. I have, therefore, decided to emphasize some of the main points and recurrent themes of his approach by means of an abbreviated conceptual discussion and outline of what I consider to be the key elements of Weber's work. This outline reflects the substantive structure of this volume, the details of which are presented at the end of this introduction (A Note on the Present Edition).

Weber's categorical framework has an inherently dualistic structure, that is, it exhibits a series of nested distinctions between logically or empirically opposed concepts that are not reducible to each other. The overriding binary oppositions are those between tradition and rationality, values and interests, community and society, legitimacy and social action, and understanding and explanation. With the help of these and other subordinate distinctions, Weber sought to grasp the variety of human conduct under different social and cultural conditions, to attempt an understanding of their meaning from within human social experience, and to provide an explanation from the point of view of the detached observer.

Weber defined a social relationship as the probability of recurrent interaction among social actors. He identified four types of value orientations underlying social action: traditional (as in family and community relationships), affective (as in friendship and love relationships), value-rational (as in the inner-directed choice of a given ethical or normative value system as the basis for one's conduct), and purposive-rational (as in the instrumental, rational choice of the most cost-effective means to achieve given ends). In this typology, the first two orientations are seen as occurring in the nonrational context of primary groups and primordial communities, whereas the last two tend to occur in secondary groups such as voluntary associations and modern industrial societies. But while the first two are more or less commonsensical, the difference between value-rationality and instrumental rationality needs some explication. Value-rationality in one's orientation presupposes a conscious search among alternative values and a decisive commitment to one chosen set of values. The moral basis for this kind of decision making is what Weber calls an ethics of conviction, since one's choice will be defended no matter what the cost or consequences of one's conduct. Thus, the basis of the choice is rational, but the subsequent commitment to it is not, since it is beyond discussion, so to speak. The extreme case of value-rationality is a religious or political conviction which social actors may affirm and defend until death; for example, self-sacrifice in religious martyrdom or a holy war, or the defense of the honor of one's status group by suicide. The crucial difference between traditional and value-rational conduct is that the latter involves consciously and rationally articulated patterns of orientation and action, whereas the former does not.

Purposive or instrumental rationality is much closer to our modern notion of rationally weighing the costs and consequences of our actions and implementing our decisions on the basis of formal criteria of efficiency and cost-benefit analysis. The search for the economically and technically most efficient means to achieve given ends may dominate an actor's conduct even to the point of changing one's goals or choosing new ones. Thus, the process of rationally implementing a substantive policy may come to dominate the fate and content of the policy even if it means modifying it, lowering its claims, or abandoning it for an alternative policy rather than pursuing it irrespective of the costs. The pragmatic, everyday version of this sober evaluation of the means and resources available to implement a given policy is the notion that "the devil is in the detail." While the weighing of the consequences of one's actions leads to what Weber calls an ethics of responsibility, the practical upshot of this kind of utilitarian and instrumental rationality is to maximize one's gains and to minimize one's losses according to a formal calculus such as game theory or similar methods of rational decision making. It is the responsiveness to scaled incentives and to the systematic evaluation of positive and negative expectations or reinforcements that characterizes this type of means-ends rationality. Purposive-rationality is, according to Weber, the dominant basis of conduct in modern society.

This typology of rational and nonrational orientations, which Weber believes to be exhaustive, may serve to characterize essentially voluntary relations, agreements, and contracts among more or less equal actors who enter into relationships with each other, collectively form groups, communities, associations, and markets, and seek to pursue their material and ideal interests. Each type of relationship is meaningful to those who engage in it, and it can be understood by anyone who takes the trouble to interpret its meaning from the perspective of the actors. It can even serve to explain the varieties of social conduct under different social, economic, political, and cultural conditions. Moreover, adjudication in the arena of private law and contract can be analyzed in terms of this typology, since much of it (in the form of common law and civil law) serves to regulate and coordinate the conduct of social actors and takes cognizance of the different orientations underlying social action. It is also important to note that Weber's emphasis on social orientations includes much that psychologists might relegate to the category of individual motivation without, however, lapsing into psychological reductionism or simplistic behaviorism.

A second major typology of Weber's deals with legitimate power or authority. It parallels in many respects the previous typology, but now the accent is on the impact of values, the normative control exercised by the moral order of legitimacy, the authoritative imposition of hierarchical control, and the domination by tradition, charisma, religion, expert knowledge, and the state. Weber assumes that power—the probability that someone's will shall be obeyed by another—must be legitimate in order to be socially effective. There are four bases of legitimation which permit power to become authority. The first one is again tradition, which bestows legitimacy by default, as it were. The three great corresponding forms of traditional authority are patriarchal, patrimonial, and feudal authority. It is significant to note that modern students of Chinese, Japanese, and Korean organizations and authority structures find much that can be understood in terms of neo-traditionalism and neo-patrimonialism. The second, "affective," basis of legitimacy generates Weber's famous authority of charisma, an unstable amalgam of extraordinary personal leadership and emotionally grounded followership in structurally contingent and historically uncertain situations. The charisma of a person can be converted into the charisma of office (e.g., priest, pope, president), but in either case it is subject to the probability of routinization and the constraints of everyday life, especially if problems of securing material resources and leadership succession push the nonrational basis of charisma into a more rational and bureaucratic direction.

Of greatest interest, however, are the two rational bases of legitimacy. Substantive rationality is an attribute of a structure or policy that is governed by an ideological system such as ethics, religion, science, technical expertise, or power politics. Thus, the policies of a theocracy, a socialist state, the modern welfare state, the scientific establishment, and the modern professions such as law and medicine are substantively rational. The corresponding type of authority can be religious, political, scientific, or collegial-professional. While value-rationality in the previous typology applies to a set of values at the level of conduct, substantive rationality applies to belief systems at the level of social structure, for example, large-scale organizations, the professions, social movements, or nation-states and their policies.

In contrast to substantive rationality as a basis of legitimation, Weber defines formal-legal rationality as a relatively autonomous system of rules and abstract concepts created by legal thought itself, or by the democratic sovereign in the form of a legislature. It is this type of legitimacy which forms the basis of authority both in a law-governed state and in a bureaucracy. Thus, democracies and bureaucracies ultimately have a political underpinning and, of course, a political form of leadership at the top, but their system of positive laws and procedures, constitutional rights and guarantees, rules and regulations, due process, appeals, reviews, and checks and balances is established with a view toward creating a formal authority independent of politics and designed to protect the sanctity of rules against the encroachment by arbitrary power, substantive policy making, and ad hoc decision making. Thus bureaucratic and political authority, while representing formidable bases of power, are nevertheless bound by the legitimacy of the charter and the constitutional system of rules under which they operate.

This second typology of the forms of legitimacy and authority focuses on the normative constraints of shared values and beliefs, on the authoritative imposition of a political or legal order, and on the major types of domination and hierarchy. Insofar as it deals with law, it highlights the nature of public, statutory, and criminal law as a code of subordination rather than coordination. The second typology, then, emphasizes what could be seen as a vertical dimension of social organization, in contrast to the more horizontal nature of orientations, actions, relationships, private contracts, and the articulation and aggregation of interests that inform the first typology. Both typologies share the subordinate distinctions between nonrational and rational forms and, within the latter, between value-oriented, substantive as compared to formal, logical aspects of rationality. Thus, the categorical distinctions that differentiate between these typologies reappear within them as well, just as they pervade Weber's entire opus. Let us now take a closer look at the methodological nature of these typologies and their central ingredient, the ideal-type.

Weber's Method: The Ideal-Type

It may be useful to illustrate Weber's procedure by means of two of his most celebrated contributions to social theory: his analysis of bureaucracy and of the Protestant ethic. It will not be difficult for the careful reader to discern the inner connection and substantive correspondence between these two ideal-types, in addition to their formal similarity.

For Weber, bureaucracy, defined as a system of control based on technical knowledge, emerges as a new organizational form designed to deal with the increasingly large and complex administrative tasks of Western urban industrial societies. Weber seeks to understand this peculiarly "modern" form of organizing the state, economic corporations, and even voluntary associations such as political parties and labor unions by means of a method which became his intellectual trademark: the ideal-type. Ideal-types are conceptual or analytical models that are always constructed for comparative purposes by selecting a series of culturally significant facets of a complex socio-historical formation, relating them to each other as parts of a meaningful whole, and contrasting it with a different (often opposed) type of formation.

For example, certain aspects of the world religions can be grasped in terms of two analytical dimensions: other-worldliness vs. this-worldliness, and asceticism vs. mysticism. Thus, Buddhism is an example of other-worldly mysticism, and Roman Catholicism has aspects of other-worldly asceticism. By contrast, Confucianism can be seen as a type of mysticism, but with a this-worldly emphasis which might be a key to understanding the economic successes of some of the Pacific Rim nations. Finally, Calvinism or the "Protestant Ethic" can be understood as a form of this-worldly asceticism that emphasizes one's unique "vocation" in life, as well as the values of discipline, obedience, regularity, efficiency, and methodical rigor in one's work habits, the suppression of one's passions and desires by a kind of self-rationalization, i.e., the subordination of feelings and emotions to cognitive control and, ultimately, the devotion of one's whole life to God's plan. The individualizing outcome of these comparisons is a result of Weber's interest in explaining not only the general link between economic rationality and religious ethics, but the peculiarities of one case, viz., the possible influence of Western puritanism on the rise of European capitalism and economic rationality. In its Calvinist form, the Protestant ethic did not envisage working, saving, or conducting a business as a means for making a profit, but saw work and rational conduct as ends in themselves. As a system of religious and economic norms, the Protestant ethic is therefore not the same as the ethics of modern business management, which is oriented toward maximizing productivity and profits, but it did feed into it and thus may have helped to foster attitudes and beliefs that were favorable to the rise of Western entrepreneurial capitalism and its increasingly bureaucratic institutional forms.

In a similar fashion, the ideal-type of bureaucracy can itself be characterized by a series of salient, partly historical, partly analytic concepts. These concepts and their interrelationships form a framework, syndrome, or configuration of the most significant attributes of modern (late nineteenth century) public administration compared to traditional authority as well as prebureaucratic, nonbureaucratic, and postbureaucratic forms of administration. Among the concepts identified by Weber are the following. First, the administration of large and complex tasks is typically performed by a system of division of labor and specialization based on expertise in different spheres of competence. Second, there is a hierarchy of offices based on the super- and subordination of different levels or ranks of authority, whereby the lower levels can appeal to those above them, but the higher levels have ultimate and final authority to make decisions. It is interesting to note that while a bureaucratic hierarchy emphasizes rank authority as compared to the collegial and professional expertise of a legal hierarchy (as, for example, in the hierarchically superior jurisdiction of the Supreme Court over lower appeals courts and trial courts), the two authority structures share, in Weber's mind, the element of formal-legal rationality as the basis of their legitimacy. In Weber's rational model of organization, in other words, bureaucratic and expert authority are fused. By contrast, postmodern and postindustrial organizations or those that deviate from the ideal-type may exhibit a conflict between managers and technical experts or develop altogether different forms of authority and administration that Weber did not envisage.

A third dominant element in the bureaucratic ideal-type is the system of formal, written rules which are meant to insure objectivity, consistency, and routine conformity to certain procedural standards in the disposition of "cases." Conformity to rules implies the importance of precedent in decision making, which, in turn, requires files and dossiers documenting past correspondence, case histories, opinions, and decisions. While clerks and files filled nineteenth century bureaucracies, the advent of the computer and its "informating" capacities (storing information about cases as well as the processing of cases) has changed much of this. But rule orientation and the case processing method still dominate the work of large bureaucracies like insurance companies, utilities, or the Internal Revenue Service.

Weber was not an efficiency expert and, hence, had no interest in judging the adequacy of bureaucratic administration to its task except in terms of formal rationality. Thus, it was only for a later generation of students of bureaucracy to discover that an excessive preoccupation with enforcing rules and formalistic procedures might actually be counterproductive and thus subvert the bureaucracy's mission or displace its overall goals. The rational model assumes that "red tape" is the result of insufficient rationality, not a built-in structural tension. Also, while a system of rules may require hierarchical supervision, audit, and review to ensure compliance or enforce conformity with the rules, hierarchy, in turn, may spawn rules and regulations in the interest of control rather than efficiency. Similarly, division of labor may give rise to hierarchical coordination, but top-level management may also add a new product line, assign people to new jobs, create new departments and divisions, and restructure the system of specialization by introducing a new technology such as computers. Thus, the analysis of empirical or historical ideal-types suggests links between their constituent elements, even though establishing their causal direction may be a matter of empirical research.

A fourth element of bureaucracy stressed by Weber was impersonality in the dealings among officials and between officials and clients. Echoing the norm of cognitive control over emotions embedded in the Protestant ethic, the detached, disinterested elimination of personal preferences and human relations from the bureaucratic work environment was to ensure maximum efficiency, objectivity, and procedural consistency. The idea that a "user-friendly" service orientation, personal ties among workers, and a philosophy of enhancing human relations could actually promote cooperation and productivity is foreign to the rational model.

Still another set of elements emphasized by Weber, the notion of a life-long career pattern, regular compensation on the basis of a salary, and the orientation toward having a regular and continuous position within the same organization and being promoted on the basis of qualifications and credentials (e.g., civil service exams) or performance and merit summarizes much that used to be true of an official's status in late nineteenth century British and continental military or governmental bureaucracies, and may still be true for middle- and upper-level managers in modern Japanese corporations. The most important aspect of this notion of a career pattern, however, is that it provides a formal, methodical basis for the regular and continuous discharge of duties, which distinguishes bureaucracies from the arbitrary, informal, frequently changing, and unreliable allocation of family members and loyal vassals to ill-defined tasks under the traditional authority of personal rulership.

Weber used the method of ideal-type construction to analyze a wide variety of complex social phenomena, for example, economic classes, social status groups, and political parties, the intelligentsia in imperial China, the characteristics of Western Capitalism, religious formations such as ancient Judaism and the economic ethics of other major world religions, and the rational and irrational, substantive and formal types of law. Given such voluminous and wide-ranging scholarship, how can we evaluate the success of Weber's efforts without violating the cardinal rule of interpretive sociology: to understand ideas and practices from within their own intellectual and cultural horizon and on the basis of categories that are grounded in a meaningful social and historical context?

Appraisal and Conclusion

The process of ideal-type construction inherently tends to accentuate the consistency and goodness of fit among its diverse elements. As a result, it tends to suppress or minimize conflicts and contradictory tendencies within the socio-historical formation under consideration. Nevertheless, the ideal-type helps the culturally embedded observer to make sense of a complex and more or less transient reality and to see it as a meaningful whole, although Weber rejected Hegelian historical teleology or Darwinian social evolutionism. It can be argued that the imposition of a unifying, integrative conceptual unity on the perceived diversity of social life and the flux of history is part of the fundamentally modernist legacy of German philosophical idealism, especially neo-Kantian conceptual subjectivism, which Weber shared and cherished. Analytical categorizations and binary oppositions may help the observer to understand the social world insofar as they respond both to the diversity of cognition and to a need for order and unity. Ultimately, then, such binary categories represent the observer's way of ordering reality by reducing its complexity to manageable proportions. Such an activist, if not compulsive need for order and pure, well-bounded categories may also betray a low tolerance for ambiguity and diversity, and an aversion to being merely a passive participant in what may appear to be a chaotic, anarchic, disorderly, and rapidly changing social universe. These considerations suggest, of course, the not sufficiently appreciated affinity between the activist and subjectivist element in philosophical idealism and Weber's thought, on the one hand, and between the scientific mentality and the legacy of positivism, objectivism, and modernism, on the other.

Yet Weber saw himself more in the tradition of the cultural analysis of the human sciences than in that of the natural sciences and positivism, although it is precisely the ideal-type that seeks to bridge the gap between the recurrent phenomena of the natural world and the unique, yet meaningful events of social history. As a methodological device in the social sciences, the ideal-type offers a way of understanding that comes closest to the notion of grounded theory, reflecting the categories of cognition as they appear to, and are selected by, the participant observer situated in a given social and cultural universe of discourse. The ambiguity and ambivalence of this epistemological position, but also its potential for reflexive and critical interpretation and its sociological eye for empirical detail and concrete historical mixtures of analytical elements is what carries fruitfully over from Weber's dualism.

A final point concerns the question of whether Weber saw himself as having produced a theory of society. There is no doubt that he contributed profoundly to theorizing in sociology and in the social sciences, especially at the level of the "middle range," but I believe the answer is probably negative. While categorizations may be necessary for developing theories, they are not in themselves testable theories, only ways of seeing and ordering. Weber painted a great variety of unforgettable images of social and historical reality. But he did not, in my view, develop a social theory in the narrow sense of the term. The closest Weber comes to formulating a theoretical generalization is in his view of the transition from traditional to modern society, from community to society, a view that is as important compared to that of Marx and Durkheim as it is different from them. For Weber, the raw material of this transition are status-conscious groups and collectivities, the conditions are those of conflict, and the mechanism is a cultural force, namely rationalization. By positing rationalization as a master trend and as a meta-narrative, as one might say from a postmodern perspective, Weber could analyze the Protestant Reformation, bureaucracy, the rise of the nation-state, and the rise of industrial capitalism as manifestations of the same process. Weber's work could thus be seen as implying a cultural theory of social change. As he saw it, the rise of Western rationalism had its roots in ancient Judaism and found its eighteenth and nineteenth century culmination in the Protestant economic ethic and its "elective affinity" to the spirit of capitalism. Only the German sociologist Wolfgang Schluchter has endeavored to push Max Weber's account of the rise of Western rationalism further and to define it as a form of "developmental history" by linking it to a stage theory of historical rationalization and to the neo-evolutionary models of modern systems theory. While judging the result of Weber's effort as being superior to that of others, Schluchter stops short of calling it a theory and prefers to talk about forms of theoretical analysis, albeit on a very high level.

But Weber did strain toward theoretical explanation. Implicit in his ideal-types are the beginnings of theoretical propositions which suggest causal connections between the constitutive elements of the type. Moreover, his notion of "elective affinity" acts as a category of causal explanation. As such, it is comparable to the concept of purposive or intentional explanation, which is crucial to theoretical explanation in the social sciences because it takes into account human agency at the individual and collective level. At the same time, Weber distances himself from conventional scientific or positivist causal explanation insofar as it subsumes events under causal laws, which, in the social sciences, are largely replaced by probabilistic models that seek to "explain variance" in the dependent variable by means of estimating the effects of a series of independent and intervening variables. And he generally avoids functional explanations which assign causal powers to the positive, but unintended and unidentified consequences of social patterns.

If Weber's lasting contribution was that of producing highly influential conceptual distinctions, ideal-types, and taxonomies, the fruitful theoretical content of his categorizations consists in the fact that they remained close to historical detail and approached the "thick description" of the ethnographer, yet at the same time strained toward a level of analytical precision and conceptual differentiation that might provide the basis for a more dynamic reconstruction of the mysteries and motion of the social world. Perhaps the driving element behind this monumental effort was the need, influenced no doubt by the biographical contingencies of Weber's own life and political context, to make sense of the flux of history culminating in the complexities, ambiguities, and conflicts of modern existence and the demands on, and challenges to, human conduct. The search for categories and concepts, distinctions and contrasts, differences and similarities was animated by the quest for certainty in an uncertain, dangerous, and ever-changing world. It was a search for order and control in the morass of history, politics, and everyday life. It is by no means clear whether Weber thought that he had found satisfactory answers; his style of thinking moved from the historically unique detail to the categorical, almost scientific contrast, and from there back to the Talmudic ambivalence of "on the one hand . . . but on the other. . . ." But it is obvious (and thus perhaps trivial to note) that his dualistic intellectual posture was paralleled by a certain pessimism, spawned by a sense of realistic acceptance and sober resignation, if not despair, over what he felt were inevitable limits of human existence as well as inescapable constraints of social order. Weber's famous image of the "iron cage" of bureaucracy, not unlike the "iron law of oligarchy" of his contemporary Robert Michels, and his notion of the "disenchantment" of the world by science and rationality, not unlike Durkheim's "anomie" and Marx's "alienation," all testify to the struggle to comprehend the world in terms of its differences and identities, yet paradoxically to end up within the very prison house of categories constructed as a defense against flux, complexity, and uncertainty. Yet in spite of the tragic tenor, Weber agonizes time and again over the necessity to take a stand, to make a decision, to commit oneself in an almost existentialist fashion to a definitive course of action. Thus, his own value-rationality remains both an intellectual and a highly personal answer to the seemingly random challenges of modern existence. It is this moral and rational posture that compels us to appreciate Max Weber as a great social thinker and an extraordinary human being.

A Note on the Present Edition

The present volume of selections from Weber's work is organized around four key ideas: the conceptual basis of Weber's sociology, notably the different concepts of social action and social relationships; the two great social forces operating in modern societies, domination and stratification; the process of rationalization in the three important institutional spheres of economy, religion, and law; and the significance of method and scientific procedure for understanding human society. Thus, in Part I of this volume (Social Action and Social Relationships), the reader will find most of the basic definitions that are necessary to understand Weber's concepts and his idea of what makes the "social" special and unique in human society.

In Part II, the first five chapters are devoted to Weber's pivotal contribution to political sociology and the theory of bureaucracy. Here, the reader will find the famous discussion of power and the state, legitimacy and authority, charisma and collegial authority, bureaucracy and its pervasive consequences. By arranging the readings on charisma, collegiality, and bureaucracy in a sequence, I wish to emphasize both the continuities and contrasts among these concepts as well as their importance for understanding alternative forms of authority and domination; for example, the affinity between charismatic and professional authority in dealing with uncertainty, and the potential for bureaucratic-professional conflict under certain structural conditions. The last two chapters in Part II focus on stratification and especially on Weber's famous notion of status groups as a special category of stratification. With the exception of the piece on the Chinese Literati, all chapters included in Part II are new translations.

Part III deals with the nature and consequences of rationalization. The first two chapters are taken from Weber's lectures on general economic history and focus on the origins of modern capitalism and the evolution of the capitalist spirit, that special individualized, risk-taking, cognitively and instrumentally patterned mentality that Weber saw as so important for the emergence of capitalist institutions and practices. Chapters 20, 21 and 22 are taken from Weber's sociology of religion and focus especially on the economic ethics of the world religions. Finally, the last three selections (Chapters 23–25) illustrate Weber's crucial contributions to the sociology of law. Of particular interest here is the typology of legal forms and the formal qualities of modern law which are, nevertheless, gradually eroded by anti-formalist tendencies emerging in the twentieth century. This piece is critical for understanding the development of informal and flexible strategies such as plea-bargaining and settlement practices within modern judicial systems as well as the rise of mediation and alternative dispute resolution outside the courts.

The last section of this volume, Part IV, deals with the relationship between sociology and science. Here, Weber articulates his well-known approach to interpretive sociology and to the importance of understanding and explanation as the twin pillars of social science inquiry (Chapters 26 and 27). In Chapters 28 and 29 Weber develops his ideas on the need for "value-neutrality" and objectivity once the culturally embedded researcher has chosen an appropriate social scientific object for research and analysis. Weber's formulation of this issue was very influential insofar as he took consensual validation to be the core of objectivity and truth in the social sciences. After a detailed discussion of the nature and function of ideal-type constructs (Chapter 30), the volume ends with one of Weber's most famous speeches on "Science as a Vocation" (Chapter 31), in which he describes the problems facing social science inquiry in an increasingly scientific civilization. But while Weber deplores the disenchantment of the world and its destructive effect on traditional values, he reaffirms his commitment to a rationality of purpose and an ethics of responsibility as the only way to warrant human conduct in modern society and to validate it on grounds of intellectual and moral integrity.

This edition inevitably reflects my judgment as to what parts of Weber's work are most important and how his ideas can be made accessible in the most meaningful way. Accordingly, I have focused on the basic concepts, on the overriding analytical dimensions of Weber's work, and on specific examples and elaborations that show Weber's great virtuosity in the craft of sociological interpretation. Thus, it is my hope that this edition will be as useful to the general reader as to the undergraduate or graduate student who seeks to enter into the intricate intellectual realm of Weber's thought, not to mention the occasionally demanding prose and the sometimes sober, if not somber style of reasoning and writing. Many of Weber's essays, however, also show him to be the perfectly lucid and rational intellectual that he was and have nothing academic, abstract, and arid about them. Indeed, in spite of his predilection for categorical distinctions, Weber always wrote about concrete issues in a precise and intriguing way.

W. H.

Editor's Acknowledgments

I am happy to acknowledge an intellectual and personal debt to a number of persons who had a part in the publication of this volume. I want to thank Volkmar Sander, the general editor of the German Library, for inviting me to edit a selection of writings by Max Weber and for his patience, encouragement, and collaboration in the painstaking review of the newly translated sections. In this connection, I am especially grateful to Martin Black for his translation of Chapters 11–14 and 16, and to Martin Black and Lance Garmer for their translation of Chapter 15 on Bureaucratic Authority. I also want to thank my colleagues Edward Lehman, Guenther Roth, and Dennis Wrong for their helpful comments on the Introduction. Finally, I am grateful to Evander Lomke, managing editor of Continuum, for his patience and guidance. Last but not least, I want to acknowledge my great debt to Liz, Daniel, and Sophie for tolerating my absences and grounding me in reality.

Social Action and Social Relationships

1. The Concept of Social Action[1]

Social action, which includes both failure to act and passive acquiescence, may be oriented to the past, present, or expected future behavior of others. Thus it may be motivated by revenge for a past attack, defense against present, or measures of defense against future aggression. The "others" may be individual persons, and may be known to the actor as such, or may constitute an indefinite plurality and may be entirely unknown as individuals. Thus "money" is a means of exchange which the actor accepts in payment because he orients his action to the expectation that a large but unknown number of individuals he is personally unacquainted with will be ready to accept it in exchange on some future occasion.

Not every kind of action, even of overt action, is "social" in the sense of the present discussion. Overt action is nonsocial if it is oriented solely to the behavior of inanimate objects. Subjective attitudes constitute social action only so far as they are oriented to the behavior of others. For example, religious behavior is not social if it is simply a matter of contemplation or of solitary prayer. The economic activity of an individual is only social if, and then only insofar as, it takes account of the behavior of someone else. Thus very generally in formal terms it becomes social insofar as the actor's actual control over economic goods is respected by others. Concretely it is social, for instance, if in relation to the actor's own consumption the future wants of others are taken into account and this becomes one consideration affecting the actor's own saving. Or, in another connection, production may be oriented to the future wants of other people.

Not every type of contact of human beings has a social character; this is rather confined to cases where the actor's behavior is meaningfully oriented to that of others. For example, a mere collision of two cyclists may be compared to a natural event. On the other hand, their attempt to avoid hitting each other, or whatever insults, blows, or friendly discussion might follow the collision, would constitute "social action."

Social action is not identical either with the similar actions of many persons or with action influenced by other persons. Thus, if at the beginning of a shower a number of people on the street put up their umbrellas at the same time, this would not ordinarily be a case of action mutually oriented to that of each other, but rather of all reacting in the same way to the like need of protection from the rain. It is well known that the actions of the individual are strongly influenced by the mere fact that he is a member of a crowd confined within a limited space. Thus, the subject matter of studies of "crowd psychology," such as those of Le Bon, will be called "action conditioned by crowds." It is also possible for large numbers, though dispersed, to be influenced simultaneously or successively by a source of influence operating similarly on all the individuals, as by means of the press. Here also the behavior of an individual is influenced by his membership in the crowd and by the fact that he is aware of being a member. Some types of reaction are only made possible by the mere fact that the individual acts as part of a crowd. Others become more difficult under these conditions. Hence it is possible that a particular event or mode of human behavior can give rise to the most diverse kinds of feeling—gaiety, anger, enthusiasm, despair, and passions of all sorts—in a crowd situation which would not occur at all or not nearly so readily if the individual were alone. But for this to happen there need not, at least in many cases, be any meaningful relation between the behavior of the individual and the fact that he is a member of a crowd. It is not proposed in the present sense to call action "social" when it is merely a result of the effect on the individual of the existence of a crowd as such and the action is not oriented to that fact on the level of meaning. At the same time the borderline is naturally highly indefinite. In such cases as that of the influence of the demagogue, there may be a wide variation in the extent to which his mass clientele is affected by a meaningful reaction to the fact of its large numbers; and whatever this relation may be, it is open to varying interpretations.

But furthermore, mere "imitation" of the action of others, such as that on which Tarde has rightly laid emphasis, will not be considered a case of specifically social action if it is purely reactive so that there is no meaningful orientation to the actor imitated. The borderline is, however, so indefinite that it is often hardly possible to discriminate. The mere fact that a person is found to employ some apparently useful procedure which he learned from someone else does not, however, constitute, in the present sense, social action. Action such as this is not oriented to the action of the other person, but the actor has, through observing the other, become acquainted with certain objective facts; and it is these to which his action is oriented. His action is then causally determined by the action of others, but not meaningfully. On the other hand, if the action of others is imitated because it is "fashionable" or traditional or exemplary, or lends social distinction, or on similar grounds, it is meaningfully oriented either to the behavior of the source of imitation or of third persons or of both. There are of course all manner of transitional cases between the two types of imitation. Both the phenomena discussed above, the behavior of crowds and imitation, stand on the indefinite borderline of social action. The same is true, as will often appear, of traditionalism and charisma. The reason for the indefiniteness of the line in these and other cases lies in the fact that both the orientation to the behavior of others and the meaning which can be imputed to the actor himself, are by no means always capable of clear determination and are often altogether unconscious and seldom fully self-conscious. Mere "influence" and meaningful orientation cannot therefore always be clearly differentiated on the empirical level. But conceptually it is essential to distinguish them, even though merely "reactive" imitation may well have a degree of sociological importance at least equal to that of the type which can be called social action in the strict sense. Sociology, it goes without saying, is by no means confined to the study of "social action"; this is only, at least for the kind of sociology being developed here, its central subject matter, that which may be said to be decisive for its status as a science. But this does not imply any judgment on the comparative importance of this and other factors.

Translated by A. M. Henderson and Talcott Parsons

2. The Types of Social Action

Social action, like other forms of action, may be classified in the following four types according to its mode of orientation: (1) in terms of rational orientation to a system of discrete individual ends *(zweckrational)*, that is, through expectations as to the behavior of objects in the external situation and of other human individuals, making use of these expectations as "conditions" or "means" for the successful attainment of the actor's own rationally chosen ends; (2) in terms of rational orientation to an absolute value *(wertrational)*, involving a conscious belief in the absolute value of some ethical, aesthetic, religious, or other form of behavior, entirely for its own sake and independently of any prospects of external success; (3) in terms of affectual orientation, especially emotional, determined by the specific affects and states of feeling of the actor; (4) traditionally oriented, through the habituation of long practice.[1]

Strictly traditional behavior, like the reactive type of imitation discussed above, lies very close to the borderline of what can justifiably be called meaningfully oriented action, and indeed often on the other side. For it is very often a matter of almost automatic reaction to habitual stimuli which guides behavior in a course that has been repeatedly followed. The great bulk of all everyday action to which people have become habitually accustomed approaches this type. Hence, its place in a systematic classification is not merely that of a limiting case because, as will be shown later, attachment to habitual forms can be upheld with varying degrees of self-consciousness and in a variety of senses. In this case the type may shade over into number two *(Wertrationalität)*.

Purely affectual behavior also stands on the borderline of what can be considered "meaningfully" oriented, and often it, too, goes over the line. It may, for instance, consist in an uncontrolled reaction to some exceptional stimulus. It is a case of sublimation when affectually determined action occurs in the form of conscious release of emotional tension. When this happens it is usually, though not always, well on the road to rationalization in one or the other or both of the above senses.

The orientation of action in terms of absolute value is distinguished from the affectual type by its clearly self-conscious formulation of the ultimate values governing the action and the consistently planned orientation of its detailed course to these values. At the same time the two types have a common element, namely that the meaning of the action does not lie in the achievement of a result ulterior to it, but in carrying out the specific type of action for its own sake. Examples of affectual action are the satisfaction of a direct impulse to revenge, to sensual gratification, to devote oneself to a person or ideal, to contemplative bliss, or, finally, toward the working off of emotional tensions. Such impulses belong in this category regardless of how sordid or sublime they may be.

Examples of pure rational orientation to absolute values would be the action of persons who, regardless of possible cost to themselves, act to put into practice their convictions of what seems to them to be required by duty, honor, the pursuit of beauty, a religious call, personal loyalty, or the importance of some "cause," no matter in what it consists. For the purposes of this discussion, when action is oriented to absolute values, it always involves "commands" or "demands" to the fulfilment of which the actor feels obligated. It is only in cases where human action is motivated by the fulfilment of such unconditional demands that it will be described as oriented to absolute values. This is empirically the case in widely varying degrees, but for the most part only to a relatively slight extent. Nevertheless, it will be shown that the occurrence of this mode of action is important enough to justify its formulation as a distinct type; though it may be remarked that there is no intention here of attempting to formulate in any sense an exhaustive classification of types of action.

Action is rationally oriented to a system of discrete individual ends *(zweckrational)* when the end, the means, and the secondary results are all rationally taken into account and weighed. This involves rational consideration of alternative means to the end, of the relations of the end to other prospective results of employment of any given means, and finally of the relative importance of different possible ends. Determination of action, either in affectual or in traditional terms, is thus incompatible with this type. Choice between alternative and conflicting ends and results may well be determined by considerations of absolute value. In that case, action is rationally oriented to a system of discrete individual ends only in respect to the choice of means. On the other hand, the actor may, instead of deciding between alternative and conflicting ends in terms of a rational orientation to a system of values, simply take them as given subjective wants and arrange them in a scale of consciously assessed relative urgency. He may then orient his action to this scale in such a way that they are satisfied as far as possible in order of urgency, as formulated in the principle of "marginal utility." The orientation of action to absolute values may thus have various different modes of relation to the other type of rational action, in terms of a system of discrete individual ends. From the latter point of view, however, absolute values are always irrational. Indeed, the more the value to which action is oriented is elevated to the status of an absolute value, the more "irrational" in this sense the corresponding action is. For, the more unconditionally the actor devotes himself to this value for its own sake, to pure sentiment or beauty, to absolute goodness or devotion to duty, the less is he influenced by considerations of the consequences of his action. The orientation of action wholly to the rational achievement of ends without relation to fundamental values is, to be sure, essentially only a limiting case.

It would be very unusual to find concrete cases of action, especially of social action, which were oriented only in one or another of these ways. Furthermore, this classification of the modes of orientation of action is in no sense meant to exhaust the possibilities of the field, but only to formulate in conceptually pure form certain sociologically important types, to which actual action is more or less closely approximated or, in much the more common case, which constitute the elements combining to make it up. The usefulness of the classification for the purposes of this investigation can only be judged in terms of its results.

Translated by A. M. Henderson and Talcott Parsons

3. The Concept of Social Relationship

The term "social relationship" will be used to denote the behavior of a plurality of actors insofar as, in its meaningful content, the action of each takes account of that of the others and is oriented in these terms. The social relationship thus consists entirely and exclusively in the existence of a probability that there will be, in some meaningfully understandable sense, a course of social action. For purposes of definition there is no attempt to specify the basis of this probability.

Thus, as a defining criterion, it is essential that there should be at least a minimum of mutual orientation of the action of each to that of the others. Its content may be of the most varied nature; conflict, hostility, sexual attraction, friendship, loyalty, or economic exchange. It may involve the fulfilment, the evasion, or the denunciation of the terms of an agreement; economic, erotic, or some other form of "competition"; common membership in national or class groups or those sharing a common tradition of status. In the latter cases mere group membership may or may not extend to include social action; this will be discussed later. The definition, furthermore, does not specify whether the relation of the actors is "solidary" or the opposite.

The "meaning" relevant in this context is always a case of the meaning imputed to the parties in a given concrete case, on the average or in a theoretically formulated pure type—it is never a normatively "correct" or a metaphysically "true" meaning. Even in cases of such forms of social organization as a state, church, association, or marriage, the social relationship consists exclusively in the fact that there has existed, exists, or will exist a probability of action in some definite way appropriate to this meaning. It is vital to be continually clear about this in order to avoid the "reification" of these concepts. A "state," for example, ceases to exist in a sociologically relevant sense whenever there is no longer a probability that certain kinds of meaningfully oriented social action will take place. This probability may be very high or it may be negligibly low. But in any case it is only in the sense and degree in which it does exist or can be estimated that the corresponding social relationship exists. It is impossible to find any other clear meaning for the statement that, for instance, a given "state" exists or has ceased to exist.

The subjective meaning need not necessarily be the same for all the parties who are mutually oriented in a given social relationship; there need not in this sense be "reciprocity." "Friendship," "love," "loyalty," "fidelity to contracts," "patriotism," on one side, may well be faced with an entirely different attitude on the other. In such cases the parties associate different meanings with their actions and the social relationship is insofar objectively "asymmetrical" from the points of view of the two parties. It may nevertheless be a case of mutual orientation insofar as, even though partly or wholly erroneously, one party presumes a particular attitude toward him on the part of the other and orients his action to this expectation. This can, and usually will, have consequences for the course of action and the form of the relationship. A relationship is objectively symmetrical only as, according to the typical expectations of the parties, the meaning for one party is the same as that for the other. Thus the actual attitude of a child to its father may be at least approximately that which the father, in the individual case, on the average or typically, has come to expect. A social relationship in which the attitudes are completely and fully corresponding is in reality a limiting case. But the absence of reciprocity will, for terminological purposes, be held to exclude the existence of a social relationship only if it actually results in the absence of a mutual orientation of the action of the parties. Here as elsewhere all sorts of transitional cases are the rule rather than the exception.

A social relationship can be of a temporary character or of varying degrees of permanence. That is, it can be of such a kind that there is a probability of the repeated recurrence of the behavior which corresponds to its subjective meaning, behavior that is an understandable consequence of the meaning and hence is expected. In order to avoid fallacious impressions, let it be repeated and continually kept in mind, that it is only the existence of the probability that, corresponding to a given subjective meaning complex, a certain type of action will take place, which constitutes the "existence" of the social relationship. Thus that a "friendship" or a "state" exists or has existed means this and only this: that we, the observers, judge that there is or has been a probability that on the basis of certain kinds of known subjective attitude of certain individuals there will result in the average sense a certain specific type of action. For the purposes of legal reasoning it is essential to be able to decide whether a rule of law does or does not carry legal authority, hence whether a legal relationship does or does not "exist." This type of question is not, however, relevant to sociological problems.

The subjective meaning of a social relationship may change; thus a political relationship, once based on solidarity, may develop into a conflict of interests. In that case it is only a matter of terminological convenience and of the degree of continuity of the change whether we say that a new relationship has come into existence or that the old one continues but has acquired a new meaning. It is also possible for the meaning to be partly constant, partly changing.

The meaningful content which remains relatively constant in a social relationship is capable of formulation in terms of maxims that the parties concerned expect to be adhered to by their partners, on the average and approximately. The more rational in relation to values or to given ends the action is, the more is this likely to be the case. There is far less possibility of a rational formulation of subjective meaning in the case of a relation of erotic attraction or of personal loyalty or any other affectual type than, for example, in the case of a business contract.

The meaning of a social relationship may be agreed upon by mutual consent. This implies that the parties make promises covering their future behavior, whether toward each other or toward third persons. In such cases each party then normally counts, so far as he acts rationally, in some degree on the fact that the other will orient his action to the meaning of the agreement as he (the first actor) understands it. In part, they orient theii action rationally to these expectations as given facts with, to be sure, varying degrees of subjectively "loyal" intention of doing their part. But in part also they are motivated each by the value to him of his "duty" to adhere to the agreement in the sense in which he understands it. This much may be anticipated.

Translated by A. M. Henderson and Talcott Parsons

4. The Concept of Legitimate Order

Action, especially social action which involves social relationships, may be oriented by the actors to a belief *(Vorstellung)* in the existence of a "legitimate order." The probability that action will actually empirically be so oriented will be called the "validity" *(Geltung)* of the order in question.[1]

Thus, orientation to the validity of an order *(Ordnung)* means more than the mere existence of a uniformity of social action determined by custom or self-interest. If furniture movers regularly advertise at times of the large-scale expiration of leases, this uniformity is determined by self-interest in the exploitation of opportunities. If a salesman visits certain customers on particular days of the month or the week, it is either a case of customary behavior or a product of some kind of self-interested orientation. But when, on the other hand, a civil servant appears in his office daily at a fixed time, it may involve these elements, but is not determined by custom or self-interest alone, for with these he is at liberty to conform or not as he pleases. As a rule such action in addition is determined by his subjection to an order, the rules governing the department which impose obligations on him, which he is usually careful to fulfill, partly because disobedience would carry disadvantageous consequences to him, but usually also in part because it would be abhorrent to the sense of duty, which, to a greater or lesser extent, is an absolute value to him.

The subjective meaning of a social relationship will be called an "order" only if action is approximately or on the average oriented to certain determinate "maxims" or rules. Furthermore, such an order will only be called "valid" if the orientation to such maxims includes, no matter to what actual extent, the recognition that they are binding on the actor or the corresponding action constitutes a desirable model for him to imitate. Naturally, in concrete cases, the orientation of action to an order involves a wide variety of motives. But the circumstance that, along with the other sources of conformity, the order is also held by at least part of the actors to define a model or to be binding naturally increases the probability that action will in fact conform to it, often to a very considerable degree. An order which is adhered to from motives of pure expediency is generally much less stable than one upheld on a purely customary basis through the fact that the corresponding behavior has become habitual. The latter is much the most common type of subjective attitude. But even this type of order is in turn much less stable than an order which enjoys the prestige of being considered binding, or, as it may be expressed, of "legitimacy." The transitions between orientation to an order from motives of tradition or of expediency on the one hand to the case where, on the other, a belief in its legitimacy is involved, are naturally empirically gradual.

It is possible for action to be oriented to an order in other ways than through conformity with its prescriptions, as they are generally understood by the actors. Even in the cases of evasion of or deliberate disobedience to these prescriptions, the probability of its being recognized as a valid norm may have an effect on action. This may, in the first place, be true from the point of view of sheer expediency. A thief orients his action to the validity of the criminal law in that he acts surreptitiously. The fact that the order is recognized as valid in his society is made evident by the fact that he cannot violate it openly without punishment. But apart from this limiting case, it is very common for violation of an order to be confined to more or less numerous partial deviations from it, or for the attempt to be made, with varying degrees of good faith, to justify the deviation as legitimate. Furthermore, there may exist at the same time different interpretations of the meaning of the order. In such cases, for sociological purposes, each can be said to be valid insofar as it actually determines the course of action. The fact that, in the same social group, a plurality of contradictory systems of order may all be recognized as valid, is not a source of difficulty for the sociological approach. Indeed, it is even possible for the same individual to orient his action to contradictory systems of order. This can take place not only at different times, as is an everyday occurrence, but even in the case of the same concrete act. A person who fights a duel orients his action to the code of honor; but at the same time, insofar as he either keeps it secret or conversely gives himself up to the police, he takes account of the criminal law.[2] To be sure, when evasion or contravention of the generally understood meaning of an order has become the rule, the order can be said to be "valid" only in a limited degree and, in the extreme case, not at all. Thus for sociological purposes there does not exist, as there does for the law, a rigid alternative between the validity and lack of validity of a given order. On the contrary, there is a gradual transition between the two extremes; and also it is possible, as it has been pointed out, for contradictory systems of order to exist at the same time. In that case each is "valid" precisely to the extent that there is a probability that action will in fact be oriented to it.[3]

Translated by A. M. Henderson and Talcott Parsons

5. The Bases of Legitimacy of an Order

Legitimacy may be ascribed to an order by those acting subject to it in the following ways:

(a) By tradition; a belief in the legitimacy of what has always existed; (b) by virtue of affectual attitudes, especially emotional, legitimizing the validity of what is newly revealed or a model to imitate; (c) by virtue of a rational belief in its absolute value,[1] thus lending it the validity of an absolute and final commitment; (d) because it has been established in a manner which is recognized to be legal. This legality may be treated as legitimate in either of two ways: on the one hand, it may derive from a voluntary agreement of the interested parties on the relevant terms. On the other hand, it may be imposed on the basis of what is held to be a legitimate authority over the relevant persons and a corresponding claim to their obedience.

All further details, except for a few other concepts to be defined below, belong in the sociology of law and the sociology of authority. For the present, only a few remarks are necessary.

The derivation of the legitimacy of an order from a belief in the sanctity of tradition is the most universal and most primitive case. The fear of magical penalties confirms the general psychological inhibitions against any sort of change in customary modes of action. At the same time the multifarious vested interests which tend to become attached to upholding conformity with an order, once it has become established, have worked in the same direction.

Conscious departures from tradition in the establishment of a new order have originally been due almost entirely to prophetic oracles or at least to pronouncements which have been sanctioned as prophetic. This was true as late as the statutes of the Greek Aesymnetes. Conformity has then depended on belief in the legitimacy of the prophet. In times of strict traditionalism a new order, that is, one which was regarded as new, could, without being revealed in this way, only become legitimized by the claim that it had actually always been valid though not yet rightly known, or that it had been obscured for a time and was now being restored to its rightful place.

The type case of legitimacy by virtue of rational belief in an absolute value is that of "Natural Law." However limited its actual effect, as compared with its ideal claims, it cannot be denied that its logically developed reasoning has had an influence on actual action which is far from negligible. This mode of influence should be clearly distinguished from that of a revealed law, of one imposed by authority, or of one which is merely traditional.

To-day the most usual basis of legitimacy is the belief in legality, the readiness to conform with rules which are formally correct and have been imposed by accepted procedure. The distinction between an order derived from voluntary agreement and one which has been imposed is only relative. For so far as the agreement underlying the order is not unanimous, as in the past has often been held necessary for complete legitimacy, its functioning within a social group will be dependent on the willingness of individuals with deviant wishes to give way to the majority. This is very frequently the case and actually means that the order is imposed on the minority. At the same time, it is very common for minorities, by force or by the use of more ruthless and far-sighted methods, to impose an order which in the course of time comes to be regarded as legitimate by those who originally resisted it. Insofar as the ballot is used as a legal means of altering an order, it is very common for the will of a minority to attain a formal majority and for the majority to submit. In this case majority rule is a mere illusion. The belief in the legality of an order as established by voluntary agreement is relatively ancient and is occasionally found among so-called primitive peoples; but in these cases it is almost always supplemented by the authority of oracles.

So far as it is not derived merely from fear or from motives of expediency, a willingness to submit to an order imposed by one man or a small group, always in some sense implies a belief in the legitimate authority of the source imposing it.

Submission to an order is almost always determined by a variety of motives; by a wide variety of interests and by a mixture of adherence to tradition and belief in legality, unless it is a case of entirely new regulations. In a very large proportion of cases, the actors subject to the order are of course not even aware how far it is a matter of custom, of convention, or of law. In such cases the sociologist must attempt to formulate the typical basis of validity.

Translated by A. M. Henderson and Talcott Parsons

6. The Concept of Conflict

A social relationship will be referred to as "conflict" insofar as action within it is oriented intentionally to carrying out the actor's own will against the resistance of the other party or parties. The term "peaceful" conflict will be applied to cases in which actual physical violence is not employed. A peaceful conflict is "competition" insofar as it consists in a formally peaceful attempt to attain control over opportunities and advantages which are also desired by others. A competitive process is "regulated" competition to the extent that its ends and means are oriented to an order. The struggle, often latent, which takes place between human individuals or types of social status, for advantages and for survival, but without a meaningful mutual orientation in terms of conflict, will be called "selection." Insofar as it is a matter of the relative opportunities of individuals during their own lifetime, it is "social selection"; insofar as it concerns differential chances for the survival of inherited characteristics, "biological selection."

There are all manner of continuous transitions ranging from the bloody type of conflict which, setting aside all rules, aims at the destruction of the adversary to the case of the battles of medieval chivalry, bound as they were to the strictest conventions, and to the strict regulations imposed on sport by the rules of the game. A classic example of conventional regulation even in war is the herald's call before the battle of Fontenoy: "Messieurs les Anglais, tirez les premiers." There are transitions such as that from unregulated competition of, let us say, suitors for the favor of a woman to the competition for economic advantages in exchange relationships, bound as that is by the order governing the market, or to strictly regulated competitions for artistic awards or, finally, to the struggle for victory in election campaigns. The treatment of conflict involving the use of physical violence as a separate type is justified by the special characteristics of the employment of this means and the corresponding peculiarities of the sociological consequences of its use.

All typical struggles and modes of competition which take place on a large scale will lead, in the long run, despite the decisive importance in many individual cases of accidental factors and luck, to a selection of those who have in the higher degree, on the average, possessed the personal qualities important to success. What qualities are important depends on the conditions in which the conflict or competition takes place. It may be a matter of physical strength or of unscrupulous cunning, of the level of mental ability or mere lung power and skill in the technique of demagoguery, of loyalty to superiors or of ability to flatter the masses, of creative originality, or of adaptability, of qualities which are unusual, or of those which are possessed by the mediocre majority. Among the decisive conditions, it must not be forgotten, belong the systems of order to which the behavior of the parties is oriented, whether traditionally, as a matter of rationally disinterested loyalty, or of expediency. Each type of order influences opportunities in the process of social selection differently.

Not every process of social selection is, in the present sense, a case of conflict. Social selection, on the contrary, means only in the first instance that certain types of behavior, and hence of the corresponding personal qualities, are more favorable than others in procuring differential advantages in attaining to certain social relationships, as in the role of "lover," "husband," "member of parliament," "official," "contractor," "managing director," "successful business man," and so on. But the concept does not specify whether this differential advantage in selection for social success is brought to bear through conflict or not, neither does it specify whether the biological chances of survival of the type are affected one way or the other. It is only where there is a genuine competitive process that the term conflict will be used.

It is only in the sense of "selection" that it seems, according to our experience, that conflict is empirically inevitable, and it is furthermore only in the sense of biological selection that it is inevitable in principle. Selection is inevitable because apparently no way can be worked out of eliminating it completely. It is possible even for the most strictly pacific order to eliminate means of conflict and the objects of and impulses to conflict only in that it deals with each type individually. But this means that other modes of conflict would come to the fore, possibly in processes of open competition. But even on the utopian assumption that all competition were completely eliminated, conditions would still lead to a latent process of selection, biological or social, which would favor the types best adapted to the conditions, whether their relevant qualities were mainly determined by heredity or by environment. On an empirical level, the elimination of conflict cannot go beyond a point which leaves room for some social selection, and in principle a process of biological selection necessarily remains.

From the struggle of individuals for personal advantages and survival, it is naturally necessary to distinguish the "conflict" and the "selection" of social relationships. It is only in a metaphorical sense that these concepts can be applied to the latter. For relationships exist only as systems of human action with particular subjective meanings. Thus a process of selection or a conflict between them means only that one type of action has in the course of time been displaced by another, whether it is action by the same persons or by others. This may occur in various ways. Human action may in the first place be consciously aimed to alter certain social relationships—that is, to alter the corresponding action—or it may be directed to the prevention of their development or continuance. Thus a "state" may be destroyed by war or revolution, or a conspiracy may be broken up by savage suppression; prostitution may be suppressed by police action; "shady" business practices by denial of legal protection or by penalties. Furthermore, social relationships may be influenced by the creation of differential advantages which favor one type over another. It is possible either for individuals or for organized groups to pursue such ends. Secondly, it may, in various ways, be an unanticipated consequence of a course of social action and its relevant conditions that certain types of social relationships (meaning, of course, the corresponding actions) will be adversely affected in their opportunities to maintain themselves or to arise. All changes of natural and social conditions have some sort of effect on the differential probabilities of survival of social relationships. Anyone is at liberty to speak in such cases of a process of "selection" of social relationships. For instance, he may say that among several states the "strongest," in the sense of the best "adapted," is victorious. It must, however, be kept in mind that this so-called "selection" has nothing to do with the selection of types of human individuals in either the social or the biological sense. In every case it is necessary to inquire into the reasons which have led to a change in the chances of survival of one or another form of social action or social relationship, which has broken up a social relationship, or which has permitted it to continue at the expense of other competing forms. The explanation of these processes involves so many factors that it does not seem expedient to employ a single term for them. When this is done, there is always a danger of introducing uncritical value judgments into empirical investigation. There is, above all, a danger of being primarily concerned with justifying the success of an individual case. Since individual cases are often dependent on highly exceptional circumstances, they may be in a certain sense "fortuitous." In recent years there has been more than enough of this kind of argument. The fact that a given specific social relationship has been eliminated for reasons peculiar to a particular situation, proves nothing whatever about its "fitness to survive" in general terms.

Translated by A. M. Henderson and Talcott Parsons

7. Types of Solidary Social Relationships

A social relationship will be called "communal"[1] if and so far as the orientation of social action—whether in the individual case, on the average, or in the pure type—is based on a subjective feeling of the parties, whether affectual or traditional, that they belong together. A social relationship will, on the other hand, be called "associative" if and insofar as the orientation of social action within it rests on a rationally motivated adjustment of interests or a similarly motivated agreement, whether the basis of rational judgment be absolute values or reasons of expediency. It is especially common, though by no means inevitable, for the associative type of relationship to rest on a rational agreement by mutual consent. In that case the corresponding action is, at the pole of rationality, oriented either to a rational belief in the binding validity of the obligation to adhere to it, or to a rational expectation that the other party will live up to it.

The purest cases of associative relationships are: (a) rational free market exchange, which constitutes a compromise of opposed but complementary interests; (b) the pure voluntary association based on self-interest, a case of agreement as to a long-run course of action oriented purely to the promotion of specific ulterior interests, economic or other, of its members; (c) the voluntary association of individuals motivated by an adherence to a set of common absolute values, for example, the rational sect, insofar as it does not cultivate emotional and affective interests, but seeks only to serve a "cause." This last case, to be sure, seldom occurs in anything approaching the pure type.

Communal relationships may rest on various types of affectual, emotional, or traditional bases. Examples are a religious brotherhood, an erotic relationship, a relation of personal loyalty, a national community, the *esprit de corps* of a military unit. The type case is most conveniently illustrated by the family. But the great majority of social relationships has this characteristic to some degree, while it is at the same time to some degree determined by associative factors. No matter how calculating and hard-headed the ruling considerations in such a social relationship—as that of a merchant to his customers—may be, it is quite possible for it to involve emotional values which transcend its utilitarian significance. Every social relationship which goes beyond the pursuit of immediate common ends, which hence lasts for long periods, involves relatively permanent social relationships between the same persons, and these cannot be exclusively confined to the technically necessary activities. Hence, in such cases as association in the same military unit, in the same school class, in the same workshop or office, there is always some tendency in this direction, although the degree, to be sure, varies enormously.[2] Conversely, a social relationship which is normally considered primarily communal may involve action on the part of some or even all of the participants, which is to an important degree oriented to considerations of expediency. There is, for instance, a wide variation in the extent to which the members of a family group feel a genuine community of interests or, on the other hand, exploit the relationship for their own ends. The concept of communal relationship has been intentionally defined in very general terms and hence includes a very heterogeneous group of phenomena.

The communal type of relationship is, according to the usual interpretation of its subjective meaning, the most radical antithesis of conflict. This should not, however, be allowed to obscure the fact that coercion of all sorts is a very common thing in even the most intimate of such communal relationships if one party is weaker in character than the other. Furthermore, a process of the selection of types leading to differences in opportunity and survival goes on within these relationships just the same as anywhere else. Associative relationships, on the other hand, very often consist only in compromises between rival interests, where only a part of the occasion or means of conflict has been eliminated, or even an attempt has been made to do so. Hence, outside the area of compromise, the conflict of interests, with its attendant competition for supremacy, remains unchanged. Conflict and communal relationships are relative concepts. Conflict varies enormously according to the means employed, especially whether they are violent or peaceful, and to the ruthlessness with which they are used. It has already been pointed out that any type of order governing social action in some way leaves room for a process of selection among various rival human types.

It is by no means true that the existence of common qualities, a common situation, or common modes of behavior imply the existence of a communal social relationship. Thus, for instance, the possession of a common biological inheritance by virtue of which persons are classified as belonging to the same "race," naturally implies no sort of communal social relationship between them. By restrictions on social intercourse and on marriage, persons may find themselves in a similar situation, a situation of isolation from the environment which imposes these distinctions. But even if they all react to this situation in the same way, this does not constitute a communal relationship. The latter does not even exist if they have a common "feeling" about this situation and its consequences. It is only when this feeling leads to a mutual orientation of their behavior to each other that a social relationship arises between them, a social relationship to each other and not only to persons in the environment. Furthermore, it is only so far as this relationship involves feelings of belonging together that it is a "communal" relationship. In the case of the Jews, for instance, except for Zionist circles and the action of certain associations promoting specifically Jewish interests, there thus exist communal relationships only to a relatively small extent; indeed, Jews often repudiate the existence of a Jewish "community."

Community of language, which arises from a similarity of tradition through the family and the surrounding social environment, facilitates mutual understanding, and thus the formation of all types of social relationships, in the highest degree. But taken by itself it is not sufficient to constitute a communal relationship, but only for the facilitation of intercourse within the groups concerned, thus for the development of associative relationships. In the first place, this takes place between individuals, not because they speak the same language, but because they have other types of interests. Orientation to the rules of a common language is thus primarily important as a means of communication, not as the content of a social relationship. It is only with the emergence of a consciousness of difference from third persons who speak a different language that the fact that two persons speak the same language, and in that respect share a common situation, can lead them to a feeling of community and to modes of social organization consciously based on the sharing of the common language.

Participation in a "market" is of still another kind. It encourages association between the individual parties to specific acts of exchange and a social relationship, above all that, of competition between the individual participants who must mutually orient their action to each other. But no further modes of association develop except in cases where certain participants enter into agreements in order to better their competitive situations, or where they all agree on rules for the purpose of regulating transactions and of securing favorable general conditions for all. It may further be remarked that the market and the competitive economy resting on it form the most important type of the reciprocal determination of action in terms of pure self-interest, a type which is characteristic of modern economic life.

Translated by A. M. Henderson and Talcott Parsons

8. Open and Closed Relationships

A social relationship, regardless of whether it is communal or associative in character, will be spoken of as "open" to outsiders if and insofar as participation in the mutually oriented social action relevant to its subjective meaning is, according to its system of order, not denied to anyone who wishes to participate and who is actually in a position to do so. A relationship will, on the other hand, be called "closed" against outsiders so far as, according to its subjective meaning and the binding rules of its order, participation of certain persons is excluded, limited, or subjected to conditions. Whether a relationship is open or closed may be determined traditionally, affectually, or rationally in terms of values or of expediency. It is especially likely to be closed, for rational reasons, in the following type of situation: a social relationship may provide the parties to it with opportunities for the satisfaction of various interests, whether the satisfactions be spiritual or material, whether the interest be in the end of the relationship as such or in some ulterior consequence of participation, or whether it is achieved through cooperative action or by a compromise of interests. If the participants expect that the admission of others will lead to an improvement of their situation, an improvement in degree, in kind, in the security or the value of the satisfaction, their interest will be in keeping the relationship open. If, on the other hand, their expectations are of improving their position by monopolistic tactics, their interest is in a closed relationship.

There are various ways in which it is possible for a closed social relationship to guarantee its monopolized advantages to the parties. Such advantages may be left free to competitive struggle within the group; they may be regulated or rationed in amount and kind, or they may be appropriated by individuals or sub-groups on a permanent basis and become more or less inalienable. The last is a case of closure within, as well as against outsiders. Appropriated advantages will be called "rights." As determined by the relevant order, appropriation may be for the benefit of the members of particular communal or associative groups (for instance, household groups), or for the benefit of individuals. In the latter case, the individual may enjoy his rights on a purely personal basis or in such a way that in case of his death one or more other persons related to the holder of the right by birth (kinship), or by some other social relationship, may inherit the rights in question. Or the rights may pass to one or more individuals specifically designated by the holder. Finally, it may be that the holder is more or less fully empowered to alienate his rights by voluntary agreement, either to other specific persons or to anyone he chooses. This is "alienable" appropriation. A party to a closed social relationship will be called a "member"; in case his participation is regulated in such a way as to guarantee him appropriated advantages, a "privileged" member. Appropriated rights which are enjoyed by individuals through inheritance or by hereditary groups, whether communal or associative, will be called the "property" of the individual or of groups in question; and, insofar as they are alienable, "free" property.

The apparently gratuitous tediousness involved in the elaborate definition of the above concepts is an example of the fact that we often neglect to think out clearly what seems to be "obvious," because it is intuitively familiar.

(a) Examples of communal relationships, which tend to be closed on a traditional basis, are those in which membership is determined by family relationship.

(b) Personal emotional relationships are usually affectually closed. Examples are erotic relationships and, very commonly, relations of personal loyalty.

(c) Closure on the basis of rational commitment to values is usual in groups sharing a common system of explicit religious belief.

(d) Typical cases of rational closure on grounds of expediency are economic associations of a monopolistic or a plutocratic character.

A few examples may be taken at random. Whether a group of people engaged in conversation is open or closed depends on its content. General conversation is apt to be open, as contrasted with intimate conversation or the imparting of official information. Market relationships are in most, or at least in many, cases essentially open. In the case of many relationships, both communal and associative, there is a tendency to shift from a phase of expansion to one of exclusiveness. Examples are the guilds and the democratic city-states of Antiquity and the Middle Ages. At times these groups sought to increase their membership in the interest of improving the security of their position of power by adequate numbers. At other times they restricted their membership to protect the value of their monopolistic position. The same phenomenon is not uncommon in monastic orders and religious sects which have passed from a stage of religious proselytizing to one of restriction in the interest of the maintenance of an ethical standard or for the protection of material interests. There is a similar close relationship between the extension of market relationships in the interest of increased turnover on the one hand, their monopolistic restriction on the other. The promotion of linguistic uniformity is today a natural result of the interests of publishers and writers, as opposed to the earlier, not uncommon, tendency for class groups to maintain linguistic peculiarities or even for secret languages to be built up.

Both the extent and the methods of regulation and exclusion in relation to outsiders may vary widely, so that the transition from a state of openness to one of regulation and closure is gradual. Various conditions of participation may be laid down; qualifying tests, a period of probation, requirement of possession of a share which can be purchased under certain conditions, election of new members by ballot, membership or eligibility by birth or by virtue of achievements open to anyone. Finally, in the case of closure and the appropriation of rights within the group, status may be dependent on the acquisition of an appropriated right. There is a wide variety of different degrees of closure and of conditions of participation. Thus regulation and closure are relative concepts. There are all manner of gradual shadings as between an exclusive club, a theatrical audience the members of which have purchased tickets, and a party rally to which the largest possible number has been urged to come;

similarly, from a church service open to the general public through the rituals of a limited sect to the mysteries of a secret cult.

Similarly, closure within the group as between the members themselves and in their relations with each other may also assume the most varied forms. Thus a caste, a guild, or a group of stock-exchange brokers, which is closed to outsiders, may allow to its members a perfectly free competition for all the advantages which the group as a whole monopolizes for itself. Or it may assign every member strictly to the enjoyment of certain advantages, such as claims over customers or particular business opportunities, for life or even on a hereditary basis. This is particularly characteristic of India. Similarly a closed group of settlers may allow its members free use of the resources of its area or may restrict them rigidly to a plot assigned to each individual household. A closed group of colonists may allow free use of the land or sanction and guarantee permanent appropriation of separate holdings. In such cases all conceivable transitional and intermediate forms can be found. Historically, the closure of eligibility to fiefs, benefices, and offices within the group, and the appropriation on the part of those enjoying them, have occurred in the most varied forms. Similarly, the establishment of rights to and possession of particular jobs on the part of workers may develop all the way from the "closed shop" to a right to a particular job. The first step in this development may be to prohibit the dismissal of a worker without the consent of the workers' representatives. The development of the "works councils" in Germany after 1918 might be a first step in this direction, though it need not be.[1]

All the details must be reserved to particular studies. The most extreme form of permanent appropriation is found in cases where particular rights are guaranteed to an individual or to certain groups of them, such as households, clans, families, in such a way that it is specified in the order either that, in case of death, the rights descend to specific heirs, or that the possessor is free to transfer them to any other person at will. Such a person thereby becomes a party to the social relationship so that, when appropriation has reached this extreme within the group, it becomes to that extent an open group in relation to outsiders. This is true so long as acquisition of membership is not subject to the ratification of the other, prior members.

The principal motives for closure of a relationship are: (a) The maintenance of quality, which is often combined with the interest in prestige and the consequent opportunities to enjoy honor, and even profit. Examples are communities of ascetics, monastic orders, especially, for instance, the Indian mendicant orders, religious sects like the Puritans, organized groups of warriors, of retainers and other functionaries, organized citizen bodies as in the Greek states, craft guilds; (b) orientation to the scarcity of advantages in their bearing on consumption needs *(Nahrungsspielraum)*. Examples are monopolies of consumption, the most developed form of which is a self-subsistent village community; (c) orientation to the scarcity of opportunities for acquisition *(Erwerbsspielraum)*. This is found in trade monopolies such as the guilds, the ancient monopolies of fishing rights, and so on. Usually motive (a) is combined with (b) or (c).

Translated by A. M. Henderson and Talcott Parsons

9. Power, Authority, and Imperative Control

"Power" *(Macht)* is the probability that one actor within a social relationship will be in a position to carry out his own will despite resistance, regardless of the basis on which this probability rests.

"Imperative control" *(Herrschaft)*[1] is the probability that a command with a given specific content will be obeyed by a given group of persons. "Discipline" is the probability that by virtue of habituation a command will receive prompt and automatic obedience in stereotyped forms, on the part of a given group of persons.

The concept of power is highly comprehensive from the point of view of sociology. All conceivable qualities of a person and all conceivable combinations of circumstances may put him in a position to impose his will in a given situation. The sociological concept of imperative control must hence be more precise and can only mean the probability that a *command* will be obeyed.

The concept of "discipline" includes the "habituation" characteristic of uncritical and unresisting mass obedience.

The existence of imperative control turns only on the actual presence of one person successfully issuing orders to others; it does not necessarily imply either the existence of an administrative staff, or, for that matter, of a corporate group. It is, however, uncommon to find it not associated with at least one of these. A corporate group, the members of which are by virtue of their membership subjected to the legitimate exercise of imperative control, that is to "authority," will be called an "imperatively coordinated" group[2] *(Herrschaftsverband)*.

The head of a household exercises authority without an administrative staff. A Bedouin chief, who levies contributions from the caravans, persons, and shipments of goods which pass his stronghold, exercises imperative control over the total group of changing and indeterminate individuals who, though they are not members of any corporate group as such, have gotten themselves into a particular common situation. But to do this, he needs a following which, on the appropriate occasions, serves as his administrative staff in exercising the necessary compulsion. This type of imperative control is, however, conceivable as carried out by a single individual without the help of any administrative staff.

If it possesses an administrative staff, a corporate group is always, by virtue of this fact, to some degree imperatively coordinated. But the concept is relative. The usual imperatively coordinated group is at the same time an administrative organization. The character of the corporate group is determined by a variety of factors: the mode in which the administration is carried out, the character of the personnel, the objects over which it exercises control, and the extent of effective jurisdiction of its authority. The first two factors in particular are dependent in the highest degree on the way in which the authority is legitimized.

Translated by A. M. Henderson and Talcott Parsons

10. Political and Religious Corporate Groups

An imperatively coordinated corporate group will be called "political" if and insofar as the enforcement of its order is carried out continually within a given territorial area by the application and threat of physical force on the part of the administrative staff. A compulsory political association with continuous organization *(politischer Anstaltsbetrieb)* will be called a "state" if and insofar as its administrative staff successfully upholds a claim to the monopoly of the legitimate use of physical force in the enforcement of its order. A system of social action, especially that of a corporate group, will be spoken of as "politically oriented" if and insofar as it aims at exerting influence on the directing authorities of a corporate political group; especially at the appropriation, expropriation, redistribution or allocation of the powers of government.

An imperatively coordinated corporate group will be called a "hierocratic" group *(hierokratischer Verband)* if and insofar as for the enforcement of its order it employs "psychic" coercion through the distribution or denial of religious benefits ("hierocratic coercion"). A compulsory hierocratic association with continuous organization will be called a "church" if and insofar as its administrative staff claims a monopoly of the legitimate use of hierocratic coercion.

It goes without saying that the use of physical force is neither the sole, nor even the most usual, method of administration of political corporate groups. On the contrary, their heads have employed all conceivable means to bring about their ends. But, at the same time, the threat of force, and in case of need its actual use, is the method which is specific to political associations and is always the last resort when others have failed. Conversely, physical force is by no means limited to political groups, even as a legitimate method of enforcement. It has been freely used by kinship groups, household groups, the medieval guilds under certain circumstances, and everywhere by all those entitled to bear arms. In addition to the fact that it uses, among other means, physical force to enforce its system of order, the political group is further characterized by the fact that the authority of its administrative staff is claimed as binding within a territorial area and this claim is upheld by force. Whenever corporate groups which make use of force are also characterized by the claim to territorial jurisdiction, such as village communities or even some household groups, federations of guilds or of trade unions, they are, by definition, to that extent political groups.

It is not possible to define a political corporate group, including the state, in terms of the end to which its corporate action is devoted. All the way from provision for subsistence to the patronage of art, there is no conceivable end which *some* political corporation has not at some time pursued. And from the protection of personal security to the administration of justice, there is none which *all* have recognized. Thus it is possible to define the "political" character of a corporate group only in terms of the *means* peculiar to it, the use of force. This means is, however, in the above sense specific, and is indispensable to its character. It is even, under certain circumstances, elevated into an end in itself.

This usage does not exactly conform to everyday speech. But the latter is too inconsistent to be used for technical purposes. We speak of the "open market" policy[1] of a central bank, of the "financial" policy of an association, of the "educational" policy of a local authority, and mean the systematic treatment and control of a particular problem. It comes considerably closer to the present meaning when we distinguish the "political" aspect or implication of a question. Thus there is the "political" official, the "political" newspaper, the "political" revolution, the "political" club, the "political" party, and the "political" consequences of an action, as distinguished from others such as the economic, cultural, or religious aspect of the persons, affairs or processes in question. In this usage we generally mean by "political" things that have to do with relations of authority within what is, in the present terminology, a political organization, the state. The reference is to things which are likely to uphold, to change or overthrow, to hinder or promote, the interests of the state, as distinguished from persons, things, and processes which have nothing to do with it. This usage thus seeks to bring out the common features of the various means of exercising authority which are used within the state in enforcing its order, abstracting them from the ends they serve. Hence it is legitimate to claim that the definition put forward here is only a more precise formulation of what is meant in everyday usage, in that it gives sharp emphasis to what is the most characteristic of these means; the actual or threatened use of force. It is, of course, true that everyday usage applies the term "political" not only to groups which are the direct agents of the legitimate use of force itself, but also to other, often wholly peaceful groups, which attempt to influence corporate action politically. It seems best for present purposes to distinguish this type of social action, "politically oriented" action, from political action as such, the actual corporate action of political groups.

Since the concept of the state has only in modern times reached its full development, it is best to define it in terms appropriate to the modern type of state, but at the same time, in terms which abstract from the values of the present day, since these are particularly subject to change. The primary formal characteristics of the modern state are as follows: It possesses an administrative and legal order subject to change by legislation, to which the organized corporate activity of the administrative staff, which is also regulated by legislation, is oriented. This system of order claims binding authority, not only over the members of the state, the citizens, most of whom have obtained membership by birth, but also to a very large extent, over all action taking place in the area of its jurisdiction. It is thus a compulsory association with a territorial basis. Furthermore, to-day, the use of force is regarded as legitimate only so far as it is either permitted by the state or prescribed by it. Thus the right of a father to discipline his children is recognized—a survival of the former independent authority of the head of a household, which in the right to use force has sometimes extended to a power of life and death over children and slaves. The claim of the modern state to monopolize the use of force is as essential to it as its character of compulsory jurisdiction and of continuous organization.

In formulating the concept of a hierocratic corporate group, it is not possible to use the character of the religious sanctions it commands, whether worldly or other-worldly, material or spiritual, as the decisive criterion. What is important is rather the fact that its control over these sanctions can form the basis of a system of spiritual imperative control over human beings. What is most characteristic of the church, even in the common usage of the term, is the fact that it is a rational, compulsory association with continuous organization and that it claims a monopolistic authority. It is normal for a church to strive for complete imperative control on a territorial basis and to attempt to set up the corresponding territorial or parochial organization. So far as this takes place, the means by which this claim to monopoly is upheld, will vary from case to case. But historically, its control over territorial areas has not been nearly so essential to the church as to political corporations; and this is particularly true to-day. It is its character as a compulsory association, particularly the fact that one becomes a member of the church by birth, which distinguishes a church from a "sect." It is characteristic of the latter that it is a voluntary association and admits only persons with specific religious qualifications. This subject will be further discussed in the Sociology of Religion.[2]

Translated by A. M. Henderson and Talcott Parsons

Domination and Stratification

11. Legitimacy and the Types of Authority

Authority is the probability that specific commands (or all commands) will be obeyed by a given group of people. Thus not every means for exercising power and influence over other people is involved here. Authority, in this sense, can be based in each individual case on the most varied motives for compliance: from dull habit to purely rational calculation. A certain minimal willingness to obey; that is, an interest (external or internalized) in obeying is essential in every real model of domination.

Not every system of authority employs economic means, and it is even less likely to have economic purposes. But every system of authority exercising power over a number of people normally requires a staff of individuals (administrative staff); that is, certain reliable, obedient individuals who normally can be trusted to order their conduct so as to execute general instructions as well as specific commands. This administrative staff may base obedience to their superiors simply on custom, on pure affection, on material interests, or value-rational motives. The type of motive largely determines the mode of authority. When purely material interests and opportunism constitute the basis of the relation between the administrator and his staff, this signifies here, as elsewhere, a relatively unstable condition. Normally other motives—affectual or value-rational interests—are also involved. In exceptional cases these alone can be decisive. In everyday experience, these relationships, like others, are ruled by custom and material, purposive-rational interests. But neither custom and material interests, nor purely affectional and value-rational motives constitute a sufficiently reliable basis for authority. To these must be added an additional component: the belief in legitimacy.

No authority voluntarily limits itself solely to material, affectual, or value-rational means of appeal for its survival. Rather, each system attempts to establish and maintain belief in its legitimacy. All differ fundamentally, however, in respect to the nature of the legitimacy claim, the type of obedience, the specific administrative staff guaranteeing it and the character of the authority being exercised. The effect, too, differs markedly. For this reason it is useful to distinguish types of authority according to their typical claim to legitimacy. In achieving this it will be expedient to begin with modern and therefore familiar conditions.

That this particular criterion for differentiation is chosen over any other can only be justified by the result. That certain other typical distinguishing criteria are avoided for the present and incorporated later will not create significant difficulty. The legitimacy of an authority, due to its definite connection to the legitimacy of ownership, is by no means based solely on its ideal component.

Not every conventional or legally grounded "claim" can be called an authority relationship. Otherwise a worker, in receiving his contractual wage, could be considered "master" of his employer in that the latter can be taken to court by the worker if the wage agreement is not fulfilled. In reality, the worker is formally, "by rights," an equal party to his employer in a contractual agreement involving the exchange of services. But that this exchange developed in a formally free manner by no means excludes the concept of an authority relationship here: just as the voluntarily accepted authority of the employer is represented to the worker in his work regulations and instructions, so too is the freely accepted authority of the feudal lord represented to the vassal in his fealty. That obedience to military discipline is formally "involuntary," and that of the workplace "voluntary," does not in itself differentiate the two; the discipline of the workplace also represents subjugation to authority. The position of the bureaucrat, too, is accepted on a contractual basis and can be terminated, and even the role of the subject can be freely accepted and (to a certain degree) dissolved. Absolute compulsion exists only in slavery. On the other hand, however, if a party manages to achieve a monopolistic position and exert economic power; that is, in this case, the possibility for the contractual partner to "dictate" the contractual terms, this should not be considered an exercise of authority. In the same way, erotic appeal or superior influence in sports or discussion cannot be termed an exercise of authority. If a large bank is in a position to force other banks into a cartel arrangement, this alone should not be considered authority. Authority is exercised when a direct hierarchical relationship is created, whereby the instructions of the management of the one bank explicitly place a claim on another bank with the probability that the instructions will be carried out with supervision and regardless of their content. Of course the line of distinction is here, as elsewhere, fluid: there are a great number of intermediary levels between indebtedness and debt slavery. The dealings of a "salon" might border on authoritarian power without actually constituting "authority." Clear distinction is in reality often not possible; clear concepts are therefore all the more necessary.

The legitimacy of an authority can, of course, only be regarded as probability insofar as it is relevant and practical. It is certainly not the case that every submissive party is primarily (or even at all) oriented toward this belief in respect to the organ of authority. Whether in individual cases or collectively, compliance may well be spawned by hypocrisy for opportunistic reasons: out of material self-interest and therefore for practical reasons, or out of individual weakness and dependence, and thus practiced unavoidably and without alternative. But this is not crucial for the determination of authority. Rather, it is essential that the particular legitimacy claim actually be valid in accordance with its type, and, to a relevant degree, that it establish its position, and designate the chosen means to exercise authority. Furthermore, a system of authority can frequently protect itself so absolutely through the clearly shared interests between the chief administrator and his staff (bodyguards, Pretorians, "red" or "white" guards) in contrast to the subordinates, that, assured of the latter's dependence, those in authority themselves may scorn their own claim to legitimacy. It is then always the case that the type of legitimacy relations between administrator and staff are very differently structured according to the existing relations for authority between them, and this arrangement will prove to be highly significant for the structure of the system of domination, as will be shown.

Obedience ideally signifies that the conduct of the obeyer proceed as if he has made the content of the command a maxim for his own activity and for its own sake. Without concern for his own valuation of the command as such, his activity ideally occurs exclusively for the sake of the formal obligation.

Purely psychologically, the chain of causality can vary broadly, and especially between suggestion and empathy. This distinction, however, is not relevant for the typology of authority.

The scope of the authoritative influence in the social and cultural spheres is fundamentally broader than appears at first glance. This authority, for example, is that practiced in the schools, where it determines orthodox forms of speech and writing. The language of the chancellery, and of politically autocephalous groups; that is, the functional codes of the administrators, are counted among these orthodox forms of speech and writing, and have even led to the political separation of nations (e.g., Holland from Germany). Parental and educational authority, however, extend far beyond the seemingly formal determination of culture, in the impression they exercise on youth, and therefore people generally.

That administrator and staff represent themselves as servants of the ruled proves, of course, nothing about the actual character of authority. Later on, there will be more to say concerning the substantive characteristics of so-called democracy. In almost all conceivable cases, a certain minimum amount of guaranteed power, (i.e., "authority"), must always be present for the issuing of commands.

There are three pure types of legitimate authority. The basis for their claim to legitimacy may be primarily one of:

(1) *Rational* character—resting on the common belief in the legality of rules and the right of those empowered to exercise authority (i.e., legal authority); or

(2) *Traditional* character—resting on the common belief in the sanctity of existing traditions and the legitimacy of that authority thereby empowered (i.e., traditional authority); or finally

(3) *Charismatic* character—resting on an uncommon devotion to the sanctity, heroism or otherwise impressive character of an individual and to the dispositions openly enacted by that person (i.e., charismatic authority).

In the case of statutory authority, obedience is accorded the legally prescribed technically impersonal order. This obedience is further accorded specific persons in whom authority is vested on the basis of the formal legitimacy of this legally prescribed order, its dispositions and its scope. In the case of traditional authority, obedience is accorded that individual empowered by the tradition who is (within its domain) bound to that tradition. Obedience is accorded on the basis of loyalty to the leader within the scope of custom. In the case of charismatic authority, it is the charismatically qualified leader to whom obedience is accorded and on the basis of a personal trust in the leader's revelation, his heroism or his exemplary character within the parameters of the individual's willingness to believe in this charisma.

The utility of this classification can only be established by the results of systematic analysis. The concept of charisma ("gift of grace") is drawn from early Christian terminology. For the Christian hierocracy, Rudolph Sohm, in his *Church Law,* is the first to introduce the concept, if not the actual terminology. Others (Karl Holl in his *Enthusiasm and Power of Atonement* [1898], for example) have further clarified certain important consequences of this phenomenon. The concept is thus not a new one.

That none of these three ideal types, a discussion of which is to follow, really occur historically in their pure form should certainly not prevent us from expressing them in as sharply focused a conceptual framework as possible. Later on (chapter 13) we will discuss the transformation of pure charisma into its routinized form, thereby enhancing the essential relevancy of this concept to empirical forms of authority. But even so, for every empirical historical incidence of authority, it can be said that the study doesn't attempt to be the definitive text on the subject. Sociological typology offers empirical historical research an essential advantage which cannot be underestimated: it can determine, in individual cases involving concrete forms of authority, what most closely approximates such types as: "charisma," "hereditary charisma," "charisma of office," and "patriarchical," "bureaucratic," "status" authority, etc. In this way, consistent, unambiguous concepts can be employed. One thing is certain: it is by no means the author's viewpoint that a totalistic historical reality can be captured in the conceptual framework to be developed.

Translated by Martin Black

12. Charismatic Authority

Charisma is to be considered an uncommon quality of an individual personality (originally deemed a magical quality, whether of prophets, healers, wisemen, leaders of the hunt, or war heroes). It invests that personality with supernatural, superhuman or at least specifically extraordinary powers which are not accessible to other individuals. These qualities are thought to be either of divine origin or exemplary personal characteristics, and therefore designate the individual as a leader. How the relevant quality might be "objectively" assessed from an ethical, aesthetic, or any other point of view is obviously immaterial: of sole importance is how the charismatically ruled, (i.e., the "followers"), assess this quality.

Examples of this type of authority are the charisma of a "berserk" (whose manic seizures had been apparently incorrectly attributed to the use of certain drugs: in Medieval Byzantium, a number of these individuals possessing a charismatic war frenzy were assembled as a kind of instrument of war), the charisma of a "showman" (a magician for whose ecstacies, in the pure type, the capacity for epileptic seizures was considered a pre-condition), the charisma of the founder of Mormonism, Joseph Smith, (who actually may have been a refined swindler, although this cannot be established with certainty) or the charisma possessed by writers such as Kurt Eisner who is his own best audience in proclaiming his demagogic success. These examples will all be treated by a value-free sociology in the same manner as the charisma of those figures conventionally judged to be the greatest heroes, prophets, and saints.

(1) It is recognition on the part of the ruled which is decisive for the validity of charisma. This recognition is guaranteed on the basis of proof (originally always a miracle), and is freely given out of devotion to the manifest revelation, hero worship, or trust in the leader. But this recognition is not (in the case of genuine charisma) the basis for legitimacy; it is rather the duty of those who, by virtue of their commitment and provenness, are summoned to the recognition of this quality. This recognition, psychologically born of enthusiasm or adversity and hope, involves complete personal devotion.

No prophet has ever considered his qualification dependent upon the opinion of the masses, no chosen king or charismatic duke has treated an opposing or reticent faction as other than delinquent in their duty: those who have not taken part in the military campaign of a leader, for which the recruitment is formally voluntary, have been universally treated with disdain.

(2) If charismatic proof is not forthcoming, if the charismatically gifted leader appears abandoned by his god, his magical or his heroic powers, if success is repeatedly denied him and, above all, if his leadership does not enhance the well-being of those subject to his authority, then there is every possibility that his charismatic author-

ity may vanish. This is the genuine charismatic meaning of divine power.

Even among old Germanic kings there was occasionally a "scorned one." The same is true among so-called primitive peoples. In China, the charismatic qualification of the monarch (transmitted by heredity; see Chapter 13, below) was so strictly observed that any misfortune, regardless of its nature (not only defeat in war, but also droughts, floods, unsavory astronomical phenomena etc.), required public penance of him and could potentially force his abdication. If such were the case, it indicated that he did not possess the charisma of virtue required by the heavenly spirit and he was therefore not a legitimate "son of heaven."

(3) A group or community subject to charismatic authority is cohesive for reasons of emotional communal integration. The administrative staff of the charismatic leader is not characterized by an "official" bureaucracy and its members are not technically trained. The staff is selected neither on the basis of social status, nor for reasons of domestic or personal dependency. Rather, selection occurs according to charismatic qualities in the same way that disciples correspond to their prophet, adherents to their warlord and, in general, loyal retainers to their leader. There is no appointment or dismissal, no career track and no promotion. Appointees are rather summoned by the leader on the grounds of charismatic qualification. There is no hierarchy; the leader will intervene on a general basis or in specific cases when the administrative staff proves charismatically incompetent for a certain task or appeals to the leader for assistance. There are neither administrative districts and specific spheres of competence, nor appropriations of bureaucratic authority on the basis of social privilege. Possible limitations on charismatic impact and mission are, therefore, territorial or functional in nature. While there is neither salary nor a living per se, disciples or followers live primarily in an honor-bound communistic relationship with their leader on means solicited from patrons. There are no established authorities, but rather emissaries who either have been invested with the charismatic authority of their leader, or themselves possess the charisma necessary to fulfill their obligations. There are no formal regulations, no abstract legal axioms, no rational systems of judicial rulings oriented to them, and no judicial decisions and legal axioms based on traditional precedent. In the place of these, formal legal judgments are newly created from case to case, originally possessing the authority of divine judgments and revelations. Substantive to all

genuine types of charismatic authority, however, is the tenet: "thus it is written—and yet I say unto you." The genuine prophet, like the genuine military leader or any other genuine leader, proclaims, creates, or demands new precepts in the original sense of charisma; that is, either by virtue of revelation, oracle, inspiration, or by the strength of his own will which is recognized by his spiritual, military, or political community as emanating from the same source. This recognition is obligatory. Should one authority come into conflict with a competing charismatic authority, a resolution can only occur by means of magic or, when necessary, via a decisive physical battle between the leaders involving obligatory acknowledgement by the community. Of necessity, only one side can be proven right in this conflict, while the other side represents a wrong which must be expiated.

Charismatic authority, due to its extraordinary character, stands opposed to rational forms of authority (bureaucratic forms in particular), as well as to traditional forms (especially those characterized by a patriarchal, patrimonial, or estate structure). Both of these primary types are specific everyday forms of authority; the genuine charismatic form is specifically the opposite. Bureaucratic authority is specifically rational in the sense of its debt to intellectually analyzable rules; charismatic authority, in contrast, is specifically irrational in the sense of its inherent freedom from rules. Traditional authority is bound to the precedents of the past, and as such, is likewise associated with rules. Within its sphere of influence, charismatic authority subverts the past, and in this sense is specifically revolutionary. Whether it be on the part of the leader or socially privileged status groups, no authority of this type recognizes the appropriation of power on the basis of the possession of property. On the contrary, authority is only legitimate to the extent and for the duration that the leader is able to sustain his personal charisma; that is, as long as it is accorded recognition and as long as loyal subjects, disciples and other followers are charismatically useful over time.

The above hardly requires further elucidation. It applies to the purely plebiscitary charismatic leader (Napoleon's "rule of genius," which elevated plebians to kings and generals) as well as to prophets and war heroes.

(4) Pure charisma is specifically foreign to economic calculation. It constitutes, wherever it appears, a "calling" in the emphatic sense of the word—as a mission or spiritual task. It disdains and repudi-

ates, in its purest form, the economic utilization of the gift of grace as a source of income. This, of course, often remains more an intent than a reality. It is not that charisma renounces the possession and acquisition of property as do prophets and their disciples under certain circumstances (see below). The war hero and his followers seek the spoils of war, the plebiscitary leader or the charismatic party chief target the material means to power. Aside from this, the former also seeks a material splendor for his authority in order to secure his prestige. But what all forms do repudiate, provided they are of the genuine charismatic type, are the traditional or rational routine ("everyday") market strategies; that is, the securing of a regular "income" by means of strategic, continuous, economic activity. Typical charismatic means of providing for its needs are, on the one hand, voluntary, involving patronage either on the grand scale such as donations, endowments, bribery, and gratuities, or by begging. On the other hand, needs can be met by either violent forms of exploitation (war spoils) or formally peaceful means (extortion). From the point of view of rational economy, charismatic procurement is a typical "anti-economic" force. This is because it repudiates the establishment of everyday routine. Displaying complete indifference, it can only partake of occasional irregular acquisitions. For some of its forms, the dependence on property income as a type of release from economic concerns can constitute the economic basis of charismatic existence. For the average charismatic "revolutionary," however, this is not the case.

The manner in which the Jesuits refused to assume official positions within the church is a rationalized application of this principle of discipleship. Certainly all heroes of asceticism, the mendicant orders, and religious libertinism can be included in this category. Almost all prophets have been supported by patrons. The words of Saint Paul: "If a man does not work, neither shall he eat," intended as a criticism of the parasitic missionaries of the time, was obviously not meant as an affirmation of the economy, but rather referred to the individual's obligation, regardless of how, to provide for his own support by means of a secondary occupation. The charismatic parable of the "lilies of the field" was not literally feasible whereas "take no thought for the morrow" potentially was. On the other hand, when considering a primarily artistic charismatic discipleship, it is conceivable that the requisite liberation from economic need actually limits "the truly called" to those who are, as a rule, economically independent, that is, those supported by property income (such as was at least the primary intention of the Stefan George circle).

(5) Charisma is the great revolutionary force of traditionalist historical periods. Distinct from a similarly revolutionary form, the power of reason, which either effects change externally by changing living conditions, living problems, and the attitudes toward them, or via intellectualizing, charisma can cause transformation from within. Whether born of privation, adversity, or inspiration, this redirecting of thought and energy might signify a completely new orientation to the many different forms of life and to the concept of "world" in general. In pre-rationalistic times, tradition and charisma accounted for almost the entire compass of human activity.

Translated by Martin Black

13. The Routinization of Charisma

Charismatic authority, in its genuine form, is of a character specifically foreign to everyday routine. Social relationships subject to it are of a strictly personal nature and play an important role in the validity of charismatic personal qualities and their confirmation. If these, however, are not to remain purely ephemeral, but demonstrate a quality of permanence, such as a community of fellow worshipers, warriors, disciples, a party organization, or any type of political or hierocratic group, it is necessary that the character of charismatic authority be fundamentally altered. In its purely ideal form, charismatic authority only exists, so to speak, *in statu nascendi.* It will become either traditionalized, or rationalized (i.e., legalized), or a combination of both. The primary reasons for this are the following:

(1) the ideal or material interests of the followers in the perpetuation and continual rejuvenation of the community,

(2) the even stronger ideal and material interests of the administrative staff, be it comprised of disciples, royal retainers, followers, etc. Their interests are:
    (a) to perpetuate the existence of the relationship, and
    (b) to perpetuate it in such a way that their own positions, both ideal and material, are placed on a permanent, ordinary basis. This is achieved by outwardly creating the possibility for family life or at least a secure, absorbing situation in place of the type of mission that isolates one from the spheres of the family and the market place.

These problems typically arise with the disappearance of the charismatic leader's person and the subsequent question of a successor. The manner in which this problem is solved (if, in fact, at all) and the means by which the charismatic community continues to exist (or now first emerges), are essential in determining the nature of the developing social relationships.

The problems can have the following types of solutions:

(1) A new search for a charismatic leader, qualified according to certain criteria. An example of a relatively pure type is the selection process of a new Dalai Lama (involving a child whose characteristics suggest that it is the incarnation of the godhead, in a manner similar to the search for the Bull of Apis).

In this case, the legitimacy of the new charismatic leader is based on criteria; that is, rules from which a tradition then arises. This, in turn, leads to a process of traditionalization reducing the purely personal character of charismatic leadership.

(2) By means of revelation: oracle, lot, divine judgment or other techniques of selection. Here the legitimacy of the new charismatic leader is acquired from the legitimacy of the selection technique; hence a form of legalization. The Israelite *Shofetim* [Judges] are said occasionally to have been of this character. Saul is to have been designated by the old war oracle.
(3) By means of the designation of the successor by the former charismatic leader and his recognition by the community. This is a very common form. The creation of the Roman magistracies was originally entirely of this character (most clearly surviving in the appointment of the dictator and in the institution of the "*interrex*"). Legitimacy in this case is acquired by means of designation.
(4) Through designation of the successor by the charismatically qualified administrative staff and the recognition of the community. In its intended form, this should be differentiated from the concept of the vote, nomination, party nomination, etc. It is not an issue of free selection or a majority designation, but rather a strictly obligatory selection; that is, the correct designation of the right person, of the truly charismatic leader—one who might well be correctly selected by the minority. Unanimity may be required, acknowledgement of error an obligation, and the per-

sistence of error a serious delinquency. A wrong choice is an offense (originally magical) which must be expiated.

In any case, legitimacy can thus easily take on the appearance of an acquired right which, observing all due precautions, is correctly obtained chiefly via certain formalities (coronations, etc.). This was the original intention of bishops' and kings' coronations as performed by the clergy or the princes with the approval of the community. Such was the custom in the Western world, with numerous analogous ceremonies around the globe. That the idea of election originated in this process will be the subject of later discussion.

(5) By means of the conception that charisma is a quality of hereditary nature and transmitted through the family blood-line, especially to the next of kin; that is, hereditary charisma. The line of hereditary succession is not necessarily that of appropriated rights, but is often distinct from it. Selection of the correct heir within the clan might also need to be determined by means of the criteria (1) through (4) listed above.

Among indigenous black cultures, duels between brothers often determine succession. The line of succession is often followed in such a way that the relationship of the next generation to the ancestral spirits is not disturbed as, for example, in China. Rule by seniority or designation via the followers is very often practiced in the Orient (for this reason it was one's "duty" to kill off all other conceivable aspirants in the House of Osman).

Except for a few other individual cases, the unambiguous principle of primogeniture has prevailed only in medieval Europe and in Japan. The result has led to a consolidation of political groups and the avoidance of undue conflict between several candidates from the same charismatic clan.

Under these circumstances, belief is no longer accorded by dint of the charismatic qualities of the person, but rather on the basis of the hereditary line of legitimate acquisition (i.e., through traditionalization and legalization). The concept of divine grace comes to be wholly changed in meaning. No longer dependent upon gaining the recognition of the ruled, authority is now based on hereditary right. Personal charisma may be altogether absent.

The hereditary monarchy, the enormous number of hereditary hierarchies in Asia, and the hereditary charisma of clan groups have all served as criteria of rank and qualification for fiefs and sinecures.

(6) By means of the impression that charisma can be transferred or can be nurtured (originally by magic) by the bearer of charisma using ritualistic means; that is, the objectification of charisma especially as exemplified in the charisma of office. The belief in legitimacy is, in this case, no longer associated with the individual, but rather with the acquired qualities and the effectiveness of the ritual acts.

The most important example is the transmission or confirmation of priestly charisma by means of anointment, consecration and coronation. The *character indelebilis* signifies the inherent separation of the powers of the charismatic office from those of the person of the priest. For this very reason, there has been, beginning with Donatism and Montanism through the Puritan (baptist) revolution, the occasion for constant dispute (the "hireling" of the Quakers is the preacher possessing the charisma of office.)

Concomitant with the interest in routinizing charisma for the purpose of securing successors is that of the administrative staff in the routinization of charisma. It is only *in statu nascendi* and as long as the rule of the charismatic leader is genuinely extra-ordinary, that the administrative staff, whether from patronage, spoils, or occasional acquisitions, is able to survive together with a leader whom it serves for reasons of faith and enthusiasm. Rarely does the number of those prepared to "make" this "idealistic calling" their living extend beyond the relatively small enthusiastic circle of disciples and followers. The vast majority of disciples and followers will choose (in the long run) to make a material living out of their "calling" as well. This is, in fact, necessary lest the group disintegrate.

As a result, the routinization of charisma also occurs:

(1) in the form of the followers' or disciples' appropriation of power and their earning opportunities, as well as from the regulation of their recruitment.

(2) This traditionalization or legalization (depending upon whether rational precepts are involved or not) can take any one of a number of typical forms.

(a) The genuine form of recruitment is one based upon personal charisma. In the process of routinization, the followers or discipleship may set up standards for recruitment, in particular (1) standards of education, and (2) standards of testing.

Charisma can only be awakened and tested, but not learned or taught. All types of magical asceticism (whether practiced by magicians or heroes), and all novitiates belong in this category, in which the administrative staff exhibits a closed form. Only the tested novices will be granted access to positions of authority. The genuine charismatic leader can successfully oppose prerequisites of this sort; his successor, at least if selected by the administrative staff, cannot.

The asceticism of magicians' and warriors' groups in the "man's world," along with their initiation ceremonies and age groups, belong in this category. He who doesn't successfully pass the initiation remains a "woman," that is, excluded from the circle of followers.

(b) Charismatic standards can easily be transformed into those defining traditional social status (hereditary charismatic) norms. If the leader is in power on the basis of hereditary charisma, both his administrative staff and, possibly, his followers are likely to be selected and deployed on a similar basis. In cases where a political organization strictly and completely adheres to the principle of hereditary charisma and all appropriations of authority, fiefs, sinecures, and earning opportunities occur on this basis, this type exists as a "clan state" *(Geschlechterstaat)*. In such a case, all powers and opportunities become traditionalized. The family heads, traditional gerontocrats, or patriarchs who have not been legitimized on the basis of personal charisma, regulate the exercise of these powers which cannot be expropriated from the family. It is not the type of position he holds which determines the "rank" of the man or his family, but the hereditary charismatic *family* rank which determines the positions he can occupy.

Classic examples of this are Japan, prior to the development of bureaucracy, and without a doubt, China, to a large extent (the "old families"), before the influx of rationalization to the provinces; India, with its caste system; Russia, prior to the introduction of *mestnichestvo* and in other forms later on. In the same way, in fact, all hereditary social statuses enjoying established privileges throughout the world belong in this category.

(c) The administrative staff can require and bring about the creation and appropriation of individual positions and economic opportunities for its members. In such a case, whether by means of traditionalization or legalization, the following emerge: (1) Sinecures (leading to prebendary forms of organization—see above) (2) Offices (the development of patrimonialism and bureaucracy—see above) (3) Fiefs (feudalization).

All of the above revenue sources become appropriated, thereby replacing the original purely noneconomic forms of provision by means of charity or booty.

In reference to case (1), sinecures may consist of proceeds from begging, payments in kind, monetary tax proceeds or proceeds from fees. The above may be appropriated through regulation of provisions initially in the form of patronage (compare to regulated begging) or spoils (compare to payments in kind and monetary taxes) by a rational organization of finance.

Examples of the above are to be found in Buddhism (regulated begging), and Chinese and Japanese rice taxes (payments in kind). Monetary taxes have been the rule in all rationalized states of conquest, and individual cases of proceeds from fees can be found everywhere, in particular among priests and judges, but also among military authorities, as in India.

In reference to case (2), the "institutionalization" of the charismatic mission can take the form either of patrimonialization or bureaucratization. The former case is generally the rule, whereas the latter case is more a phenomenon of antiquity and the modern Western world, occurring less frequently and as an exception elsewhere.

In reference to case (3), two different situations are possible: one in which only the land itself is appropriated as a fief, allowing the position as such to retain its missionlike character; or one in which there is a full fief-like appropriation of the powers and authority. The two cases are difficult to distinguish. The orientation to the mission-like character of the position, however, was slow to disappear, even during the Middle Ages.

A prerequisite for the routinization of charisma is the elimination of its noneconomic predisposition, its adaptation to financial forms of fulfilling needs, and therefore, to economic conditions necessary to raising taxes and duties. When a charismatic mission begins to develop a prebendary nature, the laity becomes differentiated from the clergy. The clergy, who are participating members of the charismatic administrative staff, now become routinized (as priests of the emerging church). In an emerging political organization, the routinized administrative staff of vassals, sinecurists and officials (rather than the loyal retainers) become differentiated from the taxpayer (in the rational case it is the state and the functionaries rather than the voluntary party workers who stand differentiated from the taxpayer).

This can be typically observed among the Buddhists and the Hindu sects. The same can be seen in all long-lasting rationalized empires of conquest, as well as in political parties and other frameworks initially intended as purely charismatic.

With the routinization process, the charismatic authority is essentially transformed into one of the everyday authorities—the patrimonial form, especially in its estate or bureaucratic variant. Its original unusual character expresses itself in the charismatic status honor enjoyed, whether it be acquired by heredity or office-holding. This is shared by all who are subject to the appropriation, the leader as well as the administrative staff, and constitutes a type of prestige among ruling groups. An hereditary monarch ruling by "divine right" is no simple patrimonial lord, patriarch or sheik; a vassal is different from a medieval or modern official. A more detailed discussion belongs in the analysis of "status groups" (see chapter 16, below).

Routinization does not occur, as a rule, without a struggle. Initially, personal claims on the charisma of the leader are not forgotten, and the struggle between office-based, or hereditary, charisma and personal charisma is a typical historical process. Consider the following examples:

(1) The transformation of the power of absolution (dispensation of mortal sins) from a personal power held only by charismatic martyrs and ascetics into a power of the office of a bishop or a priest is an event which occurred much more slowly in the Orient than in the Occident under the influence of the Roman concept of "office." Revolutions led by charismatic leaders against the powers of charismatic heredity or office can be found in the history of any

organization, from the state to the trade unions (as is the case now! [1918–20]). But the more developed the economic interdependencies of the monetary economy, the greater the pressure of the charismatic subject's everyday needs becomes. The result is the tendency toward routinization, which is in operation everywhere and, in general, took effect very quickly. Charisma typically appears early on in the development of a religious (prophetic) or political (conquering) authority. It will give way before long, however, to routine powers as soon as its authority has been assured and, above all, as soon as it has gained sway over the masses.

(2) In all cases, one primary motive for the routinization of charisma is, naturally, a striving for security. This entails the legitimization, on the one hand, of the social prestige of positions of authority and, on the other, the economic opportunities for the followers and supporters of the leader. An additional motive develops, however, out of the objective necessity of adapting the orders and the administrative staff to the average everyday exigencies and conditions of an administration. Connected to this is the particular need for guiding principles to establish an administrative and jurisdictional tradition, a need equally necessary to both the administrative staff and those subject to its authority. Furthermore, there is a need for the ranking of positions held by members of the administrative staff. Finally, and of greatest importance, it is necessary that all administrative regulations be adapted to the everyday economic terms (this will be discussed in greater detail below). It is not feasible to fund a permanent, everyday administration in a fashion similar to that of a warring or prophetic charismatic authority; that is, via booty, contributions, gifts, hospitality, and the like.

(3) The problems of the routinization process, therefore, are not confined to the problem of succession and, in fact, involve much more than just this. The primary problem involves the transition from charismatic administrative staffs and corresponding administrative principles to a routinized system. But the problem of succession is crucial because it concerns the routinization of the charismatic core—the leader himself and his claim to legitimacy. In contrast to the problems of transition to traditional or legal structures and their accompanying administrative staffs, the charismatic succession problem reveals the peculiar and characteristic conceptions involved, which are only comprehensible when viewed in the context of this process. The most important of these conceptions are the charismatic designation of a successor and hereditary charisma.

(4) As was mentioned, the most important historical example of

successor designation by a charismatic leader is that of Rome. In respect to the *rex,* this arrangement is attested to by tradition, while the naming of the dictator, the co-emperor, and successor in the *Principat* are historically recorded. The style of appointing all upper-level officials with full powers clearly indicates that even they were designated as successors by the military commander, pending the approval of the citizen army. The nature of this development is clearly indicated by the fact that candidates were examined by the magistrate in office and originally could be excluded on an obviously arbitrary basis.

(5) The most important example of successor designation by the charismatic followers is the appointment of the bishops. Of special interest is that of the Pope, whose designation, in the original system, was in the hands of the clergy, while his recognition was the part of the lay community. It is probable (as U. Stutz has shown) that the election of the German Kaiser was later modelled on that of the appointment of bishops, in which designation was undertaken by certain princes and recognition granted by the "people" (i.e., those who bore arms). Similar forms are found throughout history.

(6) The classic country of origin for the development of hereditary charisma was India. All occupational skills, and especially, qualifications for positions of authority and power there were considered strictly bound to charismatic heredity. Any claim to fiefs and the accompanying powers was dependent upon membership in the royal clan and was granted by the eldest of the clan. Every level of religious office, including the extremely important and influential position of guru *(directeur de l'âme),* all traditional client relations, all positions within the village establishment (priests, barbers, laundrymen, guards, etc.) were also considered charismatically hereditary. The founding of every sect signified the foundation of a hereditary hierarchy (as was the case with Taoism in China as well). Prior to the introduction of the Chinese model of the patrimonial bureaucracy, which then led to prebendary forms and feudalism, the social framework of the Japanese "clan state" was based on purely charismatic heredity (as will be discussed later on in another connection).

The charismatic hereditary right to positions of authority developed in a similar way throughout the world. Qualification on the basis of self-achievement was replaced by a system in which qualification was based on genealogy. The appearance of this phenomenon became the basis for the development of status by birth as exemplified by the Roman nobility; by the concept of the *stirps regia* among the Germanic peoples as recorded by Tacitus; and by the competency qualifications for entry to tournaments and the right to make donations of the late Middle Ages. It can also be found in modern genealogical studies conducted at the request of the American *nouveau* aristocracy. In fact, the importance of genealogy becomes manifest wherever differentiation by "social status" has become established (more on this below).

Relationship between Charisma and Economy

The routinization of charisma is, in a very important respect, identical with the adaptation to the conditions of the economy as is required of the continually functioning forces of everyday life. In this respect, the economy is the determining, not the determined force. To the largest extent, the transformation of hereditary or office-related charisma serves as a means of legitimation for the existing or acquired economic powers of control. Not discounting the commitment of the ideological loyalists, the clinging to hereditary monarchy is conditioned by other considerations as well. The fact that all inherited and legitimately acquired possessions are shaken in the event that the divinely sanctioned inheritance of the crown is thrown into question is indication enough that it is more than coincidence alone that makes the monarchy more suited to the needs of the propertied classes than to those of the proletariat.

Aside from this, it is impossible to make generalizations (which are simultaneously objective observations of substance and value) about the relations of various possible modes of adaptation to the economic order; this will have to be reserved for a more specific analysis. The prebendary and feudalization process, and the appropriation of opportunities of all sorts on a hereditary charismatic basis, may, in all cases, have the same stereotyping effects on the economy, whether this process developed from initially charismatic circumstances or issued out of patrimonial and bureaucratic conditions. While the power of charisma, both economically and otherwise, is one of great revolutionary as well as destructive force (due to the fact that it is potentially ever oriented toward the new and the "unconditional"), with routinization, this initial impact is subverted. The economics of charismatic revolutions ought to be treated separately as it is a different matter altogether.

Translated by Martin Black

14. Collegiality and the Division of Powers

Whether on a traditional or rational basis, authority can be limited and controlled by specific means. The topic of concern here is not the traditional and legalistic limitations of authority as such. The present focus is rather on the specific social relationships and associations which effect these limitations and controls.

(1) A patrimonial or feudal authority is limited as a result of the privileges of status groups. This is especially pronounced when the division of power occurs in relation to the estates of the realm.

(2) A bureaucratic authority can be limited (and must actually be limited—normally at that point when the legality type reaches fullest development—to ensure that administrative actions occur only in accordance with the rules) by official agencies which function on the basis of their own authority alongside the bureaucratic hierarchy. In addition such agencies:

 (a) supervise and possibly verify the observance of the standing rules,

 (b) monopolize the creation of all rules pertaining to the powers of officials, or at least those concerning the scope of their authority required for fulfilling the duties of office.

 (c) potentially, and of greatest importance, monopolize the granting of the means necessary to effective administration.

(3) Any type of authority can be stripped of its monocratic character (based on one-person rule) via the principle of collegiality. This principle, however, can operate in a variety of ways:

 (a) in the sense that alongside of monocratic institutions of power, other similarly monocratic authorities exist which, whether by tradition or law, are invested with the power to enact a delay or a veto of decrees of the former, hence "veto collegiality."

 The most important examples of this are the tribune (and originally the ephor) of Antiquity, the *capitano del popolo* of the Middle Ages, and the Council of Workers and Soldiers and their delegates who were accorded, as a control, a "countersigning" entitlement in the period after November 9, 1918, until the regular administration was emancipated from this control.

 (b) in the entirely opposite sense that the powers of non-monocratic officials are only enacted after previous consultation and a vote; this is according to the regulation that not one individual, but a majority of individuals must agree in order for an enactment to become binding. This is then "functional collegiality," where a collegial network equals functional collegiality. In this case either unanimous rule or rule by majority can serve as the standard.

(c) the case of (a) "veto collegiality" corresponds in effect to the case in which, for the purpose of weakening the monocratic power, multiple, monocratic, equally-empowered agents of authority exist alongside one another without a clear demarcation of duties. The resulting competition between agents to accomplish the same task requires mechanical means (by lot, turn, oracle, intervention by a controlling agent [2a]) to determine delegation of responsibilities, with the effect that every empowered agent becomes a vetoing agent of all other collegial bodies. The most important example of this case is the Roman collegiality of the legitimate magistrates such as the consuls and the praetors.

(d) the case of (b) "functional collegiality" is similar to this next case in which, despite there being an agent with the materially monocratic rights of *primus inter pares*, his directives nonetheless are normally exercised only after consultation with formally equal members. In this case great divergence of opinion regarding important matters may result in a breaking up of the collegial body by means of resignation or secession, thereby endangering the position of the monocratic leader (functional collegiality with a preeminent leader). The most important example of this case is the position of the British "Prime Minister" in respect to his "cabinet." This has changed considerably. The cabinet, however, corresponded substantively in most cases to the above formulation during the period of cabinet government.

Advisory collegial bodies do not necessarily weaken the power structures of monocratic leaders. In fact they can effect a tempering of monocratic authority by means of rationalization. It is possible, however, that they win the upper hand from the leader. This is especially possible if these collegial bodies represent status groups. The following are the primary cases:

(e) the case of (d) is similar to that in which a collegial body operates formally only in an advisory capacity in observing its commitment to a monocratic leader. The leader is by no means bound by their conclusions; rather, by precedent or ruling, he is only bound to solicit their formally nonbinding advice, the neglect of which, however, may make him responsible in the case of some policy failure.

The most important example of this case is the development of the senate. Initially acting as an advisory body to the magistrates, it actually assumed a degree of control over the magistrates (through control of the finances). This was approximately how it began. The combination of actual financial control, but even more, the collegial social identity shared between the senators and the formally elected magistrates, allowed for the development of a situation in which the magistrates were actually bound by senatorial decisions. The phrase "*si dis placeret,*" which expresses this lack of obligation, later came to mean something similar to our "if you please" when accompanied by urgent instructions.

(f) A further distinction can be found in the case in which a collegial body is comprised of individuals with specified functions. That is to say, the preparation and presentation of a particular subject is entrusted to the expert—or, potentially, experts, in a situation large enough to require several—possessing competence for the appropriate situation. Decisions, however, are based on the collective vote of the entire body.

In most state councils and similar forms of governmental bodies of the past, this was always more or less the case (as in the example of the English Privy Council in the period before the development of the cabinet government). Despite occasional periods in which their powers have been great, they have never disempowered ruling princes. In fact, it is the exact opposite of this which has often taken place: under certain circumstances, princes have sought the support of their councils in an attempt to topple the cabinet form of government consisting of party leaders, as in England, albeit in vain. This type of council also approximates the panel of specialized experts associated with the charismatic hereditary leader or the elected official (the American type), the members of which are appointed to their particular posts by the ruler (king, president) based on their qualifications and in order to lend him support.

(g) A collegial body whose members have specified functions may play a purely advisory role leaving ultimate acceptance or rejection of their recommendations, as in case (e), to the free choice of the leader. Hence the only difference between the two is one of greater specialization by function. This corresponds, in part, to the practice by the Prussians under Friedrich Wilhelm I (1713–1740). Without exception this arrangement consolidates the power of the ruler.

(h) A body comprised of rationally specified forms of collegiality contrasts most strongly with traditional forms of collegiality, this latter consisting of "elders," whose collegial gesture serves as a guarantee for the preservation of authentically traditional rights. Potentially, these elders can serve as a means to preserve the tradition by exercising their veto against anti-traditionalist legislation. Examples of this include the "*gerousia*" of Antiquity; for the veto power it is the Areopagus in Athens and the "*patres*" in Rome (although the latter is primarily related to type 1 below).

(i) Authority can be weakened by the implementation of the collegial principle against the highest ruling body (whether its authority is of formal or substantive nature and including, potentially, the ruler himself). Such a case is quite similar to cases (d) through (g) discussed above. Individual responsibilities can either be rotated or assigned to individuals as an administrative "domain" on a more permanent basis. Collegiality will only persist as long as the performance of legitimate acts requires the formal participation of all members.

The most important examples include the Swiss Federal Council with its ambiguous division of responsibilities and use of the rotation principle; the revolutionary assemblies of the "People's Commissars" in Russia, Hungary, and, for a short time, in Germany; and from the past, the Venetian "Council of Eleven," the Assemblies of the Elders, etc.

A large number of the cases involving collegiality within a *patrimonial* or feudal hierarchy can fall into the following categories:

(1) cases involving the division of power on the basis of estate (collegiality of the estate administrative staff or those appropriated by the estate);
(2) cases involving the organization of collegial bodies consisting of patrimonial officials in solidarity with the ruler and opposed to

the authority of the social status groups (as in the case of the state councils in example (f) above);

(3) cases involving the creation of advisory and, under certain circumstances, executive bodies over which the ruler presides, or whose meetings he attends, or about whose proceedings and record he is informed. Through the composition of such bodies, which are in part specialized experts and in part persons of particular social prestige, the ruler hopes—in the face of the increasingly specialized demands of his position—that, with briefings from these bodies, his increasingly limited posture of informed dilettantism will still allow for intelligent personal decisions (case g above).

In cases of this third type, the leader will naturally be most interested in the representation, if possible, of heterogeneous and conflicting technical opinions and interests so that he might be more fully informed and able to play the alternatives against one another.

In cases of the second type, on the contrary, the leader is often (though not always) more interested in a consensus of opinions and positions (hence the source of "solidary" ministries and cabinets in so-called "constitutional" states or other states possessing an effective division of powers).

In cases of the first type, the assembly which represents the co-opted interests will favor the uniformity of opinions and solidarity. These will not always be attainable, however, as every co-optation on the basis of social privilege will result in conflicting special interests.

For case (1), typical examples are the assemblies of estates, class delegations, and, prior to them, the assemblies of vassals, which were also found frequently outside of Europe (as in China). An example of case (2) can be found in the first administrative agencies of the developing modern monarchies which were, without exception, collegial and primarily (though not entirely) comprised of legal and financial experts. For case (3) there are the state councils of these emerging modern western monarchies, as well as numerous others throughout the world (as late as the eighteenth century it was occasionally the case that an Archbishop had a seat in the English "cabinet"), all with their temporary councillors and a mixture of *honoratiores* and specialized officials.

Every situation involving conflict of interests between status groups can work to the advantage of the ruler through negotiation and struggle.

(j) For though it be only on the basis of external form, those associations may be termed "collegial" whose conflicting interests, be they economic, ideal, or power-based causes, are compromised by delegated representatives in order to smooth over the differences (i.e., "compromise collegiality" in contrast to bureaucratic and parliamentary collegiality). The crude form of this type is revealed in the case of a division of power among "status groups" in such a way that compromise between the privileged parties is continually required in order to arrive at decisions (see below). A more rationalized form of this type is in evidence when delegates are selected on the basis of lasting status or class affiliation or in terms of the existing conflict of interests. As long as the character of such a body remains constant, the role of the vote is of little consequence. Rather, action is taken on the basis of a negotiated compromise among the represented interests, or a compromise is ordained by the ruler after hearing out the positions of the interest groups involved.

The peculiar structure of the so-called "*Ständestaat*" will be discussed later. The stratification of the electorate as found in England (the House of "Lords" and the House of "Commons," the separate "convocations" of the Church), in France (the nobility, the clergy and the *tiers etat*), and in the numerous divisions of the German status groups serve as appropriate examples here. These divisions were all characterized by the necessity for compromise, both within the status groups and between them, in arriving at decisions. Their decisions were then often treated by the ruler simply as nonbinding recommendations. In contemporary times a primary fault with the modern theory of "occupational representation" is that its advocates fail to realize that the solely adequate means to its success is not consensus, but compromise. Within free Workers Councils of this nature, concerns would be settled on the basis of economically determined power, not by majority decision.

(k) Finally there is the related type of "voting collegiality" in cases where a number of formerly autocephalous and autonomous groups come together to form a new association, thereby achieving for themselves the right to influence decisions (to some degree gradated) through the delegation of votes to individual leaders or their representatives (merger collegiality).

Examples of this include the representation of the phylae, the phratries, and the clans of the governing councils of Antiquity, the medieval clan association in the time of the *consuls*, the *mercadanza* of the guilds, the formation of the delegates of "vocational councils" into a central council for labor, the "federal council" or senate in the federal republics and the real collegiality achieved in coalition ministries and coalition cabinets. This is maximized in systems where government posts are assigned according to the proportion of the vote, as in Switzerland.

(l) The voting collegiality of elected parliamentary representatives possesses a special character and therefore requires special attention. The basis for this form of collegiality is either that of leadership, whereby collegiality represents its constituency, or that of collegial party management, resulting in a parliament which lacks a single strong leader. Elucidation requires a full discussion of political parties.

Except in the case of monocratic veto collegiality, collegiality presents, almost without exception, an obstacle to precise, unequivocal, and above all, rapid decisions (this carries over into irrational manifestations, as well, in such cases when even technical experts find themselves hampered). It might be noted that at that point in time when the nobility was first beginning to rely on specialized officials, the effects of these consequences were not unwelcome. But as the necessary tempo for decision-making and implementation steadily increased, these hitherto welcome delays were increasingly eliminated. In general, and in instances where collegial bodies have possessed *executive* authority, the power of their leading members has tended to grow to a point of formal and substantive preeminence (as in the case with the positions of Bishop and Pope in the Catholic Church and the Prime Minister in the cabinet). Any interest shown in the revitalization of the collegiality of leadership generally originates out of the need for a weakening of the leader as such. This, in turn, originates out of mistrust and jealousy; not on the part of the ruled, who clamor for strong leadership, but on the part of the members of the administrative staff who are opposed to monocratic leadership. But this does not only, and by no means primarily, apply to the under-privileged strata, but rather especially to the privileged ones. Collegiality is by no means specifically "democratic." Where privileged strata have had to protect themselves from the threat presented by groups outside of their circle, they have also continually attempted to prevent the rise of monocratic power, which might base its ascent on the underprivileged stratum. Hence, while maintaining strict equality among its own members, the privileged stratum created a collegial system of officials for establishing a supervisory and even a governing capacity. Examples are Sparta, Venice, the Roman Senate before the time of the Gracchi and Sulla, England repeatedly during the 18th century, Bern and other Swiss cantons, the medieval patrician cities with their collegial consules, the *mercadanza* which comprised the merchant guilds, but not those of the craftsmen. The latter of these often fell easy prey to the *nobili* or *signori*.

Collegiality ensures a greater degree of "thoroughness" in administrative decisions. Allowing for the above-mentioned considerations, where collegiality is favored at the expense of precision and rapidity, it still tends to be resorted to today. After all, it does normally have the effect of dividing responsibility and, in the case of larger bodies, responsibility virtually disappears altogether, whereas under a monocracy it is very clearly and unequivocally assumed. Large undertakings and those requiring rapid and consistent solutions tend, in general, (and, at least technically, with good reason) to be placed into the hands of the monocratic "dictator" who alone assumes complete responsibility.

Neither a strongly unified foreign nor domestic policy of a large state can be effectively carried out on a collegial basis. The "dictatorship of the proletariat," especially for the purpose of nationalizing industry, requires a "dictator" who enjoys the trust of the masses. Though "the people," as such, may not be so ill-disposed toward a dictator, those holding power in the massive bureaucracies of the parliament, the parties, and, what amounts to little difference, the "soviets," neither can nor will tolerate such a despot. Only in Russia did such a leader manage to come to power with both the support of the military and the peasant's interest in a program of solidarity.

Finally, the following remarks are meant to summarize and supplement that which has already been said:

Historically, collegiality has had a dual significance:

(a) It has involved multiple incumbency of the same office or several overlapping offices in direct competition with one another, all possessing a mutual power of veto. The primary concern is therefore one of a technical division of powers for the purpose of minimizing authority. It was "collegiality" in this sense that was, most notably, the characteristic of the Roman magistrates. Their most important significance lay in the authority of any *par potestas* magistrate to intervene in any official act for the purpose of limiting the power of any one magistrate. The office of magistrate, however, remained that of an individual office, but in multiple issue.

(b) The second major point of significance involves collegial decision-making. In this case, the enactment of a command is only legitimate if based on unanimous or majority cooperation of the group. Hence the modern concept of collegiality, a concept not unknown in Antiquity but not characteristic of the age. This type of collegiality can be that of 1. the highest leadership, that is, the authority itself, 2. administrative officials, 3. advisory officials.

1. Collegiality in the highest leadership can have its basis in:

(a) The fact that the governing authority in question rests upon the communal bonding or association of several autocephalous groups, and that all of these groups demand their own share of power (as in the case of the "synoikism" of the ancients, with the division of their collegial councils into clans, phratries and phylae; the medieval association of clans with the stratified council of families; the medieval association of the guilds in the *mercadanza,* with the council of the "Elders" or guild deputies; in the "Federal Council"—a body representing the component states—in the modern federal state system; in the effective collegiality of the ministries which are appointed on the basis of party coalition [this achieves maximum effect with the stratification of power according to the proportion of the vote, which is increasingly the case in Switzerland]. Collegiality can thus also be a special case of the status or territorial principle of representation).

(b) Or, as a consequence of the absence of a leader, in turn perhaps resulting from jealousy among those competing for the leadership position, or the attempts on the part of the ruled to minimize the authority of one individual. In the majority of revolutions, collegiality will arise from a combi-

nation of these reasons in the form of a "council" of officers, or even the soldiers of revolutionary troops as in the case of the Committee of Public Safety or the Committee of "People's Commissars." In most peacetime administrations, it has almost always been this aforementioned unpopularity of the individual "strong man" theory which has served as the motive for the establishment of collegiality among leading officials. This was the case in Switzerland and in the Baden Constitution of 1919. (In this last instance, it was the socialists who were responsible for encouraging this unpopularity and who, in their concern to prevent an "elected monarch," sacrificed their strict administrative unity, an absolutely essential ingredient to successful nationalization. The suspicious attitudes of union, party, and local government officials in the party toward the powers of leadership were especially decisive.)

(c) The status or "lordly" social position of a candidate as a determining factor in the filling of administrative positions and in the possession of the same by the monopolizing stratum; that is, in short, collegiality as a product of privileged, aristocratic authority. Every socially privileged stratum fears leadership based on the emotional support of the masses at least as strongly as true democracies fear strong leaders. The senatorial structure [of Rome], and the tactical attempts to rule via closed councils belong here as examples along with the Venetian and similar constitutions.

(d) Or, in the struggle of the monarchs against increasing disempowerment at the hands of a technically trained bureaucracy. Without exception in the occidental states, the modern concept of administrative organization was introduced at the highest levels of leadership with the establishment of collegial bodies. This was also the case in the development of patrimonial states as models in the Orient, such as China, Persia, the Caliph Empire and the Ottoman Empire. The prince not only fears the power of individuals, but hopes, above all, through a collegial system involving votes and counter-votes, to maintain the decisive position himself. Because his position is increasingly that of the dilettante, only by maintaining this margin, and not abdicating in favor of individual officials, does he feel that the necessary control over the administration is preserved. (The func-

tion of the highest officials has been an intermediary one between advisory and executive capacities; only in the case of finance, where arbitrariness results in particularly irrational consequences was the power of the prince immediately rescinded, forcing him to give way, for pressing reasons, to the technically adept officials.)

(e) Or, in the hope of reconciling specialized professional points of view and conflicting interests of a technical or personal nature by means of collegial discussion with the intent of making compromise possible. Such has been the case in the organization of municipal administrations which confront, on the one hand, locally relevant and highly technical problems and, on the other hand, require a strong reliance upon compromise both by nature and due to material interests. This will continue as long as the masses leave leadership and authority to the strata privileged with property and education. The collegiality of ministries technically has a similar basis: where it has been found to be lacking historically, as, for example, in Russia and, less apparently, in Imperial Germany (until 1918), an effective solidarity of the different branches of government has never been achieved. On the contrary, the result has been that of embittered governmental conflict.

The bases for cases *(a)*, *(c)*, and *(d)* are purely historical. The modern development of bureaucratic authority as manifested in large scale associations—by the states or cities—has led to an overall weakening of effective collegial control. Reasons for this are that collegiality unavoidably diminishes: (1) the promptness of decision-making, (2) the unity of leadership, (3) the unambiguous responsibility of the individual, and (4) the reckless indifference to outsiders and the maintenance of discipline within. Hence, for these and other economic and technical reasons in large states involved in world politics, where collegiality has survived, it has been weakened in favor of the prominence of the political *leader* (such as that of the Prime Minister). This happens to be similar, in fact, to almost all large patrimonial associations, especially the strictly sultanistic. There has constantly been the need for a winning personality (such as the Grand Vizier) in addition to the reigning prince, provided that those enjoying special favor did not supply a substitute. One person, at least, had to bear responsibility; from a *legal* perspective, however, this could not be the prince.

2. The collegiality of those authorities entrusted with enforcing higher directives exists for the purpose of promoting objectivity and, above all, the integrity of the administration. In this interest, collegiality seeks to weaken the power of the individual. For the same reasons, this collegiality has, without exception, given way to the technical superiority of monocratic organizations (such was the case with the provincial "governments" in Prussia).

3. The collegiality of bodies whose function is solely advisory has always existed and will probably always exist. Though very important in the historical development of authority, especially in those cases where the "advice" to the magistrates or princes was, due to the power structure, "decisive," its analysis is not necessary to the present discussion.

The term "collegiality" has consistently been used here to mean collegiality of authority—that of authorities which themselves either govern or directly influence (advise) administrative bodies. The conduct of assemblies representing status groups or parliamentary bodies is not relevant here.

Historically, it has been collegiality which has led to the development of the concept of "administrative agency." This was due to its steady differentiation of the "office" from the "household," of public from private staff, and means of administration from personal property. It is therefore hardly coincidental that the history of modern western administration was ushered in by the development of collegial agencies composed of technical specialists. Though in a different way, collegial administration has also played an important constitutive role in every permanent organization involving patrimonial, status, feudal or other traditional types of political association. Only those collegial bodies of officials that demonstrated cohesiveness were able, over time, to politically disempower especially those western monarchs who became "dilettantes." Had the officials been individually appointed, due to their obligation of personal obedience, the prince could have easily prevailed against their inevitable opposition to his irrational stewardship. After what became acknowledged as the irreversible transition to a technical bureaucracy, the prince regularly attempted to use his voting and veto power to undermine the advisory collegial system (state council system) to maintain control despite his dilettantism. With the eventual and conclusive victory of the rational technical bureaucracy, the need for a monocratically led solidarity among the highest officials first began to emerge through the person of a prime minister. This was especially the case in parliamentary systems. These bodies were initially intended to legitimize the prince who, in turn, legitimized them. Since then, the general tendency toward monocracy, and therefore bureaucracy, has prevailed in administrative organization.

Two examples may suffice. First, collegiality became significant in the early stages of modern administration in the case of Kaiser Maximilian I and, in particular, his struggle with his own financial agency which he specifically created to raise emergency funds for countering the Turkish invasion, but which came to oppose his practice of going over the heads of his officials to issue orders and securities according to his own whim. The disempowerment of the princes began with problems of finance, as it was here that their lack of technical know-how first became apparent. This development came first to the Italian city-states with their commercially oriented accounting system, then to the French and Burgundians, then to the German territorial states, with Norman-controlled Sicily and the English exchequer developing independently of these. The Divans in the Orient, the Yamen in China and the Bakafu in Japan played a corresponding role, but one that did not lead to bureaucratization. Due to the absence of rationally trained technical experts, it was necessary to refer to the empirical knowledge of the "experienced" officials. In Rome this role was played by the Senate.

Secondly, in separating the private household from the office environment, collegiality played a role similar to that of large, voluntary trading houses which promoted the separation of the household from profit-making business, and personal property from capital.

Translated by Martin Black

15. Bureaucratic Authority

Modern bureaucracy functions by way of the following specific means:

I. The principle of strictly observed official areas of jurisdiction which are generally ordered by rules, that is, by laws or administrative regulations. This means: (1) There is a fixed delegation of those regular activities necessary to the purposes of the bureaucratically controlled structure; these are the official duties; (2) The authority to issue the orders necessary for the fulfilling of these official duties is delegated in an equally controlled fashion, and its allotted means of coercion (physical, sacerdotal, or otherwise) strictly limited by rules; (3) For the regular and ongoing fulfillment of these assigned duties and for the exercise of the corresponding rights, systematic provision is made by employing only those individuals whose qualifications meet the general regulations.

In the sphere of public-legal authority, these three instances constitute a bureaucratic "agency," and in the sphere of private-economic authority, that of a bureaucratic "enterprise." In this sense, in political and ecclesiastical communities, bureaucracy achieves maturity for the first time only with the advent of the modern state. In the private economy, maturity comes only in the most advanced stages of capitalism. For an established agency to have a fixed area of competence is not the rule but the exception. This holds true for expansive political structures as well as those of the ancient Orient, the Germanic and Mongolian empires of conquest, and in many feudal state structures. In these structures, the ruler carries out the most important measures by means of personal confidantes, table companions, or court servants hired for the occasion, and whose commissions and authority are not strictly delimited.

II. The principle of the office hierarchy and of the successive stages of appeal requires a clearly ordered system of authority and subordination involving supervision of the lower offices by the higher ones; a system which simultaneously accords the governed the possibility of appealing, in a regulated fashion, the finding of a lower agency to the corresponding superior agency. With the full development of this type, the office hierarchy is monocratically ordered. The principle of the office hierarchy is found in state, ecclesiastical, and all other bureaucratic structures such as large party organizations, as well as large-scale private enterprises; the characteristics of bureaucracy are not affected regardless of whether it is called private or public. With full implementation of the principle of "jurisdiction," however, hierarchical subordination, at least in public offices, does not result in a situation in which the authority of the "superior" agency simply incorporates the business of the "lower" level. The opposite, in fact, is the rule and, therefore, should a vacancy occur in a well-established office, the position must not go unfilled.

III. Management of the modern office is based upon written documents (files) maintained in the original or in rough draft, and upon a staff of subordinate officials and clerks of every kind. The whole of the officials employed by an agency, along with the corresponding material and file apparatus, constitutes a "*bureau*" (often called an "office" [*Kontor*] in private enterprises). Modern organization of the governmental agency fundamentally separates the office from the private dwelling. Office activity, considered a special function, is wholly divorced from the sphere of private life; official monies and means are likewise divorced from the private property of the official. This is a condition that has everywhere been the product of a long development. Today this condition is found in public as well as private enterprises and, indeed, in the latter group, even extends to include leading entrepreneurs themselves. The office from the household, business from private correspondence, business assets from private wealth—the more consistently the modern type of business conduct has been implemented, the more these things, in principle, are separated one from the other. The rudimentary stages of this process can already be found in the Middle Ages. One peculiarity of the modern entrepreneur is that he considers himself the "first official" of his enterprise, just as a certain ruler of a specifically bureaucratic modern state designated himself the "first servant" of the state [Friedrich the Great]. The concept of there being an inherent difference between public office work and service in the private sector is a continental European notion and utterly foreign to the American way of thinking.

IV. The official function of an office, at least that which is functionally specialized—and it is this that is specifically modern—normally presumes a thorough training in an area of specialization. This is also increasingly the case for executives and employees of a private concern as well as for public officials.

V. With full development of an office, the official activity demands the entire working capacity of the official regardless of the fact that his obligatory working hours in the office may be strictly delimited. Normally this, too, is only the product of a long development in public as well as private-sector offices. Previously and under normal circumstances, this state of affairs was the reverse: the official activity of an office was executed as a secondary priority.

VI. Office management by officials is conducted according to general rules that are more or less fixed, more or less exhaustive, and can be learned. The knowledge of these rules, therefore, represents a special technical expertise (respectively: jurisprudence, administrative and office management) which the officials possess. The attachment to rules is so firmly rooted in the character of modern office management that modern scientific theory, for example, assumes that the authority lawfully ceded to an agency for the ordering of certain matters by decree would not entitle this agency to regulate via individual orders on a case-by-case basis, but rather only to regulate on an abstract basis. This stands in stark contrast to the regulation of all relationships through individual privileges and the granting of favor. As we shall see, this practice is plainly the dominant type of regulation in patrimonialism, for example, at least insofar as these relationships are not determined by sacred tradition.

Position of Officials

For the internal and external position of officials, all of this has the following consequences:

I. The office is a vocation. This initially finds expression in the requirement of a strictly prescribed course of education that is demanding to the point of requiring the full working capacities of the student for a protracted period of time. This, as well as generally prescribed special examinations, are the prerequisites of employment. An additional dimension is the sense of duty inherent in the position of the official. The nature of this duty determines the internal structure of the official's relation in the following manner: The holding of an office is treated neither legally nor actually as a possession to be exploited as a source of revenue and fees in return for the rendering of specific services, as was the norm in the Middle Ages and, frequently, right up to the threshold of modern times. It is also not to be treated as a common remunerative exchange of services as in the case of a free employment contract. On the contrary, accepting an office, in the private sector as well, carries with it the assumption of a specific office loyalty in exchange for the guarantee of a secure existence. Decisive for the character of this modern office loyalty is that, in its pure form, it does not establish a relationship (as in feudal or patrimonial authoritarian structures) to a person, after the manner of a vassal's or disciple's loyalty. Rather, the loyalty serves an impersonal, technical purpose. Behind this technical purpose, of course, stand ideologically sanctifying cultural values, be they state, church, community, party, or enterprise. In all cases, these serve as surrogates for an earthly or celestial personal master and are embodied within the group. The political official, for example, at least in the fully developed modern state, does not function as the personal servant to a ruler. Even a bishop, priest or preacher no longer serves, as in early Christian times, as the bearer of a purely personal charisma whose divine sacred values under the personal mandate of a master—and, in principle, responsible only to him—he would offer to all those who appeared worthy of them and sought them. Rather, despite the partial lingering of the old theory, he has become an official in the service of a technical purpose, which, in the contemporary "church," is at once rendered mundane and ideologically resanctified.

II. The *personal* position of the official in all of this is shaped in the following manner:

(1) The modern official, whether in a public or private office, always seeks and normally enjoys a specifically elevated status-related social esteem vis-a-vis the governed. His social position is guaranteed by means of hierarchical regulations, and, in the case of political officials, by special punitive provisions for the "slandering of officials," and the disparagement of the authorities of church and state, etc. The actual social position of the officials is normally the highest in those cases where, in a country possessing an older cultural tradition, there exists a strong demand for a technically trained administration, and a strong and stable social differentiation. Here, the officials, either because of the social distribution of power or as a consequence of the expense of the prescribed training and their ties to class conventions, come from socially and economically privileged classes. The influence of educational credentials (the possession of which is normally closely connected with qualification for office) naturally enhances the element of prestige in the social position of officials. In addition, as in the case of the German army, there is explicit acknowledgement of this element of prestige in the prescription that the acceptance of those aspiring to the career of official is contingent upon the consent ("election") of the members of the official body (or here, the officers corps). Similar instances, such as those promoting a guild-like exclusiveness of the official establishment, are typically found in the patrimonial and, particularly, in the prebendal bureaucracy of the past. Efforts to allow these structures to recur in a changed form are by no means infrequent in modern bureaucratic hierarchies, and also played a role, for example, in the demands of the heavily proletarianized, specialized officials during the Russian revolution [of 1905].

The social esteem of the officials as such is normally especially low in areas where—as is often the case in newly settled regions—

as a consequence of great economic opportunity and great instability of social stratification, the demand for a specially trained administration as well as the authority of status conventions are especially weak—as, for example, in the United States.

(2) In its pure form, the appointment of the bureaucratic official is typically carried out by a superior agency. An official elected by the governed is no longer a purely bureaucratic figure. The formal existence of an election, of course, does not necessarily signify that an appointment didn't actually take place behind the scenes—especially by the party chiefs in the context of government. Whether or not this is the case does not depend upon the legal statutes, but rather upon the way in which the party mechanisms function. Where they are strictly organized, these can transform the formally free election into a simple acclamation of a candidate designated by the party chief; more frequently, however, they result in a competition, conducted according to set regulations, for one of two designated candidates. Under all circumstances, however, the placement of officials by means of election by the governed modifies the severity of hierarchical subordination. An official appointed by means of election possesses a basic autonomy in respect to his superiors, as he derives his office "from below" rather than "from above," or at least from the party power brokers (bosses) who will also determine his future career, and not from superior agencies in the official hierarchy. His career is not, or at least not directly dependent upon his superiors within the administration. From a purely technical perspective, the unelected official who has been appointed by a leader normally functions with more exactitude, due to the fact that, under similar circumstances, it is more likely that purely technical considerations and qualities will determine his selection and career. As laymen, the electorate can only acquaint itself with the degree to which a candidate for office is technically qualified for the position by virtue of experience; that is, after the fact. Wherever officials are appointed to office by means of election—whether this be a designation of otherwise freely elected officials through the party head's creation of a candidate slate, or a free appointment of officials by an elected party head—parties quite naturally do not give priority to considerations of technical competence but rather to the services a candidate renders the party bosses. In any case, the contrast is relative, however, since similar circumstances also apply where legitimate monarchs and their subordinates appoint officials. In these cases, though, influences of allegiance are less controllable.

Where the demand for a technically trained administration is significant, or becomes so, as is presently the case in the United States, and where the party adherents are forced to reckon with an intellectual, highly developed and independent "public opinion" (which, of course, is lacking everywhere in the U.S., where the immigrant element functions in the cities like a block vote), the appointment of unqualified officials reverts back upon the ruling party during [subsequent] elections. This is quite naturally the case where the officials are appointed by the party chief. Popular election of the administrative chief as well as his subordinate officials, therefore, more severely endangers the expert qualification of the officials and the precise functioning of the bureaucratic mechanism, besides weakening the dependence upon the hierarchical model. This is at least the case with large and therefore not easily supervised administrative bodies. In the United States, the superior qualification and integrity of the federal judges, appointed by the president, compared to those judges who are elected, is well known even though both types of officials will be primarily selected according to party considerations. In America, the great transformations of the local metropolitan administrations, which were demanded by reformers, were undertaken essentially by elected mayors who worked with a bureaucratic apparatus appointed by them; hence these changes occurred in "Caesaristic" fashion. As an organized authoritarian apparatus, the effectiveness of this "Caesarism," itself often immanent within democratic structures, is based in general, from a technical point of view, upon the position of the "Caesar" as an independent trustee of the masses (of the army or of the citizenry), unbound by tradition. As such, he is thus the unlimited leader of a personally and freely chosen select cadre of highly qualified officers and officials, whose appointment is undertaken independently of tradition or other special considerations. This "rule by personal genius," however, stands in contradiction to the formally "democratic" principle of the generally elected officialdom.

(3) At least in public and related bureaucratic frameworks, but increasingly so in others as well, appointments are normally lifelong positions. This is a factual rule even where it is presupposed that resignations and periodic reappointments will occur. In the private sphere as well, the tenure rule normally distinguishes the official from the worker. This legal or factual life-long tenure, however, is not considered the entitlement of the office incumbent, as was the case in many forms of authority in the past. On the contrary, as is

the case in Germany for all judicial and, increasingly, administrative officials, wherever legal guarantees are in place to prevent arbitrary dismissal or transfer from office, they are there for the sole purpose of guaranteeing that the specific duties of office in question will be discharged on strictly technical grounds, independently of any personal considerations. Within the bureaucracy, then, even the measure of "independence" granted by this legal guarantee of tenure is by no means always a source of enhanced conventional esteem of the official whose position is thus secured. Often the reverse, in fact, is true, especially in communities with older cultural traditions and a greater degree of social differentiation. For the subordination under the arbitrary rule of the leader ensures, relative to the strictness of its exercise, the maintenance of the conventional lordly style of living. In this way, the conventional esteem of the official can actually be enhanced as a direct consequence of the absence of these legal guarantees. This was the case in the Middle Ages when the esteem of the court officials was enhanced at the expense of the freemen, and that of the king's judge at the expense of the folk magistrate. In Germany, it is much easier, at any time or for whatever reason, to remove an officer or an administrative official from office than it is an "independent" judge, whose behavior would never cost him his office even in cases of the grossest breach of the "honor code" or offense to the formal, social conventions. But, for exactly this reason, the "social acceptability" of the position of judge, in the view of the ruling class (all other circumstances being equal), is lower than that of those officials (officers and administrators) whose greater dependence on the ruler is a stronger guarantee of the status conformity. The average official quite naturally seeks to establish a body of administrative law which, in addition to providing material security in his old age, enhances the guarantees against his arbitrary removal from office. Yet this ambition has its limit. Proliferation of the "right to office" naturally increases the difficulty of filling offices according to considerations of technical competence, and also serves to hamper the career opportunities of ambitious candidates. This circumstance, but also the tendency among officials to depend upon peers rather than upon the governed who are socially subordinate, has the consequence that officials in general are untroubled by dependency upon "those above." The conservative movement before 1914 among the clerics of the German province of Baden, occasioned by their fear of the alleged threatening separation of church and state, was expressly determined by the desire not to be turned "from a master into a servant of the congregation."

(4) The official regularly receives monetary compensation in the form of a normally fixed salary and old-age security by means of a pension. In principle, salary is measured less as a wage proportionate to service rendered, but rather according to "status," that is, according to the type of function (the "rank") and, potentially, to the length of service. The relatively high degree of security provided by the official's income, as well as the compensation afforded by social esteem make the office highly sought after in countries no longer offering colonial profit opportunities. In such cases, these benefits serve to permit a relatively low apportionment in terms of salary.

(5) Corresponding to the hierarchical order of the office, the official is placed on a career track that extends from the lower, less important, lesser paid positions to the higher ones. The average official naturally seeks to have the terms of advancement as mechanically fixed as possible. If promotion does not come in the form of office positions, then it will appear in the level of salary and according to seniority, or possibly, according to the grades achieved on a professional examination in such places where an examination board exists. Now and then, low grades can actually form an effective, permanent stigma which may follow the official throughout his life. This development, in connection with the intended strengthening of the right to an office and the increasing tendency toward professional stratification and the economic security of the official, reveals a trend toward the treatment of the offices like "personal benefits" of those qualified on the basis of their educational degrees. The necessity of considering the general personal and mental qualification of an individual, independently of the often subaltern character of certificates of specialized education, has led to a situation in which especially the highest political offices, and in particular the ministry posts, are consistently filled on a basis essentially independent of educational achievement.

Prerequisites and Correlates of Bureaucratization

The social and economic presuppositions of the modern bureaucracy are the following.

1. The Effect of Money Economy. The development of the money economy, insofar as it is money which clearly prevails as a form of compensating officials in the modern era, is of great importance to the entire phenomenon of modern bureaucracy, although by no means solely decisive. The quantitatively most significant historical examples of a relatively clearly developed officialdom are: (a) Egypt at the time of the new empire; (b) the later Roman Principate, and especially the Diocletian monarchy, and the Byzantine state which developed out of it, all with strong feudal and patrimonial elements; (c) the Roman Catholic Church, increasingly since the end of the 13th century; (d) China from the times of Shi Houng Ti to the present, but with a strong patrimonial and prebendal element; (e) in an ever purer form of the modern European state and increasingly all public entities since the development of princely absolutism; (f) the large modern capitalist enterprise, the more so the larger and more complex it is. To a very large degree, and sometimes predominantly, cases (a) through (d) were based on compensation of the officials in kind. And yet they display many of the characteristic qualities and effects of bureaucracy. The historical model of all later bureaucracies—the new empire in Egypt—is simultaneously one of the finest examples of an exchange economy. This juncture of bureaucracy and exchange economy can only be understood here in view of the entirely unique conditions of the period. For, in general, the considerable reservations appropriate in attributing these structures to bureaucracy are actually contingent upon an operating exchange economy. A certain degree of a developed money economy is a normal prerequisite of pure bureaucratic administrations; if not for its creation, at least for its unaltered preservation. After all, historical experience indicates that, without a money economy, it is scarcely avoidable that the bureaucratic structure will alter its internal mechanisms or transform altogether into a different structure. Beginning with the allocation of fixed allowances and other forms of running income-in-kind from the stocks and provisions in the storehouses of the ruler, as was the case for thousands of years in Egypt and China, and otherwise played a significant role during the late Roman monarchy as well, the first steps were taken toward the appropriation of the sources of taxation by officials, and their use as private property. Payments-in-kind have served to protect officials from the often abrupt fluctuations in the purchasing power of money. Should those fees and salaries that are based on taxation-in-kind be paid in an irregular fashion, however, as is the rule whenever the exercise of the lord's power subsides, then the official, whether authorized or not, will maintain direct claim on the taxables of his particular domain. The idea of protecting the official against these fluctuations by changing or transferring tax assessments, and therefore the power to tax, or by granting the official the use of profitable land or properties belonging to the ruler is now not farfetched. Every central authority which is not strictly empowered will attempt to pursue this course either voluntarily or through pressure applied by the officials. This can occur in such a way that the official satisfies himself with these resources in the amount of his salary and returns the surplus. But since this system contains strong temptations and therefore generally gives rise to unsatisfactory results for the ruler, a more likely alternative involves assigning the official a fixed monetary obligation. This was frequently the case in the period preceding the advent of the German bureaucracy, but was especially prevalent in all of the satrap administrations in the East. In such instances, the official was obligated to surrender a fixed sum, and retained the surplus.

From an economic point of view, then, the official is very much like a leasing entrepreneur, and the leasing of offices occurs on a regular basis, including even the awarding of offices according to the best offer. In the private economic sphere, the transformation of the manorial structure into a leasing relationship is one of the most important among many. In this way, the ruler can easily shift the trouble of transforming his income-in-kind into money onto the leasing official and/or the official who is obligated to surrender a fixed sum. This was apparently the case with some Oriental governors of Antiquity. Above all, the leasing out of the public tax-collection process itself, rather than its direct management by the ruler, served this purpose. The most important result of this practice was the possibility for significant progress toward organizing the ruler's finances into a budget system. That is to say, rather than having to live hand-to-mouth on an unpredictable flow of receipts, as is the typical case for all early stages of public finance, the ruler could have, with a budget system, a firm estimation of revenues and, correspondingly, of expenses. On the other hand, with this kind of a system, the control and full exploitation of the tax-levying power for use by the ruler are surrendered. Depending upon the respective degree of freedom remaining for the official or office and tax-leaser, the resources are even endangered by careless exploitation, since a capitalist does not have the same lasting, vested interest in these resources as does the ruler. To protect himself against these dangers, the ruler seeks the safeguard of regulations. The configuration of the leaseholding or transfer of taxes can, therefore, vary greatly.

Thus, according to the balance of power between the ruler and the leaseholder, what prevails is either the interest of the latter in uninhibited exploitation of the taxability of the governed, or the interest of the ruler in conserving these resources. The configuration of the tax-leasing system in the Ptolemaic empire, for example, was based essentially on the joint and opposing effects of the motives mentioned: the elimination of fluctuations in the receipts, the possibility of budgeting, protection of the tax-paying capability of the subjects by safe-guarding against their uneconomical exploitation, and state control of the leaseholder's receipts for the purpose of appropriating the maximum possible. In such a system, as in Hellas and Rome as well, the leaseholder still functioned as a private capitalist, but the collecting of taxes occurred bureaucratically and was state-controlled. Furthermore, the profit of the leaseholder was only a share of any surplus over and above his lease fee, which, in fact, served as a guarantee; his risk-factor consisted in the possibility of actual tax receipts being lower than this sum.

If the ruler finds himself in the predicament of requiring not so much regular income as investment capital, as in the case of war or the dispensing of debts, the purely economic constitution of the office as a private source of income for the official can also lead directly to its sale. Sale of office as a regular institution has existed especially in the states of modern times, in the Papal State as well as in France and England, and for sinecures as well as for very important offices, as in the case of officer's commissions, well into the nineteenth century. Though not the rule, in individual cases the economic meaning of a relationship of this sort can be altered to the degree that the purchase price partially or fully bears the aspect of a security deposit, paid to assure loyalty to the office.

But the transfer of revenues, fees, and services by the ruler to the official for his personal exploitation always signifies a sacrifice of the pure form of bureaucratic organization. The official in this situation has his own right of ownership to his office. This is the case to an even greater degree when the duty of office is related to compensation in such a way that the official does not turn over to the ruler any receipts from the property in his purview, but retains these entirely for his own private use in exchange for services rendered the ruler of a personal, military, or other political or clerical nature.

We speak of "prebends" and of "prebendal" office organization in cases of the life-long assignment of materially determined rent payments or essentially economic revenues from land or other sources of rent intended as compensation for the fulfillment of real or fabricated duties of office, for the economic security of which these assets have been permanently allocated by the ruler. In Antiquity and the Middle Ages, but also right up to modern times as well, the transition from this system of compensation to that of salaried officialdom is fluid. "Prebendal" structures have very often been the economic form employed for compensating the priesthood, but the same form has also been employed in other areas during virtually all periods of history. In Chinese priestly law, the specific "prebendal" character of all offices had the consequence that, during the ritual mourning of the father or head of the household, the obligatory abstention from enjoying [newly acquired] possessions (originally intended to avoid the ill-will of the deceased lord) forced the mourner to surrender his office, which was viewed for its prebendal quality simply as a source of income. An additional level of distinction from salaried bureaucracy is attained when not only economic rights, but also political rights are bestowed, in return for which personal services to the ruler are stipulated. Political rights bestowed in this manner can themselves vary in nature. In the case of political officials, for example, they may tend more toward a manorial character or toward that of bureaucratic authority. In both cases, but especially in the case of the latter, the specific character of bureaucratic organization is completely destroyed, and we have entered the realm of "feudal" organization of authority.

All forms of assigning services—or revenues-in-kind as compensation to officials have the tendency of loosening the bureaucratic mechanism, and especially of weakening hierarchical subordination. This subordination is most strictly developed in the discipline of modern bureaucracy. Only where the subjection of the official in respect to the ruler has been absolute in personal terms as well, as in the administrative employment of slaves or of employees treated like slaves, has a similar precision been attained, at least under energetic leadership, such as that displayed by contractually employed officials in the modern-day Western world.

In the natural economies of Antiquity, the Egyptian officials, when not legally the slaves of the Pharaoh, were, in point of fact, slaves nonetheless. In the Roman manorial system, it was preferred to entrust slaves with the direct management of money because of the possibility of inflicting torture. In China, the bamboo switch was employed liberally as a disciplinary measure in an attempt to achieve similar results. But the chances of the constant success of direct means of coercion are highly unfavorable. Experience seems to reveal that relatively optimal conditions for the success and endurance of a strictly mechanized form of the bureaucratic apparatus are offered by a secure salary along with the opportunity for pursuing a career that has been assigned under conditions other than mere chance or arbitrariness. Additional factors include strict discipline and control, which are closely related with a sense of honor, the development of a sense of honor within the status group, and the possibility for public criticism. These factors alone assure a more successfully mechanized form of bureaucracy than all legal forms of slavery. And, in fact, the official's strong sense of status consciousness is not only compatible with his readiness to utterly subordinate his own will to that of his superiors, but—as in the case of the officer—it has the consequence of serving as internal reward for his self-esteem. The purely impersonal work character of the office, with its principal separation of the private sphere of the official from the aspects of his official activities, simplifies his assimilation into the fixed, functional conditions of a mechanism based on discipline.

Even if the full development of the money economy is thus not considered an indispensable precondition of bureaucratization, as a specifically permanent structure, bureaucracy nonetheless requires as a prerequisite for its maintenance the availability of continuous revenues. Where this cannot be channeled from private profit—as is the case with the bureaucratic organization of large modern concerns—or from fixed land assets—as in the case of the manorial system—then an established system of taxation is the precondition for the enduring existence of bureaucratic administration. For well-known general reasons, however, the fully developed money economy alone offers the most secure basis for a taxation system of this sort. The degree of bureaucratization of an administration in urban commonwealths possessing a fully developed money economy, therefore, has not infrequently been greater than that in much larger territorial states of the same period. As soon as these latter administrations were able to develop a regulated tax system, of course, their own bureaucratic manifestations evolved into a much more comprehensive system than that of the city-state. For its part, assuming that its dimensions remained within moderate bounds, the city-state has demonstrated a tendency to find a plutocratic collegial administration of ranking citizens to be the most effective for its purposes. This is because the actual foundation of bureaucratization has always been a specific development of administrative tasks, the quantitative development of which will be taken up next.

2. Quantitative Development of Administrative Duties. In the political arena, for example, the classical basis of bureaucratization is formed by the large state and the mass political party.

This is not to imply, however, that every actual historically acknowledged formation process of the large state was automatically accompanied by its own bureaucratic administration. For, in the first place, the purely temporal life of an existing large state of this sort, or the homogeneity of the culture borne by it, were not necessarily always attached to its bureaucratic structure. Both, however, were to a large degree the case in the Chinese empire. The ephemeral nature of numerous large Black African empires and similar developments can be directly traced to the absence of a bureaucratic apparatus. In the same way, the central organization of the Carolingian empire disintegrated with the decline of its bureaucratic organization, though it was primarily of a patrimonial character, rather than bureaucratic. In contrast, from a purely temporal perspective, the Caliphal Empire and its predecessors in Asia managed to survive for a considerable period of time with essentially patrimonial and prebendal forms of bureaucratic organization, as did the Holy Roman Empire despite the virtually total absence of any bureaucracy. At the same time, these empires all demonstrated a cultural homogeneity almost as pronounced as that achieved by bureaucratic entities. The Ancient Roman Empire caved in on itself despite increasing bureaucratization; in fact, simultaneous to its implementation, as a result of the manner in which the related public burden was distributed which, in turn, favored an exchange economy. In any event, the temporal survival of those formations mentioned initially were, from the perspective of the intensity of their purely political unity, essentially of an unstable and nominal conglomerative cohesion, and generally demonstrated a steadily decreasing capacity for political action. Their relatively large degree of cultural unity was, on the one hand, the product of the strictly unified and, in the Medieval West, increasingly bureaucratic, ecclesiastical framework. On the other hand, it was the product of an extensive homogeneity in the social structures which, in turn, resulted from the repercussions and transformation of their former political unity. Both are phenomena of a traditional cultural stereotyping process that favors the persistence of an unstable equilibrium. Both offered, as well, such a powerful foundation that even huge expansionary attempts like the Crusades were able to take place, despite the absence of an intensive political unity, as what one might call "private undertakings." Their failure and the somewhat irrational course of political events were in many ways directly connected to the absence of the coordinating influence of a unified and strong state power. Doubtlessly the seeds of strong "modern" state formation appeared everywhere in the Middle Ages simultaneously with the development of bureaucratic structures. Similarly, it was the bureaucratically most developed political structures which finally shattered those conglomerates which were essentially based on conditions of unstable equilibria.

The disintegration of the Ancient Roman Empire was in part actually brought on by the bureaucratization of its army and official apparatus. This bureaucratization could only be sustained by means of the simultaneous implementation of a method of distributing the government expenditures that could only lead to the increasing relative significance of the exchange economy. Hence, there are always individual factors involved. Furthermore, the intensity of state action directed outwardly (its expansive thrust) and inwardly (the state influence on culture) does not necessarily stand in a direct proportion to the degree of bureaucratization. A direct proportion can only be ascribed to the former activity and, even here, not inevitably but only as a rule. After all, two of the most expansive political formations ever, the Roman and British empires, were based only marginally upon a bureaucratic structure in their periods of early expansion. In England, the Norman state erected a strict, efficient organization on the basis of the feudal hierarchy. In large part, however, this particular state structure owed its unity and momentum to the management of the royal treasury. In comparison to other political formations of the feudal period, the Norman treasury was bureaucratized to an unusually high degree. That the English state did not continue to participate in the continental development toward bureaucratization, but retained an administration drawn from local people of rank, was a result of the relative absence of the continental character—as was the case with the republican administration of Rome—and some entirely unique preconditions that in England are presently disappearing. One of these preconditions peculiar to England is the superfluousness of maintaining the kind of *standing* army required by continental states that, having similar expansionistic tendencies, must protect their land borders. For this reason, in Rome as well, bureaucratization progressed along with the empire's transition from a coastal to a continental empire. In addition, the Roman power structure possessed a level of technical efficiency that doubled as a bureaucratic apparatus. The precision and functional unity of the administration effected by the strictly military character of the magistrate's powers—developed to a point hitherto unknown to any other people—made this possible for an executive administration, especially outside city limits. And the continuity of the administration was guaranteed by the equally peculiar position of the Senate. One prerequisite not to be forgotten for this dispensability of bureaucracy applied in Rome as well as in England. This was the fact that state officials increasingly "minimized" the scope of their activities directed toward *domestic* affairs; that is, they limited themselves domestically to those things which were absolutely demanded by direct "reasons of state." On the continent, however, state power in the emerging modern period was consistently concentrated, in the hands of those princes who most recklessly pursued a course of administrative bureaucratization. It is clearly evident that the longer the large modern state endures, the more likely it is technically to absolutely require a bureaucratic basis. In similar fashion, the larger the state is, and, above all, the more it is regarded as a superpower, the more indispensable this bureaucratic basis becomes. Currently, the United States government is still not wholly bureaucratic, at least not in the technical sense, but this will unavoidably and increasingly change in a formal bureaucratic direction as external friction grows and the need for internal administrative unity becomes more pressing. Moreover, the partially non-bureaucratic form of the state structure of the United States is substantively offset by an even stricter bureaucratic structure of what, in actuality, are the politically dominant formations, these being the political parties themselves under the direction of career experts of organizational and election strategy. The most conspicuous example of the significance of purely quantitative factors as a lever to the bureaucratization of social formations happens to be the increasingly bureaucratic organization of all genuine mass parties. In Germany, it is the Social Democratic party above all which belongs to this phenomenon, while abroad both of the "historic" American parties are its finest expression.

3. Qualitative Changes. Of greater inducement to bureaucratization than extensive and quantitative factors, however, is the intensive and qualitative expansion of the administrative tasks. Both the direction in which this development is realized and the reasons for its inducement can be, therefore, of vastly differing types. In Egypt, the oldest country with a bureaucratic state administration, it was the technical necessity of common regulation of the water supply for the entire country from above that created the system of scribes and officials. Early on, this system then found its second great mission in the extraordinary, militarily organized construction projects. As previously mentioned, of special importance in aiding the process of bureaucratization have been demands resulting from the creation of standing armies, for reasons of power politics, and the related development of systems of finance. Further promotion of the same process can be found in the modern state, however, where the administration, in general, faces growing demands associated with the increasing complexity of the culture itself. During periods of significant expansion outward, in particular, overseas expansion has especially been undertaken by states ruled by notables (Rome, England, Venice). As will soon be demonstrated, however, the intensity of the administration—that is, the assumption of as many tasks as possible by the state for continual processing and execution in the course of its own operations—was only slightly developed in the large states ruled by notables, particularly Rome and England, compared to bureaucratic forms of government. By all accounts, the structure of state authority has strongly influenced the culture in the case of both England and Rome, but had relatively little influence in the form of state operations and control. This is the case from the system of justice to that of education. These growing cultural demands are for their part determined, though to a varying degree, by the increase in wealth of the most influential strata within the state. To this extent, then, increasing bureaucratization is a function of increasing possession of consumer goods and of an increasingly refined technique of external living corresponding to the opportunities presented by enhanced wealth. In its reaction upon the general standard of living, this creates an increasing subjective indispensability of organized public, interlocal, and hence bureaucratic services for the most varied of life's needs which earlier were either unknown or provided through private or local means. Especially persistent in promoting bureaucratization from purely political impulses are the increasing needs on the part of a society grown accustomed to absolute pacification in matters of order and protection ("police") in all domains. There is a direct progression from the adjudication of the blood feud sacerdotally or by means of arbitration—which places the burden of rights and security entirely upon the sense for oath and vengeance of the individual's comrades—to the present role of the policeman as the "representative of God on earth." Other prominent impulses that promote bureaucratization are the manifold so-called sociopolitical tasks which are, in part, foisted upon the modern state by special interest groups and, in part, usurped by the state for reasons either of power politics or ideological objectives. These services are, of course, primarily economically determined. Finally, due to essentially technical factors, the specifically modern communication networks (public land and waterways, railroads, telegraph, etc.) can be considered as pacesetters of bureaucratization. These networks are administered publicly, due in part to necessity, and in part to technical expediency. As such, they play, in many ways, much the same role today as did the Mesopotamian canals and the regulation of the Nile in the ancient Orient. On the other hand, it is the degree of development of the communication and transportation network that is, if not solely decisive, then certainly an important determining prerequisite for the possibility of bureaucratic administration. In Egypt, without the natural transportation route of the Nile River, bureaucratic centralization could certainly never have attained such a degree of development in an exchange economy. In modern-day Persia, in order to promote bureaucratic centralization, telegraph officials were formally entrusted with reporting directly to the Shah over the heads of local officials about all events occurring in the provinces. In addition, with the same end in mind, everyone has been offered the right of direct protest via telegraph. In the Occident, the modern state is and can only be governed by exercising control of the telegraph system as well postal and railroad services. For their part, these phenomena are closely related to the development of inter-local mass traffic of goods, which can be included among the causal factors that appear simultaneously with the formation of the modern state. But this does not necessarily hold true for the past, as we have previously seen.

4. Technical superiority. The decisive reason for the development of bureaucratic organization has always been its purely technical superiority to every other form. A fully developed bureaucratic apparatus compares to other forms as do mechanical to non-mechanical modes of production. Precision, speed, clarity, accessibility of files, continuity, discretion, unity, strict subordination, avoidance of friction and material and personal expenses—all these attain an optimal level under bureaucratic, and especially monocratic forms of administration and by means of trained, individual officials compared to collegial or honorary and avocational forms of administration. Insofar as complicated duties are involved, paid bureaucratic work is not only more precise, but, in end effect, often even less expensive than is the formally unremunerated honorary position. Employment in an honorary position is avocational employment and is, for that reason alone, normally performed more slowly, less formulaically and less according to plan. It also tends to be less precise and unified owing to the fact that it is less dependent upon superiors, and is discontinuous. Furthermore, it is often actually very costly as a consequence of the almost unavoidably inefficient acquisition and exploitation of subordinate and ministerial offices and their personnel. This is especially the case when one takes into account not only the cash expenses of the public treasury—which a bureaucratic administration significantly increases, however, especially in comparison with honorary administration by notables—but also the frequent economic losses of the governed due to delays and a general lack of precision. Honorary administration by notables is normally only permanent in those cases where business can be satisfactorily attended to as an avocation. With the qualitative increase in the duties it faces, administration of this sort reaches its limit even in England. On the other hand, collegially organized work creates friction and hesitation, compromises between conflicting interests and views, and is therefore less precise, and less dependent upon superiors, making it therefore less unified and slower. All progress made by the Prussian administrative organization has been and will always be the progress of the bureaucratic, and especially the monocratic, principle.

Today, it is principally the modern capitalist market economy that is foremost in demanding that the official business of an administration be executed as quickly, precisely, unambiguously and continuously as possible. The largest of the modern capitalist enterprises are themselves normally unmatched models of strict bureaucratic organization. Their commerce is based entirely upon increasing precision, continuity and, above all, speed of operations. This, in turn, is determined by the nature of the modern means of communication including, among others, the news service branch of the press. The extraordinary speed with which public announcements are transmitted, whether they be of an economic or purely political content, exercises, on this basis alone, continuous sharp pressure on the administration in the direction of possible acceleration of time of response to the respective given situations. Attaining the optimum in this case is normally done only by means of strict bureaucratic organization. (That the bureaucratic apparatus can and, in fact, does produce certain obstructions to the settlement of a matter by means peculiar to the individual case, does not belong to this context.)

Above all, however, bureaucratization offers optimal conditions for the possibility of executing the principle of the division of labor at an administrative level according to purely objective considerations, and by allocating work to specially trained functionaries who, through constant exercise of their skills, become increasingly well-tooled in their expertise. Objective discharge of duties means in this case primarily discharge "without the regard for individuals" according to calculable rules. "Without regard for individuals," however, is also the language of the marketplace and, in general, the naked pursuit of economic interest. Consistent implementation of bureaucratic authority leads to the levelling of status honor. Hence, if the principle of market freedom is not simultaneously reined in, it will lead to universal domination of the class situation. If this consequence of bureaucratic authority does not everywhere emerge proportional to the degree of bureaucratization, the reason for this can be found in the differences in possible principles that various political communities demonstrate in furnishing their needs. But for modern bureaucracy, it is the second element, the "calculable rules," that is actually of greater significance. It is just this peculiarity of modern culture, but especially its technical-economic basis, that requires this "calculability" of success. In a specific sense, a fully developed bureaucracy falls under the principle of *"sine ira ac studio"* [without hatred or passion]. Bureaucracy's specific nature, quite welcome to capitalism, is increasingly perfected the more it becomes objectified or "dehumanized." Considered its virtue, the perfecting of this specific nature involves the successful exclusion of love, hate and all purely personal, irrational, and emotional elements, to which calculation is alien, from the process of discharging official business. The more complex and specialized modern culture becomes, the more its external apparatus demands replacement of the traditional lord, capable of being moved through personal sympathy, goodwill, mercy, or gratitude, with a personally unsympathetic and, therefore, strictly "objective" expert. And, in fact, the bureaucratic structure offers all of this in a favorable combination. In particular, it was first the bureaucratic structure of the administration of justice which paved the way for a conceptually systematized, rational law based upon statutes such as those created with a high degree of technical perfection during the later Roman Empire. During the Middle Ages, the reception of this law went hand in hand with the bureaucratization of legal administration, the influx of rationally trained expertise replacing the old system of justice that was bound to tradition or to irrational assumptions.

Excursus on Judicial Administration

The "rational" interpretation of law on the basis of strictly formal legal concepts stands in contrast to a type of interpretation that is tightly bound to sacred tradition. A concrete case that cannot be unambiguously decided upon on the basis of tradition will be settled either by means of concrete "revelation" (oracle, prophecies or divine judgment) in the case of "charismatic justice" or—and especially relevant here—(1) informally according to concrete ethical or other practical value judgments (as in "khadi-justice," as R. Schmidt has so appropriately termed it) or, (2) formally, but not according to a hierarchy of rational concepts; rather by means of the application of "analogies" and by reference to and interpretation of concrete "precedents" (as in the case of "empirical justice"). Neither the "khadi-justice" nor modern empirical justice in its pure form knows anything of a rational basis of judgment, at least in the sense of what we would deem rational. The concrete valuational character of the khadi-justice can continue to intensify up to the point of a prophetic break with all tradition. Empirical justice, on the other hand, can be sublimated and rationalized into an aesthetic doctrine. As discussed elsewhere, since the non-bureaucratic forms of authority demonstrate a peculiar co-existence of strict adherence to tradition on the one hand, and the discretion and mercy of the ruler on the other, combinational and transitional forms between these two principles occur frequently. In England, for example, as Mendelssohn has demonstrated, there is even at this late date a broad substratum of the justice system that is actually "khadi-justice" to a degree hardly conceivable on the Continent. In cases where juries are used in Germany where there is no requirement to reveal the bases of verdicts, they function often in the same way. Generally speaking, one ought to be wary of the belief that "democratic" principles of justice are identical with "rational" (in the sense of formal) types of adjudication. In fact, as demonstrated elsewhere, the opposite is true. And yet the English (and American) system of justice in their highest courts are still, to a large extent, empirical systems based on legal precedent. In England, the reason for the failure of all efforts at rational codification and a resistance to the reception of Roman law [at the end of the Middle Ages when this occurred elsewhere in Europe] was due to the successful opposition to such efforts by the huge, uniformly organized lawyers' guilds, a monopolistic class of notables from whose midst the judges of the highest courts were chosen. Retaining control of juristic training in empirical and technically highly developed doctrine, they successfully opposed the efforts at rationalization of the law that threatened their social and material standing, and that primarily emanated from the ecclesiastical courts as well as occasionally from the universities. The struggle of the common-law advocates against Roman and ecclesiastical law and, in general, against the power base of the church was, to a considerable degree, economically motivated by their interest in their legal fees. This is clearly demonstrated by the manner in which the throne intervened in the struggle. The lawyers' position of power, confirmed as it was by their victory, was, however, determined by political centralization. For principally political reasons, there was no socially powerful class of notables in Germany that, after the manner of the English lawyers, could stand as the bearer and administrator of a national legal system, develop the national law to the level of an art with a regulated apprenticeship, and that could withstand and oppose the intrusion of the technically superior schooling of the Roman-trained jurists. It wasn't that the substantive aspects of Roman law were better adaptable to the needs of the emerging capitalism of the period, thereby assuring its victory on the Continent—virtually all legal institutions specific to modern capitalism are alien to Roman law and are of medieval origin. On the contrary, it was its rational *form* and, above all, the technical necessity of placing the trial procedure in the hands of experts trained in rational methodology (i.e., none other than those trained in Roman law at the universities) that was decisive here. The technical necessity arose in response to the increasingly complicated practical cases of law and the demand by an increasingly rationalized economy for a rational procedure of evidence to replace the primeval means of ascertaining truth through concrete revelation or sacred guarantee, as was the universal practice. To a large extent, of course, this situation was influenced by structural changes in the economy. But this impulse was operating everywhere, even in England, where the throne introduced the rational procedure of evidence primarily for the benefit of the merchants. The predominant reasons for the present differences that have developed in the substantive law of England and Germany in spite of these common influences, had more to do, as we have seen, with the autonomous development of respective authoritarian structures: in England, the concomitant centralized justice system and rule by notables; in Germany, the absence of political centralization despite bureaucratization. England, which in modern times was the first and most highly developed capitalist country, retained, in this manner, a less rational and less bureaucratic administration of justice. But capitalism was especially well suited to circumstances in England by virtue of the fact that, up to modern times, the nature of the judiciary and judicial procedure meant a successful and far-reaching denial of justice to the economically disadvantaged. This fact, coupled with the equally time-consuming and expensive system for the transfer of real estate, itself a function of the economic interests of the career lawyers, also had a profound impact on England's agrarian system, in favor of the accumulation and entrenchment of landed wealth.

Roman law in the period of the Republic, for its part, was constituted by a unique mixture of rational and empirical elements as well as those of khadi-justice. The jury appointments as such, and the *actiones in factum* (factual prosecution) of the praetors, which undoubtedly were initially formulated "from case to case," contained an element of khadi-justice. The "precautionary jurisprudence" and everything that developed from it—including a residual part of the response practice of the classical jurists—bore an "empirical" character. The decisive turn of juristic thought toward a rational character was first brought about by the technical nature of the trial instructions, which were based on formulas of the praetorian edict coordinated with concepts of law. (Today, under the dominance of the principle of substantiation, where the presentation of facts is decisive, irrespective of the legalistic point of view from which they may justify a complaint, the same kind of compulsion to formally and unambiguously develop a point to encompass the full scope of the concepts involved, as had been produced by the technically sophisticated culture of Roman law, is now lacking.) Hence, to this extent, the factors which played a role in the development of rational law were essentially of a technical, procedural nature, and resulted only indirectly from the structure of the state. But the rationalization of Roman law into a closed, scientifically applicable system of concepts—a development which sharply distinguishes this system from that produced by Oriental and Hellenic culture—only fully came to fruition in the period when the state apparatus itself underwent bureaucratization.

The rabbinical responses in the Talmud present a typical example of a form of empirical justice which is not rational, but rationalistic, and strictly bound by tradition. A pure form of "khadi"-justice that is specifically not bound by tradition is contained in every prophetic decree following the pattern: "So it is written . . . and yet I say unto you." The more strongly the religious character of the *Khadi*'s (or similar judge's) position is emphasized, the more freely integrated the unfettered judgment of the individual case will be within that sphere unbound by sacred tradition. The fact that, in Tunisia for example, the rulings of the ecclesiastical court concerning land holdings were made on the basis of "free discretion," as the Europeans termed it, presented a tangible restraint on the development of capitalism for a full generation following the French occupation. In another context, we will familiarize ourselves with the sociological foundation of these older types of justice in the authoritarian structure.

Objectivity, Expertise and Reasons of State

It is entirely true that "matter-of-factness" and "expertness" are not necessarily identical with the primacy of general, abstract norms, not even in the arena of the modern administration of justice. It is well known that the idea of a flawless system of law is, in principle, heavily under attack. The conception of the modern judge is as a vending machine into which legal documents and fees are inserted at the top, resulting in a verdict disgorged below—complete with the mechanical presentation of substantiating reasons. This image is, of course, strongly contested, perhaps due to the fact that, with the consistent bureaucratization of the legal system, there is a certain truth to it. Even within the sphere of the administration of justice, there are areas in which "individualizing" procedures are directly brought to the attention of the bureaucratic judge by the legislator. As far as the domain of actual administrative activity is concerned, that is, for all state activities which do not fall within the realm of the creation and administration of law, it is customary to hear individualized claims of freedom and autonomy. In contrast to this, general norms are primarily perceived as playing a limiting and, hence, negative role in respect to the official's positive "creative" activity which should never be regulated. This is not the place to explore the consequences of this thesis. But what is decisive for this context is that this "freely" creative administration (and, potentially, judicial system) would not constitute a realm of free, voluntary action and goodwill and personally motivated favor and valuation, such as we do find in pre-bureaucratic forms. On the contrary, what exists in its place as a constant norm of conduct is the rule and rational weighing of objective purposes as well as a devotion to these. It is especially the view most strongly exalting the "creative" discretion of the official that appraises the specifically modern and strictly objective idea of the "reason of state" as the highest and ultimate lodestar for his conduct in the area of state administration. Inseparably fused with the canonization of this abstract and "objective" idea of the *raison d'etat* are, of course, above all, the security-conscious instincts of bureaucracy for the conditions of maintaining its own power (and therefore also by definition vis-à-vis other states). Ultimately it is bureaucracy's own power interests which lend this in no way unambiguous ideal a concretely exploitable content and, in dubious cases, tip the balance. We cannot pursue this argument here. But what is especially decisive for us at this juncture is that, in principle, behind every act of real bureaucratic administration there stands a system of rationally debatable "reasons;" that is, either subsumption under norms or a weighing of means and ends.

In this context as well, the position taken by all "democratic" movements, i.e., movements that seek to minimize domination, is necessarily ambiguous. "Equality before the law" and the demand for legal guarantees against arbitrary treatment require a formal rational "objectivity" of administration, in contrast to the free, personal discretion and the goodwill of the old patrimonial authority. Other instincts aside, however, if an "ethos" were to take hold of the masses in respect to an individual question, the postulates of substantive "justice," oriented as they are toward the concrete instance and the individual case will unavoidably collide with the formalism and regulated, cool "objectivity" of bureaucratic administration, overturning for emotional reasons what reason dictates. Demanded by the interests of the bourgeoisie, it is especially those of the propertyless masses which are not served by a formalized "equality before the law" and a "calculable" process of law and administration. For the propertyless, law and administration ought to naturally stand in the service of a fair distribution of economic and social life-chances in respect to the propertied classes, but this function, of course, can only be performed by them if they assume an essentially informal character due to its "ethical" *("Khadi")* content. Not only all types of "popular justice"—which does not concern itself with questions of rational "reasons" and "norms"—thwart the rational course of justice and administration, but also all types which seek to manipulate administration by means of so-called "public opinion;" that is, under the conditions of mass democracy, the use of community action born of irrational "sentiments," and normally staged or directed by party leaders and the press. These types of justice are equally, and, under certain circumstances, even more irrational than the "arbitrary government" of an "absolute" ruler.

Concentration of the Means of Administration

The Bureaucratic Structure Goes Hand in Hand with the Concentration of the Material Means of Administration in the Hands of the Ruler. This finds expression, in a well-known and typical fashion, in the development of large capitalist enterprises that demonstrate their essential characteristics in this process. But it also finds its complement in public organizations. The bureaucratically led armies of the pharaohs, those of the later period of the Roman Republic and the Principate and, above all, the armies of the modern military state are characterized by the fact that their equipment and provisions are government issue. In contrast, it was the norm in the people's armies of agrarian tribes as well as the civilian armies of antiquity; the militias of the early medieval cities, and all feudal armies, that those obligated to fight were responsible for their own equipment and provisions. Present-day machine warfare has made a standardized means of provisioning and supply technically indispensable in the same way that the preeminence of the machine in commerce has required the concentration of the means of production and management. Those bureaucratic armies of the past, however, that were, in fact, equipped by the ruler were thus supplied when social and economic developments limited relatively or absolutely the stratum of citizens economically capable of equipping themselves to the point that their number no longer sufficed for raising the required armies. A relative deficit, however, was not prohibitive as long as the available numbers stood in correct proportion to the power claim of the state apparatus. It has only been the bureaucratization of the military which has made professional standing armies possible; which are, in turn, necessary for the purpose of securing a lasting peace over large territories, as well as waging war against distant enemies, particularly overseas. In addition, the specific military discipline and technical training can normally only be fully developed, at least to its modern level of sophistication, in the bureaucratic army.

Historically, the bureaucratization of the army has everywhere developed parallel to the shift of military service as an honorable privilege of landowners onto the unpropertied class. (This duty first fell to native propertyless men as in the cases of the armies of the Roman generals of the late Republic, the Imperial Period, and in modern armies up to the 19th century. Military service has always been the burden of non-natives in all periods of history.) In addition to contributing factors such as the increasing population density, the accompanying intensity and strain of economic work, and the increasing "unavailability" of the higher economic strata for the purposes of war, this process of the shifting of the war burden typically goes hand in hand with the general increase in material and intellectual culture. Not taking into account times of strong ideological fluctuation, the propertied classes possessing refined and, particularly, urban culture have little aptitude or inclination for the basic war duty of the common soldier. All other things being equal, the qualifications and inclinations of the landed gentry at least make them better suited to the occupation of professional officer. This imbalance between urban and rural propertied classes becomes equalized where the increasing possibility for mechanized warfare creates a need for leaders with technical qualification. The bureaucratization of warfare can be carried out on a capitalist model in the same fashion as any other form of industry. In fact, right up to the threshold of the nineteenth century, capitalist means were regularly employed in various forms for the procuring and administering of mercenary armies, especially in the Occident. During the Thirty Years War in Brandenburg, the soldiers were generally the owners of the material implements of their profession. Though they owned their weapons, horses and clothing, the state did, in fact, "turn out" these articles and provide them for sale. Later on, in the case of the Prussian standing army, the regiment commander owned the military equipment, and it wasn't until the Peace of Tilsit [1807] that these materials became concentrated in the hands of the state. This occurred simultaneously to the general establishment of common uniforms, a matter previously left to the discretion of the regiment commander. An exception to this occurred when individual units were "loaned" specific uniforms by the king (for the first time in 1620 for the Royal Guards, and then more frequently under

Friedrich II). Terms such as "regiment" and "battalion" had entirely different meanings in the eighteenth century than they have today. Only the latter of the two terms was used to identify a tactical fighting unit (as are both today), while the former was an economic unit of operation created by the "entrepreneurial" position of the colonel. Semiofficial battle ventures at sea (such as those of the Genoese "*maone*") and army recruitment were a part of the first capitalistic giant enterprises and, to a large extent, possessed a bureaucratic structure. Their transformation to an organ of the state has its modern parallel in the nationalization of the railroads (which have been state-run from the beginning).

In other spheres as well, the bureaucratization of the administration has gone hand in hand with the concentration of the means of operation. The old satrap and gubernatorial administration, as well as administration by lease or sale of office, and especially feudal administration by vassals, had the effect of decentralizing the material means of administration. The expenses of the army and the subordinate officials were defrayed in advance from the local revenues of the province, allowing only the surplus to reach the central treasury. The feudal official was required to administer entirely out of his own pocket. In the bureaucratic state, by contrast, all total state administrative expenses are met by the state budget, and the subordinate authorities are provided with a flow of means which the state regulates and controls. This bears the same significance for the economy of public administration as it does for the large centralized capitalist enterprise. In the area of scientific research and education as well, bureaucratization of the currently proliferating "institutes" of the universities (the first large institutional example of which was Liebig's laboratory in Gießen) is a function of the increasing need for material means of operation. Due to their concentration in the hands of the privileged state directors, the bulk of researchers and educators are as disenfranchised from these means as are the workers in capitalist enterprises from the means of production.

In spite of all the unquestionable technical advantages of bureaucracy, its development everywhere was relatively late, due, in part, to a series of barriers that have only diminished for good with the emergence of specific social and political conditions.

The Leveling of Economic and Social Differences. Bureaucratic organization has regularly attained relative dominance on the basis of the leveling of economic and social differences in respect to the role they play in the assumption of administrative functions. Above all, bureaucracy is a phenomenon that inevitably accompanies modern mass democracy as opposed to democratic self-administration of small homogeneous units. This is a consequence of the abstract regularity of the exercise of authority which is its characteristic principle. This results from the demand for "equality before the law" in the personal and objective sense, that is, from a disdain for "privilege" and its principled rejection of settling matters "from case to case." But the social preconditions of its emergence also play a role. Every nonbureaucratic administration of a quantitatively large social entity is based, in one way or another, upon the understanding that existing superior social and material position or honorific rank are associated with administrative functions and duties. This normally bears the consequence that direct or indirect economic and/or social exploitation of the administrative position, the opportunity for which resides in every aspect of the office, represents the compensation for its assumption. Therefore, bureaucratization and democratization have the effect, within the administration of the state, of increasing the cash expenditures of the public treasury, in spite of the fact that the character of bureaucratic administration is typically "more economical" in contrast to other forms. The turning over of the entire burden of local administration and the jurisdiction of the lower courts to the landowners of eastern parts of Prussia proved, until recently, to be the least expensive manner for meeting the needs of administration—at least from the vantage point of state coffers. The same is true of the administration of the justices of the peace in England. Mass democracy, which does away with feudal, patrimonial, and—at least by intention—plutocratic privileges in the administration, must be unswerving in replacing with paid professionals an avocational administration by traditional notables. This is not only true for state structures. It is no coincidence that it was the mass democratic parties that broke most comprehensively, in their own party organization, with the practices of honorific authority that relied so heavily on the passing down of positions on the basis of personal connections and personal esteem; practices which persisted in old conservative party structures, but in the older liberal forms as well. This type of organization was replaced in the mass parties with a bureaucratic structure under the direction of party officials and professionally employed party and trade union secretaries (as in the case of the Social Democrats and the agrarian mass movement in Germany; the Gladstone–Chamberlain caucus democracy, first organized in the 1870s in Birmingham, England; and both parties since the Jackson Administration in America). In France, the attempt at strict organization within the political parties by dint of a coercive, electoral system failed repeatedly, primarily due to the resistance of local circles of notables. In the long run, their influence has been broken by the unavoidable spread of party bureaucracy across the entire country. Every advance of simple election techniques based on numbers, such as (at least under the conditions of the large state) the system of proportional representation, has required a strict interlocal bureaucratic organization of the parties, accompanied by the increasing domination of party bureaucracy and discipline, along with the dislodging of the local circles of notables. Within the state administration itself, it is quite obvious that the progress of bureaucratization in France, North America, and now England, is a phenomenon accompanying the progress of democracy. It is important to bear in mind, however, that the term "democratization" can be misleading: the *demos,* in the sense of an unstructured mass, never "governs" larger associations itself, but is, in fact, itself governed, and is only able to change the means of selecting the ruling administrative executive on the basis of so-called "public opinion." It does so also to the degree to which social circles from its midst are in a position to exercise influence over the content and direction of administrative activity. "Democratization," in the sense intended here, does not necessarily translate into enhanced active participation in authority on the part of the governed within the social entity in question. This may well be the result of this process, but not necessarily so.

What is especially important to bear in mind at this juncture, however, is that the political concept of democracy, founded on the principle of the "equal rights" of the governed, implies these additional postulates as well: firstly, in the interest of maintaining the universal accessibility of office, the prevention of the development of a closed "status group of officials." Secondly, a minimization of the official's power in the interest of achieving the broadest possible sphere of influence of "public opinion." Hence, insofar as possible, democratization seeks to limit office tenure through election, recall, and selection of officials on a basis other than expert qualification. As a consequence, democratization inevitably comes into conflict with the general tendencies of bureaucratization, which the former itself produced in the course of its struggle with honorific authority. Consequently, the generally imprecise term "democratization" is not of use here insofar as it is understood to mean the minimization of the power of "professional officials" in favor of the most "direct" rule of the demos possible. In practical terms, this means representation by the respective party leaders of the demos. What is much more decisive here, in fact almost exclusively so, is the leveling of the governed relative to the governing, bureaucratically structured group which, for its part, can occupy an entirely autocratic position on a factual basis, and often on a formal basis as well.

Excursus on Passive Democratization

In Russia, the shattering of the position of the old landed nobility by means of the regulation of *mjestnitschwestwo* (ranking order), and the consequent suffusion of the old nobility with an office nobility was a characteristic intermediary phenomenon in the development of bureaucratization. In China, the estimation of rank according to the number of examinations passed, and the resulting respective qualification for office, played a similar role, but, at least theoretically, with a more pronounced impact. In France, the Revolution, and especially Bonapartism, made bureaucracy all-powerful. In the Catholic Church, first feudal powers, but then also all of the independent local intermediary authorities were comprehensively abolished. This process was begun by Pope Gregory VII and was continued by the Council of Trent, the Vatican council and finally the decrees of Pope Pius X, leading to the transformation of these authorities into purely functionary positions of a central authority. This transformation was connected to the ongoing rise of the factual significance of the formally entirely dependent chaplains—based, above all, on the political party organization of Catholicism. This process too, then, assisted the advance of bureaucracy, and along with it, in this case, that of "passive" democratization, that is, the levelling of the governed. In the same way, the replacement of honorific armies, responsible for their own provisioning, with a bureaucratic army will always be a process of "passive" democratization. This is true for the establishment of any absolute military monarchy in place of a feudal state or a republic of notables. Despite all the particular details, in principle this also proves applicable to as early a case as the development of the state in Egypt. Under the Roman Principate, the bureaucratization of provincial administration, as, for example, in the area of tax administration, went hand in hand with the elimination of the plutocracy of a capitalist class that had become too powerful under the Rèpublic. This, in turn, resulted in the elimination of ancient capitalism.

Obviously, there is almost always a variety of economic conditions which play a part in "democratizing" developments such as these. It is very often the case that the origin of new classes, whether of a plutocratic, petty bourgeois, or proletarian character, is economically determined. These classes often ask the assistance, or play a role in the founding or reviving, of a political power, be it legitimate or Caesaristic, for the purpose of attaining economic or social advantages. Yet, on the other hand, cases are equally possible and historically documented in which the initiative came "from above," and was of a purely political nature, for example: turning political constellations, but especially foreign ones, to account; exploiting existing economic and social antagonisms and class interests merely as a means to acquire political power; casting the antagonistic classes out of their forever unstable equilibrium; and summoning them into conflict on the basis of their latent, conflicting interests.

It seems hardly possible to say something in general about this. The degree and nature of the way in which decisive economic events have played a role vary greatly. One can say the same, however, of the manner in which political power relations exercise an influence. In Hellenic Antiquity, the transition to the disciplined hoplite combat strategy and, later on in Athens, the increasing significance of the navy formed the basis for the overthrow of the political structure by those strata of the population upon whose shoulders the burden of military duty respectively rested. The same development in Rome, however, shook the honorific authority of the office nobility only in a temporary and superficial way. Indeed, the modern mass army has always been the ultimate means by which the power of the nobles is broken, but in and of itself, has always remained solely a passive, never an active instrument of democratization. One important consideration here, however, is that the civilian army of Antiquity equipped itself, whereas the modern army relies upon bureaucratic provisioning. That the advance of the bureaucratic structure was based upon its "technical" superiority led, as with all aspects of technology, to a situation in which progress occurred slowest in those areas where the older structures functioned through a relatively highly developed technical adaptation to existing needs. This was the case with the honorific administration in England, which is why this country has been the slowest of all to succumb to bureaucratization or, indeed, is only now partially submitting to this process. This is the same kind of phenomenon as in the case when a highly developed gas lighting utility or steam railroad, possessing large fixed capital assets, offers greater resistance to electrification than entirely undeveloped areas to be newly provided with the service.

The Basis of Bureaucratic Continuity

Once a bureaucracy has been fully established, it proves to be one of the most difficult social structures to destroy. Bureaucratization is the specific means by which concerted "communal action" is transformed into rationally organized "societal action." Therefore, as an instrument for the socialization of authority relations, bureaucracy was and is a powerful tool of the first order for those who control the bureaucratic apparatus. Under otherwise equal conditions, systematically organized and directed societal action is superior to all opposing forms of mass action or communal action. Where administration has been exhaustively bureaucratized, the authority structure created is practically invincible. The individual official is unable to extricate himself from the apparatus into which he has been harnessed. In contrast to "notables," who administer on an honorary or avocational basis, the professional bureaucrat is bound by his entire material and conceptual existence to his professional activity. As in the vast majority of cases, the bureaucrat is simply an individual cog in a ceaseless, indefatigable mechanism. Entrusted with specialized tasks, the bureaucrat normally has no control over the mechanism, which is set in motion or brought to rest only from the very top of the hierarchy, and which generally prescribes the marching route to which he is essentially bound. In this way, he is, above all, firmly forged to the common interests of all functionaries integrated into the mechanism for the sake of its continued operation and the perpetuation of the rationally organized structure of authority. In addition, the governed, for their part, can neither dispense with nor replace a bureaucratic authority structure once it is established. This is due to the fact that it is based on specialized training, the technical specialization of work, and a fixed disposition toward habitual mastery, to the point of virtuosity, of fully integrated functions. In the event of a work stoppage, or if work is violently interrupted, the resulting chaos is not easily controlled by improvising with replacements from among the governed. This proves to be true for both public and private economic administration. The degree to which the material fate of the masses is dependent upon the continuous smooth functioning of increasingly bureaucratically organized capitalist enterprises continues to climb, and any thought concerning the possibility of turning the apparatus off becomes ever more utopian. Increasingly, the basis of all order in public as well as private operations is a matter of the "filing system" and bureaucratic discipline; that is, the disposition of officials toward precise obedience within their accustomed domain. However great the practical importance of the files may be, it is "discipline" that is of greater significance here. The naive assumption of Bakuninism, that by destroying documents it is possible to simultaneously destroy the basis of "acquired rights" together with "domination," overlooks the fact that it is the fixed proclivity of human beings for routinely observing norms and regulations that will survive independently of the files. Every reorganization of defeated and dispersed troop formations as well as every restoration of administrative order destroyed by revolts, panics, or other catastrophes, occurs by means of an appeal to this conditioned orientation bred in bureaucrats, on the one hand, and the governed, on the other, to obediently yield to these structures. If the appeal is successful, it can have the effect of "throwing into gear" again the disengaged mechanism of the state. The objective indispensability of the previously existing apparatus, in connection with its unique "impersonal" character, gives this system the attribute that it—in contrast to the feudal structures based on personal piety—can be readily made to work for anyone who knows how to exercise control over it. A rationally structured system of bureaucrats will continue to function flawlessly, even if an enemy occupies the territory in question, as long as the invader merely changes the top officials. It continues to function due to the fact that it is in the vital interest of all involved, including, above all, that of the enemy. Bismarck, who in the course of long years in power had made his ministerial colleagues unconditionally and bureaucratically dependent upon him by eliminating all independent statesmen, was surprised to find, upon his retirement, that these officials continued unerringly to push on with the administration of their offices, as if it were a random individual figure being replaced in the bureaucratic mechanism, not their ingenious lord and creator. Amidst the many transitions from one ruler to the next in France since the time of the First Empire, the apparatus of authority remained essentially the same. Wherever this apparatus has controlled the modern means of news and communication (telegraph), it has made "revolution," in the sense of a violent creation of entirely new institutions of authority, increasingly impossible, either for purely technical reasons, or by means of its thoroughly rationalized internal structure. As the example of France demonstrates in classical manner, the apparatus replaces "revolutions" with "*coups d'état,*" since all successful transformations there have run their course along these lines.

Some Economic and Social Consequences of Bureaucratization

It is obvious that the bureaucratic organization of a social, and especially of a political framework, for its part, can and normally does have far-reaching economic consequences. Which consequences these are depends naturally upon the distribution of social and economic power in any individual case, and particularly upon the sphere that the emerging bureaucratic mechanism occupies; hence, upon the direction indicated by the powers making use of it. Very often, the result has been a distribution of power that is semi-plutocratic in nature. In England, and especially in America, party patrons regularly stand behind the bureaucratic party organizations, and, by financing them, have been able to influence them extensively. Well known examples of patronage systems include the breweries in England, so-called heavy industry with its campaign funds, and the Hansa League with its respective funds in Germany. Within political and especially state structures as well, bureaucratization and social levelling, together with the breaking up of the opposing local and feudal privileges, have, in modern times, frequently benefitted the interests of capitalism, and often have been carried out directly in association with these interests. Such was the case with the great historical alliance between capitalist interests and the princes possessing absolute power. For, in general, a legal levelling and breaking up of closely knit local networks ruled by notables serves to broaden the operational parameters of capitalism. There are, however, other effects of bureaucratization as well: one that satisfies petit bourgeois interests in secure, traditional "sustenance," but also a state-socialist one that hampers opportunities for private profit. These have occurred in various historically advanced cases, particularly in Antiquity, but are doubtlessly to be anticipated as a future development, perhaps here as well [in Germany]. Although the political organization that existed in Egypt under the pharaohs was, at least in principle, very similar to those of Hellenistic and Roman times, the effects of the three were very different. This serves to demonstrate that the economic significance of bureaucratization may vary quite broadly according to the respective direction of the factors generally present. The mere fact of bureaucratic organization alone says nothing unequivocally about the concrete direction of its economic effects, effects which are, in some form, always present. In any event, it says less than can be said about its social, at least relatively levelling, effects. And, in this respect, it should also be borne in mind that bureaucracy, purely in and of itself, is a precision instrument which can place itself at the disposal of a full array of very different interests of domination, be they purely political, purely economic, or of any other nature. For this reason, the degree to which its development has paralleled that of democratization, as typical as this may be, should not be exaggerated. Under certain circumstances, even feudal lords have employed this instrument in their service. In addition, the possibility exists and, in the case of the Roman Principate as well as in some forms of absolutist state structures, it has often come to pass that a bureaucratizing of the administration is purposely connected with the formation of status groups, or mixed up with it by the force of the existing social power structures. Very frequently, offices are expressly reserved for members of certain status groups; in actuality, this is even more often the case.

Bureaucracy as a Power Structure

Whether actual or perhaps only formal, the democratization of society in its totality in the modern sense of the word is indeed an especially favorable, but by no means the sole possible basis for instances of bureaucratization. Bureaucratization seeks only to level those opposing forces in those areas that, in individual cases, it seeks to occupy. One fact of particular note we have already encountered a number of times, and which bears repeating, is that "democracy," because of its unavoidable yet unintended promotion of bureaucratization, is itself opposed to the "rule" of bureaucracy. Thus, under certain circumstances, democracy creates tangible breaks in and impediments to the bureaucratic organization. Hence, the individual historical case should be analyzed with regard to the specific direction in which bureaucratization has developed.

For this reason, it will remain here an undecided issue whether the modern states, where bureaucratization continues unilaterally to progress apace, also exhibit, without exception, a universal increase of bureaucratic power within the state apparatus. The fact that the bureaucratic organization is technically the most highly developed instrument of power available to that body controlling it says nothing about the emphasis bureaucracy, as such, is able to place on its agenda within the respective social framework. The ever-increasing indispensability of officialdom, swollen into the millions, is equally inconclusive on this issue as, for example, the indispensability of the proletariat in determining the measure of its social or political power position—according to the view of some representatives of the proletarian movement. Were indispensability actually a decisive factor, in areas where slavery prevails, the slaves, who are at least equally indispensable, could themselves claim such a power position since, under such conditions, free men seek to avoid labor as degrading. Whether the power of bureaucracy as such increases cannot be determined *a priori* from such reasons. The consultation of interest groups, of other nonofficial experts or, viceversa, of lay representatives lacking expertise, the creation of local, interlocal, or central parliamentary or other representative or professional organs capable of making resolutions, *appear* to run directly counter to bureaucracy. The degree to which this appearance is, in fact, reality belongs in all its details to another chapter rather than in this purely formal and casuistic discussion. Only the following general statements can be made here:

The power position of the fully developed bureaucracy is always a very large one and, under normal conditions, a commanding one. Regardless of whether the political "ruler" the bureaucracy serves is, in fact, the "people," equipped with the power of "law-making," "referendums," and the right to dismiss officials; a parliament, elected on a more aristocratic or a more "democratic" basis and equipped with the right or the authority to cast a "vote of no confidence;" an aristocratic consortium, legally or actually based on self-recruitment and preservation; a president, elected by the people; or an "absolute" or "constitutional" hereditary monarch—in every case the "ruler" will always find himself in the position of the "dilettante" vis-à-vis the "expert" officials trained in the operation of the administration. Every bureaucracy seeks to further enhance the superiority of the professionally knowledgeable staff by means of keeping secret its knowledge and intentions. It is the tendency of bureaucratic administration to always exclude the public and, as far as possible, conceal its knowledge and actions from criticism. Prussian church officials have threatened to take disciplinary measures if any reprimands or admonitory measures they have directed at a pastor are in any way made accessible to a third party, because by so doing, a pastor would be "guilty" of enabling criticism of church authorities. The accounting officials of the Persian Shah made of their budgetary art a secret science and even employed a secret code. In general, the only official Prussian statistics to be published were those that could not be damaging to the intentions of the power-wielding bureaucracy. The tendency toward secret information in certain administrative areas is a result of their objective nature: it especially prevails where the power interests of the respective authority structure regarding the outside are involved, whether it be in respect to economic competitors of a private concern or whether, in the political arena, it be in respect to foreign, potentially hostile, political powers. If it is to be occasioned by success, the conduct of diplomacy can only be publicly supervised in a very limited sense and to a limited degree. In the face of the growing significance of purely technical aspects, the military administration must rely increasingly on the secrecy of its most important measures. The political parties operate in the same fashion: indeed, in spite of all the ostensible publicity surrounding the Catholic Conventions and party congresses, this is ever more frequently the case with increasing bureaucratization of the party machinery. In Germany, for example, trade policy leads to the concealment of production statistics. Every combative posture assumed by social institutions toward the outside has the effect of strengthening the position occupied by those forces currently in power. Simply by its nature, the pure power interests of bureaucracy alone contribute far more to this stance than those areas functionally motivated to secrecy. The concept of the "office secret" is its specific invention, and bureaucracy will defend nothing with such fanaticism as this attitude, which is external to those specifically qualified areas, and not justifiable on purely technical grounds. Faced with a parliament, a bureaucracy will fight, out of its own sure instinct for power, to oppose every attempt by the parliament to obtain, by its own means (as, for example, by the so-called "right of investigation"), expert knowledge from the interested parties: a poorly-informed and consequently powerless parliament is, of course, more welcome to the bureaucracy to the extent that this ignorance is consistent with its own interests. The absolute monarch too, and in a certain sense especially he, is powerless in the face of superior bureaucratic expertise. All the angry decrees of Friedrich the Great concerning the "abolition of serfdom" were derailed, so to speak, enroute to their realization, because the official mechanism simply ignored them as the occasional fancies of a dilettante. Wherever the constitutional monarch finds himself in agreement with a socially influential segment of the governed, he very often has a more significant influence on the conduct of the administration than does the absolute monarch. This is as a consequence of the relatively greater publicity of criticism directed at the administration under a constitutional monarch, thereby facilitating his supervision of it; the absolute monarch, however, is wholly dependent on information received solely through the bureaucracy. The Russian Czar of the old regime was seldom in a position to carry out even trivial matters over time, if it displeased his bureaucracy and was not in keeping with its power interests. His ministries, which were directly subordinate to him as the autocrat, formed, as Leroy-Beaulieu has already very accurately noted, a conglomerate of satrapies that fought among themselves with all the means of personal intrigues, especially bombarding one another continually with voluminous "reports," against which the monarch, as a dilettante, was quite helpless. Every transition to constitutionalism is accompanied by the inevitable concentration of the power of the central bureaucracy in one person; [i.e.,] its assignment beneath a monocratic head, such as a prime minister, through whose hands everything directed to the monarch must first pass. This has the effect of placing the monarch significantly beneath the guardianship of the bureaucratic chief of staff. It was against this principle that Wilhelm II struggled in his well-known conflict with Bismarck, an attack from which he was very soon required to retreat. Under the rule of expertise, the real influence of the monarch can only continue to be maintained by means of ongoing communication, well-planned and directed by and with the heads of the central bureaucracy. At the same time, constitutionalism binds the bureaucracy and the ruler together in a partnership of interests against the aspirations to power of the party chiefs in the parliamentary bodies. For this very reason the constitutional monarch is powerless against the bureaucracy, if he is unable to find support in the parliament. The desertion of the "Grandees of the Realm," the Prussian ministers and the highest officials of the Empire, brought a German monarch into approximately the same situation in November, 1918, as did the corresponding case under the feudal state structure in 1076. Nevertheless, this is an exception. For the power position of the monarch in respect to bureaucratic officials is, in the main, far stronger than it was in the feudal state or the "stereotypical" patrimonial state, owing to the ever-present supply of promotion-happy prospective candidates with whom he can easily replace disagreeable, independent officials. All other things being equal, only economically independent officials, that is, officials belonging to propertied strata, can afford to risk loss of office: recruitment from the unpropertied strata has always served to enhance the power of rulers. And only officials belonging to a socially influential stratum that the monarch believes he can entrust with his support are able to completely and permanently paralyze his will.

Solely superior to the expert knowledge of bureaucracy is the expert knowledge of private economic interests in the field of "business." This is due to the fact that exact factual knowledge in this field is a matter of direct economic survival: errors in official statistics do not have a direct economic impact upon the responsible official, whereas miscalculations in a capitalist concern are made at the expense of losses, if not the concern's very existence. Furthermore, the secret as a means of power is even more safely concealed in the books of the entrepreneur than it is in any files of public authorities. It is for this reason that public influence on economic life in the capitalist era is bound by such narrow parameters, and the measures of the state in this area so often derail in an unforeseen and unintended way, or are made illusory by means of the superior expert knowledge of the interested parties.

Excursus on Interest Groups and Collegiate Bodies

Because specialized expert knowledge increasingly became the foundation of officeholders' power, it soon became an object of the "ruler's" concern how one could make use of that expert knowledge to preserve one's own position as ruler without thereby abdicating in the experts' favor. With the increasing qualitative accumulation of administrative tasks and thus of the indispensability of expert knowledge, it typically comes to pass that occasional consultation with either individual, proven confidants or even an assembly of them intermittently called together during difficult situations, is no longer sufficient for the ruler; he henceforth surrounds himself with *collegiate* bodies—the *"Räte von Haus aus"* are a characteristic transitional manifestation of this—which constantly confer, advise, and make decisions (Conseil d'Etat, Privy Council, Generaldirektorium, Kabinett, Diwan, Tsungli-Yamen, Waiwupu, etc.). Of course, their position varies greatly, not only according to the extent that they become the highest administrative authority or whether one or several monocratic central authorities stand beside them, but also according to their procedure. When this prototype is fully developed, these collegiate bodies deliberate, actually or fictively, under the chairmanship of the ruler. Subsequent to all-round elucidation by respective experts' reports and other members' motions, all important affairs are settled by resolution, which the ruler's decree then sanctions or rejects. Thus, this sort of collegiate body is the typical form through which the ruler, who becomes more and more a "dilettante," simultaneously makes use of expert knowledge and—what often remains unnoticed—seeks to ward off the growing preeminence of expert knowledge and to assert his position as ruler vis-à-vis that knowledge. He keeps one expert in check through others, and through that intricate procedure, seeks to secure for himself a comprehensive picture and the certainty that he is not prompted into arbitrary decisions. In so doing, he often expects a guarantee of his own maximum influence, less through his personal chairmanship than through the written votes presented to him. Friedrich Wilhelm the First, whose actual influence on the administration was quite significant, almost never attended the strictly collegially organized sessions of ministers, and made decisions on written presentations by means of margin notes or decrees, which were delivered to the ministers via the courier from the "cabinet" after consultation with the personal servants of the king. In Russia as well as in Prussia and other states, the cabinet developed into a kind of personal fortress toward which the specialized bureaucracy directed its hatred, the subjects their distrust, in the case of failures, and to which the ruler fled, to a certain degree, to escape expert knowledge and the "routinization" of administration.

Furthermore, through the collegiate principle, the ruler attempted to mold a sort of synthesis of specialized experts into a collective unity. One generally can not determine the success of this. The phenomenon itself is common to greatly varying forms of state, from the patrimonial and feudal state to the early bureaucratic one. Primarily, however, it is most typical of the early absolutism of princes. It was one of the strongest devices for urging administrations to become objective. By drawing on or pooling the counsel of socially influential citizens, it also allowed a balanced combination of the authority of notables and entrepreneurial expertise with the expert knowledge of professional bureaucrats. The collegiate bodies were one of the first institutions to allow the development of the modern concept of "the authorities" in the sense of a perennial organization existing independently of the individual.

As long as expert knowledge of administrative affairs was exclusively a product of long empirical practice and the norms of administration were not regulations of law, but rather elements of tradition, the council of elders, often with the participation of the priests, the "elder statesmen," and the notables, was typically the adequate form for such authorities which initially only advised the ruler; being perennial organizations, though, they later often encroached upon the actual power of the successive rulers. Such was the case with the Roman Senate and the Venetian Council, as well as with the Athenian Areopagus until its suppression in favor of the rule of the "*demagogos.*" Of course, one must sharply distinguish such authorities as a type from the corporate bodies here under discussion, which, despite numerous alterations, are nevertheless founded on both rational expert specialization and the rule of expert knowledge. On the other hand, they must be distinguished from those select advisory bodies, comprised of private interest groups and common in the modern state, whose core is not constituted by past or present civil servants. They must also be distinguished sociologically from those collegiate supervisory authorities (boards of directors) found in the bureaucratic organizations of today's private economy (joint-stock companies), despite the fact that joint-stock companies often supplement themselves by drawing in notables from disinterested groups, be it for the sake of those groups' expert knowledge or be it as a means for representation and publicity. These organizations normally do not bring together within themselves representatives of special expertise, but rather those of the decisive economic primary interests as such (particularly the banks that finance the enterprise), who have by no means a merely advisory position, but rather a controlling, indeed often ruling one. With some reservation, they are to be compared to the assemblies of the great independent feudal vassals, officeholders, and other socially powerful interest groups of patrimonial or feudal political organizations, which, though sometimes the precursors of the "councils" that arose as a result of the increased intensity of administration, had even more often been precursors of privileged corporate bodies.

Quite regularly, this bureaucratic collegiate principle was transferred from the central authority onto the most varied lower levels of authority. As initially remarked, within locally closed and, particularly, urban units, collegiate administration was originally a form of rule by *notables* (originally by means of elected "councils," "magistrate colleges," "*Dukurionen* colleges," and "jurymen's colleges" that were later at least partially coopted). Thus, they are a normal constituent of the organization of "self-administration," that is, of the discharge of administrative tasks by local interest groups under the control of bureaucratic state authorities. The above examples of the Venetian Council and especially of the Roman Senate are cases involving the transfer to large oversea empires of the indigenous form of rule by notables, which is normally founded on local political associations. Within the bureaucratic state, collegiate administration dissipates as the necessity for speedy decisions and the abovementioned characteristics that press toward complete bureaucracy and monocracy, along with the progress of transportation networks and the technical demands on the administration, come to predominate. Above all, though, it dissipates as soon as the development of parliamentary institutions and the often simultaneous increase and publicity of outside criticism allow absolute uniformity in the administration's leadership to appear more important, from the standpoint of the ruler's interests, than the thoroughness in the preparation of its decisions. Under these modern conditions, France's thoroughly rationalized system of specialist ministers and governors, which presumably is supplemented by the already mentioned pooling of advisory boards comprised of interested parties from the economically and socially most influential classes, has considerable opportunities for pushing back the old forms everywhere; such pooling has been occurring with ever greater frequency and is also gradually becoming formally organized. This latter development, which seeks to place the interest groups's concrete experience into the service of the rational administration of expertly trained civil servants, certainly has an important future and will increase the power of the bureaucracy even more. It is well known how Bismarck sought to use the plan of a "National Economic Council" as a weapon against the German Parliament, accusing the opposition majority—to whom he would never have conceded the right of investigation as practiced in the English Parliament—of trying, in the interests of parliamentary power, to keep officialdom from becoming "too smart." This is not the context for a discussion concerning what future position the associations of interest groups can be assigned within the administration.

Not until the bureaucratization of state and law, does one also generally see the definite possibility of sharp, conceptual separation of an "objective" justice system from "subjective" rights of individuals guaranteed by that system; one also sees the separation of "public" law, which governs relations of authorities among one another and to the "subjects," from "private" law, which governs the relations of individuals among one another. This bureaucratization assumes the conceptual separation of the "state," as an abstract agent of rulers' rights and the creator of "legal norms," from all personal "rights" of individuals—notions that must have been far removed from the nature of the *pre*bureaucratic, and especially of the patrimonial and feudal, structures of rule. This idea first became conceivable and practiced in urban communities at that point in time when these began choosing their officials in periodic *elections,* for with this it became obvious that the individual "practitioner" of power, even if in the highest position, was no longer identical with the person who possessed authority "in his own right." But it was only with the complete depersonalization of office management in bureaucracy and the rational systemization of law that this separation was formally ushered in.

Bureaucracy and Cultural Capital

We cannot here analyze the far-reaching, general cultural effects that the advance of the rational bureaucratic structure of rule unfurls independently of the areas of which it seizes hold. Of course, it serves the advancement of "rationalism" of life-style. Yet this concept allows for greatly differing meanings. Quite generally, it can only be said that the development toward rational "matter-of-factness" and the establishment of "professional" and "expert classes," with all of its ramifications, is greatly hastened by the bureaucratization of all rule. Only one important constituent of this process can be briefly indicated here: the effect upon the type of upbringing and education *("Erziehung und Bildung").* Our continental, Western educational institutions, especially the higher ones—universities, technical colleges, business schools, college preparatory schools, and other intermediate schools—are controlled and influenced by the need for that type of "education" which produces the system of specialty examination increasingly indispensable for modern bureaucracy: specialty schooling. In the modern sense, the "specialty examination" was and still is found outside of actual bureaucratic organizations as well; such is the case with the "free" professions of medicine and law and in guild-organized vocations. Nor is it an indispensable phenomenon accompanying bureaucratization: the French, English, and American bureaucracies have largely or entirely done without them for a long time; they were replaced by schooling and achievement within the party organization. "Democracy" adopts a conflicted point of view toward the specialty examination, as it does toward all phenomena of bureaucratization that it itself promotes. On the one hand, the specialty examination entails or seems to entail "selection" of qualified persons from all classes of society instead of rule by notables. On the other hand, democracy fears that a privileged "caste" will arise from examinations and educational credentials, and thus fights against them. Finally, the specialty examination is already present in pre-bureaucratic times. Its first, regular, historical appearance is in prebendally organized authority structures. The expectation of prebends, initially of clerical ones—such as in the Islamic Orient and in the occidental Middle Ages—and later of secular ones, as was the case especially in China, was the typical prize for which people studied and were examined. However, these examinations only partially have an actual "specialty" character. Not until the advent of complete, modern bureaucratization did the rational organization of the specialty examination fully evolve. The civil service reform is gradually importing specialty training and the specialty examination to America; the examination is also spreading into all other countries from its primary European breeding ground, Germany. In England, the growing bureaucratization of the administration is increasing the importance of the specialty examination; the attempt to replace the semipatrimonial old bureaucracy with the new one brought the specialty examination to China (replacing the earlier and entirely different examination system); the bureaucratization of capitalism and its need for specially trained technicians, clerks, etc., has carried it throughout the world. Most of all, this development is greatly promoted by the social prestige of the educational credentials obtained by means of the specialty examination; all the more so when this prestige is converted into economic advantage. Today, educational credentials are what proof of ancestry was in the past: a precondition for equality of birth, a prerequisite for access to royal endowments *(Stiftsfähigkeit)*, and, wherever nobility remained socially powerful, necessary for qualification to state office. The establishment of university, technical, and business school diplomas, and the universal call for the creation of educational certificates in all areas serve for the creation of a privileged stratum in private and public office. The possession of an educational certificate supports its holder's claim to marriage into circles of notables (of course, there are also hopes in the office for the favor of the boss's daughter), to admission to circles observing "honor codes," to a salary "appropriate to status" instead of achievement-based pay, to certain promotion and a pension, and, most of all, to a monopolization of the socially and economically advantageous positions. If we listen closely to the desire in all areas for the institution of regulated courses of study and specialty exams, then we find that the reason for this is not a "stampede for education" that has suddenly arisen, but rather the struggle to limit supply in respect to positions, and to monopolize these in favor of the holders of educational credentials. Today, the "examination" is the universal means for this monopolization; this is the reason for its irresistible advance. And since the course of study necessary for obtaining educational credentials incurs significant costs and time for maturation, this struggle entails the repression of talent ("charisma") in favor of property—the "mental" costs of educational credentials are constantly low and do not increase, but rather decrease when these credentials are produced *en masse*. The requirement of a chivalrous life-style as an old qualification for holding a fief has been replaced in Germany by the necessity of participating in its modern remnants, namely, the fraternities of the degree-granting universities; in the Anglo-Saxon countries, it has been replaced by athletic and social clubs. On the other hand, the bureaucracy strives toward the development of a type of "right to office" by the creation of an orderly disciplinary procedure and by the elimination of the "superior's" entirely arbitrary disposition over civil servants; the bureaucracy seeks to find him a position, timely promotion, and a retirement pension. In so doing, the bureaucracy is supported by the "democratic" attitude of the governed, who desire a minimization of domination by the ruler and believe they glimpse a weakening of the ruler's power in any diminution of his arbitrary disposition over civil servants. Thus, bureaucracy within both public service and the business office is just as much a vehicle of a specifically status-related development as were the entirely different public officials of the past. And it has already been indicated that these status qualities are by their nature prone to exploitation for their technical usefulness to bureaucracy in discharging its tasks. It is exactly against this unavoidable "status" character that "democracy" reacts in its striving to replace appointed officials with the election of officials for short terms and to replace regulated disciplinary proceedings with the termination of officials by popular vote, thereby replacing the arbitrary disposition of hierarchically superior "rulers" with the arbitrary disposition of those governed, that is, of the party chiefs who govern them.

Social prestige based on the enjoyment of a particular upbringing and education is, in itself, by no means specific to bureaucracy. On the contrary, in other structures of rule it rests on substantially different foundations of content. In feudal, theocratic, and patrimonial structures of rule, in the English administration by notables, in the ancient Chinese bureaucracy by patrimony, in the demagogic rule of the so-called Hellenic democracy, the goal of upbringing and the foundation of social esteem was, regardless of the difference of the structure of rule, not the "expert," but—to use a slogan—the "cultivated" person. The expression is here used entirely value-free and only in the sense that a quality of life-style *passing* for "cultured" was the goal of upbringing, not of specialized expert training. The cultivated personality as the ideal of education, whether of the chivalrous, ascetic, literary (as in China), gymnastic-artistic (as in Greece), or gentlemanly type (as is the convention in Anglo-Saxon countries), was occasioned by the structure of rule and the social requirements for membership within the ruling class. The qualification of the ruling class as such rested not on expert knowledge, but on the possession of a surplus of "cultural capital" (in the entirely variable, value-free sense here imputed to this concept). Of course, martial, theological, and legal expertise were exhaustively cultivated. Yet in the Hellenic, medieval, and Chinese courses of study, the concentration was comprised of didactic elements entirely different from "useful" ones applicable to an area of expertise. Behind all present-day discussions about the foundations of the educational system lies the struggle of the "expert" type against the old "liberal arts" type, a struggle present at every decisive point of the irresistible expansion of the bureaucratization of all public and private authority relations and determined by the constantly increasing importance of expert knowledge; this struggle penetrates the most intimate questions of culture.

To summarize, during its advance, the bureaucratic organization has had to overcome not only the oft-mentioned substantially negative obstacles to the levelling it requires. In addition, forms of administrative structure based on heterogeneous principles have crossed and still do cross paths with bureaucratic organization; we have already touched upon these forms of administrative structure. Not all actually existing types can be discussed here—that would lead us too far afield—but a few especially important structural principles can be cursorily summarized in a greatly simplified manner. Among some of the questions that are to be asked are: (1) To what extent are bureaucratic structures subject to economic determination, or are their opportunities for development created by other circumstances, such as political ones, or by a "lawfulness" inherent in their technical structure? (2) What, if any, specific economic effects do they themselves set in motion? In answering these questions, one must keep the fluidity and overlapping of all these organizational principles in sight. Their "pure" types are to be considered solely as theoretical limits, valuable and indispensable for purposes of analysis. Between the "pure" types, historical reality has moved and continues to move in mixed forms.

The bureaucratic structure is everywhere a late product of development. The farther we go back into that development, the more typical becomes the absence of bureaucracy and officialdom as a form of authority. Bureaucracy has a "rational" character: its behavior is governed by rule, purpose, means, and a de-personalized "matter-of-factness." Thus, its rise and expansion has everywhere had a "revolutionary" effect similar to the forward march of rationalism in all areas. In this way, bureaucracy destroyed structural forms of domination that did not have a rational character.

Translated by Martin Black, with Lance W. Garmer

16. The Distribution of Power within the Political Community: Classes, Status Groups, Political Parties

Based on its structure, every legal order (not only that of the state) directly affects the distribution of power within the respective community, that of economic power or any other. Power is to be generally understood as the chance of an individual or a number of people to effect their will in social action, even when faced with opposition from others. Economically conditioned power is not, of course, identical to power in general. In fact, the development of economic power is much more likely to be the consequence of power existing on different grounds. For its part, power is not sought for purposes of economic enrichment alone. Power, even economic power, is often cherished "for its own sake" and, frequently, the attempts to achieve it are determined by the social honor it bestows. But not all forms of power bring social honor. The typical American boss, like the typical large-scale speculator, may well consciously renounce it. In general, especially blatant economic power, that is, the naked display of financial power, is by no means a recognized basis of social honor. Nor is power alone the sole basis of social honor. In fact, the reverse is possible. Social honor (prestige) may even be the basis for power of an economic nature and frequently has been. Just as the law can guarantee power, so can it also guarantee honor. Normally, however, the legal order is rarely the primary source in this case, but rather a kind of added element that may well enhance the likelihood of possessing power and honor, but cannot always ensure it. The manner in which social honor is distributed in a community among the typical participating groups we will designate as the *social order.* This social order stands in a similar relation to the law as the economic order. The social order is not identical to it however; the economic order simply reveals the nature in which economic goods and services are distributed and consumed. In large measure, however, the social order is determined by it and impacts back upon it.

"Classes," "status groups," and "political parties" are phenomena of the distribution of power within a community.

Classes

"Classes" are not themselves communities in the sense used here, but rather only represent possible and frequent bases for social action. We are speaking of a class when (1) a number of people share a specific causal component of their life-chances insofar as (2) this component is solely represented by means of its economic interests in its possessions and income, and (3) is represented under the terms of the commodities or labor markets (i.e., "class situation"). It is the most elementary of economic facts that the way in which material possessions are distributed among a multitude of individuals meeting competitively within the market place for the purpose of exchange, by its nature alone, creates specific life-chances. In accordance with the law of marginal utility, the mode of distribution serves to shut the propertyless out of the competition for all goods of higher value in favor of the propertied, and allows the latter to monopolize the procurement of these goods. All other things being equal, it monopolizes the profit opportunities for all those who, already provided with their goods, do not have to sell just to stay in business. Circumstances such as these also tend to enhance the edge of the owners (in the event of price wars) over those who, without possessions, can offer nothing other than their service or their product, and who are compelled to sell these off in order to subsist at all. The mode of distribution monopolizes the possibility for the propertied to transfer property from the sphere of utility as assets to a new sphere of valuation as capital (i.e., to the entrepreneurial function), limiting all opportunities for direct or indirect participation in capital gains to themselves. Such are conditions within the arena of pure market relations. Property and lack of property, therefore, are the basic categories of all class situations, regardless of whether these categories develop in the course of a price war (hence a consumer struggle) or product competition (producer's struggle). But within these categories, the class situations differentiate themselves even further according to types of property usable for returns, on the one hand, and the types of service to be rendered on the other. Some of the types of ownership can be: real estate; workshops; warehouses; retail stores; arable land of large and smaller proportions (quantitative differences with potentially qualitative consequences); ownership of mines, cattle, people (slaves); disposition over the means of production or capital goods of all sorts, above all money or objects easily exchanged for money; products of one's own or someone else's work, different according to the degree to which each is a finished product; or transferable monopolies of any kind. All of these distinctions serve to differentiate the class situations of the propertied. Similarly, the way in which they can and do use their property, above all their liquid possessions, differentiates them as to whether they belong to the rentier class or to that of the entrepreneurs.

In the same way, those without property who offer services are differentiated according to the manner in which they offer them, whether on a continual contractual basis, or irregularly from case to case. One thing, however, remains common to the concept of class: it is the type of chance one has in the marketplace which is of moment in portraying a common condition for the fate of the individual. Hence, "class situation" is, in this sense, ultimately "market situation." The effect of outright possession as such, which among cattle breeders places those who lack property, such as slaves or bondsmen, under the power of the cattle owner, is only a preliminary stage of actual class formation. Nonetheless, in the loan of cattle and in the naked severity of liability under the law, we see for the first time in such communities the degree to which simple possession is a determinant of individual fate, a situation in stark contrast to work in agrarian communities based on labor. The creditor-debtor relationship, the basis of class situations, first began to develop in the cities along with a rather primitive credit market, an interest rate which climbed according to demand, and a factual monopolization of lending under a budding plutocracy. It is here that the class struggles begin. That group of people, however, whose fate is not determined by the possibility of utilizing goods or services in the market—slaves, for instance—cannot, in a technical sense, be considered as a class, but rather as a status group.

According to this terminology, then, it is unambiguously economic interest, and one important to the very existence of the market, which creates class. Despite this, however, the concept of "class interest" is ambiguous. It is not a clear empirical concept if it refers to something other than the factual orientation of interests. These interests emerge with a certain probability out of the class situation, and represent a certain average constituency identified with this situation. In the same class situation and with all conditions otherwise being equal, the direction in which, say, the individual worker is likely to follow his interests may vary greatly, according to whether he is, for example, highly, regurlarly, or poorly qualified in his talents for a certain task. In the same way, the direction of interests may vary according to whether or not social conduct of a greater or lesser number of those commonly affected by the class situation, or even an association among them (such as a trade union), has grown out of the class situation from which the individual can anticipate results for himself. The development of communal or even societal conduct out of a common class situation is by no means a universal phenomenon. The effect of the class situation is more likely to be limited to the evocation of an essentially similar reaction, that is, in the appropriate terminology, a "mass action;" but this may not be the case at all. Frequently, it is the case that only an amorphous form of collective action emerges. The "grumbling" of the workers, well known in ancient Oriental ethics, is an example of this: a moral condemnation of the foreman. In its practical significance, this is probably not unlike a recent industrial development, the appearance of which is increasingly typical: the "job action," or slowdown (the intentional reduction of work productivity), applied by the work force on the basis of tacit agreement. The degree to which communal action and, potentially, associations are a function of the mass action of the members of a particular class is connected to general cultural conditions, especially to those of an intellectual nature. It is further connected to the extent to which contrasts, and especially the linkage between the causes and the consequences of the class situation, have become transparent. As starkly differentiated as the life-chances may be, experience indicates that this fact alone by no means gives birth to a "class-based action" (social action by members of a class). For this to occur, the real conditions and the effect of the class situation have to be clearly discernable. It is only then that the contrasting degrees of privilege are discovered not to be absolute givens, but the result of either (1) the given distribution of property, or (2) the structure of a concrete economic order. It is with this awareness that it becomes possible to respond not only with acts of intermittent and irrational protest, but in the form of rational association. Class situations of the first category were to be found in especially crude and transparent forms in the urban centers of Antiquity and during the Middle Ages. They especially occurred wherever large fortunes were amassed by means of factually monopolized trading in the commercial products of the respective locale, or in foodstuffs. Furthermore, the same has occurred under certain circumstances in agrarian economies of the most diverse historical periods by means of exploiting its growing profitability. The most important historical example of the second category is the class situation of the modern "proletariat."

Hence, every class can serve as the bearer of any of the innumerable forms of possible class-based action, but it is certainly not necessarily so. In any case, a class is not to be confused with a community; any attempt to conceptually equate the two results in distortions. The circumstance that has people of the same class situation reacting on a regular basis to such tangible situations as economic ones by means of mass action corresponding to the interests of the average participant is as important as it is basic to the understanding of historical events. But this fact must not lead to a pseudo-scientific way of operating with the concepts of class and class interest which is so common in modern times and received its classic expression in the assertion by a talented writer to the effect that the individual might well err in respect to his interests, but that a class was infallible in this respect.

If classes as such are not communities, it is nevertheless true that class situations only emerge on the basis of association. Communal action, however, while responsible for the emergence of class situations, is not the type involving members of the same class, but those of different classes. Forms of communal action, for example, that directly determine the class situation of the worker and the entrepreneur are the labor market, the commodities market, and the capitalist enterprise. The existence of a capitalist enterprise, however, presupposes the existence of a very special kind of protective communal action that recognizes the possession of goods purely as such, and especially grants individuals the power of principally free disposition over the means of production. This protective communal action is a system of laws and one of a specific nature. Every type of class situation, especially those that base themselves upon the power of property as such, becomes most efficacious when all other determining factors of reciprocal relations are, as much as possible, eliminated in their significance, thereby allowing the use of the power of property in the market to attain virtually sovereign significance.

Among the impediments to the consistent application of the pure market principle are the "status groups" which, for the moment, are only of interest to us in this connection. Before we briefly examine them, however, it is important to observe that there is not much of a general nature that can be said about the more specific types of antagonisms between the classes (in the sense which we have established here). The big shift, which has been continuously evolving from the past to the present day, can be summarized at the cost of some accuracy: the struggle in which class situations obtain has increasingly shifted from consumer credit toward, initially, competition in the commodities market, and then to wage disputes in the labor market. The "class struggles" of Antiquity—to the extent that they were actual class struggles and not struggles among status groups—were initially struggles between rural debtors (artisans, no doubt, among them) facing the threat of slavery or bondage, and the urban creditors. For, as among the cattle breeders, bondage was the normal consequence of property differentiation in the cities, and especially in the ports of trade. Debt relationships as such provoked class action until the time of Catalina. Along with this, the struggle for food emerged and, despite increasing provision by the city via foreign purchase of grain, chiefly involved the provisions and prices of bread. These conditions, tolerated throughout Antiquity and the Middle Ages, were protested by the propertyless in respect to the actual and intended beneficiaries of the bread-shortage/bread-price increase. The situation soon spread to other life-sustaining goods such as the tools necessary to handicraft production. Wage disputes were discussed little during Antiquity and throughout the Middle Ages, and have only slowly become an issue in modern times. Not only did they recede entirely during slavery uprisings, but also at times of conflict in the commodities market.

Monopolies, forestallings, buy-outs, and the withholding of goods from the market for the purpose of price hikes were the kinds of things protested by the propertyless during ancient and medieval times. Today, contention is over wage–price formation. The struggles for access to the market and for the determination of the price of products represent the transition to modern times, and involved clashes between the merchants and craftsmen in the cottage industry. A general phenomenon that can be acknowledged here is that class conflict, conditioned by the market situation, is most bitter between those participants who directly oppose one another in the price wars. It is the industrialist and company director, not the rentier, shareholder, or banker, who are met with the rancor of the worker, although, ironically, it is into the pockets of these latter individuals that the profits of "unemployment" are channeled; more so certainly than into those of the former, who are, nonetheless, the workers' chief opponents in wage disputes. This simple fact has often been decisive for the role played by the class situation in the formation of political parties. For one thing, it has made possible the various manifestations of patriarchal socialism and, at least earlier, the frequent attempts of threatened social status groups to form coalitions with the proletariat against the bourgeoisie.

Status Groups

Status groups *(Stände)*, in contrast to classes, are normally communities or groups *(Gemeinschaften)*, if not also often of an amorphous nature. In contrast to the purely economically-determined class situation, we mean to designate with the term "status situation" every typical component of the fate of those individuals determined by means of a specific positive or negative social estimation of honor. This honor is generally attributed to any particular common characteristic and can also be linked to a class situation; class differences and, though not always, property as such, as we have already observed, tend, in the long run, to have an extraordinarily predictable correlation with status. In the subsistence economy of neighborhood associations throughout the world, it seems frequently to be the case that the richest man is simply considered the chief, although this often signifies a purely honorary distinction. In so-called pure modern democracy (i.e., in which expressly structured status privileges of individuals are renounced), it happens, for example, that only families in approximately similar tax brackets dance together (as had been said about some of Switzerland's smaller towns). But status honor does not necessarily have to be linked to the class situation. In fact, it normally stands in direct contradiction to the pretensions of sheer ownership as such. Both propertied and propertyless individuals can belong to the same status group, as often happens with very tangible consequences. This "equality" of social esteem, however, does tend to be very precarious over time. The status equality of American gentlemen, for example, expresses itself in such a manner that—once away from the objectively determined subordination of business where the old traditions still prevail—it would be considered strictly in poor taste if even the richest boss, while playing billiards or cards at the club, did not treat his clerk like a complete equal, but should bestow upon him a place-conscious condescending sense of benevolence. This is a sentiment of which the German boss will never rid himself and is, in fact, one of the most important reasons why German clubs in America will never have the attraction that the American clubs have been able to achieve.

In content, the honor of status expresses itself in the specifically stylized way of life to which all aspiring members are expected to adhere. In connection with this expectation are limitations which may be placed on social interaction; that is, interaction which does not have a strictly economic or business purpose. This may extend to restrict normal marriage to within the status group, even to the point of complete endogamous closure. Once this is no longer a mere individual and socially irrelevant imitation of a foreign life style, but involves an agreed-upon format of social action, the status development has begun. In its characteristic form, status stratification on the basis of conventional life-style is developing along these lines in the United States out of a concept of democracy. As an example, only those residents of certain streets ("the Street") are considered members of society, can move in social circles and can be visited and invited. Above all, however, it is the strict submission to current fashion in America, among men as well, and to a degree unheard of in Germany, which may be a symptom of the fact that, for the young initiate, the state of gentlemanhood is something to which claim is laid, and the degree to which he observes this submission to fashion determines, *prima facie,* whether he will be treated as a gentleman. Whether he submits or not is as important to his employment possibilities at the best houses and, above all, to his social intercourse, including the chance of marrying into an esteemed family, as are gentlemanly "qualifications" for dueling. In other cases, status honor is usurped, for instance, by certain families such as those that have resided in a specific spot for a long time (and, of course, are correspondingly prosperous). Other examples include the "F.F.V." (the "First Families of Virginia"), the actual (or supposed) descendants of the Indian Princess Pocahontas, the

Pilgrims, the Knickerbockers, the members of virtually inaccessible sects, and other such circles distinguished by some distinctive feature. In this case, we are dealing with purely conventional stratification based essentially on usurpation (as are originally almost all typical cases of status honor). But the path from there to legal privilege (positive and negative) is easily traversed as soon as a certain stratification of the social order has factually taken root and, as a consequence of the stable distribution of economic power, has itself achieved stability. In those cases where the consequences have been realized to their fullest extent, the status group develops into a closed "caste." Along with conventional and legal distinctions, caste distinctions introduce a ritual guarantee to status group stratification to the extent that mere physical contact between members of respectively lower and higher castes is considered ritualistically impure, a blemish that must be atoned for by a religious act. Furthermore, individual castes may develop wholly distinct cults and gods.

Normally, however, the status stratification will only intensify to this degree where underlying differences are considered to be ethnic. The caste is normally the form in which ethnic communities, believing in blood relations and the exclusion of exogenous marriage and social intercourse, maintain a social framework. As has already been discussed, castes are part of a worldwide phenomenon of "pariah" peoples, communities which have acquired specific occupational traditions in handicrafts or other vocations, have maintained a belief in their ethnic commonality and, in a state of diaspora, live lives strictly segregated from all but unavoidable personal commerce. Though their legal position is usually precarious, on the basis of their economic indispensability, they are tolerated and often privileged, living interspersed throughout the political communities. The Jewish people are the most remarkable historical example.

Those castes which have emerged from a status segregation differ structurally from group segregation of a merely ethnic nature: the horizontal, unconnected coexistence of the latter is transformed, via caste structure, into a vertical, social hierarchy. To express it correctly, comprehensive organization of the ethnically disparate communities unites the groups into a specific political form of communal action. In their effect, the two structures differ in that ethnic coexistence, which results in mutual ethnic rejection and disdain, allows every ethnic community to consider its own honor the highest. In caste stratification, however, the social system of subordination accords more honor to the privileged castes, because the ethnic differences here correspond to function within the political community (soldiers, priests, craftsmen politically important to war, construction, etc.). Even the most despised pariah people, be they an ethnic or a status group, equally maintain this one peculiarity: the belief in their own specific honor (as is the case with the Jews). It is only among negatively privileged status groups that the "sense of dignity" (i.e., the subjective precipitate created by coupling social honor with the conventional demands nurtured in the members of the positively privileged status group) undergoes a specific deviation. The sense of dignity among positively privileged status groups, by its nature, does not base itself on anything extending beyond their "being," their "beauty and virtue." Their domain is "of this world," and they live for the present from their grand past. The sense of dignity among negatively privileged strata is only able to base itself in a time to come, be it in this life or in an afterlife. In other words, this dignity must be based on a belief in a providential "mission," in the group's specific honor before God as a "chosen people," and in the belief that their reward will either come in an afterlife where "the last shall be first," or in this life in which the messiah shall appear, bearing witness to the hidden honor of the despised pariah people or status group (as in the case, again, of the Jews). This rather simple set of circumstances is the source of the religiosity maintained by the pariah status group. The significance of this behavior will be discussed in another connection, but not in relation with that of Nietzsche's much vaunted construction (from *The Genealogy of Morals*) of "resentment." As we have seen, "resentment" is only applicable in a limited sense and not at all for one of Nietzsche's main examples, that of Buddhism. In most cases, an ethnic origin of status group formation is not the normal phenomenon. On the contrary, since each subjective sentiment of ethnic commonality is not entirely based upon objective racial criteria, any question of an ultimately racial foundation for status stratification is appropriately a matter of each concrete individual case. Oftentimes the status group can effect a kind of exclusiveness in its type, based, as it is, on a selection of personal qualifications (as, for example, in the knightly orders, where members were chosen on the basis of their physical and psychic preparedness for war). Thus, on its own merit, the status group can serve as a means for the development of a thoroughbred anthropological type. Individual selection, however, is a long way from being the sole, or the primary means of status group formation. Historically, political affiliation or the class situation have served as criteria at least as frequently, and, in contemporary times, the latter of these is certainly predominant. The possibility of observing status group decorum in one's way of life has certain natural economic preconditions.

From a practical point of view, status group stratification is interconnected with a monopolization of ideal or material goods and opportunities in a way we now recognize as typical. Aside from specific status honor, which has always been based upon social distance and exclusivity, and aside from the privileges of honor such as the rights to particular costume, to specific foods otherwise taboo to others, to bear arms (with all its obvious consequences), to pursue artistic endeavor for other than commercial reasons, (i.e., as a dilettante—the playing of specific musical instruments, for example); aside from all these specific rights, it is material monopolies that, while rarely wholly sufficient, nonetheless provide the most effective motive for maintaining status exclusiveness. For intermarriage within the status group, the interest of the families in maintaining a monopoly on their daughters' hands is paralleled, and perhaps superseded, by their interest in monopolizing potential member bridegrooms who can provide for these daughters. Conventional grants of preferential opportunities in specific positions are more widely practiced the more exclusive a status group tends to be. This can lead to legal monopolies on certain offices held by members of these groups. Certain goods become the objects of monopolies by status groups, among them typically manorial estates including, at times, the serfs and retainers and, eventually, specific trades and professions. This has its positive application when the respective group acts as the sole owner and operator of the goods or trades; the negative complement exists when, in order to sustain a certain standard of living, the group is restricted from their ownership and operation. Because of the decisive role played by the "standard of living" in status honor, it is a matter of course that the status groups serve as the specific bearers of all conventions. All stylization of life, however it is expressed, either originates from the status groups, or at least is sought to be conserved by them. Although the principles of status conventions may be seen to differ widely, certain typical traits are apparent, especially among the most highly privileged strata. In general, the performance of common physical labor can result in status disqualification from the privileged status groups. This trend is now taking hold in America, contrary to an old, opposing tradition of high regard for labor. Very frequently, every rational form of industry and, in particular, the entrepreneurial sort, is considered grounds for disqualification of status and, further, is regarded as degrading. The moment it is exploited for purposes of livelihood, this extends to artistic and literary activity as well, or at least to those forms requiring hard, physical labor. Hence, the sculptor dressed in smock, working like a common stonemason, is considered in a different light than is the painter in his salon-like studio, or the conventional forms of practicing music acceptable to the status group.

The very frequent disqualification of the "gainfully employed" as such, aside from being related to various individual reasons which will be taken up below, is a direct consequence of the principle of status stratification and this principle's opposition to a distribution of power exclusively regulated by the market. As we have seen, the market and the economic processes of which it is comprised do not move "in respect to the individual." Rather, the market is controlled purely on the basis of material interests. It knows nothing of honor. The status order, on the other hand, stands for the exact opposite: stratification occurs according to honor and the way of life appropriate to the status group. As such, the status order is threatened to the core when someone, on the basis of mere economic acquisition and the kind of sheer economic power which cannot conceal its "outsider" origins, is accorded equal or, depending on the measure of success, even greater honor than that claimed by status group members on the strength of their life-styles. Of course, even in cases of otherwise equal status honor, ownership of property will represent an added, if often unacknowledged, effect on status. The members of every stratum, therefore, will react with particular sharpness toward the pretensions of pure economic acquisition as such and, in general, more intensely the more threatened they feel. The respectful treatment given the peasant class in Calderon, for instance, as opposed to the ostensible disdain for the "*canaille*" found in his contemporary, Shakespeare, serves as an expression of a universally recurring state of affairs: the different reactions contrast a tightly structured status order with an economically precarious one. In reaction, then, to the pretensions of property, the privileged status groups never actually accept the parvenu personally and without condition (even if he has fully adapted his way of life to theirs), reserving this distinction for his descendants, who are educated in the status conventions of their group, and who do not threaten to besmirch the honor of the status group by their own economic industry.

While only one general effect of the status order can be determined, it is a very important one: the obstruction of the free development of the market. Initially, this occurs for those goods which the status groups directly withdraw from free trade by means of monopolization, be it by legal or conventional means. Such was the case in many of the Hellenic cities, specifically during the "status era," as well as originally in Rome (as demonstrated by the old interdiction on spendthrifts), where the inherited estate was monopolized, as were the estates of knights, peasants, and priests, but, above all, the clientele of the merchant and trade guilds. The market consequently becomes restricted and the power of naked property *per se*, which has placed its stamp on class formation, recedes. The effects of this process can vary greatly and, of course, do not necessarily result in a weakening of the contrasts in the economic situation; in fact, the opposite is often the case. But regardless of the result, whenever the status order so heavily permeates the community, as was the case in all political communities of Antiquity and the Middle Ages, the idea of there existing any actual free-market competition, in the contemporary sense, is simply out of the question. But there is something of even greater consequence than the direct exclusion of certain goods from the market. From the previously mentioned opposition between the status order and the purely economic one, it follows that the concept of status order, in most cases, utterly rejects that which is most specific to the market: the practice of haggling. Be it among status peers or even occasionally members of a status group in general, honor wholly rejects the practice. Therefore, there are status groups everywhere, often the most influential, for which almost any type of open participation in economic acquisition is plainly considered a blemish to status honor.

To summarize and to employ an oversimplification, one could perhaps say that classes stratify themselves according to their relation to the production and acquisition of goods, while status groups do so according to the principles of their consumption of goods, in the form of their specific ways of life. Status by profession is also considered as status (i.e., as successfully laying claim to social honor); normally at first by virtue of, and later determined by, the specific style of life afforded by the profession. The differences between classes and status groups will often overlap. It is especially those status communities which, on the basis of their honor, are most strictly separated from one another (the Indian castes) that today demonstrate—although admittedly within certain strict limits—a relatively high degree of indifference toward economic acquisition. It is this same type of acquisition that is especially sought by the Brahmins in a broad variety of forms.

Of the general economic conditions making for the predominance of status stratification, it can only be said very generally and in connection with that which has been previously ascertained, that a certain (relative) stability of the bases of the acquisition and distribution of goods will favor status stratification. Every technical and economic shock and upheaval, however, is a threat to this stratification, and will tend to push the class situation into the foreground. Those eras and countries in which the naked class situation is of prevailing significance represent, as a rule, situations of technical and economic upheaval. Any retardation of the process of economic redistribution, on the other hand, leads, in time, to the growth of status structures and restores the significance of social honor.

Political Parties

Although the classes find their place in the economic order and status groups theirs in that of the social order (i.e., the sphere of the distribution of honor), from which the two tend to influence, and are influenced by, each other and the legal order, "parties" are primarily of the sphere of power. Their concern is that of social power, which is to say, their influence on social action, regardless of its content. Basically, parties are as much at home in a social club as they are within the state. Party-oriented social action, unlike that of classes and status groups where this is not necessarily the case, always implies association. This is because the party is always involved in striving toward projected goals, be they material in nature, implementing a program for ideal or material purposes, or personal sinecures, power, and as a consequence, honor for the leader and followers. As is usually the case, it is toward a combination of all of these that the party strives. Because of this, however, parties can only function within a social context that is in some way associational, (i.e., that possesses a rational order and an apparatus of individuals who are prepared to implement it). For it is the goal of the party to win influence over this apparatus of individuals and, where possible, to recruit party members from its ranks. In individual cases, parties have the ability to represent interests determined by the class situation or the status stratification, and thereby solicit recruits from the respective memberships. But parties need to be neither pure class nor pure status organizations. Parties can represent both ephemeral and perennial institutions, and their means of acquiring power are of great variety. These means can extend from the use of unconcealed force of any type to the solicitation of votes by cruder or more refined means: money, social influence, the power of speech, suggestion and clumsy chicanery, but also cruder as well as more artful tactics of obstruction within parliamentary bodies. Necessarily, a party's sociological structure will differ fundamentally according to the respective social conduct it is striving to influence: according to the community (i.e., whether or not its structure is status- or class-oriented), and, above all, according to the structure of authority within the community. For it is the acquisition of power for which their leaders typically strive. In the general sense we are observing here, parties are not only products of specific modern forms of authority: we will designate those forms from Antiquity and the Middle Ages as parties as well, in spite of a structure fundamentally different from that of modern times. As a consequence of these structural differences in authority, however, there is not much that can be said about party structure without first discussing these structural forms of social authority. Party structure, because it constantly strives for control, purposely organizes itself in a strictly authoritarian manner.

To summarize once again, there is one more generalization to be made about "classes," "status groups," and "parties:" although these groups necessarily presuppose larger, more comprehensive associations (specifically, those within a political community), this does not imply that they would be confined to the boundaries of such a political community. On the contrary, the order of the day has always been that the association, and indeed, even a type of association aiming at the use of military force, extends beyond the political boundaries. Examples of this extend from the solidarity of interests of the oligarchs and democrats in Greece, the Guelphs and Ghibellines during the Middle Ages, and the Calvinist party in the time of religious struggles; up to and including the solidarity of the landowners (International Congresses of Agriculture), monarchs (Holy Alliance, Karlsbad Decrees), socialist workers, and conservatives (the yearning for Russian intervention on the part of the Prussian Conservatives in 1850). Toward this end, however, the goal is not necessarily the development of a new international, political, (i.e., territorial) domain. Most frequently the aim is simply to influence the existing order.

Translated by Martin Black

17. The Chinese Literati*

For twelve centuries social rank in China has been determined more by qualification for office than by wealth. This qualification, in turn, has been determined by education, and especially by examinations. China has made literary education the yardstick of social prestige in the most exclusive fashion, far more exclusively than did Europe during the period of the humanists, or as Germany has done. Even during the period of the Warring States, the stratum of aspirants for office who were educated in literature—and originally this only meant that they had a scriptural knowledge—extended through all the individual states. Literati have been the bearers of progress toward a rational administration and of all 'intelligence.'

As with Brahmanism in India, in China the literati have been the decisive exponents of the unity of culture. Territories (as well as enclaves) not administered by officials educated in literature, according to the model of the orthodox state idea, were considered heterodox and barbarian, in the same way as were the tribal lands that were within the territory of Hinduism but not regulated by the Brahmans, as well as areas not organized as *polis* by the Greeks. The increasingly bureaucratic structure of Chinese polities and of their carriers has given to the whole literary tradition of China its characteristic stamp. For more than two thousand years the literati have definitely been the ruling stratum in China and they still are. Their dominance has been interrupted; often it has been hotly contested; but always it has been renewed and expanded. According to the *Annals*, the Emperor addressed the literati, and them alone, as 'My lords'[1] for the first time in 1496.

It has been of immeasurable importance for the way in which Chinese culture has developed that this leading stratum of intellectuals has never had the character of the clerics of Christianity or of Islam, or of Jewish rabbis, or Indian Brahmans, or Ancient Egyptian priests, or Egyptian or Indian scribes. It is significant that the stratum of literati in China, although developed from ritual training, grew

---

*From 'Konfuzianismus und Taoismus,' chap. 5, Der Literatenstand, in *Gesammelte Aufsaetze zur Religionssoziologie*, vol. 1, pp. 395–430. This chapter was originally included in the *Archiv* series, 'Die Wirtschaftsethik der Weltreligionen.'

out of an education for genteel laymen. The 'literati' of the feudal period, then officially called *puo che*, that is, 'living libraries,' were first of all proficient in ritualism. They did not, however, stem from the sibs of a priestly nobility, as did the *Rishi* sibs of the *Rig-Veda*, or from a guild of sorcerers, as did in all likelihood the Brahmans of the *Atharva-Veda*.

In China, the literati go back, at least in the main, to the descendants, probably the younger sons, of feudal families who had acquired a literary education, especially the knowledge of writing, and whose social position rested upon this knowledge of writing and of literature. A plebeian could also acquire a knowledge of writing, although, considering the Chinese system of writing, it was difficult. But if the plebian succeeded, he shared the prestige of any other scholar. Even in the feudal period, the stratum of literati was not hereditary or exclusive—another contrast with the Brahmans.

Until late historical times, Vedic education rested upon oral transmission; it abhorred the fixing of tradition in writing, an abhorrence which all guilds of organized professional magicians are apt to share. In contrast to this, in China the writing of the ritual books, of the calendar, and of the *Annals* go back to prehistoric times.[2] Even in the oldest tradition the ancient scriptures were considered magical objects,[3] and the men conversant with them were considered holders of a magical charisma. As we shall see, these have been persistent facts in China. The prestige of the literati has not consisted in a charisma of magical powers of sorcery, but rather in a knowledge of writing and of literature as such; perhaps their prestige originally rested in addition upon a knowledge of astrology. But it has not been their task to aid private persons through sorcery, to heal the sick, for instance, as the magician does. For such purposes there were special professions, which we shall discuss later. Certainly the significance of magic in China, as everywhere, was a self-understood presupposition. Yet, so far as the interests of the community were concerned, it was up to its representatives to influence the spirits.

The emperor as the supreme pontifex, as well as the princes, functioned for the political community. And for the family, the head of the sib and the housefather influenced the spirits. The fate of the community, above all of the harvest, has been influenced since olden times by rational means, that is, by water regulation; and therefore the correct 'order' of administration has always been the basic means of influencing the world of the spirits.

Apart from knowledge of scriptures as a means of discerning tradition, a knowledge of the calendar and of the stars was required for discerning the heavenly will and, above all, for knowing the *dies fasti* and *nefasti*, and it seems that the position of the literati has also evolved from the dignified role of the court astrologer.[4] The scribes, and they alone, could recognize this important order ritually (and originally probably also by means of horoscopes) and accordingly advise the appropriate political authorities. An anecdote of the *Annals*[5] shows the results in a striking manner.

In the feudal state of the Wei, a proved general—U KI, the alleged author of the textbook in ritually correct strategy which was authoritative until our time—and a literary man competed for the position of first minister. A violent dispute arose between the two after the literary man had been appointed to the post. He readily admitted that he could neither conduct wars nor master similar political tasks in the manner of the general. But when the general thereupon declared himself to be the better man, the literary man remarked that a revolution threatened the dynasty, whereupon the general admitted without any hesitation that the literary man was the better man to prevent it.

Only the adept of scriptures and of tradition has been considered competent for correctly ordering the internal administration and the charismatically correct life conduct of the prince, ritually and politically. In sharpest contrast to the Jewish prophets, who were essentially interested in foreign policy, the Chinese literati-politicians, trained in ritual, were primarily oriented toward problems of internal administration, even if these problems involved absolute power politics, and even though while in charge of the prince's correspondence and of the chancellery they might personally be deeply involved in the guidance of diplomacy.

This constant orientation toward problems of the 'correct' administration of the state determined a far-reaching, practical, and political rationalism among the intellectual stratum of the feudal period. In contrast to the strict traditionalism of the later period, the *Annals* occasionally reveal the literati to be audacious political innovators.[6] Their pride in education knew no limit,[7] and the princes—at least according to the lay-out of the *Annals*—paid them great deference.[8] Their intimate relations to the service of patrimonial princes existed from ancient times and has been decisive for the peculiar character of the literati.

The origin of the literati is veiled from us in darkness. Apparently they were the Chinese augurs. The pontifical Cesaro-papist character of imperial power has been decisive for their position, and the character of Chinese literature has also been determined by it. There were official *Annals,* magically proved hymns of war and sacrifice, calendars, as well as books of ritual and ceremony. With their knowledge the literati supported the character of the state, which was in the nature of an ecclesiastic and compulsory institution; they took the state for granted as an axiomatic presupposition.

In their literature, the literati created the concept of "office," above all, the ethos of "official duty" and of the "public weal."[9] If one may trust the *Annals,* the literati, being adherents of the bureaucratic organization of the state as a compulsory institution, were opponents of feudalism from the very beginning. This is quite understandable because, from the standpoint of their interests, the administrators should be only men who were personally qualified by a literary education.[10] On the other hand, they claimed for themselves to have shown the princes the way toward autonomous administration, toward government manufacture of arms and construction of fortifications, ways and means by which the princes became "masters of their lands."[11]

This close relation of the literati to princely service came about during the struggle of the prince with the feudal powers. It distinguishes the Chinese literati from the educated laymen of Hellas, as well as from those of Ancient India *(Kshatriya).* It makes them similar to the Brahmans, from whom, however, they differ greatly in their ritualist subordination under a Cesaro-papist pontifex. In addition, no caste order has existed in China, a fact intimately connected with the literary education and the subordination under a pontifex.

The relation of the literati to the office has changed its nature [in the course of time]. During the Period of the Feudal States, the various courts competed for the services of the literati, who were seeking opportunities for power and, we must not forget, for the best chances for income.[12] A whole stratum of vagrant "sophists" *(che-she)* emerged, comparable to the wayfaring knights and scholars of the Occidental Middle Ages. As we shall later see, there were also Chinese literati who, in principle, remained unattached to any office. This free and mobile stratum of literati were carriers of philosophical schools and antagonisms, a situation comparable to those of India, of Hellenic Antiquity, and of the Middle Ages with its monks and scholars. Yet, the literati as such felt themselves to be a unitary status group. They claimed common status honors[13] and were united in the feeling of being the sole bearers of the homogeneous culture of China.

The relation of the Chinese literati to princely service as the normal source of income differentiated them as a status group from the philosophers of Antiquity and from at least the educated laymen of India, who, in the main, were socially anchored in fields remote from any office. As a rule, the Chinese literati strove for princely service both as a source of income and as a normal field of activity. Confucius, like Lao-tse, was an official before he lived as a teacher and writer without attachment to office. We shall see that this relation to state-office (or office in a "church state") was of fundamental importance for the nature of the mentality of this stratum. For this orientation became increasingly important and exclusive. The opportunities of the princes to compete for the literati ceased to exist in the unified empire. The literati and their disciples then came to compete for the existing offices, and this development could not fail to result in a unified orthodox doctrine adjusted to the situation. This doctrine was to be *Confucianism.*

As Chinese prebendalism grew, the originally free mental mobility of the literati came to a halt. This development was fully underway even at the time when the *Annals* and most of the systematic writings of the literati originated and when the sacred books, which Shi-Hwang-Ti had destroyed, were "rediscovered."[14] They were "rediscovered" in order that they might be revised, retouched, and interpreted by the literati and therewith gain canonical value.

It is evident from the *Annals* that this whole development came about with the pacification of the empire, or rather, that it was pushed to its conclusions during this period. Everywhere war has been the business of youth, and the sentence *sexagenarios de ponte* has been a slogan of warriors directed against the "senate." The Chinese literati, however, were the "old men," or they represented the old men. The *Annals,* as a paradigmatic public confession of the prince Mu kong (of Tsin), transmitted the idea that the prince had sinned by having listened to "youth" (the warriors) and not to the "elders," who, although having no strength, did have experience.[15] In fact, this was the decisive point in the turn toward pacifism and therewith toward traditionalism. Tradition displaced charisma.

Confucius

Even the oldest sections of the classic writings connected with the name of Kung Tse, that is, with Confucius as editor, permit us to recognize the conditions of charismatic warrior kings. (Confucius died in the year 478 B.C.) The heroic songs of the hymnbook *(Shi-king)* tell of kings fighting from war chariots, as do the Hellenic and Indian epics. But considering their character as a whole, even these songs are no longer heralds of individual, and in general, purely human heroism, as are the Homeric and Germanic epics. Even when the *Shi-king* was edited, the king's army had nothing of the romance of the warrior followings or the Homeric adventures. The army already had the character of a disciplined bureaucracy, and above all it had "officers." The kings, even in the *Shi-king* no longer win simply because they are the greater heroes. And that is decisive for the spirit of the army. They win because before the Spirit of Heaven they are morally right and because their charismatic virtues are superior, whereas their enemies are godless criminals who, by oppression and trespass upon the ancient customs, have wronged their subjects' weal and thus have forgone their charisma. Victory is the occasion for moralizing reflections rather than heroic joy. In contrast to the sacred scriptures of almost all other ethics, one is struck at once by the lack of any "shocking" expression, of any even conceivably "indecent" image. Obviously, a very systematic expurgation has taken place here, and this may well have been the specific contribution of Confucius.

The pragmatic transformation of the ancient tradition in the *Annals,* produced by official historiography and by the literati, obviously went beyond the priestly paradigms performed in the Old Testament, for example, in the Book of Judges. The chronicle expressly ascribed to Confucius' authorship contains the driest and most sober enumeration of military campaigns and punitive expeditions against rebels; in this respect it is comparable to the hieroglyphic protocols of Assyria. If Confucius really expressed the opinion that his character could be recognized with special clarity from this work—as tradition maintains—then one would have to endorse the view of those (Chinese and European) scholars who interpret this to mean that his characteristic achievement was this systematic and pragmatic correction of facts from the point of view of "propriety." His work must have appeared in this light to his contemporaries, but for us its pragmatic meaning, in the main, has become opaque.[16]

The princes and ministers of the classics act and speak like paradigms of rulers whose ethical conduct is rewarded by Heaven. Officialdom and the promotion of officials according to merit are topics for glorification. The princely realms are still ruled hereditarily; some of the local offices are hereditary fiefs; but the classics view this system skeptically, at least the hereditary offices. Ultimately they consider this system to be merely provisional. In theory, this pertains even to the hereditary nature of the dignity of the emperor. The ideal and legendary emperors (Yao and Shun) designate their successors (Shun and Yü) without regard to birth, from the circle of their ministers and over the heads of their own sons, solely according to their personal charisma as certified by the highest court officials. The emperors designate their ministers in the same way, and only the third Emperor, Yü, does not name his first minister (Y) but his son (Ki) to become his successor.

In contrast with the old and genuine documents and monuments, one looks in vain for genuinely heroic minds in most of the classic writings. The traditional view held by Confucius is that caution is the better part of valor and that it ill behooves the wise man to risk his own life inappropriately. The profound pacification of the country, especially after the rule of the Mongols, greatly enhanced this mood. The empire became an empire of peace. According to Mencius, there were no "just" wars within the frontiers of the empire, as it was considered as one unit. Compared to the size of the empire, the army had finally become very tiny. After having separated the training of the literati from that of the knights, the Emperors retained sport and literary contests and gave military certificates[17] in addition to the state examinations of the literati. Yet for a long time the attainment of such military certificates had hardly any connection with an actual career in the army.[18] And the fact remained that the military were just as despised in China as they were in England for two hundred years, and that a cultivated literary man would not engage in social intercourse on an equal footing with army officers.[19]

The Development of the Examination System

During the period of the central monarchy, the mandarins became a status group of certified claimants to office prebends. All categories of Chinese civil servants were recruited from their midst, and their qualification for office and rank depended upon the number of examinations they had successfully passed.

These examinations consisted of three major degrees,[20] which were considerably augmented by intermediary, repetitive, and preliminary examinations as well as by numerous special conditions.

For the first degree alone there were ten types of examinations. The question usually put to a stranger of unknown rank was how many examinations he had passed. Thus, in spite of the ancestor cult, how many ancestors one had was not decisive for social rank. The very reverse held: it depended upon one's official rank whether one was allowed to have an ancestral temple (or a mere table of ancestors, which was the case with illiterates). How many ancestors one was permitted to mention was determined by official rank.[21] Even the rank of a city god in the Pantheon depended upon the rank of the city's mandarin.

In the Confucian period (sixth to fifth century B.C.), the possibility of ascent into official positions as well as the system of examinations was still unknown. It appears that as a rule, at least in the feudal states, the "great families" were in the possession of power. It was not until the Han dynasty—which was established by a parvenu—that the bestowal of offices according to merit was raised to the level of a principle. And not until the Tang dynasty, in A.D. 690, were regulations set up for the highest degree. As we have already mentioned, it is highly probable that literary education, perhaps with a few exceptions, was at first actually, and perhaps also legally, monopolized by the "great families," just as the Vedic education in India was monopolized. Vestiges of this continued to the end. Members of the imperial sib, although not freed from all examinations, were freed from the examination for the first degree. And the trustees, whom every candidate for examinations, until recently, had to name, had to testify to the candidate's "good family background." During modern times this testimony has only meant the exclusion of descendants of barbers, bailiffs, musicians, janitors, carriers, and others. Yet alongside this exclusion there was the institution of "candidates for the mandarinate," that is, the descendants of mandarins enjoyed a special and preferred position in fixing the maximum quota of examination candidates from each province. The promotion lists used the official formula "from a mandarin family and from the people." The sons of well-deserved officials held the lowest degree as a title of honor. All of which represent residues of ancient conditions.

The examination system has been fully carried through since the end of the seventh century. This system was one of the means the patrimonial ruler used in preventing the formation of a closed estate, which, in the manner of feudal vassals and office nobles, would have monopolized the rights to the office prebends. The first traces of the examination system *seem* to emerge about the time of Confucius (and Huang K'an) in the sub-state of Chin, a locality which later became autocratic. The selection of candidates was determined essentially by military merit. Yet, even the *Li Chi* and the *Chou Li*[22] demand, in a quite rationalist way, that the district chiefs examine their lower officials periodically with regard to their morals, and then propose to the emperor which of them should be promoted. In the unified state of the Han emperors, pacifism began to direct the selection of officials. The power of the literati was tremendously consolidated after they had succeeded in elevating the correct Kuang wu to the throne in A.D. 21 and in maintaining him against the popular "usurper" Wang Mang. During the struggle for prebends, which raged during the following period and which we shall deal with later, the literati developed into a unified status group.

Even today the Tang dynasty irradiates the glory of having been the actual creator of China's greatness and culture. The Tang dynasty, for the first time, regulated the literati's position and established colleges for their education (in the seventh century). It also created the *Han lin yuan*, the so-called "academy," which first edited the *Annals* in order to gain precedents, and then controlled the emperor's correct deportment. Finally, after the Mongol storms, the national Ming dynasty in the fourteenth century decreed statutes which, in essence, were definitive.[23] Schools were to be set up in every village, one for every twenty-five families. As the schools were not subsidized, the decree remained a dead letter—or rather we have already seen which powers gained control over the schools. Officials selected the best pupils and enrolled a certain number in the colleges. In the main, these colleges have decayed, although in part they have been newly founded. In 1382, prebends in the form of rice rents were set aside for the "students." In 1393, the number of students was fixed. After 1370, only examined men had claims to offices.

At once a fight set in between the various regions, especially between the North and the South. The South even then supplied candidates for examinations who were more cultured, having experienced a more comprehensive environment. But the North was the military foundation stone of the empire. Hence, the emperor intervened and punished (!) the examiners who had given the "first place" to a Southerner. Separate lists for the North and the South were set up, and moreover, a struggle for the patronage of offices began immediately. Even in 1387 special examinations were given to officers' sons. The officers and officials, however, went further, and demanded the right to designate their successors, which meant a demand for refeudalization. In 1393 this was conceded, but in the end only in a modified form. The candidates presented were preferentially enrolled in the colleges, and prebends were to be reserved for them: in 1465 for three sons, in 1482 for one son. In 1453 we meet with the purchase of college places, and in 1454 with the purchase of offices. During the fifteenth century, as is always the case, these developments arose from the need for military funds. In 1492 these measures were abolished, but in 1529 they were reintroduced.

The departments also fought against one another. The Board of Rites was in charge of the examinations after 736, but the Board of Civil Office appointed the officials. The examined candidates were not infrequently boycotted by the latter department, the former answering by going on strike during the examinations. Formally, the minister of rites, actually, the minister of offices (the major-domo) were in the end the most powerful men in China. Then merchants, who were expected to be less "stingy," came into office.[24] Of course, this hope was quite unjustified. The Manchus favored the old traditions and thus the literati and, as far as possible, "purity" in the distribution of offices. But now, as before, three routes to office existed side by side (1) imperial favors for the sons of the "princely" families (examination privileges), (2) easy examinations (officially every three to six years) for the lower officials by the higher officials who controlled patronage; this inevitably led each time to advancement also to higher positions, (3) the only legal way : to qualify effectively and purely by examination.

In the main, the system of examinations has actually fulfilled the functions as conceived by the emperor. Occasionally (in 1372), it was suggested to the emperor—one can imagine by whom—that he draw the conclusion from the orthodox charisma of virtues by abolishing the examinations, since virtue alone legitimizes and qualifies. This conclusion was soon dropped, which is quite understandable. For after all, both parties, emperor and graduates, had a stake in the examination system, or at least they thought they had. From the emperor's standpoint, the examination system corresponded entirely to the role which the *mjestnitshestvo,* a technically heterogeneous means, of Russian despotism played for the Russian nobility. The system facilitated a competitive struggle for prebends and offices among the candidates, which stopped them from joining together into a feudal office nobility. Admittance to the ranks of aspirants was open to everybody who was proved to be educationally qualified. The examination system thus fulfilled its purpose.

The Typological Position of Confucian Education

We shall now discuss the position of this educational system among the great types of education. To be sure, we cannot here, in passing, give a sociological typology of pedagogical ends and means, but perhaps some comments may be in place.

Historically, the two polar opposites in the field of educational ends are: to awaken charisma, that is, heroic qualities or magical gifts; and, to impart specialized expert training. The first type corresponds to the charismatic structure of domination; the latter type corresponds to the rational and bureaucratic (modern) structure of domination. The two types do not stand opposed, with no connections or transitions between them. The warrior hero or the magician also needs special training, and the expert official is generally not trained exclusively for knowledge. However, they are polar opposites of types of education and they form the most radical contrasts. Between them are found all those types which aim at cultivating the pupil for a conduct of life, whether it is of a mundane or of a religious character. In either case, the life conduct is the conduct of a status group.

The charismatic procedure of ancient magical asceticism and the hero trials, which sorcerers and warrior heroes have applied to boys, tried to aid the novice to acquire a "new soul," in the animist sense, and hence, to be reborn. Expressed in our language, this means that they merely wished to awaken and to test a capacity which was considered a purely personal gift of grace. For one can neither teach nor train for charisma. Either it exists *in nuce*, or it is infiltrated through a miracle of magical rebirth—otherwise it cannot be attained.

Specialized and expert schooling attempts to train the pupil for practical usefulness for administrative purposes—in the organization of public authorities, business offices, workshops, scientific or industrial laboratories, disciplined armies. In principle, this can be accomplished with anybody, though to varying extent.

The pedagogy of cultivation, finally, attempts to educate a cultivated type of man, whose nature depends on the decisive stratum's respective ideal of cultivation. And this means to educate a man for a certain internal and external deportment in life. In principle this can be done with everybody, only the goal differs. If a separate stratum of warriors form the decisive status group—as in Japan—

education will aim at making the pupil a stylized knight and courtier, who despises the pen-pushers as the Japanese Samurai have despised them. In particular cases, the stratum may display great variations of type. If a priestly stratum is decisive, it will aim at making the disciple a scribe, or at least an intellectual, likewise of greatly varying character. In reality, none of these types ever occurs in pure form. The numerous combinations and intermediary links cannot be discussed in this context. What is important here is to define the position of Chinese education in terms of these forms.

The holdovers of the primeval charismatic training for regeneration, the milk name, the initiation rites of youth, the bridegroom's change of name, and so on, have for a long time in China been a formula (in the manner of the Protestant confirmation) standing beside the testing of educational qualifications. Such tests have been monopolized by the political authorities. The educational qualification, however, in view of the educational means employed, has been a "cultural" qualification, in the sense of a general education. It was of a similar, yet of a more specific nature than, for instance, the humanist educational qualification of the Occident.

In Germany, such an education, until recently and almost exclusively, was a prerequisite for the official career leading to positions of command in civil and military administration. At the same time this humanist education has stamped the pupils who were to be prepared for such careers as belonging socially to the cultured status group. In Germany, however—and this is a very important difference between China and the Occident—rational and specialized expert training has been added to, and in part has displaced, this educational status qualification.

The Chinese examinations did not test any special skills, as do our modern rational and bureaucratic examination regulations for jurists, medical doctors, or technicians. Nor did the Chinese examinations test the possession of charisma, as do the typical "trials" of magicians and bachelor leagues. To be sure, we shall presently see the qualifications which this statement requires. Yet it holds at least for the technique of the examinations.

The examinations of China tested whether or not the candidate's mind was thoroughly steeped in literature and whether or not he possessed the ways of thought suitable to a cultured man and resulting from cultivation in literature. These qualifications held far more specifically with China than with the German humanist gymnasium. Today one is used to justifying the gymnasium by pointing to the practical value of formal education through the study of Antiquity. As far as one may judge from the assignments[25] given to the pupils of the lower grades in China, they were rather similar to the essay topics assigned to the top grades of a German gymnasium, or perhaps better still, to the select class of a German girls' college. All the grades were intended as tests in penmanship, style, mastery of classic writings,[26] and finally—similar to our lessons in religion, history, and German—in conformity with the prescribed mental outlook.[27] In our context it is decisive that this education was on the one hand purely secular in nature, but, on the other, was bound to the fixed norm of the orthodox interpretation of the classic authors. It was a highly exclusive and bookish literary education.

The literary character of education in India, Judaism, Christianity, and Islam resulted from the fact that it was completely in the hands of Brahmans and Rabbis trained in literature, or of clerics and monks of book religions who were professionally trained in literature. As long as education was Hellenic and not "Hellenist," the Hellenic man of culture was and remained primarily ephebe and hoplite. The effect of this was nowhere thrown into relief more clearly than in the conversation of the Symposium, where it is said of Plato's Socrates that he had never "flinched" in the field, to use a student term. For Plato to state this is obviously at least of equal importance with everything else he makes Alcibiades say.

During the Middle Ages, the military education of the knight, and later the genteel education of the Renaissance salon, provided a corresponding though socially different supplement to the education transmitted by books, priests, and monks. In Judaism and in China, such a counterbalance was, in part altogether, and in part as good as altogether, absent. In India, as in China, the literary means of education consisted substantially of hymns, epic tales, and casuistry in ritual and ceremony. In India, however, this was underpinned by cosmogonic as well as religious and philosophical speculations. Such speculations were not entirely absent from the classics and from the transmitted commentaries in China, but obviously they have always played only a very minor role there. The Chinese authors developed rational systems of social ethics. The educated stratum of China simply has never been an autonomous status group of scholars, as were the Brahmans, but rather a stratum of officials and aspirants to office.

Higher education in China has not always had the character it has today. The public educational institutions *(Pan kung)* of the feudal princes taught the arts of the dance and of arms in addition to the knowledge of rites and literature. Only the pacification of the empire into a patrimonial and unified state, and finally, the pure system of examinations for office, transformed this older education, which was far closer to early Hellenic education, into what has existed into the twentieth century. Medieval education, as represented in the authoritative and orthodox *Siao-Hio,* that is "schoolbook," still placed considerable weight upon dance and music. To be sure, the old war dance seems to have existed only in rudimentary form, but for the rest, the children, according to age groups, learned certain dances. The purpose of this was stated to be the taming of evil passions. If a child did not do well during his instruction, one should let him dance and sing. Music improves man, and rites and music form the basis of self-control.[28] The magical significance of music was a primary aspect of all this. "Correct music"—that is, music used according to the old rules and strictly following the old measures—"keeps the spirits in their fetters."[29] As late as the Middle Ages, archery and charioteering were still considered general educational subjects for genteel children.[30] But this was essentially mere theory. Going through the schoolbook one finds that from the seventh year of life, domestic education was strictly separated according to sex; it consisted essentially of instilling a ceremonial, which went far beyond all Occidental ideas, a ceremonial especially of piety and awe toward parents and all superiors and older persons in general. For the rest, the schoolbook consisted almost exclusively of rules for self-control.

This domestic education was supplemented by school instruction. There was supposed to be a grade school in every *Hsien*. Higher education presupposed the passing of the first entrance examination. Thus two things were peculiar to Chinese higher education. First, it was entirely non-military and purely literary, as all education established by priesthoods has been. Second, its literary character, that is, its written character, was pushed to extremes. In part, this appears to have been a result of the peculiarity of the Chinese script and of the literary art which grew out of it.[31]

As the script retained its pictorial character and was not rationalized into an alphabetical form, such as the trading peoples of the Mediterranean created, the literary product was addressed at once to both the eyes and the ears, and essentially more to the former. Any "reading aloud" of the classic books was in itself a translation from the pictorial script into the (unwritten) word. The visual character, especially of the old script, was by its very nature remote from the spoken word. The monosyllabic language requires sound perception as well as the perception of pitched tone. With its sober brevity and its compulsion of syntactical logic, it stands in extreme contrast to the purely visual character of script. But in spite of this, or rather—as Grube has shown in an ingenious way—in part because of the very rational qualities of its structure, the Chinese tongue has been unable to offer its services to poetry or to systematic thinking. Nor could it serve the development of the oratorical arts as have the structures of the Hellenic, Latin, French, German, and Russian languages, each in its own way. The stock of written symbols remained far richer than the stock of monosyllabic words, which was inevitably quite delimited. Hence, all fantasy and ardor fled from the poor and formalistic intellectualism of the spoken word and into the quiet beauty of the written symbols. The usual poetic speech was held fundamentally subordinate to the script. Not speaking but writing and reading were valued artistically and considered as worthy of a gentleman, for they were receptive of the artful products of script. Speech remained truly an affair of the plebs. This contrasts sharply with Hellenism, to which conversation meant everything and a translation into the style of the dialogue was the adequate form of all experience and contemplation. In China the very finest blossoms of literary culture lingered, so to speak, deaf and mute in their silken splendor. They were valued far higher than was the art of drama, which, characteristically, flowered during the period of the Mongols.

Among the renowned social philosophers, Meng Tse (Mencius) made systematic use of the dialogue form. That is precisely why he readily appears to us as the one representative of Confucianism who matured to full "lucidity." The very strong impact upon us of the "Confucian Analects" (as Legge called them) also rests upon the fact that in China (as occasionally elsewhere) the doctrine is clothed in the form of (in part, probably authentic) sententious responses of the master to questions from the disciples. Hence, to us, it is transposed into the form of speech. For the rest, the epic literature contains the addresses of the early warrior kings to the army; in their lapidary forcefulness, they are highly impressive. Part of the didactic *Analects* consists of speeches, the character of which rather corresponds to pontifical "allocutions." Otherwise speech plays no part in the official literature. Its lack of development, as we shall see presently, has been determined by both social and political reasons.

In spite of the logical qualities of the language, Chinese thought has remained rather stuck in the pictorial and the descriptive. The power of *logos,* of defining and reasoning, has not been accessible to the Chinese. Yet, on the other hand, this purely scriptural education detached thought from gesture and expressive movement still more than is usual with the literary nature of any education. For two years before he was introduced to their meaning, the pupil learned merely to paint about 2,000 characters. Furthermore, the examiners focused attention upon style, the art of versification, a firm grounding in the classics, and finally, upon the expressed mentality of the candidate.

The lack of all training in calculation, even in grade schools, is a very striking feature of Chinese education. The idea of positional numbers, however, was developed[32] during the sixth century before Christ, that is, during the period of warring states. A calculative attitude in commercial intercourse had permeated all strata of the population, and the final calculations of the administrative offices were as detailed as they were difficult to survey, for reasons mentioned above. The medieval schoolbook (*Siao-Hio* 1, 29), enumerates calculation among the six "arts." And at the time of the warring states, there existed a mathematics which allegedly included trigonometry as well as the rule of three and commercial calculation. Presumably this literature, apart from fragments, was lost during Shi-Hwang-Ti's burning of the books.[33] In any case, calculation is not even mentioned in later pedagogy. And in the course of history, calculation receded more and more into the background of the education of the genteel mandarins, finally to disappear altogether. The educated merchants learned calculation in their business offices. Since the empire had been unified and the tendency toward a rational administration of the state had weakened, the mandarin became a genteel literary man, who was not one to occupy himself with the "σχολή" of calculation.

The mundane character of this education contrasts with other educational systems, which are nevertheless related to it by their literary stamp. The literary examinations in China were purely political affairs. Instruction was given partly by individual and private tutors and partly by the teaching staffs of college foundations. But no priest took part in them.

The Christian universities of the Middle Ages originated from the practical and ideal need for a rational, mundane, and ecclesiastic legal doctrine and a rational (dialectical) theology. The universities of Islam, following the model of the late Roman law schools and of

Christian theology, practiced sacred case law and the doctrine of faith; the Rabbis practiced interpretation of the law; the philosophers' schools of the Brahmans engaged in speculative philosophy, in ritual, as well as in sacred law. Always ecclesiastic dignitaries or theologians have formed either the sole teaching staff or at least its basic corps. To this corps were attached mundane teachers, in whose hands the other branches of study rested. In Christianity, Islam, and Hinduism, prebends were the goals, and for the sake of them educational certificates were striven after. In addition, of course, the aspirant wished to qualify for ritual activity and the curing of souls. With the ancient Jewish teachers (precursors of the Rabbis), who worked "gratis," the goal was solely to qualify for instructing the laymen in the law, for this instruction was religiously indispensable. But in all this, education was always bound by sacred or cultic scriptures. Only the Hellenic philosophers' schools engaged in an education solely of laymen and freed from all ties to scriptures, freed from all direct interests in prebends, and solely devoted to the education of Hellenic "gentlemen" *(Caloicagathoi)*.

Chinese education served the interest in prebends and was tied to a script, but at the same time it was purely lay education, partly of a ritualist and ceremonial character and partly of a traditionalist and ethical character. The schools were concerned with neither mathematics nor natural sciences, with neither geography nor grammar. Chinese philosophy itself did not have a speculative, systematic character, as Hellenic philosophy had and as, in part and in a different sense, Indian and Occidental theological schooling had. Chinese philosophy did not have a rational-formalist character, as Occidental jurisprudence has. And it was not of an empirical casuist character, as Rabbinic, Islamite, and, partly, Indian philosophy. Chinese philosophy did not give birth to scholasticism because it was not professionally engaged in logic, as were the philosophies of the Occident and the Middle East, both of them being based on Hellenist thought. The very concept of logic remained absolutely alien to Chinese philosophy, which was bound to script, was not dialectical, and remained oriented to purely practical problems as well as to the status interests of the patrimonial bureaucracy.

This means that the problems that have been basic to all Occidental philosophy have remained unknown to Chinese philosophy, a fact which comes to the fore in the Chinese philosophers' manner of categorical thought, and above all in Confucius. With the greatest practical matter-of-factness, the intellectual tools remained in the form of parables, reminding us of the means of expression of Indian chieftains rather than of rational argumentation. This holds precisely for some of the truly ingenious statements ascribed to Confucius. The absence of speech is palpable, that is, speech as a rational means for attaining political and forensic effects, speech as it was first cultivated in the Hellenic *polis*. Such speech could not be developed in a bureaucratic patrimonial state which had no formalized justice. Chinese justice remained, in part, a summary Star Chamber procedure (of the high officials), and, in part, it relied solely on documents. No oral pleading of cases existed, only the written petitions and oral hearings of the parties concerned. The Chinese bureaucracy was interested in conventional propriety, and these bonds prevailed and worked in the same direction of obstructing forensic speech. The bureaucracy rejected the argument of "ultimate" speculative problems as practically sterile. The bureaucracy considered such arguments improper and rejected them as too delicate for one's own position because of the danger of innovations.

If the technique and the substance of the examinations were purely mundane in nature and represented a sort of "cultural examination for the literati," the popular view of them was very different: it gave them a magical–charismatic meaning. In the eyes of the Chinese masses, a successfully examined candidate and official was by no means a mere applicant for office qualified by knowledge. He was a proved holder of magical qualities, which, as we shall see, were attached to the certified mandarin just as much as to an examined and ordained priest of an ecclesiastic institution of grace, or to a magician tried and proved by his guild.[34]

The position of the successfully examined candidate and official corresponded in important points, for example, to that of a Catholic chaplain. For the pupil to complete his period of instruction and his examinations did not mean the end of his immaturity. Having passed the "baccalaureate," the candidate came under the discipline of the school director and the examiners. In case of bad conduct his name was dropped from the lists. Under certain conditions his hands were caned. In the localities' secluded cells for examinations, candidates not infrequently fell seriously ill and suicides occurred. According to the charismatic interpretation of the examination as a magical "trial," such happenings were considered proof of the wicked conduct of the person in question. After the applicant for office had luckily passed the examinations for the higher degrees with their strict seclusion, and after, at long last, he had moved into an office corresponding to the number and rank of examinations passed and depending on his patronage, he still remained throughout his life under the control of the school. And in addition to being under the authority of his superiors, he was under the constant surveillance and criticism of the censors. Their criticism extended even to the ritualist correctness of the very Son of Heaven. The impeachment of the officials[35] was prescribed from olden times and was valued as meritorious in the way of the Catholic confession of sins. Periodically, as a rule every three years, his record of conduct, that is, a list of his merits and faults as determined by official investigations of the censors and his superiors, was to be published in the *Imperial Gazette*.[36] According to his published grades, he was allowed to retain his post, was promoted, or was demoted.[37] As a rule, not only objective factors determined the outcome of these records of conduct. What mattered was the "spirit," and this spirit was that of a lifelong harassment by official authority.

The Status-Honor of the Literati

As a status group, the literati were privileged, even those who had only been examined but were not employed. Soon after their position had been strengthened, the literati enjoyed status privileges. The most important of these were: first, freedom from the *sordida munera*, the *corvée;* second, freedom from corporal punishment; third, prebends (stipends). For a long time this third privilege had been rather severely reduced in its bearing, through the financial position of the state. The *Seng* (baccalaureate) still got stipends of $10.00 yearly, with the condition that they had to submit every three to six years to the *Chu jen* or Master's examination. But this, of course, did not mean anything decisive. The burden of the education and of the periods of nominal pay actually fell upon the sib, as we have seen. The sib hoped to recover their expenses by seeing their member finally enter the harbor of an office. The first two privileges were of importance to the very end; for the *corvée* still existed, although to a decreasing extent. The rod, however, remained the national means of punishment. Caning stemmed from the terrible pedagogy of corporal punishment in the elementary schools of China. Its unique character is said to have consisted in the following traits, which remind one of our Middle Ages but were obviously developed to even greater extremes.[38] The fathers of the sibs or of the villages compiled the "red cards," that is, the list of pupils *(Kuan-tan)*. Then for a certain period they engaged a schoolmaster from among the over-supply of literati without office, which always existed. The ancestral temple (or other unused rooms) was the preferred schoolroom. From early until late the howling in unison of the written "lines" was to be heard. All day long the pupil was in a condition of mental daze, which is denoted by a Chinese character, the component parts of which signify a pig in the weeds *(meng)*. The student and graduate received slaps on the palm of his hand, no longer on what, in the terminology of German mothers of the old hue, was called "the God-ordained spot."

The graduates of high rank were entirely free from such punishment so long as they were not demoted. And in the Middle Ages freedom from the *corvée* was firmly established. Nevertheless, in spite and also because of these privileges, the development of feudal ideas of honor was impossible on their basis. Moreover, as has been observed, these privileges were precarious because they were immediately voided in the case of demotion, which frequently occurred. Feudal honor could not be developed on the bases of examination certificates as a qualification for status, possible degradation, corporal punishment during youth, and the not quite infrequent case of degradation even in old age. But *once*, in the past, such feudal notions of honor had dominated Chinese life with great intensity.

The old *Annals* praise "frankness" and "loyalty" as cardinal virtues.[39] "To die with honor" was the old watchword. "To be unfortunate and not to know how to die is cowardly." This applied particularly to an officer who did not fight "unto the death."[40] Suicide was a death which a general, having lost a battle, valued as a *privilege*. To permit him to commit suicide meant to forego the right to punish him and therefore was considered with hesitation.[41] The meaning of feudal concepts was changed by the patriarchal idea of *hiao*. *Hiao* meant that one should suffer calumny and even meet death as its consequence if it served the honor of the master. One could, and in general should, compensate for all the mistakes of the lord by loyal service. The *kotow* before the father, the older brother, the creditor, the official, and the emperor was certainly not a symptom of feudal honor. For the correct Chinese to kneel before his love, on the other hand, would have been entirely taboo. All this was the reverse of what held for the knights and the *cortegiani* of the Occident.

To a great extent, the official's honor retained an element of student honor regulated by examination achievements and public censures by superiors. This was the case even if he had passed the highest examinations. In a certain sense, it is true of every bureaucracy (at least on its lower levels; and in Württemberg, with its famous "Grade A, Fischer," even in the highest positions of office); but it held to quite a different extent in China.

The Gentleman Ideal

The peculiar spirit of the scholars, bred by the system of examinations, was intimately connected with the basic presuppositions from which the orthodox and also, by the way, nearly all heterodox, Chinese theories proceeded. The dualism of the *shen* and *kwei,* of good and evil spirits, of heavenly *yang* substance as over against earthly *yin* substance, also within the soul of the individual, necessarily made the sole task of education, including self-education, to appear to be the unfolding of the *yang* substance in the soul of man.[42] For the man in whom the *yang* substance has completely gained the upper hand over the demonic *kwei* powers resting within him also has power over the spirits; that is, according to the ancient notion, he has magical power. The good spirits, however, are those who protect order and beauty and harmony in the world. To perfect oneself and thus to mirror this harmony is the supreme and the only means by which one may attain such power. During the time of the literati, the *Kiün-tse,* the "princely man," and once the "hero," was the man who had attained all-around self-perfection, who had become a "work of art" in the sense of a classical, eternally valid, canon of psychical beauty, which literary tradition implemented in the souls of disciples. On the other hand, since the Han period at the latest,[43] it was a firmly established belief among the literati that the spirits reward "beneficence," in the sense of social and ethical excellence. Benevolence tempered by classical (canonical) beauty was therefore the goal of self-perfection.

Canonically perfect and beautiful achievements were the highest aspiration of every scholar as well as the ultimate yardstick of the highest qualification certified by examination. Li Hung Chang's youthful ambition was to become a perfect literary man,[44] that is, a "crowned poet," by attainment of the highest degrees. He was, and he remained, proud of being a calligrapher of great craftsmanship and of being able to recite the classics by heart, especially Confucius' "Spring and Autumn." This ability occasioned his uncle, after having tested it, to pardon the imperfections of his youth and to procure him an office. To Li Hung Chang all other branches of knowledge (algebra, astronomy) were only the indispensable means of "becoming a great poet." The classical perfection of the poem he conceived in the name of the Empress-Dowager, as a prayer in the temple of the tutelary goddess of silk-culture, brought him the Empress's favor.

Puns, euphemisms, allusions to classical quotations, and a refined and purely literary intellectuality were considered the conversational ideal of the genteel man. All politics of the day were excluded from such conversation.[45] It may appear strange to us that this sublimated "salon" cultivation, tied to the classics, should enable man to administer large territories. And in fact, one did not manage the administration with mere poetry even in China. But the Chinese prebendary official proved his status quality, that is, his charisma, through the canonical correctness of his literary forms. Therefore, considerable weight was placed on these forms in official communications. Numerous important declarations of the Emperors, the high priests of literary art, were in the form of didactic poems. On the other hand, the official had to prove his charisma by the "harmonious" course of his administration; that is, there must be no disturbances caused by the restless spirits of nature or of men. The actual administrative "work" could rest on the shoulders of subordinate officials. We have noticed that above the official stood the imperial pontifex, his academy of literati, and his collegiate body of censors. They publicly rewarded, punished, scolded, exhorted, encouraged, or lauded the officials.

Because of the publication of the "personal files" and all the reports, petitions, and memorials, the whole administration and the fateful careers of the officials, with their (alleged) causes, took place before the broadest public, far more so than is the case with any of our administrations under parliamentary control, an administration which puts the greatest weight upon the keeping of "official secrets." At least according to the official fiction, the official *Gazette* in China was a sort of running account of the Emperor before Heaven and before his subjects. This *Gazette* was the classic expression for the kind of responsibility which followed from the emperor's charismatic qualification. However dubious in reality the official argumentation and the completeness of publication may have been—that, after all, also holds for the communications of our bureaucracy to our parliaments—the Chinese procedure at least tended to open a rather strong and often a quite effective safety-valve for the pressure of public opinion with regard to the official's administrative activities.

The Prestige of Officialdom

The hatred and the distrust of the subjects, which is common to all patrimonialism, in China as everywhere turned above all against the lower levels of the hierarchy, who came into the closest practical contact with the population. The subjects' apolitical avoidance of all contact with "the state" which was not absolutely necessary was typical for China as for all other patrimonial systems. But this apolitical attitude did not detract from the significance of the official education for the character formation of the Chinese people.

The strong demands of the training period were due partly to the peculiarity of Chinese script and partly to the peculiarity of the subject matter. These demands, as well as the waiting periods which were often quite long, forced those who were unable to live on a fortune of their own, on loans, or on family savings of the sort discussed above, to take up practical occupations of all sorts, from merchant to miracle doctor, before completing their educational careers. Then they did not reach the classics themselves, but only the study of the last (the sixth) textbook, the "schoolbook" *(Siao Hio)*,[46] which was hallowed by age and contained mainly excerpts from the classic authors. Only this difference in the level of education and not differences in the kind of education set these circles off from the bureaucracy. For only classic education existed.

The percentage of candidates who failed the examinations was extraordinarily high. In consequence of the fixed quotas,[47] the fraction of graduates of the higher examinations was proportionately small, yet they always outnumbered many times the available office prebends. They competed for the prebends by personal patronage,[48] by purchase money of their own, or by loans. The sale of prebends functioned here as in Europe; it was a means of raising capital for the purposes of state, and very frequently it replaced merit ratings.[49] The protests of the reformers against the sale of offices persisted until the last days of the old system, as is shown by the numerous petitions of this sort in the *Peking Gazette*.

The officials' short terms of office (three years), corresponding to similar Islamic institutions, allowed for intensive and rational influencing of the economy through the administration as such only in an intermittent and jerky way. This was the case in spite of the administration's theoretical omnipotence. It is astonishing how few permanent officials the administration believed to be sufficient. The figures alone make it perfectly obvious that as a rule things must have been permitted to take their own course, as long as the interests of the state power and of the treasury remained untouched and as long as the forces of tradition, the sibs, villages, guilds, and other occupational associations remained the normal carriers of order.

Yet in spite of the apolitical attitude of the masses, which we have just mentioned, the views of the stratum of applicants for office exerted a very considerable influence upon the way of life of the middle classes. This resulted, first and above all, from the popular magical–charismatic conception of the qualification for office as tested by examination. By passing the examination, the graduate proved that he was to an eminent degree a holder of *shen*. High mandarins were considered magically qualified. They could always become objects of a cult, after their death as well as during their lifetime, provided that their charisma was "proved." The primeval magical significance of written work and of documents lent apotropaic and therapeutic significance to their seals and to their handwriting, and this could extend to the examination paraphernalia of the candidate. A province considered it an honor and an advantage to have one of its own sons selected by the emperor as the best graduate of the highest degree,[50] and all whose names were publicly posted after having passed their examinations had "a name in the village." All guilds and other clubs of any significance had to have a literary man as a secretary, and these and similar positions were open to those graduates for whom office prebends were not available. The officeholders and the examined candidates for office, by virtue of their magical charisma and of their patronage relations—especially when they stemmed from petit bourgeois circles—were the natural "father confessors" and advisers in all important affairs of their sibs. In this they corresponded to the Brahmins *(Gurus)* who performed the same function in India.

Alongside the purveyor to the state and the great trader, the officeholder, as we have seen, was the personage with the most opportunities for accumulating possessions. Economically and personally, therefore, the influence on the population of this stratum, outside as well as inside their own sibs, was approximately as great as was the combined influence of the scribes and priests in Egypt. Within the sib, however, the authority of old age was a strong counterweight, as we have already emphasized. Quite independent of the "worthiness" of the individual officials, who were often ridiculed in popular dramas, the prestige of this literary education as such was firmly grounded in the population until it came to be undermined by modern Western-trained members of the mandarin strata.

Views on Economic Policy

The social character of the educated stratum determined its stand toward economic policy. According to its own legend, for millennia, the polity had the character of a religious and utilitarian welfare state, a character which is in line with so many other typical traits of patrimonial bureaucratic structures bearing theocratic stamps.

Since olden times, to be sure, actual state policy, for reasons discussed above, had again and again let economic life alone, at least so far as production and the profit economy were concerned. This happened in China just as in the ancient Orient—unless new settlements, melioration through irrigation, and fiscal or military interests entered the picture. But military interests and interests in military finance had always called forth liturgical interventions in economic life. These interventions were monopolistically or financially determined, and often they were quite incisive. They were partly mercantilist regulations and partly in the nature of regulations of status stratification. Toward the end of national militarism, such planned "economic policy" eventually fell into abeyance. The government, conscious of the weakness of its administrative apparatus, confined itself to the care of the tide and the maintenance of the water routes, which were indispensable for provisioning the leading provinces with rice; for the rest, to the typically patrimonial policy of dearth and consumption. It had no "commercial policy" in the modern sense.[51] The tolls the mandarins had established along the waterways were, so far as is known, merely fiscal in nature and never served any economic policy. The government on the whole pursued only fiscal and mercantilist interests, if one disregards emergency situations which, considering the charismatic nature of authority, were always politically dangerous. So far as is known, the most grandiose attempts to establish a unified economic organization were planned by Wang An Shi, who during the eleventh century tried to establish a state trading monopoly for the entire harvest. In addition to fiscal gains, the plan was intended to serve the equalization of prices and was connected with a reform in land taxes. The attempt failed.

As the economy was left to itself to a large extent, the aversion against "state intervention" in economic matters became a lasting and basic sentiment. It was directed particularly against monopolistic privileges,[52] which, as fiscal measures, are habitual to patrimonialism everywhere. This sentiment, however, was only one among the quite different attitudes which resulted from the conviction that the welfare of the subjects was dependent upon the charisma of the ruler. These ideas often stood in unmediated fashion beside the basic aversion to state intervention, and continually, or at least occasionally, made for bureaucratic meddling in everything, which again is typical of patrimonialism. Moreover, the administration of course reserved the right to regulate consumption in times of dearth—a policy which is also part of the theory of Confucianism [as reflected] in numerous special norms concerning all sorts of expenditures. Above all, there was the typical aversion against too sharp a social differentiation as determined in a purely economic manner by free exchange in markets. This aversion, of course, goes without saying in every bureaucracy. The increasing stability of the economic situation under conditions of the economically self-sufficient and the socially homogeneously composed world-empire did not allow for the emergence of such economic problems as were discussed in the English literature of the seventeenth century. There was no self-conscious bourgeois stratum which could not be politically ignored by the government and to whose interests the "pamphleteers" of the time in England primarily addressed themselves. As always under patrimonial bureaucratic conditions, the administration had to take serious notice of the attitude of the merchants' guilds only in a "static" way and when the maintenance of tradition and of the guilds' special privileges were at stake. Dynamically, however, the merchant guilds did not enter into the balance, because there were no expansive capitalist interests (no longer!) of sufficient strength, as in England, to be capable of forcing the state administration into their service.

Sultanism and the Eunuchs as Political Opponents of the Literati

The total political situation of the literati can be understood only when one realizes the forces against which they had to fight. We may disregard the heterodoxies here, for they will be dealt with below.

In early times the main adversaries of the literati were the "great families" of the feudal period who did not want to be pushed out of their office monopolies. Having to accommodate themselves to the needs of patrimonialism and to the superiority of the knowledge of script, they found ways and means of paving the way for their sons by imperial favor.

Then there were the capitalist purchasers of office: a natural result of the leveling of status groups and of the fiscal money economy. Here the struggle could not lead to constant and absolute success, but only to relative success, because every demand of war pushed the impecunious central administration toward the jobbery of office-prebends as the sole means of war finance. This held until recent times.

The literati also had to fight the administration's rationalist interests in an expert officialdom. Specialist, expert officials came to the fore as early as 601 under Wen ti. During the distress of the defensive wars in 1068 under Wang An Shi, they enjoyed a short-lived and full triumph. But again tradition won out and this time for good.

There remained only one major and permanent enemy of the literati: sultanism and the eunuch-system which supported it.[53] The influence of the harem was therefore viewed with profound suspicion by the Confucians. Without insight into this struggle, Chinese history is most difficult to understand.

The constant struggle of the literati and sultanism, which lasted for two millennia, began under Shi-Hwang-Ti. It continued under all the dynasties, for of course energetic rulers continually sought to shake off their bonds to the cultured status group of the literati with the aid of eunuchs and plebeian parvenus. Numerous literati who took a stand against this form of absolutism had to give their lives in order to maintain their status group in power. But in the long run and again and again the literati won out.[54] Every drought, inundation, eclipse of the sun, defeat in arms, and every generally threatening event at once placed power in the hands of the literati. For such events were considered the result of a breach of tradition and a desertion of the classic way of life, which the literati guarded and which was represented by the censors and the Hanlin Academy. In all such cases "free discussion" was granted, the advice of the throne was asked, and the result was always the cessation of the unclassical form of government, execution or banishment of the eunuchs, a retraction of conduct to the classical schemata; in short, adjustments to the demands of the literati.

The harem system was of considerable danger because of the way in which successorship to the throne was ordered. The emperors who were not of age were under the tutelage of women; at times, this petticoat-government had come to be the very rule. The last Empress-Dowager, Tsu hsi, tried to rule with the aid of eunuchs.[55] We will not discuss at this point the roles which Taoists and Buddhists have played in these struggles, which run through all of Chinese history—why and how far they have been natural allies, specifically of the eunuchs, and how far they have been allies by constellation.

Let us mention in passing that, at least by modern Confucianism, astrology has been considered an unclassical superstition.[56] It has been thought to compete with the exclusive significance of the Emperor's *Tao* charisma for the course of government. Originally this had not been the case. The departmental competition of the Hanlin

Academy against the collegiate body of astrologers may have played a decisive part;[57] perhaps also the Jesuit origin of the astronomic measures had a hand in it.

In the conviction of the Confucians, the trust in magic which the eunuchs cultivate brought about all misfortune. Tao Mo in his Memorial of the year 1901 reproached the Empress that in the year 1875 the true heir to the throne had been eliminated through her fault and in spite of the censors' protest, for the censor Wu Ko Tu had acknowledged this by his suicide. Tao Mo's posthumous memorial to the Empress and his letter to his son were distinguished by their manly beauty.[58] There cannot be the slightest doubt of his sincere and profound conviction. Also the belief of the Empress and of numerous princes in the magical charisma of the Boxers, a belief which alone explains her whole policy, was certainly to be ascribed to the influence of eunuchs.[59] On her death-bed this impressive woman left as her counsel: (1) never again to let a woman rule in China, and (2) to abolish the eunuch system forever.[60] This counsel was fulfilled in a different way than she had undoubtedly intended—if the report is accurate. But one may not doubt that for the genuine Confucian everything that has happened since, above all the "revolution" and the downfall of the dynasty, only confirms the correctness of the belief in the significance of the charisma of the dynasty's classic virtue. In the improbable but possible event of a Confucian restoration, the belief would be exploited in this sense. The Confucianists, who are ultimately pacifist literati oriented to inner political welfare, naturally faced military powers with aversion or with lack of understanding. We have already spoken of their relationship to the officers, and we have seen that the whole *Annals* are paradigmatically filled with it. There are protests to be found in the *Annals* against making "praetorians" into censors (and officials).[61] As the eunuchs were especially popular as favorites and generals in the way of Narses, the enmity against the purely sultanist patrimonial army suggested itself. The literati took pride in having overthrown the popular military usurper Wang Mang. The danger of ruling with plebeians has simply always been great with dictators, yet only this one attempt is known in China. The literati, however, have submitted to *de facto* established power even when it was created purely by usurpation, as was the power of the Han, or by conquest, as was the power of the Mongol Manchus. They submitted even though they had to make sacrifices—the Manchus took over 50 percent of the offices without having the educational qualifications. The literati have submitted to the ruler if the ruler in turn submitted to their ritualist and ceremonial demands; only then, in modern language, have they accommodated themselves and taken a "realistic" stand.

"Constitutionally"—and this was the theory of the Confucians—the emperor could rule only by using certified literati as officials; "classically" he could rule only by using orthodox Confucian officials. Every deviation from this rule was thought capable of bringing disaster and, in case of obstinacy, the downfall of the emperor and the ruin of the dynasty.

Translated by Hans H. Gerth
and C. Wright Mills

Rationalization in Economy, Religion, and Law

18. The Origins of Modern Capitalism

The Meaning and Presuppositions of Modern Capitalism

Capitalism is present wherever the industrial provision for the needs of a human group is carried out by the method of enterprise, irrespective of what need is involved. More specifically, a rational capitalistic establishment is one with capital accounting, that is, an establishment which determines its income yielding power by calculation according to the methods of modern bookkeeping and the striking of a balance. The device of the balance was first insisted upon by the Dutch theorist Simon Stevin in the year 1698.

It goes without saying that an individual economy may be conducted along capitalist lines to the most widely varying extent; parts of the economic provision may be organized capitalistically and other parts on the handicraft or the manorial pattern. Thus at a very early time the city of Genoa had a part of its political needs, namely those for the prosecution of war, provided in capitalistic fashion, through stock companies. In the Roman empire, the supply of the population of the capital city with grain was carried out by officials, who however for this purpose, besides control over their subalterns, had the right to command the services of transport organizations; thus the forced contribution type of organization was combined with administration of public resources. Today, in contrast with the greater part of the past, our everyday needs are supplied capitalistically; our political needs, however, through compulsory contributions; that is, by the performance of political duties of citizenship such as the obligation to military service, jury duty, etc. A whole epoch can be designated as typically capitalistic only as the provision for wants is capitalistically organized to such a predominant degree that if we imagine this form of organization taken away the whole economic system must collapse.

While capitalism of various forms is met with in all periods of history, the provision of the everyday wants by capitalistic methods is characteristic of the West alone and even here has been the inevitable method only since the middle of the nineteenth century. Such capitalistic beginnings as are found in earlier centuries were merely anticipatory, and even the somewhat capitalistic establishments of the sixteenth century may be removed in thought from the economic life of the time without introducing any overwhelming change.

The most general presupposition for the existence of this present-day capitalism is that of rational capital accounting as the norm for all large industrial undertakings which are concerned with provision for everyday wants. Such accounting involves, again, first, the appropriation of all physical means of production—land, apparatus, machinery, tools, etc. as disposable property of autonomous private industrial enterprises. This is a phenomenon known only to our time, when the army alone forms a universal exception to it. In the second place, it involves freedom of the market, that is, the absence of irrational limitations on trading in the market. Such limitations might be of a class character if a certain mode of life were prescribed for a certain class, or consumption were standardized along class lines, or if class monopoly existed, as for example if the townsman were not allowed to own an estate or the knight or peasant to carry on industry; in such cases neither a free labor market nor a commodity market exists. Third, capitalistic accounting presupposes rational technology, that is, one reduced to calculation to the largest possible degree, which implies mechanization. This applies to both production and commerce, the outlays for preparing as well as moving goods.

The fourth characteristic is that of calculable law. The capitalist form of industrial organization, if it is to operate rationally, must be able to depend upon calculable adjudication and administration. Neither in the age of the Greek city-state (polis) nor in the patrimonial states of Asia nor in western countries down to the Stuarts was this condition fulfilled. The royal "cheap justice" with its remissions by royal grace introduced continual disturbances into the calculations of economic life. The proposition that the Bank of England was suited only to a republic, not to a monarchy, . . . was related in this way to the conditions of the time. The fifth feature is free labor. Persons must be present who are not only legally in the position, but are also economically compelled, to sell their labor on the market without restriction. It is in contradiction to the essence of capitalism, and the development of capitalism is impossible, if such a propertyless stratum is absent, a class compelled to sell its labor services to live; and it is likewise impossible if only unfree labor is at hand. Rational capitalistic calculation is possible only on the basis of free labor; only where, in consequence of the existence of workers who in the formal sense voluntarily, but actually under the compulsion of the whip of hunger offer themselves, the costs of products may be unambiguously determined by agreement in advance. The sixth and final condition is the commercialization of economic life. By this we mean the general use of commercial instruments to represent share rights in enterprise, and also in property ownership.

To sum up, it must be possible to conduct the provision for needs exclusively on the basis of market opportunities and the calculation of net income. The addition of this commercialization to the other characteristics of capitalism involves intensification of the significance of another factor not yet mentioned, namely speculation. Speculation reaches its full significance only from the moment when property takes on the form of negotiable paper.

The First Great Speculative Crises

We have recognized as characteristics and prerequisites of capitalistic enterprise the following: appropriation of the physical means of production by the entrepreneur, freedom of the market, rational technology, rational law, free labor, and finally the commercialization of economic life. A further motif is speculation, which becomes important from the moment when property can be represented by freely negotiable paper. Its early development is marked by the great economic crises which it called forth.

The great tulip craze of Holland in the 1630s is often numbered among the great speculative crises, but it should not be so included. Tulips had become an article of luxury among the patricians who had grown rich in colonial trade, and suddenly commanded fantastic prices. The public was misled by the wish to make easy profits until with equal suddenness the whole craze collapsed and many individuals were ruined. But all of that had no significance for the economic development of Holland; in all periods it has happened that objects connected with gaming have become subject to speculation and led to crises. It is quite otherwise with John Law and the great speculation in France and the contemporary South Sea speculation in England, in the second decade of the eighteenth century.

In the financial practice of the large states it had long been customary to anticipate revenues by the issue of certificates, to be redeemed later. In consequence of the War of the Spanish Succession, the financial requirements of the government rose to an extraordinary height in England as well as in France. The founding of the Bank of England supplied the financial needs of that country, but in France the state was already hopelessly in debt, and on the death of Louis XIV no one knew how the excessive debt was to be taken care of. Under the regency came forward the Scotchman, John Law, who thought he had learned something from the founding of the Bank of England, and had a theory of his own regarding financial affairs, although he had had no luck with it in England. He saw in inflation, that is the utmost possible increase in the medium of circulation, a stimulus to production.

In 1716, Law received a concession for a private bank which at first presented no exceptional character. It was merely specified that the credit obligations of the state must be received in payment for the capital, while the notes of the bank were to be accepted in the payment of taxes. In contrast with the Bank of England there was no clear plan as to the manner in which the bank was to have a regular and secure income so as to maintain the liquid character of its issues. In connection with this bank Law founded the Mississippi Company. The Louisiana territory was to be financed to the extent of a hundred million livres; the company accepted the same amount of obligations of the state as payment for stock and received in exchange the monopoly of the trade in a territory to be determined. If one examines the Louisiana plan it will be observed that a century would have been required before Louisiana would have yielded sufficient revenue to make possible the repayment of the capital. To begin with, Law intended to carry out an undertaking similar to the East India Company, entirely overlooking the fact that Louisiana was not, like India, an ancient civilized country, but a forest preserve inhabited by Indians.

When, in 1718, he saw himself threatened by the competition of a stock company which wished to lease the indirect taxes, he combined the Mississippi Company with the Compagnie des Indes. The new company was to carry on the trade with India and China, but the political power was not available to secure for France the share in the Asiatic trade which England already possessed. However, the regency was induced to give to Law the right of coinage and the lease on all the taxes, involving power of life and death over the state, in exchange for a loan at 3 percent by means of which the gigantic floating debt was to be taken care of. At this point the public embarked on an insane course of speculation. The first year a 200 percent dividend was declared and the price of shares rose from 500 to 9,000. This phase of the development can be explained only by the fact that short selling was impracticable since there was as yet no systematic exchange mechanism.

In 1720 Law succeeded in getting himself appointed Comptroller General of Finances. But the whole enterprise quickly disintegrated. In vain the state decreed that only John-Law-notes should be legal money; in vain it sought to sustain them by drastic restriction on the trade in precious metals. Law's fall was inevitable simply because neither Louisiana nor the Chinese or East India trade had yielded sufficient profit to pay interest on even a fraction of his capital. It is true that the bank had received deposits, but it possessed no liquid external resources for repayment. The end was a complete bankruptcy and the declaration that the notes were of no value. A result was an enduring discouragement on the part of the French public, but at the same time freely transferable share certificates, made to bearer, had been popularized.

In the same years a parallel phenomenon was exhibited by England, except that the course of development was not so wild as that in France. Soon after founding of the Bank of England, the idea of a competing institution became current (1696). This was the land bank project resting on the same ideas later presented in the proposals of the German agrarians; namely, of using land credit instead of bills of exchange as a cover for bank notes. But this project was not carried out because in England it was well understood that the necessary liquidity would be absent. This, however, did not prevent the occurrence that in 1711, after the fall of the Whig government, the Tories adopted a course similar to that followed a few years later by John Law.

The English nobility wished to create a centralized power in opposition to the specifically Puritan basis of the Bank of England, and at the same time the gigantic public debt was to be paid off. For this purpose was founded the South Sea Company, which made considerable advances to the state and in return received a monopoly of the South Pacific trade. The Bank of England was not shrewd enough to keep aloof from the project; it even outbid the founders and it was due only to the Tories, who on the ground of political repugnance refused it participation, that its offer was not accepted.

The course of events was similar to that of John Law's institution. Here also bankruptcy was unavoidable because the South Sea trade was not sufficient to pay interest on the sums advanced. Yet prior to this eventuality, just as in France, speculation gave rise to transferable certificates. The result was that enormous property was dissipated while many adventurers came out of it smiling, and the state—in a way none too honorable—achieved a substantial lightening of its burden of interest. The Bank of England remained standing in all its former prestige, being the only financial institution based on the rational discounting of exchange and hence possessing the requisite current liquidity. The explanation is that exchange represents nothing but goods already sold, and such a regular and sufficient turnover of goods no place in the world except London at that time could provide.

Speculative crises of a similar sort have taken place from that time forward, but never since on the same scale. The first crises in rational speculation began a full hundred years later, after the conclusion of the Wars of Liberation, and since that time they have recurred almost regularly at intervals of about 10 years—1815, 1825, 1835, 1847 etc. It was these which Karl Marx had in view when in the Communist Manifesto he prophesied the downfall of capitalism. The first of these crises and their periodic recurrence were based on the possibility of speculation and the resultant participation of outside interests in large business undertakings.

The collapse has resulted from the fact that in consequence of overspeculation, means of production, though not production itself, grew faster than the need for consumption of goods. In 1815 the prospect of the lifting of the continental blockade had led to a regular rage for founding factories; but the war had destroyed the buying power of the continent and it could no longer take the English products. This crisis was barely overcome, and the continent had begun to develop buying power when, in 1825, a new crisis set in because means of production, though not goods, had been speculatively produced on a scale never known before and out of correspondence with the needs.

That it was possible to create means of production to such an extent is due to the fact that with the nineteenth century the age of iron had begun. The discovery of the coking process, the blast furnace, and the carrying of mining operations to unprecedented depths, introduced iron as the basis of creating means of production, where the machines of the eighteenth century were built only of wood. Thus production was freed from the organic limitations in which nature had held it confined. At the same time, however, crises became an imminent factor of the economic order. Crises in the broader sense of chronic unemployment, destitution, glutting of the market and political disturbances which destroy all industrial life, have existed always and everywhere. But there is great difference between the fact that a Chinese or Japanese peasant is hungry and knows the while that the Deity is unfavorable to him or the spirits are disturbed and consequently nature does not give rain or sunshine at the right time, and the fact that the social order itself may be held responsible for the crisis, even to the poorest laborer. In the first case, men turn to religion; in the second, the work of men is held at fault and the laboring man draws the conclusion that it must be changed. Rational socialism would never have originated in the absence of crises.

Colonial Policy from the Sixteenth to the Eighteenth Century

At this point it is pertinent to inquire into the significance which the acquisition and exploitation of the great non-European regions had for the development of modern capitalism, although only the most characteristic features of the older colonial policy can be mentioned here. The acquisition of colonies by the European states led to a gigantic acquisition of wealth in Europe for all of them. The means of this accumulation was the monopolizing of colonial products, and also of the markets of the colonies; that is, the right to take goods into them, and, finally, the profits of transportation between motherland and colony; the last were ensured especially by the English Navigation Act of 1651. This accumulation was secured by force, without exception and by all countries. The operations might take various forms. Either the state drew a profit from the colonies directly, administering them by its own agencies, or it leased them, in return for a payment, to companies. Two main types of exploitation are met with: the feudal type in the Spanish and Portuguese colonies, the capitalistic in the Dutch and English.

Forerunners of the feudal colonization form are especially the Venetian and Genoese colonies in the Levant, and those of the Templars. In both cases the opportunity for securing a money income was afforded by the subdivision of the region to be exploited into fiefs, "encomiendas" in the case of Spain.

The capitalistic colonies regularly developed into plantations. Labor power was furnished by the natives. The opportunities for application of this labor system, from which favorable results had been secured in Asia and Africa, seemed about to expand enormously when it was transferred to transoceanic lands. It was found however that the American Indians were entirely unsuitable for plantation labor, and importation of black slaves to the West Indies took the place of their use and gradually grew into a regular commerce of enormous extent.[1] It was carried on on the basis of slave-trading privileges (*"assiento"*), the first of which was granted by the emperor Charles V in 1517 to the Flemings. These slave-trading privileges played a large role in international relations well into the eighteenth century. In the treaty of Utrecht, England secured the right to import slaves into the Spanish possessions in South America, to the exclusion of all other powers, and at the same time assumed the obligation of delivering a certain minimum number. The results of the slave trade were considerable. It may be estimated that at the beginning of the nineteenth century some seven million slaves were living in the territory of the European colonies. Their mortality was extraordinarily high, running in the nineteenth century to 25 percent and to a multiple of that figure earlier. From 1807 to 1848, a further five million slaves were imported from Africa, and the aggregate of slaves transported thence overseas can be set equal to the population of a first-class European power in the eighteenth century.

In addition to the black slaves there were white half-slaves, the "indentured servants;" they were especially numerous in the English North American colonies where in the seventeenth century their number surpassed that of the Negroes. In part they were deported criminals, in part poor wretches who attempted in this way to earn their passage money, a small fortune.

The profits of the slave labor were by no means small. In England in the eighteenth century they were estimated at fifteen to twenty pounds sterling per slave per year. The profitableness of slave labor depended upon strict plantation discipline, ruthless driving of the slave, and perpetual importation—since the slaves did not perpetuate themselves—and finally exploitative agriculture.

This accumulation of wealth brought about through colonial trade has been of little significance for the developmentt of modern capitalism—a fact which must be emphasized in opposition to Werner Sombart. It is true that the colonial trade made possible the accumulation of wealth to an enormous extent, but this did not further the specifically occidental form of the organization of labor, since colonial trade itself rested on the principle of exploitation and not that of securing an income through market operations. Furthermore, we know that in Bengal for example, the English garrison cost five times as much as the money value of all the goods carried thither. It follows that the markets for domestic industry furnished by the colonies under the conditions of the time were relatively unimportant, and that the main profit was derived from the transport business.

The end of the capitalistic method of exploiting colonies coincides with the abolition of slavery. Only in part did this come about through ethical motives. The only Christian sect which persistently and uniformly combated slavery was the Quakers; neither the Calvinists nor the Catholics nor any other denomination consistently and constantly advocated its abolition. A decisive event was the loss of the North American colonies. Even during the War for Independence, the northern colonies prohibited slavery, and in fact from purely democratic political principles, because the people wished to avoid the development of a plantation system and a planter aristocracy. A religious motive also played a part in the shape of the traditional repugnance of the Puritans to feudalism of any sort. In 1794 the French Convention declared for the abolition of slavery on political equalitarian grounds, which were dressed up in an appropriate ideology. In the meantime, in 1815, the Congress of Vienna prohibited the slave trade. The interest of England in slavery was much reduced through the loss of the principal slave-consuming region, its North American colonies. The decrees of the Congress made it possible for the English to suppress the foreign slave trade and at the same time themselves to carry on a buoyant smuggling business. From 1807 to 1847, five million human beings were carried from Africa to the English colonial territories in this way, with the actual sufferance of the government. Only after the parliamentary reform, in 1833, was slavery really prohibited in England and by England for all its colonies, and the prohibition was at once treated seriously.

In the period from the sixteenth to the eighteenth century, slavery signified as little for the economic organization of Europe as it did much for the accumulation of wealth in Europe. It produced a large number of annuitants, but contributed in very small degree toward bringing about the development of the capitalistic organization of industry and of economic life.

Characteristics of Western Capitalism

Drawing together once more the *distinguishing characteristics of western capitalism* and its causes, we find the following factors.

First, this institution alone produced a rational organization of labor, which nowhere previously existed. Everywhere and always there has been trade; it can be traced back into the stone age. Likewise we find in the most varied epochs and cultures war finance, state contributions, tax farming, farming of offices, etc., but not a rational organization of labor. Furthermore we find everywhere else a primitive, strictly integrated internal economy such that there is no question of any freedom of economic action between members of the same tribe or clan, associated with absolute freedom of trade externally. Internal and external ethics are distinguished, and in connection with the latter there is complete ruthlessness in financial procedure; nothing can be more rigidly prescribed than the clan economy of China or the caste economy of India, and on the other hand nothing is so unscrupulous as the conduct of the Hindu foreign trader. In contrast with this, the second characteristic of western capitalism is a lifting of the barrier between the internal economy and external economy, between internal and external ethics, and the entry of the commercial principle into the internal economy, with the organization of labor on this basis. Finally, the disintegration of primitive economic fixity is also met with elsewhere, as for example in Babylon; but nowhere else do we find the entrepreneurial organization of labor as it is known in the western world.

If this development took place only in the Occident the reason is to be found in the special features of its general cultural evolution which are peculiar to it. Only the Occident knows the state in the modern sense, with a professional administration, specialized officialdom, and law based on the concept of citizenship. Beginnings of this institution in antiquity and in the Orient were never able to develop. Only the Occident knows rational law, made by jurists and rationally interpreted and applied, and only in the Occident is found the concept of citizen *(civis Romanus, citoyen, bourgeois)* because only in the Occident again are there cities in the specific sense. Furthermore, only the Occident possesses science in the present-day sense of the word. Theology, philosophy, reflection on the ultimate problems of life, were known to the Chinese and the Hindu, perhaps even of a depth unreached by the European; but a rational science and in connection with it a rational technology remained unknown to those civilizations. Finally, western civilization is further distinguished from every other by the presence of men with a rational ethic for the conduct of life. Magic and religion are found everywhere; but a religious basis for the ordering of life which, consistently followed through, must lead to explicit rationalism is again peculiar to western civilization alone.

Translated by Frank H. Knight

19. The Evolution of the Capitalistic Spirit

It is a widespread error that the increase of population is to be included as a really crucial agent in the evolution of western capitalism. In opposition to this view, Karl Marx made the assertion that every economic epoch has its own law of population, and although this proposition is untenable in so general a form, it is justified in the present case. The growth of population in the west made most rapid progress from the beginning of the eighteenth century to the end of the nineteenth. In the same period China experienced a population growth of at least equal extent—from 60 or 70 to 400 millions, allowing for the inevitable exaggerations; this corresponds approximately with the increase in the west. In spite of this fact, capitalism went backward in China and not forward. The increase in the population took place there in different strata than with us. It made China the seat of a swarming mass of small peasants; the increase of a class corresponding to our proletariat was involved only to the extent that a foreign market made possible the employment of coolies ("coolie" is originally an Indian expression, and signifies neighbor or fellow member of a clan). The growth of population in Europe did indeed favor the development of capitalism, to the extent that in a small population the system would have been unable to secure the necessary labor force, but in itself it never called forth that development.

Nor can the influx of precious metals be regarded, as Sombart suggests, as the primary cause of the appearance of capitalism. It is certainly true that in a given situation an increase in the supply of precious metals may give rise to price revolutions, such as that which took place after 1530 in Europe, and when other favorable conditions are present, as when a certain form of labor organization is in process of development, the progress may be stimulated by the fact that large stocks of cash come into the hands of certain groups. But the case of India proves that such an importation of precious metal will not alone bring about capitalism. In India in the period of the Roman power, an enormous mass of precious metal—some twenty-five million *sestertii* annually—came in in exchange for domestic goods, but this inflow gave rise to commercial capitalism to only a slight extent. The greater part of the precious metal disappeared in the hoards of the rajahs instead of being converted into cash and applied in the establishment of enterprises of a rational capitalistic character. This fact proves that it depends entirely upon the nature of the labor system what tendency will result from an inflow of precious metal. The gold and silver from America, after the discovery, flowed in the first place to Spain; but in that country a recession of capitalistic development took place parallel with the importation. There followed, on the one hand, the suppression of the *communeros* and the destruction of the commercial interests of the Spanish grandees, and, on the other hand, the employment of the money for military ends. Consequently, the stream of precious metal flowed through Spain, scarcely touching it, and fertilized other countries, which in the fifteenth century were already undergoing a process of transformation in labor relations which was favorable to capitalism.

Hence neither the growth of population nor the importation of precious metal called forth western capitalism. The external conditions for the development of capitalism are rather, first, geographical in character. In China and India the enormous costs of transportation, connected with the decisively inland commerce of the regions, necessarily formed serious obstructions for the classes who were in a position to make profits through trade and to use trading capital in the construction of a capitalistic system, while in the west the position of the Mediterranean as an inland sea, and the abundant interconnections through the rivers, favored the opposite development of international commerce. But this factor in its turn must not be overestimated. The civilization of antiquity was distinctively coastal. Here the opportunities for commerce were very favorable, (thanks to the character of the Mediterranean Sea,) in contrast with the Chinese waters with their typhoons, and yet no capitalism arose in antiquity. Even in the modern period the capitalistic development was much more intense in Florence than in Genoa or in Venice. Capitalism in the west was born in the industrial cities of the interior, not in the cities which were centers of sea trade.

Military requirements were also favorable, though not as such but because of the special nature of the particular needs of the western armies. Favorable also was the luxury demand, though again not in itself. In many cases, rather, it led to the development of irrational forms, such as small workshops in France and compulsory settlements of workers in connection with the courts of many German princes. In the last resort the factor which produced capitalism is the rational permanent enterprise, rational accounting, rational technology and rational law, but again not these alone. Necessary complementary factors were the rational spirit, the rationalization of the conduct of life in general, and a rationalistic economic ethic.

At the beginning of all ethics and the economic relations which result, is traditionalism, the sanctity of tradition, the exclusive reliance upon such trade and industry as have come down from the fathers. This traditionalism survives far down into the present; only a human lifetime in the past it was futile to double the wages of an agricultural laborer in Silesia who mowed a certain tract of land on a contract, in the hope of inducing him to increase his exertions. He would simply have reduced by half the work expended because with this half he would have been able to earn twice as much as before (sic). This general incapacity and indisposition to depart from the beaten paths is the motive for the maintenance of tradition.

Primitive traditionalism may, however undergo essential intensification through two circumstances. In the first place, material interests may be tied up with the maintenance of the tradition. When for example in China, the attempt was made to change certain roads or to introduce more rational means or routes of transportation, the perquisites of certain officials were threatened; and the same was the case in the middle ages in the west, and in modern times when railroads were introduced. Such special interests of officials, landholders and merchants assisted decisively in restricting a tendency toward rationalization. Stronger still is the effect of the stereotyping of trade on magical grounds, the deep repugnance to undertaking any change in the established conduct of life because supernatural evils are feared. Generally some injury to economic privilege is concealed in this opposition, but its effectiveness depends on a general belief in the potency of the magical processes which are feared.

Traditional obstructions are not overcome by the economic impulse alone. The notion that our rationalistic and capitalistic age is characterized by a stronger economic interest than other periods is childish; the moving spirits of modern capitalism are not possessed of a stronger economic impulse than, for example, an oriental trader. The unchaining of the economic interest merely as such has produced only irrational results; such men as Cortez and Pizarro, who were perhaps its strongest embodiment, were far from having an idea of a rationalistic economic life. If the economic impulse in itself is universal, it is an interesting question as to the conditions under which it becomes rationalized and rationally tempered in such fashion as to produce rational institutions of the character of capitalistic enterprise.

Originally, two opposite attitudes toward the pursuit of profit exist in combination. Internally, there is attachment to tradition and to the pietistic relations of fellow members of tribe, clan, and house-community, with the exclusion of the unrestricted quest of gain within the circle of those bound together by religious ties; externally, there is absolutely unrestricted play of the profit spirit in economic relations, every foreigner being originally an enemy in relation to whom no ethical restrictions apply; that is, the ethics of internal and external relations are categorically distinct. The course of development involves on the one hand the bringing in of calculation into the traditional brotherhood, displacing the old religious relationship. As soon as accountability is established within the family community, and economic relations are no longer strictly communistic, there is an end of the naive piety and its repression of the economic impulse. This side of the development is especially characteristic in the west. At the same time there is a tempering of the unrestricted quest of gain with the adoption of the economic principle into the internal economy. The result is a regulated economic life with the economic impulse functioning within bounds.

In detail, the course of development has been varied. In India, the restrictions upon gain-seeking apply only to the two uppermost strata, the Brahmins and the Rajputs. A member of these castes is forbidden to practice certain callings. A Brahmin may conduct an eating house, as he alone has clean hands; but he, like the Rajput, would be unclassed if he were to lend money for interest. The latter, however, is permitted to the mercantile castes, and within it we find a degree of unscrupulousness in trade which is unmatched anywhere in the world. Finally, antiquity had only legal limitations on interest, and the proposition *caveat emptor* characterizes Roman economic ethics. Nevertheless no modern capitalism developed there.

The final result is the peculiar fact that the germs of modern capitalism must be sought in a region where officially a theory was dominant which was distinct from that of the east and of classical antiquity and in principle strongly hostile to capitalism. The *ethos* of the classical economic morality is summed up in the old judgment passed on the merchant, which was probably taken from primitive Arianism: *homo mercator vix aut numquam potest Deo placere;* he may conduct himself without sin but cannot be pleasing to God. This proposition was valid down to the fifteenth century, and the first attempt to modify it slowly matured in Florence under pressure of the shift in economic relations.

The typical antipathy of Catholic ethics, and following that the Lutheran, to every capitalistic tendency, rests essentially on the repugnance of the impersonality of relations within a capitalist economy. It is this fact of impersonal relations which places certain human affairs outside the church and its influence, and prevents the latter from penetrating them and transforming them along ethical lines. The relations between master and slave could be subjected to immediate ethical regulation; but the relations between the mortgage creditor and the property which was pledged for the debt, or between an endorser and the bill of exchange, would at least be exceedingly difficult if not impossible to moralize. The final consequence of the resulting position assumed by the church was that medieval economic ethics excluded haggling, overpricing and free competition, and were based on the principle of just price and the assurance to everyone of a chance to live.

For the breaking up of this circle of ideas the Jews cannot be made responsible as Sombart does. The position of the Jews during the Middle Ages may be compared sociologically with that of an Indian caste in a world otherwise free from castes; they were an outcast people. However, there is the distinction that according to the promise of the Indian religion the caste system is valid for eternity. The individual may in the course of time reach heaven through a course of reincarnations, the time depending upon his deserts; but this is possible only within the caste system. The caste organization is eternal, and one who attempted to leave it would be accursed and condemned to pass in hell into the bowels of a dog. The Jewish promise, on the contrary, points toward a reversal of caste relations in the future world as compared with this. In the present world the Jews are stamped as an outcast people, either as punishment for the sins of their fathers, as Deutero-Isaiah holds, or for the salvation of the world, which is the presupposition of the mission of Jesus of Nazareth; from this position they are to be released by a social revolution. In the Middle Ages the Jews were a guest-people standing outside of political society; they could not be received into any town citizenship group because they could not participate in the communion of the Lord's Supper, and hence could not belong to the *coniuratio*.

The Jews were not the only guest-people; besides them the Caursines, for example, occupied a similar position. These were Christian merchants who dealt in money and in consequence were, like the

Jews, under the protection of the princes and on consideration of a payment enjoyed the privilege of carrying on monetary dealings. What distinguished the Jews in a striking way from the Christian guest-peoples was the impossibility in their case of entering into *commercium* and *conubium* with the Christians. Originally the Christians did not hesitate to accept Jewish hospitality, in contrast with the Jews themselves who feared that their ritualistic prescriptions as to food would not be observed by their hosts. On the occasion of the first outbreak of medieval anti-semitism, the faithful were warned by the synods not to conduct themselves unworthily and hence not to accept entertainment from the Jews, who on their side despised the hospitality of the Christians. Marriage with Christians was strictly impossible, going back to Ezra and Nehemiah.

A further ground for the outcast position of the Jews arose from the fact that Jewish craftsmen existed; in Syria there had even been a Jewish knightly class, though only exceptionally Jewish peasants, for the conduct of agriculture was not to be reconciled with the requirements of the ritual. Ritualistic considerations were responsible for the concentration of Jewish economic life in monetary dealings. Jewish piety set a premium on the knowledge of the law and continuous study was very much easier to combine with exchange dealings than with other occupations. In addition, the prohibition against usury on the part of the church condemned exchange dealings, yet the trade was indispensable and the Jews were not subject to the ecclesiastical law.

Finally, Judaism had maintained the originally universal dualism of internal and external moral attitudes, under which it was permissible to accept interest from foreigners who did not belong to the brotherhood or established association. Out of this dualism followed the sanctioning of other irrational economic affairs, especially tax farming and political financing of all sorts. In the course of the centuries the Jews acquired a special skill in these matters which made them useful and in demand. But all this was pariah capitalism, not rational capitalism such as originated in the west. In consequence, hardly a Jew is found among the creators of the modern economic situation, the large entrepreneurs; this type was Christian and only conceivable in the field of Christianity. The Jewish manufacturer, on the contrary, is a modern phenomenon. If for no other reason, it was impossible for the Jews to have a part in the establishment of rational capitalism because they were outside the craft organizations. But even alongside the guilds they could hardly maintain themselves, even where, as in Poland, they had command over a numerous proletariat which they might have organized in the capacity of entrepreneurs in domestic industry or as manufacturers. After all, the genuine Jewish ethic is specifically traditionalism, as the Talmud shows. The horror of the pious Jew in the face of any innovation is quite as great as that of an individual among any primitive people with institutions fixed by the belief in magic.

However, Judaism was nonetheless of notable significance for modern rational capitalism, insofar as it transmitted to Christianity the latter's hostility to magic. Apart from Judaism and Christianity, and two or three oriental sects (one of which is in Japan), there is no religion with the character of outspoken hostility to magic. Probably this hostility arose through the circumstance that what the Israelites found in Canaan was the magic of the agricultural god Baal, while Yahweh was a god of volcanoes, earthquakes, and pestilences. The hostility between the two priesthoods and the victory of the priests of Yahweh discredited the fertility magic of the priests of Baal and stigmatized it with a character of decadence and godlessness. Since Judaism made Christianity possible and gave it the character of a religion essentially free from magic, it rendered an important service from the point of view of economic history. For the dominance of magic outside the sphere in which Christianity has prevailed is one of the most serious obstructions to the rationalization of economic life. Magic involves a stereotyping of technology and economic relations. When attempts were made in China to inaugurate the building of railroads and factories a conflict with geomancy ensued. The latter demanded that in the location of structures on certain mountains, forests, rivers, and cemetery hills, foresight should be exercised in order not to disturb the rest of the spirits.

Similar is the relation to capitalism of the castes in India. Every new technical process which an Indian employs signifies for him first of all that he leaves his caste and falls into another, necessarily lower. Since he believes in the transmigration of souls, the immediate significance of this is that his chance of purification is put off until another rebirth. He will hardly consent to such a change. An additional fact is that every caste makes every other impure. In consequence, workmen who dare not accept a vessel filled with water from each other's hands cannot be employed together in the same factory room. Not until the present time, after the possession of the country by the English for almost a century, could this obstacle be overcome. Obviously, capitalism could not develop in an economic group thus bound hand and foot by magical beliefs.

In all times there has been but one means of breaking down the power of magic and establishing a rational conduct of life; this means is great rational prophecy. Not every prophecy by any means destroys the power of magic; but it is possible for a prophet who furnishes credentials in the shape of miracles and otherwise, to break down the traditional sacred rules. Prophecies have released the world from magic and in doing so have created the basis for our modern science and technology, and for capitalism. In China such prophecy has been wanting. What prophecy there was has come from the outside as in the case of Lao-Tse and Taoism. India, however, produced a religion of salvation; in contrast with China it has known great prophetic missions. But they were prophecies by example; that is, the typical Hindu prophet, such as Buddha, lives before the world the life which leads to salvation, but does not regard himself as one sent from God to insist upon the obligation to lead it; he takes the position that whoever wishes salvation, as an end freely chosen, should lead the life. However, one may reject salvation, as it is not the destiny of everyone to enter at death into Nirvana, and only philosophers in the strictest sense are prepared by hatred of this world to adopt the stoical resolution and withdraw from life.

The result was that Hindu prophecy was of immediate significance for the intellectual classes. These became forest dwellers and poor monks. For the masses, however, the significance of the founding of a Buddhistic sect was quite different, namely the opportunity of praying to the saints. There came to be holy men who were believed to work miracles, who must be well fed so that they would repay this good deed by guaranteeing a better reincarnation or through granting wealth, long life, and the like, that is, this world's goods. Hence Buddhism in its pure form was restricted to a thin stratum of monks. The laity found no ethical precepts according to which life should be molded; Buddhism indeed had its decalogue, but in distinction from that of the Jews it gave no binding commands but only recommendations. The most important act of service was and remained the physical maintenance of the monks. Such a religious spirit could never be in a position to displace magic but at best could only put another magic in its place.

In contrast with the ascetic religion of salvation of India and its defective action upon the masses, are Judaism and Christianity, which from the beginning have been plebeian religions and have deliberately remained such. The struggle of the ancient church against the Gnostics was nothing else than a struggle against the aristocracy of the intellectuals, such as is common to ascetic religions, with the object of preventing their seizing the leadership in the church. This struggle was crucial for the success of Christianity among the masses, and hence for the fact that magic was suppressed among the general population to the greatest possible extent. True, it has not been possible even down to today to overcome it entirely, but it was reduced to the character of something unholy, something diabolic.

The germ of this development as regards magic is found far back in ancient Jewish ethics, which is much concerned with views such as we also meet with in the proverbs and the so-called prophetic texts of the Egyptians. But the most important prescriptions of Egyptian ethics were futile when by laying a scarab on the region of the heart one could prepare the dead man to successfully conceal the sins committed, deceive the judge of the dead, and thus get into paradise. The Jewish ethics knows no such sophisticated subterfuges and as little does Christianity. In the Eucharist the latter has indeed sublimated magic into the form of a sacrament, but it gave its adherents no such means for evading the final judgment as were contained in Egyptian religion. If one wishes to study at all the influence of a religion on life one must distinguish between its official teachings and this sort of actual procedure upon which in reality, perhaps against its own will, it places a premium, in this world or the next.

It is also necessary to distinguish between the virtuoso religion of adepts and the religion of the masses. Virtuoso religion is significant for everyday life only as a pattern; its claims are of the highest, but they fail to determine everyday ethics. The relation between the two is different in different religions. In Catholicism, they are brought into harmonious union insofar as the claims of the religious virtuoso are held up alongside the duties of the laymen as *consilia evangelica*. The really complete Christian is the monk; but his mode of life is not required of everyone, although some of his virtues in a qualified form are held up as ideals. The advantage of this combination was that ethics was not split asunder as in Buddhism. After all the distinction between monk ethics and mass ethics meant that the most worthy individuals in the religious sense withdrew from the world and established a separate community.

Christianity was not alone in this phenomenon, which rather recurs frequently in the history of religions, as is shown by the powerful influence of asceticism, which signifies the carrying out of a definite, methodical conduct of life. Asceticism has always worked in this sense. The enormous achievements possible to such an ascetically determined methodical conduct of life are demonstrated by the example of Tibet. The country seems condemned by nature to be an eternal desert; but a community of celibate ascetics has carried out colossal construction works in Lhasa and saturated the country with the religious doctrines of Buddhism. An analogous phenomenon is present in the Middle Ages in the West. In that epoch the monk is the first human being who lives rationally, who works methodically and by rational means toward a goal, namely the future life. Only for him did the clock strike, only for him were the hours of the day divided—for prayer. The economic life of the monastic communities was also rational. The monks in part furnished the officialdom for the early Middle Ages; the power of the doges of Venice collapsed when the investiture struggle deprived them of the possibility of employing churchmen for oversea enterprises.

But the rational mode of life remained restricted to the monastic circles. The Franciscan movement indeed attempted through the institution of the tertiaries to extend it to the laity, but the institution of the confessional was a barrier to such an extension. The church domesticated medieval Europe by means of its system of confession and penance, but for the men of the Middle Ages the possibility of unburdening themselves through the channel of the confessional, when they had rendered themselves liable to punishment, meant a release from the consciousness of sin which the teachings of the church had called into being. The unity and strength of the methodical conduct of life were thus in fact broken up. In its knowledge of human nature the church did not reckon with the fact that the individual is a closed unitary ethical personality, but steadfastly held to the view that in spite of the warnings of the confessional and of penances, however strong, he would again fall away morally; that is, it shed its grace on the just and the unjust.

The Reformation made a decisive break with this system. The dropping of the *concilia evangelica* by the Lutheran Reformation meant the disappearance of the dualistic ethics, of the distinction between a universally binding morality and a specifically advantageous code for virtuosi. The other-worldly asceticism came to an end. The stern religious characters who had previously gone into monasteries had now to practice their religion in the life of the world. For such an asceticism within the world the ascetic dogmas of

Protestantism created an adequate ethics. Celibacy was not required, marriage being viewed simply as an institution for the rational bringing up of children. Poverty was not required, but the pursuit of riches must not lead one astray into reckless enjoyment. Thus Sebastian Franck was correct in summing up the spirit of the Reformation in the words, "you think you have escaped from the monastery, but everyone must now be a monk throughout his life."

The wide significance of this transformation of the ascetic ideal can be followed down to the present in the classical lands of Protestant ascetic religiosity. It is especially discernible in the import of the religious denominations in America. Although state and church are separated, still, as late as fifteen or twenty years ago no banker or physician took up a residence or established connections without being asked to what religious community he belonged, and his prospects were good or bad according to the character of his answer. Acceptance into a sect was conditioned upon a strict inquiry into one's ethical conduct. Membership in a sect which did not recognize the Jewish distinction between internal and external moral codes guaranteed one's business honor and reliability and this in turn guaranteed success. Hence the principle, "honesty is the best policy," and hence among Quakers, Baptists, and Methodists the ceaseless repetition of the proposition based on experience that God would take care of his own: "The Godless cannot trust each other across the road; they turn to us when they want to do business; piety is the surest road to wealth." This is by no means "cant," but a combination of religiosity with consequences which were originally unknown to it and which were never intended.

It is true that the acquisition of wealth, attributed to piety, led to a dilemma, in all respects similar to that into which the medieval monasteries constantly fell; the religious guild led to wealth, wealth to fall from grace, and this again to the necessity of reconstitution. Calvinism sought to avoid this difficulty through the idea that man was only an administrator of what God had given him; it condemned enjoyment, yet permitted no flight from the world but rather regarded working together, with its rational discipline, as the religious task of the individual. Out of this system of thought came our word "calling," which is known only to the languages influenced by the Protestant translations of the Bible. It expresses the value placed upon rational activity carried on according to the rational capitalistic principle, as the fulfillment of a God-given task. Here lay also in the last analysis the basis of the contrast between the Puritans and the Stuarts. The ideas of both were capitalistically directed; but in a characteristic way the Jew was for the Puritan the embodiment of everything repugnant because he devoted himself to irrational and illegal occupations such as war loans, tax farming, and leasing of offices, in the fashion of the court favorite.

This development of the concept of the calling quickly gave to the modern entrepreneur a fabulously clear conscience—and also industrious workers; he gave to his employees as the wages of their ascetic devotion to the calling, and of co-operation in his ruthless exploitation of them through capitalism, the prospect of eternal salvation, which in an age when ecclesiastical discipline took control of the whole of life to an extent inconceivable to us now, represented a reality quite different from any it has today. The Catholic and Lutheran churches also recognized and practiced ecclesiastical discipline. But in the Protestant ascetic communities admission to the Lord's Supper was conditioned on ethical fitness, which again was identified with business honor, while into the content of one's faith no one inquired. Such a powerful, unconsciously refined organization for the production of capitalistic individuals has never existed in any other church or religion, and in comparison with it what the Renaissance did for capitalism shrinks into insignificance. Its practitioners occupied themselves with technical problems and were experimenters of the first rank. From art and mining experimentation was taken over into science.

The world-view of the Renaissance, however, determined the policy of rulers in a large measure, though it did not transform the soul of man as did the innovations of the Reformation. Almost all the great scientific discoveries of the sixteenth and even the beginning of the seventeenth century were made against the background of Catholicism. Copernicus was a Catholic, while Luther and Melanchthon repudiated his discoveries. Scientific progress and Protestantism must not at all be unquestioningly identified. The Catholic church has indeed occasionally obstructed scientific progress; but the ascetic sects of Protestantism have also been disposed to have nothing to do with science, except in a situation where material requirements of everyday life were involved. On the other hand it is its specific contribution to have placed science in the service of technology and economics.

The religious root of modern economic humanity is dead; today the concept of the calling is a *caput mortuum* in the world. Ascetic religiosity has been displaced by a pessimistic though by no means ascetic view of the world, such as that portrayed in Mandeville's "Fable of the Bees," which teaches that private vices may under certain conditions be for the good of the public. With the complete disappearance of all the remains of the original enormous religious pathos of the sects, the optimism of the Enlightenment which believed in the harmony of interests, appeared as the heir of Protestant asceticism in the field of economic ideas; it guided the hands of the princes, statesmen, and writers of the later eighteenth and early nineteenth century. Economic ethics arose against the background of the ascetic ideal; now it has been stripped of its religious import. It was possible for the working class to accept its lot as long as the promise of eternal happiness could be held out to it. When this consolation fell away it was inevitable that those strains and stresses should appear in economic society which since then have grown so rapidly. This point had been reached at the end of the early period of capitalism, at the beginning of the age of iron, in the nineteenth century.

Translated by Frank H. Knight

20. The Dualism of In-Group and Out-Group Morality

The separation of economic in-group and out-group ethics has remained permanently significant for the religious evaluation of economic activity. Rational economic activity on the basis of formal legality never could and never has been religiously valued in the manner characteristic of Puritanism. It was prevented by the dualism of the economic ethic which stamped as adiaphorous certain forms of behavior toward the outsiders which were strictly forbidden with respect to brothers in belief. This was decisive. It posed difficulties for Jewish ethical theorists.

Maimonides was inclined to view interest-taking from strangers as indeed religiously commanded. Besides the historical situation of the Jews at the time this was doubtlessly co-determined by the disinclination against the admission of such adiaphorous acts which endangers all ethical formalism. The late Judaic ethic disapproved of usury in the sense of an inconsiderate exploitation, also of non-Jews. The success of such disapproval had, however, to be precarious in the face of the robust words of the Torah and the social situation which meanwhile had developed. In any case, the dualism in the interest question remained.

The theoretical difficulties of ethical thinkers are naturally matters of secondary importance. Practically, however, this all-pervasive ethical dualism meant that the specific Puritan idea of "proving" one's self religiously through "inner-worldly asceticism" was unavailable. For this idea could not rest on a basis which was as such objectionable, but "permissible" toward certain classes of people. Thus the religious conception of "vocational" life of ascetic Protestantism was absent from the outset. The exceptionally high (traditionalistic) esteem for religiously pursuing one's daily work which we will find (with Jesus Sirach) could not alter this. The difference is plain.

To be sure, the rabbis, especially in the time of the proselytizing propaganda, greatly stressed righteous and honorable behavior of the Jews toward their host nations. In this point, the Talmudic teaching is in no way different from the ethical principles of other religious communities. Especially early Christendom (Clement of Alexandria) has, with respect to economic ethics, inclined to the same dualism which confined the law of usury of the Old Testament. The Puritanical crusader faced non-Puritans with the same abhorrence—in part fed on the Old Testament mood—as did the priestly law of Israel the Canaanite. Moreover, no Puritan could ever have said that an unbelieving king could be a "Servant of God" as Israelite prophecy expressly declared, for example, of Nebuchadnezzar and Cyrus. In the area of economic ethics, however, the Christian sects of the seventeenth and eighteenth centuries (particularly the Baptists and Quakers) pointed with pride to the fact that precisely in economic intercourse with the godless they had substituted legality, honesty, and fairness for falseness, overreaching, and unreliability; that they had carried through the system of fixed prices, that their patrons, even when sending only their children, would receive always real value at a fair price, that deposits and credits are sure with them, that precisely therefore, the godless prefer to patronize their stores, their banks and their workshops before all others: in short, that their superior, religiously-determined economic ethics gave them superiority over the competition of the godless according to the principle "honesty is the best policy."

This is in complete agreement with what could be concretely discerned in the United States during recent decades as characteristic of the middle class way of life. It held, similarly, for the Jains and Parsees in India—only here ritualistic fetters firmly delimited the possible extension of rationalization of economic enterprise. As little as the correct Jain or Parsee would a pious Puritan ever place himself at the disposition of colonial capitalism, of the state purveyor, ancient tax- and custom-farmer, or monopolist. These specific forms of ancient, non-European and pre-bourgeois capitalism to him were ethically objectionable and God-disapproved forms of brutal accumulation of money.

Jewish economic ethic was quite different. First, it was impossible that the ethic of precisely the patriarchs was without effect which implied with respect to "non-members" quite distinctly the maxim: "*Qui trompe-t-on?*" In any case, there was no soteriological motive whatever for ethically rationalizing out-group economic relations. No religious premium existed for it. That had far-reaching consequences for the economic behavior of the Jews. Since Antiquity, Jewish pariah capitalism, like that of the Hindu trader castes, felt at home in the very forms of state- and booty-capitalism along with pure money usury and trade, precisely what Puritanism abhorred. This was held in both cases as unobjectionable on ethical principles. Although whoever practiced usury as a tax farmer in the services of a godless Jewish prince or, worse, of a foreign power against one's own people was deeply objectionable and held by the rabbis as impure. However, against foreign peoples this way of acquisition was ethically adiaphorous. The moralists, naturally, made the reservation that outright deception was always abominable. Thus, economic pursuits could never furnish the setting for "proving" one's self religiously. If God "blessed" his own with economic success, it was not because they had "proven" themselves to be pious Jews in business conduct, but because they had lived a god-fearing life outside their economic pursuits (so, already, in the Deuteronomic usury teaching). As we shall see later, the area of proving one's piety in practice, for the Jew, lay in quite a different area than that of rationally mastering the "world" and especially the economy. The elements of the religiously determined way of life which enabled the Jews to play a role in our economic development will be considered later. In any case, the oriental and South and East European regions where the Jews were most and longest at home have failed to develop the specific traits of modern capitalism. This is true of Antiquity as well as of the Middle Ages and modern times. Their actual part in the development of the Occident rested essentially on their character as a guest-people, which their voluntary segregation imposed on them.

This place as a guest-people was established through ritualistic closure which, in Deuteronomic times, as we saw, was diffused, and during the time of the Exile was carried through by Ezra's and Nehemiah's enactments.

What interests us here is primarily the consummation of the ritualistic segregation of the community. It was carried out in exile after the North Israelites, deported by the Assyrians, had been almost completely absorbed by the environment. This absorption taught the priests and Torah teachers the decisive importance of such ritualistic protective barriers for their own interests.

The absolute prohibition of mixed marriages was practically the most important point. Ezra put it over by quite theatrical means and it was at once enforced with all relentlessness including the dissolution of the existing mixed marriages. The previous irrelevance of this prohibition is indicated in the old sources (Gen. chs. 34, 38; Jud. 3:5, 6; Deut. 21:10 f.) and the mixed blood of the Davidians (Ruth!). Furthermore, among those settled in Israel, alongside the distinguished sibs and quite a few priests and Levites, the family of the high priest was guilty of the abomination (Ezra 10:18 f.). In the priestly revision this struggle against mixed marriages has found expression in a whole series of theological constructions. So, in the objection to the use of mixed seeds in the field, mixed threads in weaving, and bastard animals. It is possible that these prohibitions were at least partially linked to ancient superstitions of unknown origin. But generally it is more probable that one and all of the prohibitions represent late theological constructions of formalist-minded priests occasioned by the tabooing of "mixture" with Gentiles. For example, the use of the mule as a matter of course is established for preexilic times.

Next to connubium we have to consider the role of commensalism for the caste-like closure against outsiders. We saw that commensalism was readily practiced also with ritualistic strangers, but as is natural elsewhere only within the circle of either permanent *berith* affiliates or temporary affiliates by guest right. At the separate meal of the Egyptians and Hebrews in the Joseph story the denial of commensalism is laid at the door of the Egyptians in contrast to the Israelites. Only the extraordinary stress in the priestly law on dietary prescriptions created tangible difficulties in practice.

The cultic Decalogue contained a highly specialized dietary prescription which was later extended with important consequences, namely, the prescription not to cook the kid in the milk of the mother. But neither here nor in other certainly preexilic statutes were the later and most characteristic dietary prohibitions of the Israelites carried or mentioned, except the prohibition of numerous and, in part, very important animals (Lev. 11). Such prohibitions pertain to (1) the hip nerve, which in its later specialization almost precluded all enjoyment of the hind quarters; (2) fat (Lev. 3:17; 7:23, 25), which prohibition in later interpretation was restricted to four-footed animals, forcing the Israelites to use goose fat; (3) blood; this necessitated the salting and watering of meat; (4) fallen and lacerated meat, which in combination with (3) determined the ritualistic regulation of slaughtering.

Some of these prohibitions (Lev. 3:17) are already characterized by their form as amendments of priestly enactments. The enjoyment of meat of the ass is presupposed in II Kings 6:25. The prohibition of fallen and lacerated meat is presupposed by Ezekiel (4:14, compare with 44:31) as holding only for the priests, and in Trito-Isaiah (66:3) only the sacrifice of sow's blood is mentioned as an abomination. Some features of these prohibitions must go back to ancient times, in part as general taboos, in part as sacrificial taboos for the benefit of God,[1] in part as priestly purity taboos. This holds, presumably, for the objection to pork and hare's meat and the prohibition mentioned in the tradition of Samuel (I Sam. 14:33 f.) against the enjoyment of blood. The etiological saga, generally a certain indication of great age, is to be found only for the usage not to eat the hip-nerve, a metaphysical, hence relatively late, interpretation (from the belief in souls) of the blood prohibition.

In later Judaism the prohibition of the Decalogue against cooking young kids in their mother's milk was extended to any joint cooking of meat and milk. This seems to derive from a local taboo of the Shechemite cult and is found there without motivation as a positive statute. The denial of enjoyment of fallen or lacerated cattle may be related to sacrificial prescriptions. There is nowhere to be found an etiological legend for the prohibition of certain kinds of animals. In its place appears, rather, a kind of scientific distinction, certainly not old, but a product of priestly schematization. It is similar and partially equivalent in manner to that in Manu (V. § 11 ff.) and presumably has considerably extended the range of prohibited meats.

To trace the grounds for establishment of individual prohibitions would seem to be a vain endeavor. It is ascertained for the time of the Evangels that the pig was still raised, also as a herd animal, in Palestine. Even later the bristles were not held to be impure, only the eating of the meat. All small-stock-breeders, including goat breeders, once representative of pious Yahwism, were considered impure only in Talmudic times, though not because of pork eating, but for their Levitically impure way of life. The most likely reason would be that here, as in the case of the church taboo of horse meat in Germany, the sacrificial feats of strange cults were forbidden. The rather widespread prohibition—also diffused in India and Egypt—can, however, also have been borrowed from the outside.

The prohibition of the enjoyment of blood and the increasing anxiety of avoiding all cattle not specifically killed by slaughtering had to be more incisive for possible commensalism than this rejection of a number of elsewhere quite favored meat dishes. This inhibition of commensalism had to be especially effective when the necessity was deduced of introducing a ritually controlled and regulated special method of butchering *(shachat)* for all animals, as occurred in postexilic times. All cattle incorrectly slaughtered were considered carcass *(nebelah)* even when the mistake was due, for instance, to a notch in the knife (because then it had been torn) or some other oversight of the butcher, who could learn his art only after long practice.

The difficulty, for correct Jews, of living isolated or in small communities resulted from the indispensability of *kosher* neighborhood butchers. This has promoted, to this day in the United States, the dense concentration of Orthodox Jews in the great cities (while the Reform Jews in isolation were able to pursue the very profitable business of usuriously exploiting the rural Negro). The casuistic elaboration of this dietary and butchering ritual falls only into late Antiquity, but basically goes back to the exilic priestly teaching.

This ritualization of dietary habits made commensalism very difficult. No true prohibition of commensalism was ever known to official Jewry. The admonition of the (apocryphal) Jubilee Book (22:16) to separate from the Gentile and not to eat with him has been accepted as little as a general impurity of the houses of Gentiles or of their personal touch. Only the Jew going to enact a religious rite, in later times was placed under the commandment of rigid segregation from all things pagan (John 18:23). All the same, the reports of the Hellenic and Roman authors bear out that correct Jews naturally had considerable scruples in the face of any commensalism with Gentiles. Undoubtedly this is primarily responsible for the reproach of the "*odium generis humani*."[2]

In Exile times the strict observance of the Sabbath came to the fore as one of the most important "differentiating commandments," for, in contrast to mere circumcision, it furnished a sure and generally visible sign that the respective person actually took his membership in the community seriously, then, because the religious festivals were bound up with Jerusalem as the place of worship and the Sabbath represented the one festival independent of all cultic apparatus. Naturally, the Sabbath rest rendered cooperation with non-members in the workshop quite difficult. This, besides the high visibility of Sabbath observance, actually contributed greatly to segregation.

The majestic account of creation in the priestly revision sanctioned the Sabbath with a very impressive etiological myth by means of the six days of divine work. The ritualization of the Sabbath found expression in comprehensive insertions in the text of the Decalogue. The commandment to cease all field work, stemming from the Yahwist (Ex. 34:21) and the Elohistic general prescription of rest from work (Ex.23:12) now became a prohibition of all activity, a prohibition of leaving one's home (Ex. 16:29), later softened through the delimitation of the Sabbath way with all sorts of possible evasions—of lighting fire (Ex. 35:3) so that one had to cook already on Friday—for the lamp tempered by possible evasions—of carrying loads and burying beasts of burden, of going to market, of contracting any sort of business, of fighting and loud speech (Jer. 17:19 ff.; Trito-Isaiah 58:13 f.; Neh. 10:31; 13:15 ff.). The performance of war service, in Seleucid times, was declared impossible essentially because of the Sabbath and dietary prohibitions. This sealed the definitive demilitarization of the pious Jews, except in case of Crusades when according to Maccabean view the end justifies the means.

There are indications of incipient creation of a special costume, as the late "*tefillin*" presented in similar manner for the exemplary pious, but, at first, these beginnings were not further developed.

Translated by Hans H. Gerth
and Don Martindale

21. Judaism, Christianity, and the Socioeconomic Order

Judaism, in its postexilic and particularly its Talmudic form, belongs among those religions that are in some sense accommodated to the world. Judaism is at least oriented to the world in the sense that it does not reject the world as such but only rejects the prevailing system of social classes in the world.

We have already made some observations concerning the total

sociological structure and attitude of Judaism. Its religious promises, in the customary meaning of the word, apply to this world, and any notions of contemplative or ascetic world-flight are as rare in Judaism as in Chinese religion and in Protestantism. Judaism differs from Puritanism only in the relative (as always) absence of systematic asceticism. The ascetic elements of the early Christian religion did not derive from Judaism, but emerged primarily in the heathen Christian communities of the Pauline mission. There is as little justification for equating the observance of the Jewish law with asceticism as for equating it with the fulfillment of any ritual or tabooistic norms.

Moreover, the relationship of the Jewish religion to both wealth and sexual indulgence is not in the least ascetic, but rather highly naturalistic. For wealth was regarded as a gift of God, and the satisfaction of the sexual impulse—naturally in the prescribed legal form—was thought to be so imperative that the Talmud actually regarded a person who had remained unmarried after a certain age as morally suspect. The interpretation of marriage as an economic institution for the production and rearing of children is universal and has nothing specifically Jewish about it. Judaism's strict prohibition of illegitimate sexual intercourse, a prohibition that was highly effective among the pious, was also found in Islam and all other prophetic religions, as well as in Hinduism. Moreover, the majority of ritualistic religions shared with Judaism the institution of periods of abstention from sexual relations for purposes of purification. For these reasons, it is not possible to speak of an idiosyncratic emphasis upon sexual asceticism in Judaism. The sexual regulations cited by Sombart do not go as far as the Catholic casuistry of the seventeenth century and in any case have analogies in many other casuistical systems of taboo.

Nor did Judaism forbid the uninhibited enjoyment of life or even of luxury as such, provided that the positive prohibitions and taboos of the law were observed. The denunciation of wealth in the prophetic books, the Psalms, the Wisdom Literature, and subsequent writings was evoked by the social injustices which were so frequently perpetrated against fellow Jews in connection with the acquisition of wealth and in violation of the spirit of the Mosaic law. Wealth was also condemned in response to arrogant disregard of the commandments and promises of God and in response to the rise of temptations to laxity in religious observance. To escape the temptations of wealth is not easy, but is for this reason all the more meritorious. "Hail to the man of wealth who has been found to be blameless." Moreover, since Judaism possessed no doctrine of predestination and no comparable idea producing the same ethical effects, incessant labor and success in business life could not be regarded or interpreted in the sense of certification, which appears most strongly among the Calvinist Puritans and which is found to some extent in all ascetic Protestant religions, as shown in John Wesley's remark on this point. Of course a certain tendency to regard success in one's economic activity as a sign of God's gracious direction existed in the religion of the Jews, as in the religions of the Chinese and the lay Buddhists and generally in every religion that has not turned its back upon the world. This view was especially likely to be manifested by a religion like Judaism, which had before it very specific promises of a transcendental God together with very visible signs of this God's indignation against the people he had chosen. It is clear that any success achieved in one's economic activities while keeping the commandments of God could be, and indeed had to be, interpreted as a sign that one was personally acceptable to God. This actually occurred again and again.

But the situation of the pious Jews engaged in business was altogether different from that of the Puritan, and this difference remained of practical significance for the role of Judaism in the history of economics. Let us now consider what this role has been. In the polemic against Sombart's book, one fact could not be seriously questioned, namely that Judaism played a conspicuous role in the evolution of the modern capitalistic system. However, this thesis of Sombart's book needs to be made more precise. What were the distinctive economic achievements of Judaism in the Middle Ages and in modern times? We can easily list: moneylending, from pawnbroking to the financing of great states; certain types of commodity business, particularly retailing, peddling, and produce trade of a distinctively rural type; certain branches of wholesale business; and brokerage, above all the brokerage of stocks. To this list of Jewish economic achievements should be added: money-changing; money-forwarding or check-cashing, which normally accompanies money-changing; the financing of state agencies, wars, and the establishment of colonial enterprises; tax-farming, naturally excluding the collection of prohibited taxes such as those directed to the Romans; banking; credit; and the floating of bond issues. But of all these businesses only a few, though very important ones, display the legal and economic forms characteristic of modern occidental capitalism in contrast to the forms characteristic of commerce in ancient times, the Middle Ages, and the earlier period in Eastern Asia. The distinctively modern legal forms include stock corporations and business organizations, but these are not of specifically Jewish provenience. The Jews may have introduced these forms into the Occident, but the forms themselves have a common oriental (probably Babylonian) origin, and their influence on the Occident was mediated through Hellenistic and Byzantine sources. In any event they were common to both the Jews and the Arabs. It is even true that the specifically modern forms of these institutions were in part occidental and medieval creations, with some specifically German infusions of influence. To adduce detailed proof of this here would take us too far afield. However, it can be said by way of example that the exchange, as a "market of tradesmen," was created not by Jews but by Christian merchants. Again, the particular manner in which medieval legal regulations were adapted to make possible rationalized economic enterprises (e.g., limited liability companies; privileged companies of all types—*Kommanditen, Maonen, privilegierte Kompagnien aller Art;* and stock companies) was not at all dependent on specifically Jewish influences, no matter how large a part Jews played in the formation of such rationalized economic enterprises. Finally, it must be noted that the characteristically modern principles of public and private financing first arose *in nuce* on the soil of the medieval city. Only later were the medieval legal forms of finance, which were quite un-Jewish in certain respects, adapted to the economic needs of modern states and other modern recipients of credit.

Above all, one element particularly characteristic of modern capitalism was strikingly—and perhaps completely—missing from the extensive list of Jewish economic activities. This was the organization of industrial production *(gewerbliche Arbeit)* or manufacturing in domestic industry and in the factory system. How does one explain the fact that no pious Jew succeeded in establishing an industry employing pious Jewish workers of the ghetto (as so many pious Puritan entrepreneurs had done with devout Christian workers and artisans) at times when numerous proletarians were present in the ghettos, princely patents and privileges for the establishment of any sort of industry were available for a financial remuneration, and areas of industrial activity uncontrolled by guild monopoly were open? Again, how does one explain the fact that no modern and distinctively industrial bourgeoisie of any significance emerged among the Jews to employ the Jewish workers available for home industry, despite the presence of numerous impecunious artisan groups at almost the threshold of the modern period?

All over the world, for several millennia, the characteristic forms of the capitalist employment of wealth have been state-provisioning, the financing of states, tax-farming, the financing of military colonies, the establishment of great plantations, trade, and moneylending. One finds these again and again. One finds Jews involved in just these activities, found at all times and places but especially characteristic of Antiquity, as well as involved in those specifically modern legal and organizational forms of economic activity which were evolved by the Middle Ages and not by the Jews. On the other hand, the Jews were relatively or altogether absent from the new and distinctive forms of modern capitalism, the rational organization of labor, especially production in an industrial enterprise of the factory type. The Jews evinced the ancient and medieval business temper which had been and remained typical of all primitive traders, whether small businessmen or largescale moneylenders, in Antiquity, the Far East, India, the Mediterranean littoral area, and the Occident of the Middle Ages: the will and the wit to employ mercilessly every chance of profit, "for the sake of profit to ride through Hell even if it singes the sails." But this temper is far from distinctive of modern capitalism, as distinguished from the capitalism of other eras. Precisely the reverse is true. Hence, neither that which is new in the modern economic system nor that which is distinctive of the modern economic temper is specifically Jewish in origin.

The ultimate theoretical reasons for this fact, that the distinctive elements of modern capitalism originated and developed quite apart from the Jews, are to be found in the peculiar character of the Jews as a pariah people and in the idiosyncracy of their religion. Their pariah status presented purely external difficulties impeding their participation in the organization of industrial labor. The legally and factually precarious position of the Jews hardly permitted continuous, systematic, and rationalized industrial enterprise with fixed capital, but only trade and above all dealing in money. Also of fundamental importance was the subjective ethical situation of the Jews. As a pariah people, they retained the double standard of morals which is characteristic of primordial economic practice in all communities: what is prohibited in relation to one's brothers is permitted in relation to strangers. It is unquestionable that the Jewish ethic was thoroughly traditionalistic in demanding of Jews an attitude of sustenance toward fellow Jews. As Sombart correctly notes, the rabbis made concessions in these matters, even in regard to business associations with fellow Jews, but these remained nothing more than concessions to laxity, with those who resorted to the employment of these concessions remaining far behind the highest requirements of Jewish business ethics. In any case, it is certain that economic behavior was not the realm in which a Jew could demonstrate his religious merit.

However, for the Jews the realm of economic relations with strangers, particularly economic relations prohibited in regard to fellow Jews, was an area of ethical indifference. This is of course the primordial economic ethics of all peoples everywhere. That this should have remained the Jewish economic ethic was a foregone conclusion, for even in Antiquity the Jews almost always regarded strangers as enemies. All the well-known admonitions of the rabbis enjoining honor and faithfulness toward Gentiles could not change the impression that the religious law prohibited taking usury from fellow Jews but permitted it in transactions with non-Jews. Nor could the rabbinical counsels enjoining honesty and reliability in dealing with Gentiles alter the fact, which again Sombart has rightly stressed, that a lesser degree of legality was required by the law in dealing with a stranger, (i.e., an enemy), than in dealing with another Jew, in such a matter as taking advantage of an error made by the other party. In fine, no proof is required to establish that the pariah condition of the Jews, which we have seen resulted from the promises of Yahweh, and the resulting incessant humiliation of the Jews by Gentiles necessarily led to the Jewish people's retaining different economic moralities for its relations with strangers and with fellow Jews.

Let us summarize the respective situations in which Catholics, Jews, and Protestants found themselves in regard to economic enterprises. The devout Catholic, as he went about his economic affairs, found himself continually behaving—or on the verge of behaving—in a manner that transgressed papal injunctions. His economic behavior could be ignored in the confessional only on the principle of *rebus sic stantibus,* and it could be permissible only on the basis of a lax, probabilistic morality. To a certain extent, therefore, the life of business itself had to be regarded as reprehensible or, at best, as not positively favorable to God. The inevitable result of this Catholic situation was that pious Jews were encouraged to perform economic activities among Christians which if performed among Jews would have been regarded by the Jewish community as unequivocally contrary to the law or at least as suspect from the point of view of Jewish tradition. At best these transactions were permissible on the basis of a lax interpretation of the Judaic religious code, and then only in economic relations with strangers. Never were they infused with positive ethical value. Thus, the Jew's economic conduct appeared to be permitted by God, in the absence of any formal contradiction with the religious law of the Jews, but ethically indifferent, in view of such conduct's correspondence with the average evils in the society's economy. This is the basis of whatever factual truth there was in the observations concerning the inferior standard of economic legality among Jews. That God crowned such economic activity with success could be a sign to the Jewish businessman that he had done nothing clearly objectionable or prohibited in this area and that indeed he had held fast to God's commandments in other areas. But it would still have been difficult for the Jew to demonstrate his ethical merit by means of characteristically modern business behavior.

But this was precisely the case with the pious Puritan. He could demonstrate his religious merit through his economic activity because he did nothing ethically reprehensible, he did not resort to any lax interpretations of religious codes or to systems of double moralities, and he did not act in a manner that could be indifferent or even reprehensible in the general realm of ethical validity. On the contrary, the Puritan could demonstrate his religious merit precisely in his economic activity. He acted in business with the best possible conscience, since through his rationalistic and legal behavior in his business activity he was factually objectifying the rational methodology of his total life pattern. He legitimated his ethical pattern in his own eyes, and indeed within the circle of his community, by the extent to which the absolute—not relativized—unassailability of his economic conduct remained beyond question. No really pious Puritan—and this is the crucial point—could have regarded as pleasing to God any profit derived from usury, exploitation of another's mistake (which was permissible to the Jew), haggling and sharp dealing, or participation in political or colonial exploitation. Quakers and Baptists believed their religious merit to be certified before all mankind by such practices as their fixed prices and their absolutely reliable business relationships with everyone, unconditionally legal and devoid of cupidity. Precisely such practices promoted the irreligious to trade with them rather than with their own kind, and to entrust their money to the trust companies or limited-liability enterprises of the religious sectarians rather than those of their own people—all of which made the religious sectarians wealthy, even as their business practices certified them before their God.

By contrast, the Jewish law applying to strangers, which in practice was the pariah law of the Jews, enabled them, notwithstanding innumerable reservations, to engage in dealings with non-Jews which the Puritans rejected violently as showing the cupidity of the trader. Yet the pious Jew could combine such an attitude with strict legality, with complete fulfillment of the law, with all the inwardness of his religion, with the most sacrificial love for his family and community, and indeed with pity and mercy toward all God's creatures. For in view of the operation of the laws regarding strangers, Jewish piety never in actual practice regarded the realm of permitted economic behavior as one in which the genuineness of a person's obedience to God's commandments could be demonstrated. The pious Jew never gauged his inner ethical standards by what he regarded as permissible in the economic context. Just as the Confucian's authentic ideal of life was the gentleman who had undergone a comprehensive education in ceremonial esthetics and literature and who devoted lifelong study to the classics, so the Jew set up as his ethical ideal the scholar learned in law and casuistry, the intellectual who continuously immersed himself in the sacred writings and commentaries at the expense of his business, which he very frequently left to the management of his wife.

It was this intellectualist trait of authentic late Judaism, with its preoccupation with literary scholarship, that Jesus criticized. His criticism was not motivated by the proletarian instincts which some have attributed to him, but rather by his type of piety and his type of obedience to the law, both of which were appropriate to the rural artisan or the inhabitant of a small town, and constituted his basic opposition to the virtuosi of legalistic lore who had grown up on the soil of the *polis* of Jerusalem. Members of such urban legalistic circles asked "What good can come out of Nazareth?"—the kind of question that might have been posed by any dweller of a metropolis in the classical world. Jesus' knowledge of the law and his observance of it was representative of that average lawfulness which was actually demonstrated by men engaged in practical work, who could not afford to let their sheep lie in wells, even on the Sabbath. On the other hand, the knowledge of the law obligatory for the really pious Jews, as well as their legalistic education of the young, surpassed both quantitatively and qualitatively the preoccupation with the Bible characteristic of the Puritans. The scope of religious law of which knowledge was obligatory for the pious Jew may be compared only with the scope of ritual laws among the Hindus and Persians, but the Jewish law far exceeded these in its inclusion of ethical prescriptions as well as merely ritual and tabooistic norms.

The economic behavior of the Jews simply moved in the direction of least resistance which was permitted them by these legalistic ethical norms. This meant in practice that the acquisitive drive, which is found in varying degrees in all groups and nations, was here directed primarily to trade with strangers, who were usually regarded as enemies. Even at the time of Josiah and certainly in the exilic period, the pious Jew was an urban dweller, and the entire Jewish law was oriented to this urban status. Since the orthodox Jew required the services of a ritual slaughterer, he had necessarily to live in a community rather than in isolation. Even today, urban residence is characteristic of Orthodox Jews when they are contrasted with Jews of the Reform group, as for example in the United States. Similarly, the Sabbatical year, which in its present form is certainly a product of postexilic urban scholars learned in the law, made it impossible for Jews to carry on systematic intensive cultivation of the land. Even at the present time,* German rabbis endeavor to apply the prescription of the Sabbatical year to Zionist colonization in Palestine, which would be ruined thereby. In the age of the Pharisees a rustic Jew was of second rank, since he did not and could not observe the law strictly. Jewish law also prohibited the participation of Jews in the procedures of the guilds, particularly participation in commensality with non-Jews, although in Antiquity as well as in the Middle Ages commensality was the indispensable foundation for any kind of integration or naturalization *(Einbürgerung)* in the surrounding world. But the Jewish institution of the dowry, common to the Orient and based originally on the exclusion of daughters from inheritance, favored the establishing of the Jewish groom at marriage as a small merchant; and indeed, the custom still tends toward this result. Traces of this phenomenon are still apparent in the relatively undeveloped class consciousness of Jewish apprentices.

In all his other dealings, as well as those we have just discussed, the Jew—like the pious Hindu—was controlled by scruples concerning his law. As Guttmann has correctly emphasized, genuine study of the law could be combined most easily with the occupation of

*[Before World War I. Translator's note.]

moneylending, which requires relatively little continuous labor. The outcome of Jewish legalism and intellectualist education was the Jew's methodical patterning of life and his rationalism. It is a prescription of the Talmud that "A man must never change a practice." Only in the realm of economic relationships with strangers, and in no other area of life, did tradition leave a sphere of behavior that was relatively indifferent ethically. Indeed, the entire domain of things relevant before God was determined by tradition and the systematic casuistry concerned with its interpretation, rather than determined by rational purposes derived from laws of nature and oriented without further presupposition to methodical plans of individual action *(nicht ein rational voraussetsungslos, aus einem "Naturrecht" heraus, selbstorientiertes methodisches Zweckhandeln)*. The tendency of scrupulosity before the law to develop rationalization is thoroughly pervasive but entirely indirect.

Self-control—usually accompanied by alertness, equableness, and serenity—was found among Confucians, Puritans, Buddhists and other types of monks, Arab sheiks, and Roman senators, as well as among Jews. But the basis and significance of self-control were different in each case. The alert self-control of the Puritan flowed from the necessity of his subjugating all creaturely impulses to a rational and methodical plan of conduct, so that he might secure his certainty of his own salvation. Self-control appeared to the Confucian as a personal necessity which followed from his disesteem for plebeian irrationality, the disesteem of an educated gentleman who had received classical training and had been bred along lines of honor and dignity. On the other hand, the self-control of the devout Jew of ancient times was a consequence of the preoccupation with the law in which his mind had been trained, and of the necessity of his continuous concern with the law's precise fulfillment. The pious Jew's self-control received a characteristic coloring and effect from the situation of being piously engaged in fulfilling the law. The Jew felt that only he and his people possessed this law, for which reason the world persecuted them and imposed degradation upon them. Yet this law was binding; and one day, by an act that might come suddenly at any time but that no one could accelerate, God would transform the social structure of the world, creating a messianic realm for those who had remained faithful to his law. The pious Jew knew that innumerable generations had awaited this messianic event, despite all mockery, and were continuing to await it. This produced in the pious Jew an excessive feeling of alertness. But since it remained necessary for him to continue waiting in vain, he nurtured his feelings of self-esteem by a meticulous observance of the law for its own sake. Last but not least, the pious Jew had always to stay on guard, never permitting himself the free expression of his passions against powerful and merciless enemies. This repression was inevitably combined with the aforementioned feeling of *ressentiment* which resulted from Yahweh's promises and the unparalleled history of his people who had sinned against him.

These circumstances basically determined the rationalism of Judaism, but this is not "asceticism" in our sense. To be sure, there are ascetic traits in Judaism, but they are not central. Rather, they are by-products of the law, which have arisen in part from the peculiar problem-complex of Jewish piety. In any case, ascetic traits are of secondary importance in Judaism, as are any mystical traits developed within this religion. We need say nothing more here about Jewish mysticism, since neither cabalism, Hassidism nor any of its other forms—whatever symptomatic importance they held for Jews—produced any significant motivations toward practical behavior in the economic sphere.

The ascetic aversion of pious Jews toward everything esthetic was originally based on the second commandment of the Decalogue, which actually prevented the once well-developed angelology of the Jews from assuming artistic form. But another important cause of aversion to things esthetic is the purely pedagogic and jussive character of the divine service in the synagogue, even as it was practiced in the Diaspora, long before the disruption of the Temple cult. Even at that time, Hebrew prophecy had virtually removed plastic elements from the cult, effectively extirpating orgiastic, orchestral, and terpsichorean activities. It is of interest that Roman religion and Puritanism pursued similar paths in regard to esthetic elements, though for reasons quite different from the Jewish reasons. Thus, among the Jews the plastic arts, painting, and drama lacked those points of contact with religion which were elsewhere quite normal. This is the reason for the marked diminution of secular lyricism and especially of the erotic sublimation of sexuality, when contrasted with the marked sensuality of the earlier Song of Solomon. The basis of all this is to be found in the naturalism of the Jewish ethical treatment of sexuality.

All these traits of Judaism are characterized by one overall theme: that the mute, faithful, and questioning expectation of a redemption from the hellish character of the life enforced upon the people who had been chosen by God (and definitely chosen, despite their present status) was ultimately refocused upon the ancient promises and laws of the religion. Conversely, it was held—although there are no corresponding utterances of the rabbis on this point—that any uninhibited surrender to the artistic or poetic glorification of this world is completely vain and apt to divert the Jews from the ways and purposes of God. Even the purpose of the creation of this world had already on occasion been problematic to the Jews of the later Maccabean period.

Above all, what was lacking in Judaism was the decisive hallmark of that inner-worldly type of asceticism which is directed toward the control of this world: an integrated relationship to the world from the point of view of the individual's proof of salvation *(certitudo salutis),* which proof in conduct nurtures all else. Again in this important matter, what was ultimately decisive for Judaism was the pariah character of the religion and the promises of Yahweh. An ascetic management of this world, such as that characteristic of Calvinism, was the very last thing of which a traditionally pious Jew would have thought. He could not think of methodically controlling the present world, which was so topsy-turvey because of Israel's sins, and which could not be set right by any human action but only by some free miracle of God that could not be hastened. He could not take as his "mission," as the sphere of his religious "vocation," the bringing of this world and its very sins under the rational norms of the revealed divine will, for the glory of God and as an identifying mark of his own salvation. The pious Jew had a far more difficult inner destiny to overcome than did the Puritan, who could be certain of his election to the world beyond. It was incumbent upon the individual Jew to make peace with the fact that the world would remain recalcitrant to the promises of God as long as God permitted the world to stand as it is. The Jew's responsibility was to make peace with this recalcitrancy of the world, while finding contentment if God sent him grace and success in his dealings with the enemies of his people, toward whom he must act soberly and legalistically, in fulfillment of the injunctions of the rabbis. This meant acting toward non-Jews in an objective or impersonal manner, without love and without hate, solely in accordance with what was permissible.

The frequent assertion that Judaism required only an external observance of the law is incorrect. Naturally, this is the average tendency; but the requirements for real religious piety stood on a much higher plane. In any case, Judaic law fostered in its adherents a tendency to compare individual actions with each other and to compute the net result of them all. This conception of man's relationship to God as a bookkeeping operation of single good and evil acts with an uncertain total (a conception which may occasionally be found among the Puritans as well) may not have been the dominant official view of Judaism. Yet it was sufficient, together with the double-standard morality of Judaism, to prevent the development within Judaism of a methodical and ascetic orientation to the conduct of life on the scale that such an orientation developed in Puritanism. It is also important that in Judaism, as in Catholicism, the individual's activities in fulfilling particular religious injunctions were tantamount to his assuring his own chances of salvation. However, in both Judaism and Catholicism, God's grace was needed to supplement human inadequacy, although this dependence upon God's grace was not as universally recognized in Judaism as in Catholicism.

The ecclesiastical provision of grace was much less developed in Judaism, after the decline of the older Palestinian confessional, than in Catholicism. In practice, this resulted in the Jew's having a greater religious responsibility for himself. This responsibility for oneself and the absence of any mediating religious personality necessarily made the Jewish pattern of life more systematic and personally responsible than the corresponding Catholic pattern of life. Still, the methodical control of life was limited in Judaism by the absence of the distinctively ascetic motivation characteristic of Puritans and by the continued presence of Jewish internal morality's traditionalism, which in principle remained unbroken. To be sure, there were present in Judaism numerous single stimuli toward practices that might be called ascetic, but the unifying force of a basically ascetic religious motivation was lacking. The highest form of Jewish piety is found in the religious mood *(Stimmung)* and not in active behavior. How could it be possible for the Jew to feel that by imposing a new rational order upon the world he would become the human executor of God's will, when for the Jew this world was thoroughly contradictory, hostile, and—as he had known since the time of Hadrian—impossible to change by human action? This might have been possible for the Jewish freethinker, but not for the pious Jew.

Puritanism always felt its inner similarity to Judaism, but also felt the limits of this similarity. The similarity in principle between Christianity and Judaism, despite all their differences, remained the same for the Puritans as it had been for the Christian followers of

Paul. Both the Puritans and the pristine Christians saw the Jews as the people who had once and for all been chosen by God. But the unexampled activities of Paul had the following significant effects for early Christianity. On the one hand, Paul made the sacred book of the Jews into one of the sacred books of the Christians, and at the beginning the only one. He thereby erected a stout fence against all intrusions of Greek, especially Gnostic, intellectualism, as Wernle in particular has pointed out. But on the other hand, by the aid of a dialectic that only a rabbi could possess, Paul here and there broke through what was most distinctive and effective in the Jewish law, namely the tabooistic norms and the unique messianic promises. Since these taboos and promises linked the whole religious worth of the Jews to their pariah position, Paul's breakthrough was fateful in its effect. Paul accomplished this breakthrough by interpreting these promises as having been partly fulfilled and partly abrogated by the birth of Christ. He triumphantly employed the highly impressive proof that the patriarchs of Israel had lived in accordance with God's will long before the issuance of the Jewish taboos and messianic promises, showing that they found blessedness through faith, which was the surety of God's election.

The dynamic power behind the incomparable missionary labors of Paul was his offer to the Jews of a tremendous release, the release provided by the consciousness of having escaped the fate of pariah status. A Jew could henceforth be a Greek among Greeks as well as a Jew among Jews, and could achieve this within the paradox of faith rather than through an enlightened hostility to religion. This was the passionate feeling of liberation brought by Paul. The Jew could actually free himself from the ancient promises of his God, by placing his faith in the new savior who had believed himself abandoned upon the cross by that very God.

Various consequences flowed from this rending of the sturdy chains that had bound the Jews firmly to their pariah position. One was the intense hatred of this one man Paul by the Jews of the Diaspora, sufficiently authenticated as fact. Among the other consequences may be mentioned the oscillations and utter uncertainty of the pristine Christian community; the attempt of James and the "pillar apostles" to establish an ethical minimum of law which would be valid and binding for all, in harmony with Jesus' own layman's understanding of the law; and finally, the open hostility of the Jewish Christians toward Judaism. In every line that Paul wrote we can feel his overpowering joy at having emerged from the hopeless "slave law" into freedom, through the blood of the Messiah. The overall consequence was the possibility of a Christian world mission.

The Puritans, like Paul, rejected the Talmudic law and even the characteristic ritual laws of the Old Testament, while taking over and considering as binding—for all their elasticity—various other expressions of God's will witnessed in the Old Testament. As the Puritans took these over, they always conjoined norms derived from the New Testament, even in matters of detail. The Jews who were actually welcomed by Puritan nations, especially the Americans, were not pious Orthodox Jews but rather Reformed Jews who had abandoned Orthodoxy, Jews such as those of the present time who have been trained in the Educational Alliance, and finally baptized Jews. These groups of Jews were at first welcomed without any ado whatsoever and are even now welcomed fairly readily, so that they have been absorbed to the point of the absolute loss of any trace of difference. This situation in Puritan countries contrasts with the situation in Germany, where the Jews remain—even after long generations—"assimilated Jews." These phenomena clearly manifest the actual kinship of Puritanism to Judaism. Yet precisely the non-Jewish element in Puritanism enabled Puritanism to play its special role in the creation of the modern economic temper, and also to carry through the aforementioned absorption of Jewish proselytes, which was not accomplished by nations with other than Puritan orientations.

Translated by E. Fischoff

22. The Attitude of the Other World Religions (Islam, Buddhism, Christianity) to the Social and Economic Order

Islam, a comparatively late product of Near Eastern monotheism, in which Old Testament and Jewish-Christian elements played a very important role, "accommodated" itself to the world in a very unique sense. In the first Meccan period of Islam, the eschatological religion of Muhammad developed in pietistic urban conventicles which displayed a tendency to withdraw from the world. But in the subsequent developments in Medina and in the evolution of the early Islamic communities, the religion was transformed from its pristine form into a national Arabic warrior religion, and even later into a religion with very strong class emphases. Those followers whose conversion to Islam made possible the decisive success of the prophets were consistently members of powerful families.

The religious commandments of the holy law were not directed in the first instance to the purpose of conversion. Rather, the primary purpose was war "until they (the followers of alien religions of the book) will humbly pay the tribute *(jizyah);*" i.e., until Islam should rise to the top of this world's social scale, by exacting tribute from other religions. This is not the only factor that stamps Islam as the religion of a warrior class. Military booty is important in the ordinances, in the promises, and above all in the expectations characterizing even the most ancient period of the religion. Even the ultimate elements of its economic ethic were purely feudal. The most pious adherents of the religion in its first generation became the wealthiest, or more correctly, enriched themselves with military booty—in the widest sense—more than did other members of the faith.

The role played by wealth accruing from spoils of war and from political aggrandizement in Islam is diametrically opposed to the role played by wealth in the Puritan religion. The Muslim tradition depicts with pleasure the luxurious raiment, perfume, and meticulous beard-coiffure of the pious. The saying that "when god blesses a man with prosperity he likes to see the signs thereof visible upon him"—made by Muhammad, according to tradition, to well-circumstanced people who appeared before him in ragged attire—stands in extreme opposition to any Puritan economic ethic and thoroughly corresponds with feudal conceptions of status. This saying would mean, in our language, that a wealthy man is obligated "to live in keeping with his status." In the Quran, Muhammad is represented as completely rejecting every type of monasticism, though not all asceticism, for he did accord respect to fasting, begging, and penitential mortification. Muhammad's attitude in opposition to chastity sprang from personal motivations similar to those which are apparent in Luther's famous remarks so expressive of his strongly sensual nature. A comparable attitude comes to light in the Talmud's expression of the conviction that whoever has not married by a certain age must be a sinner. But we must regard as unique in the hagiology of ethical religions of salvation Muhammad's dictum expressing doubt about the ethical character of a person who has abstained from eating flesh for forty days; as well as the reply of a renowned pillar of ancient Islam, celebrated by some as a Mahdi, to the question why he, unlike his father Ali, had used cosmetics for his hair: "In order to be more successful with women."

But Islam was never really a religion of salvation; the ethical concept of salvation was actually alien to Islam. The god it taught was a lord of unlimited power, although merciful, the fulfillment of whose commandments was not beyond human power. An essentially political character marked all the chief ordinances of Islam: the elimination of private feuds in the interest of increasing the group's striking power against external foes; the proscription of illegitimate forms of sexual behavior and the regulation of legitimate sexual relations along strongly patriarchal lines (actually creating sexual privileges only for the wealthy, in view of the facility of divorce and the maintenance of concubinage with female slaves); the prohibition of usury; the prescription of taxes for war; and the injunction to support the poor. Equally political in character is the distinctive religious obligation in Islam, its only required dogma: the recognition of Allah as the one god and of Muhammad as his prophet. In addition, there were the obligations to journey to Mecca once during a lifetime, to fast by day during the month of fasting, to attend services once a week, and to observe the obligation of daily prayers. Finally, Islam imposed such requirements for everyday living as the wearing of distinctive clothing (a requirement that even today has important economic consequences whenever savage tribes are converted to Islam) and the avoidance of certain unclean foods, of wine, and of gambling. The restriction against gambling obviously had important consequences for the religion's attitude toward speculative business enterprises.

There was nothing in ancient Islam like an individual quest for salvation, nor was there any mysticism. The religious promises in the earliest period of Islam pertained to this world. Wealth, power, and glory were all martial promises, and even the world beyond is pictured in Islam as a soldier's sensual paradise. Moreover, the original Islamic conception of sin has a similar feudal orientation. The depiction of the prohpet of Islam as devoid of sin is a late theological construction, scarcely consistent with the actual nature of Muhammad's strong sensual passions and his explosions of wrath over very small provocations. Indeed, such a picture is strange even to the Quran, for even after Muhammad's transfer to Medina he lacked any sort of tragic sense of sin. The original feudal conception of sin remained dominant in orthodox Islam, for which sin is a composite of ritual impurity, ritual sacrilege (*shirk*, i.e., polytheism), disobedience to the positive injunctions of the prophet; and the dishonoring of a noble class by infractions of convention or etiquette. Islam displays other characteristics of a distinctively feudal spirit: the obviously unquestioned acceptance of slavery, serfdom, and polygamy; the disesteem for and subjection of women; the essentially ritualistic character of religious obligations; and finally, the great simplicity of religious requirements and the even greater simplicity of the modest ethical requirements.

Islam was not brought any closer to Judaism and to Christianity in decisive matters by such Islamic developments as the achievement of great scope through the rise of theological and juristic casuistry, the appearance of both pietistic and enlightenment schools of philosophy (following the intrusion of Persian Sufism, derived from India), and the formation of the order of dervishes (which shows strong traces of Hindu influence). Judaism and Christianity were specifically civic and urban religions, but the city had only political importance for Islam. To be sure, a certain sobriety in the conduct of life might be produced by the nature of the official cult in Islam and by its sexual and ritual commandments. But the lower middle class was largely the carrier of the dervish religion, which was disseminated practically everywhere and gradually grew in power, finally surpassing the official ecclesiastical religion. This type of religion, with its orgiastic and mystical elements, with its essentially irrational and extraordinary character, and with its official and thoroughly traditionalistic ethic of everyday life, became influential in Islam's missionary enterprise because of its great simplicity. It directed the conduct of life into paths whose effect was plainly opposite to the methodical control of life found among Puritans, and indeed, found in every type of asceticism oriented toward the control of the world.

Islam, in contrast to Judaism, lacked the requirement of a comprehensive knowledge of the law and lacked that intellectual training in casuistry which nurtured the rationalism of Judaism. The ideal personality type in the religion of Islam was not the scholarly scribe *(Literat)*, but the warrior. Moreover, Islam lacked all those promises of a messianic realm upon earth which in Israel were linked with meticulous fidelity to the law, and which—together with election, sin, the priestly doctrine of history, and the dispersion of the Jews—determined the pariah character of the Jewish religion, so fraught with consequences.

To be sure, there were ascetic sects among the Muslims. Large groups of ancient Islamic warriors were characterized by a trend toward simplicity; this prompted them from the outset to oppose the rule of the Umayyads. The latter's merry enjoyment of the world presented the strongest contrast to the rigid discipline of the encampment fortresses in which Umar had concentrated Islamic warriors in the conquered domains; in their stead there now arose a very different feudal aristocracy. But this was the asceticism of a military caste, of a martial order of knights, not of monks. Certainly it was not a middle-class ascetic systematization of the conduct of life. Moreoever, it was effective only periodically, and even then it tended to merge into fatalism. We have already spoken of the quite different effect which is engendered in such circumstances by a belief in providence. Islam was diverted completely from any really methodical control of life by the advent of the cult of saints, and finally by magic.

At the opposite extreme from systems of religious ethics preoccupied with the control of economic affairs within the world stands the ultimate ethic of world-rejection, the mystical illuminative concentration of authentic ancient Buddhism (naturally not the completely altered manifestations Buddhism assumed in Tibetan, Chinese, and Japanese popular religions). Even this most world-rejecting ethic is "rational," in the sense that it produces a constantly alert control of all natural instinctive drives, though for purposes entirely different from those of inner-worldly asceticism. Salvation is sought, not from sin and suffering alone, but also from ephemeralness as such; escape from the wheel of *karma* causality and arrival into eternal rest are sought. This search is, and can only be, the highly individualized task of a particular person. There is no predestination, but neither is there any divine grace, any prayer, or any religious service. Rewards and punishments for every good and every evil deed are automatically established by the *karma* causality of the cosmic mechanism of compensation. This retribution is always proportional, and hence always limited in time. So long as the individual is driven to action by the thirst for life, he must experience in full measure the fruits of his behavior in ever-new human existences. Whether his momentary human situation is animal, heavenly, or hellish, he necessarily creates new chances for himself in the future. The most noble enthusiasm and the most sordid sensuality lead equally into new existence in this chain of individuation (it is quite incorrect to term this process transmigration of souls, since Buddhist metaphysics knows nothing of a soul). This process of individuation continues on as long as the thirst for life, in this world or in the world beyond, is not absolutely extinguished. The process is but perpetuated by the individual's impotent struggle for his personal existence with all its illusions, above all the illusion of a distinctive soul or personality.

All rational purposive activity is regarded as leading away from salvation, except of course the subjective activity of concentrated contemplation, which empties the soul of the passion for life and every connection with worldly interests. The achievement of salvation is possible for only a few, even of those who have resolved to live in poverty, chastity, and unemployment (for labor is purposive action), and hence in mendicancy. These chosen few are required to wander ceaselessly—except at the time of the heavy rains—freed from all personal ties to family and world, pursuing the goal of mystical illumination by fulfilling the injunctions relating to the correct path *(dharma)*. When such salvation is gained, the deep joy and tender, undifferentiated love characterizing such illumination provides the highest blessing possible in this existence, short of absorption into the eternal dreamless sleep of *Nirvana*, the only state in which no change occurs. All other human beings may improve their situations in future existences by approximating the prescriptions of the rule of life and by avoiding major sins in this existence. Such future existences are inevitable, according to the *karma* doctrine of causality, because the ethical account has not been straightened out, the thirst for life has not been "abreacted," so to speak (acted out). For most people, therefore, some new individuation is inevitable when the present life has ended, and truly eternal salvation remains inaccessible.

There is no path leading from this only really consistent position of world-flight to any economic ethic or to any rational social ethic. The universal mood of pity, extending to all creatures, cannot be the carrier of any rational behavior and in fact leads away from it. This mood of pity is the logical consequence of contemplative mysticism's position regarding the solidarity of all living, and hence transitory, beings. This solidarity follows from the common *karma* causality which overarches all living beings. In Buddhism, the psychological basis for this universal pity is the religion's mystical, euphoric, universal, and acosmistic love.

Buddhism is the most systematic of the doctrines of salvation produced in large numbers at many periods by the elite intellectual classes of Hinduism. Its cool and proud emancipation of the individual from life as such, which in effect stood the individual on his own feet, could never become a popular salvation faith. Buddhism's influence beyond the circle of the educated was due to the tremendous prestige traditionally enjoyed by the *shramana* (ascetics), who possessed magical traits of anthropolatry. As soon as Buddhism became a missionizing popular religion, it duly transformed itself into a savior religion based on *karma* compensation, with hopes for the world beyond guaranteed by devotional techniques, cultic and sacramental grace, and deeds of mercy. Naturally, Buddhism also tended to welcome purely magical notions.

In India itself, Buddhism met competition among the upper classes from a renascent philosophy of salvation based on the Vedas; and met competition among the masses from Hinduistic salvation religions, especially the various forms of Vishnuism, from Tantristic magic, and from orgiastic mystery religions, notably the *bhakti* piety (love of god). In Lamaism, Buddhism became the purely monastic religion of a theocracy which controlled the laity by ecclesiastical powers of a thoroughly magical nature. Wherever Buddhism was diffused in the Orient, its idiosyncratic character underwent striking transformation as it competed and entered into diverse combinations with Chinese Taoism, thus becoming the region's typical mass religion, which pointed beyond this world and the ancestral cult and which distributed grace and salvation.

At all events, no motivation toward a rational system for the methodical control of life flowed from Buddhist, Taoist, or Hindu piety. Hindu piety in particular, as we have already suggested, maintained the strongest possible power of tradition, since the presuppositions of Hinduism constituted the most consistent religious expression of the organic view of society. The existing order of the world was provided absolutely unconditional justification, in terms of the mechanical operation of a proportional retribution in the distribution of power and happiness to individuals on the basis of their merits and failures in their earlier existences.

All these popular religions of Asia left room for the acquisitive drive of the tradesman, the interest of the artisan in sustenance *(Nahrungs-Interesse)*, and the traditionalism of the peasant. These popular religions also left undisturbed both philosophical speculation and the conventional class-oriented life patterns of privileged groups. These class-oriented patterns of the privileged evinced feudal characteristics in Japan; patrimonial, bureaucratic, and hence strongly utilitarian features in China; and a mixture of knightly, patrimonial, and intellectualistic traits in India. None of these mass religions of Asia, however, provided the motives or orientations for a rationalized ethical patterning of the creaturely world in accordance with divine commandments. Rather, they all accepted this world as eternally given, and so the best of all possible worlds. The only choice open to the sages, who possessed the highest type of piety, was whether to accommodate themselves to the Tao, the impersonal order of the world and the only thing specifically divine, or to save themselves from the inexorable chain of causality by passing into the only eternal being, the dreamless sleep of *Nirvana*.

"Capitalism" existed among all these religions, even those religions of the type known in occidental Antiquity and the medieval period. But there was no development toward modern capitalism, nor even any stirrings in that direction, in these religions. Above all, there evolved no "capitalist spirit," in the sense that is distinctive of ascetic Protestantism. But to assume that the Hindu, Chinese, or Muslim merchant, trader, artisan, or coolie was animated by a weaker "acquisitive drive" than the ascetic Protestant is to fly in the face of the facts. Indeed, the reverse would seem to be true, for what is distinctive of Puritanism is the rational and ethical limitation of the quest for profit. There is no proof whatever that a weaker natural potentiality for technical and economic rationalism was responsible for the actual differences in this respect. At the present time, all these peoples import economic rationalism as the most important product of the Occident, and their capitalistic development is impeded only by the presence among them of rigid traditions, such as existed among us in the Middle Ages, not by any lack of ability or will. The impediments to the development of capitalism must be sought primarily in the domain of religion, although certain purely political factors, such as the inner structural forms of domination (which we shall discuss later on), also played important roles.

Only ascetic Protestantism completely eliminated magic and the supernatural quest for salvation, of which the highest form was intellectualist, contemplative illumination. It alone created the religious motivations for seeking salvation primarily through immersion in one's worldly vocation *(Beruf)*. This Protestant stress upon the methodically rationalized fulfillment of one's vocational responsibility was diametrically opposite to Hinduism's strongly traditionalistic concept of vocations. For the various popular religions of Asia, in contrast to ascetic Protestantism, the world remained a great enchanted garden, in which the practical way to orient oneself, or to find security in this world or the next, was to revere or coerce the spirits and seek salvation through ritualistic, idolatrous, or sacramental procedures. No path led from the magical religiosity of the nonintellectual classes of Asia to a rational, methodical control of life. Nor did any path lead to that methodical control from the world–accommodation of Confucianism, from the world-rejection of Buddhism, from the world-conquest of Islam, or from the messianic expectations and economic pariah law of Judaism.

The second great religion of world-rejection, in our special sense of the term, was early Christianity, at the cradle of which magic and belief in demons were also present. Its savior was primarily a magician whose magical charisma was an ineluctable source of his unique feeling of individuality. But the absolutely unique religious promises of Judaism contributed to the determination of the distinctive character of early Christianity. It will be recalled that Jesus appeared during the period of the most intensive messianic expectations. Still another factor contributing to the distinctive message of Christianity was the unique concern for erudition in the law characteristic of Jewish piety. The Christian evangel arose in opposition to this legalistic erudition, as a nonintellectual's proclamation directed to nonintellectuals, to the "poor in spirit." Jesus understood and interpreted the "law," from which he desired to remove not even a letter, in a fashion common to the lowly and the unlearned, the pious folk of the countryside and the small towns, who understood the law in their own way and in accordance with the needs of their own occupations. This handling of the law presented a striking contrast to the treatments of the law by the Hellenized, wealthy and upper-class people and by the erudite scholars and Pharisees trained in casuistry. Jesus' interpretation of the Jewish law was milder than theirs in regard to ritual prescriptions, particularly in regard to the keeping of the Sabbath, but stricter than theirs in other respects, e.g., in regard to the grounds for divorce. There already appears to have been an anticipation of the Pauline view that the requirements of the Mosaic law were conditioned by the sinfulness of the superficially pious. There were, in any case, instances in which Jesus squarely opposed specific injunctions of the ancient tradition.

Jesus' distinctive feeling of self-esteem did not come from anything like a "proletarian instinct" and did not come from knowledge that the way to God necessarily led through him, because of his identity with the divine patriarch. The basis of Jesus' distinctive self-esteem was his knowledge that he, a non-scholar, possessed both the charisma requisite for the control of demons and a tremendous preaching ability, far surpassing that of any scholar or Pharisee. Another basis of his self-esteem was his power to exorcise demons, but this power was only operative with respect to people who believed in him. His power to exorcise demons was inoperative with respect to heathens, his own family, the natives of his own town, the wealthy and high-born of the land, the scholars, and the legalistic virtuosi—among none of these did he find the faith that gave him his magical power to work miracles. He did find such a faith among the poor, the oppressed, publicans and sinners, and even Roman soldiers. These various charismatic powers were the absolutely decisive components in Jesus' feelings concerning his messiahship. It should never be forgotten that these powers of his own were the fundamental issue in his denunciation of the Galilean cities and in his angry curse upon the recalcitrant fig tree. His feeling about his own powers also explains why the election of Israel became ever more problematical to him and the importance of the Temple ever more dubious, while the rejection of the Pharisees and the scholars became increasingly certain to him.

Jesus recognized two absolutely mortal sins. One was the "sin against the spirit" committed by the scriptural scholar who disesteemed charisma and its bearers. The other was unbrotherly arrogance, such as the arrogance of the intellectual toward the poor in spirit, when the intellectual hurls at his brother the exclamation "Thou fool!" This anti-intellectualist rejection of scholarly arrogance and of Hellenic and rabbinic wisdom is the only "class element" of Jesus' message, though it is very distinctive. In general, Jesus' message is far from being a simple proclamation for every Tom, Dick, and Harry, for all the weak of the world. True, the yoke is light, but only for those who can once again become as little children. In truth, Jesus set up the most tremendous requirements for salvation; his doctrine has real aristocratic qualities.

Nothing was further from Jesus' mind than the notion of the universalism of divine grace. On the contrary, he directed his whole preaching against this notion. Few are chosen to pass through the narrow gate, to repent and to believe in Jesus. God himself impedes the salvation of the others and hardens their hearts, and naturally it is the proud and the rich who are most overtaken by this fate. Of course this element is not new, since it can be found in the older prophecies. The older Jewish prophets had taught that, in view of the arrogant behavior of the highly placed, the Messiah would be a king who would enter Jerusalem upon the beast of burden used by the poor. This general orientation implies no "social equality." Jesus lodged with the wealthy, which was ritually reprehensible in the eyes of the virtuosi of the law, but when he bade the rich young man give away his wealth, Jesus expressly enjoined this act only if the young man wished to be "perfect," i.e., a disciple. Complete emancipation from all ties of the world, from family as well as possessions, such as we find in the teachings of the Buddha and similar prophets, was required only of disciples. Yet, although all things are possible for God, continued attachment to Mammon constitutes one of the most difficult impediments to salvation into the Kingdom of God—for attachment to Mammon diverts the individual from religious salvation, the most important thing in the world.

Jesus nowhere explicitly states that preoccupation with wealth leads to unbrotherliness, but this notion is at the heart of the matter, for the prescribed injunctions definitely contain the primordial ethic of mutual help which is characteristic of neighborhood associations of poorer people. The chief difference is that in Jesus' message acts of mutual help have been systematized into an ethic with a religious mood and a fraternalistic sentiment of love. The injunction of mutual help was also construed universalistically, extended to everyone. The "neighbor" is the one nearest at hand. Indeed, the notion of mutual help was enlarged into an acosmistic paradox, based on the axiom that God alone can and will reward. Unconditional forgiveness, unconditional charity, unconditional love even of enemies, unconditional suffering of injustice without requiting evil by force—these products of a mystically conditioned acosmism of love indeed constituted demands for religious heroism. But it must not be overlooked, as it so often has been, that Jesus combined acosmistic love with the Jewish notion of retribution. Man must not boast of his virtue in having performed any of the aforementioned deeds of love, since his boasting would presuppose his subsequent reward, while it is believed that God alone will one day compensate, avenge, and reward. To amass treasures in heaven one must in this world lend money to those from whom no repayment can be expected; otherwise, there is no merit in the deed. A strong emphasis upon the just equalization of destinies was expressed by Jesus in the legend of Lazarus and elsewhere. From this perspective alone, wealth is already a dangerous gift.

But Jesus held in general that what is most decisive for salvation is an absolute indifference to the world and its concerns. The kingdom of heaven, a realm of joy upon earth, utterly without suffering and sin, is at hand; indeed, this generation will not die before seeing it. It will come like a thief at night; it is already in the process of appearing among mankind. Let man be free with the wealth of Mammon, instead of clutching it fast; let man give to Caesar that which is Caesar's own—for what profit is there in such matters? Let man pray to God for daily bread and remain unconcerned for the morrow. No human action can accelerate the coming of the kingdom, but man should prepare himself for its coming. Although this message did not formally abrogate law, it did place the emphasis throughout upon religious sentiment. The entire content of the law and the prophets was condensed into the simple commandment to love God and one's fellow man, to which was added the one far-reaching conception that the true religious mood is to be judged by its fruits, by its faithful demonstration *(Bewährung)*.

The visions of the resurrection, doubtless under the influence of the widely diffused soteriological myths, generated a tremendous growth in pneumatic manifestations of charisma; in the formation of communities, beginning with Jesus' own family, which originally had not shared Jesus' faith; and in missionary activity among the heathens. Though nascent Christianity maintained continuity with the older Jewish prophecies even after the fateful conversion of Paul had resulted in a breaking away from the pariah religion, still two new attitudes toward the world became decisive in the Christian missionary communities. One was the expectation of the Second Coming, and the other was the recognition of the tremendous importance of charismatic gifts of the spirit. The world would remain as it was until the master would come again. The individual was required to abide in his position and in his calling (Kinois), subordinated to the ruling authority, save where it commanded him to perpetrate a sinful deed.

Translated by Ephraim Fischoff

23. Rationality and Formalism in Law

Both lawmaking and lawfinding may be either rational or irrational. They are "formally irrational" when one applies in lawmaking or lawfinding means which cannot be controlled by the intellect; for instance when recourse is had to oracles or substitutes therefor. Lawmaking and lawfinding are "substantively irrational" on the other hand to the extent that decision is influenced by concrete factors of the particular case as evaluated upon an ethical, emotional, or political basis rather than by general norms. "Rational" lawmaking and lawfinding may be of either a formal or a substantive kind. All formal law is, formally at least, relatively rational. Law, however, is "formal" to the extent that, in both substantive and procedural matters, only unambiguous general characteristics of the facts of the case are taken into account. This formalism can, again, be of two different kinds. It is possible that the legally relevant characteristics are of a tangible nature, (i.e., that they are perceptible as sense data). This adherence to external characteristics of the facts, for instance, the utterance of certain words, the execution of a signature, or the performance of a certain symbolic act with a fixed meaning, represents the most rigorous type of legal formalism. The other type of formalistic law is found where the legally relevant characteristics of the facts are disclosed through the logical analysis of meaning and where, accordingly, definitely fixed legal concepts in the form of highly abstract rules are formulated and applied. This process of "logical rationality" diminishes the significance of extrinsic elements and thus softens the rigidity of concrete formalism. But the contrast to "substantive rationality" is sharpened, because the latter means that the decision of legal problems is influenced by norms different from those obtained through logical generalization of abstract interpretations of meaning. The norms to which substantive rationality accords predominance include ethical imperatives, utilitarian and other expediential rules, and political maxims, all of which diverge from the formalism of the "external characteristics" variety as well as from that which uses logical abstraction. However, the peculiarly professional, legalistic, and abstract approach to law in the modern sense is possible only in the measure that the law is formal in character. Insofar as the absolute formalism of classification according to "sense-data characteristics" prevails, it exhausts itself in casuistry. Only that abstract method which employs the logical interpretation of meaning allows the execution of the specifically systematic task, i.e., the collection and rationalization by logical means of all the several rules recognized as legally valid into an internally consistent complex of abstract legal propositions.

Translated by Edward Shils
and Max Rheinstern

24. Formal and Substantive Rationalization of Law

The older forms of popular justice had originated in *conciliatory proceedings between kinship-groups.* The primitive formalistic irrationality of these older forms of justice was everywhere *cast off under the impact of the authority of princes or magistrates,* or, in certain situations, of an *organized priesthood*. With this impact, the substance of the law, too, was lastingly influenced, although the character of this influence varied with the various types of authority. The more rational the authority exercising the administrative machinery of the princes or hierarchs became, that is, the greater the extent to which administrative "officials" were used in the exercise of the power, the greater was the likelihood that the legal procedure would also become rational both in form and substance. To the extent to which the rationality of the organization of authority increased, irrational forms of procedure were eliminated and the substantive law was systematized, i.e., the law as a whole was rationalized. This process occurred, for instance, in Antiquity in the *jus honorarium* and the praetorian remedies,[1] in the capitularies of the Frankish Kings, in the procedural innovations of the English Kings and Lords Chancellor, or in the inquisitorial procedure of the Catholic Church.[2] However, these rationalizing tendencies were not part of an articulate and unambiguous policy on the part of the wielders of power; they were rather driven in this direction by the needs of their own rational administration, as, for instance, in the case of the administrative machinery of the Papacy; or by powerful interest groups with whom they were allied and to whom rationality in substantive law and procedure constituted an advantage, as, for instance, to the bourgeois classes of Rome, of the late Middle Ages, or of modern times. Where these interests were absent the secularization of the law and the growth of a specialized, strictly formal mode of juridical thought either remained in an incipient stage or was even positively counteracted. In general terms, this may be attributed to the fact that the rationality of ecclesiastical hierarchies as well as of patrimonial sovereigns is substantive in character, so that their aim is not that of achieving that highest degree of formal juridical precision which would maximize the chances for the correct prediction of legal consequences and for the rational systematization of law and procedure. The aim is rather to find a type of law which is most appropriate to the expediential and ethical goals of the authorities in question. To these carriers of legal development the self-contained and specialized "juridical" treatment of legal questions is an alien idea, and they are not at all interested in any separation of law from ethics. This is particularly true, generally speaking, of theocratically influenced legal systems, which are characterized by a combination of legal rules and ethical demands. Yet in the course of this kind of rationalization of legal thinking, on the one hand, and of the forms of social relationships, on the other, the most diverse consequences could emerge from the nonjuridical components of a legal doctrine of priestly make. One of these possible consequences was the separation of *fas,* the religious command, from *jus,* the established law for the settlement of such human conflicts which had no religious relevance.[3] In this situation, it was possible for *jus* to pass through an independent course of development into a rational and formal legal system, in which emphasis might be either upon logical or upon empirical elements. This actually happened both in Rome and in the Middle Ages. We shall discuss later the ways in which the relationship between the religiously fixed and the freely established components of the law were determined in these cases. As we shall see hereafter, it was quite possible, as thinking became increasingly secular, for the sacred law to encounter as a rival, or to be replaced by, a "natural law" which would operate beside the positive law partly as an ideal postulate and partly as a doctrine with varying actual influence upon legislation or legal practice. It was also possible, however, that the religious prescriptions were never differentiated from secular rules and that the characteristically theocratic combination of religious and ritualistic prescriptions with legal rules remained unchanged. In this case, there arose an inextricable conglomeration of ethical and legal duties, moral exhortations and legal commandments without formalized explicitness and the result was a specifically nonformal type of law. Just which of these two possibilities actually occurred depended upon the already-mentioned characteristics of the religion in question and the principles that governed its relation to the legal system and the state; in part it depended upon the power position of the priesthood vis-à-vis the state; and finally, upon the structure of the state. It was because of their special structure of authority that in almost all the Asiatic civilizations the last-mentioned of these courses of development came to emerge and persist.

But although certain features in the logical structure of different legal systems may be similar, they may nevertheless be the result of diverse types of authority. Authoritarian powers, especially those resting on personal loyalty, and more particularly theocracy and patrimonial monarchy, have usually created a nonformal type of law. But a nonformal type of law may also be produced by certain types of democracy. The explanation lies in the fact that not only such power-wielders as hierarchs and despots, and particularly enlightened despots, but also democratic demagogues may refuse to be bound by formal rules, even by those they have made themselves, excepting, however, those norms which they regard as religiously sacred and hence as absolutely binding. They all are confronted by the inevitable conflict between an abstract formalism of legal certainty and their desire to realize substantive goals. Juridical formalism enables the legal system to operate like a technically rational machine. Thus it guarantees to individuals and groups within the system a relative maximum of freedom, and greatly increases for them the possibility of predicting the legal consequences of their actions. Procedure becomes a specific type of pacified contest, bound to fixed and inviolable "rules of the game."

Primitive procedures for adjusting conflicts of interest between kinship groups are characterized by rigorously formalistic rules of evidence. The same is true of judicial procedure in *Dinggenossenschaften*. These rules were at first influenced by magical beliefs which required that the questions of evidence should be asked in the proper way and by the proper party. Even afterwards it took a long time for procedure to develop the idea that a fact, as understood today, could be "established" by a rational procedure, particularly by the examination of witnesses, which is the most important method now, not to speak at all of circumstantial evidence. The compurgators of earlier epochs did not swear that a statement of fact was true but confirmed the rightness of their side by exposing themselves to the divine wrath. We may observe that this practice was not much less realistic than that of our days when a great many people, perhaps a majority, believe their task as witnesses to be simply that of "swearing" as to which party is "in the right." In ancient law, proof was therefore not regarded as a "burden" but rather as a "right" of one or the other of the contending parties, and ancient law was liberal in allowing a party this right. The judge, however, was strictly bound by rules and the traditional methods of proof. The modern theory of as late a period as that of common-law procedure[4] is different from ancient procedure only in that it would treat proof as a burden. It, too, binds the judge to the motions of, and the evidence offered by, the parties and, indeed, the same principle applies to the entire conduct of the suit: in accordance with the principle of adversary procedure the judge has to wait for the motions of the parties. Facts which are neither stipulated nor alleged and proved, and facts which remain undisclosed by the recognized methods of proof, be they rational or irrational, do not exist as far as the judge is concerned, who aims at establishing only that relative truth which is attainable within the limits set by the procedural acts of the parties.

Exactly alike in this respect were the oldest clear-cut forms of adjudication, i.e., arbitration and composition between contending kinship groups, with oracle or ordeal constituting the trial procedure. This ancient legal procedure was rigorously formal like all activities oriented toward the invocation of magical or divine powers; but, by means of the irrational supernatural character of the decisive acts of procedure, it tried to obtain the substantively "right" decision. When, however, the authority of, and the belief in, these irrational powers came to be lost and when they were replaced by rational proof and the logical derivation of decisions, the formalistic adjudication had to become a mere contest between litigants, regulated so as to aim at the relatively optimal chance of finding the truth. The promotion of the progress of the suit is the concern of the parties rather than that of the state. They are not compelled by the judge to do anything they do not wish to do at their own initiative. It is for this very reason that the judge cannot comply with the quest for the optimal realization of substantive demands of a political, ethical or effective character by means of an adjudication which could give effect to considerations of concrete expediency or equity in individual cases. Formal justice guarantees the maximum freedom for the interested parties to represent their formal legal interests. But because of the unequal distribution of economic power, which the system of formal justice legalizes, this very freedom must time and again produce consequences which are contrary to the substantive postulates of religious ethics or of political expediency. Formal justice is thus repugnant to all authoritarian powers, theocratic as well as patriarchic, because it diminishes the dependency of the individual upon the grace and power of the authorities.[5] To democracy, however, it has been repugnant because it decreases the dependency of the legal practice and therewith of the individuals upon the decisions of their fellow citizens.[6] Furthermore, the development of the trial into a peaceful contest of conflicting interests can contribute to the further concentration of economic and social power. In all these cases formal justice, due to its necessarily abstract character, infringes upon the ideals of substantive justice. It is precisely this abstract character which constitutes the decisive merit of formal justice to those who wield the economic power at any given time and who are therefore interested in its unhampered operation, and also to those who on ideological grounds attempt to break down authoritarian control or to restrain irrational mass emotions for the purpose of opening up individual opportunities and liberating capacities. To all these groups nonformal justice simply represents the likelihood of absolute arbitrariness and subjectivistic instability. Among those groups who favor formal justice we must include all those political and economic interest groups to whom the stability and predictability of legal procedure are of very great importance, i.e., particularly rational, economic, and political organizations intended to have a permanent character. Above all, those in possession of economic power look upon a formal rational administration of justice as a guarantee of "freedom," a value which is repudiated not only by theocratic or patriarchal-authoritarian groups but, under certain conditions, also by democratic groups. Formal justice and the "freedom" which it guarantees are indeed rejected by all groups ideologically interested in substantive justice. Such groups are better served by khadi-justice than by the formal type. The popular justice of the direct Attic democracy, for example, was decidedly a form of khadi-justice. Modern trial by jury, too, is frequently khadi-justice in actual practice although, perhaps, not according to formal law; even in this highly formalized type of a limited adjudication one can observe a tendency to be bound by formal legal rules only to the extent directly required by procedural technique. Quite generally, in all forms of popular justice decisions are reached on the basis of concrete, ethical, or political considerations or of feelings oriented toward social justice. The latter type of justice prevailed particularly in Athens, but it can be found even today. In this respect, there are similar tendencies displayed by popular democracy on the one hand and the authoritarian power of theocracy or of patriarchal monarchs on the other.

When, for example, French jurors, contrary to formal law, regularly acquit a husband who has killed his wife's paramour caught in the act, they are doing exactly what Frederick the Great did when he dispensed "royal justice" for the benefit of Arnold, the miller.[7]

The distinctive characteristic of a theocratic administration of justice consists entirely in the primacy of concrete ethical considerations; its indifference or aversion to formalism is limited only insofar as the rules of the sacred law are explicitly formulated. But insofar as norms of the latter apply, the theocratic type of law results in the exact opposite, viz., a law which, in order to be adaptable to changing circumstances, develops an extremely formalistic casuistry. Secular, patrimonial-authoritarian administration of justice is much freer than theocratic justice, even where it has to conform with tradition, which usually allows quite a degree of flexibility.

Finally, the administration of justice by *honoratiores* presents two aspects depending on what legal interests there are involved; those of the honoratiores' own class or those of the class dominated by them. In England, for instance, all cases coming before the central courts were adjudicated in a strictly formalistic way. But the courts of justices of the peace, which dealt with the daily troubles and misdemeanors of the masses, were informal and representative of khadi-justice to an extent completely unknown on the Continent. Furthermore, the high cost of litigation and legal services amounted for those who could not afford to purchase them to a denial of justice, which was rather similar to that which existed, for other reasons, in the judicial system of the Roman Republic.[8] This denial of justice was in close conformity with the interests of the propertied, especially the capitalistic, classes. But such a dual judicial policy of formal adjudication of disputes within the upper class, combined with arbitrariness or de facto denegation of justice for the economically weak, is not always possible. If it cannot be had, capitalistic interests will fare best under a rigorously formal system of adjudication, which applies in all cases and operates under the adversary system of procedure. In any case adjudication by *honoratiores* inclines to be essentially empirical, and its procedure is complicated and expensive. It may thus well stand in the way of the interests of the bourgeois classes and it may indeed be said that England achieved capitalistic supremacy among the nations not because but rather in spite of its judicial system. For these very reasons the bourgeois strata have generally tended to be intensely interested in a rational procedural system and therefore in a systematized and unambiguously formal and purposefully constructed substantive law which eliminates both obsolete traditions and arbitrariness and in which rights can have their source exclusively in general objective norms. Such a systematically codified law was thus demanded by the English Puritans, the Roman Plebeians[9] and the German bourgeoisie of the fifteenth century.[10] But in all these cases such a system was still a long way off.

Translated by Edward Shils
and Max Rheinstein

25. The Formal Qualities of Modern Law

Specialization in Modern Law. As we have seen, the specifically modern Occidental type of administration of justice has arisen on the basis of rational and systematic legislation. However, its basic formal qualities are by no means unambiguously definable. Indeed, this ambiguity is a direct result of more recent developments.

The ancient principles which were decisive for the interlocking of "right" and law have disappeared, especially the idea that one's right has a "valid" quality only by virtue of one's membership in a group of persons by whom this quality is monopolized. To the past now also belongs the tribal or status-group quality of the sum total of a person's rights and, with it, their "particularity" as it once existed on the basis of free association or of usurped or legalized privilege. Equally gone are the estatist and other special courts and procedures. Yet neither all special and personal law nor all special jurisdictions have disappeared completely. On the contrary, very recent legal developments have brought an increasing specialization within the legal system. Only the principle of demarcation of the various spheres has been characteristically changed. A typical case is that of commercial law, which is, indeed, one of the most important instances of modern specialization. Under the German Commercial Code this special law applies to certain types of contracts,[1] the most important of which is the contract for acquisition of goods with the intention of profitable resale. This definition of commercial contract is entirely in accordance with a rationalized legal system; the definition does not refer to formal qualities, but to the intended functional meaning of the concrete transaction. On the other hand, commercial law also applies to certain categories of persons whose decisive characteristic consists in the fact that contracts are made by them in the course of their business.[2] What is thus really decisive for the demarcation of the sphere of this type of law is the concept of "enterprise." An enterprise is a commercial enterprise when transactions of such peculiar kind are its constitutive elements. Thus every contract which "belongs" substantively, i.e., in its intention, to a commercial enterprise is under the Commercial Code, even though, when regarded alone and by itself, it does not belong to that category of transactions which are generically defined as commercial and even though, in a particular case, such a contract may happen to be made by a nonmerchant. The application of this body of special law is thus determined either by substantive qualities of an individual transaction, especially its intended meaning, or by the objective association of a transaction with the rational organization of an enterprise. It is not determined, however, by a person's membership in an estate legally constituted by free agreement or privilege, which was in the past the operative factor for the application of a special law.

Commercial law, then, inasmuch as its application is personally delimited, is a class law rather than a status-group law. However, this contrast with the past is but a relative one. Indeed, so far as the law of commerce and the law of other purely economic "occupations" are concerned, the principle of jurisdictional delimitation has always had a purely substantive character, which, while often varying in externals, has essentially been the same throughout. But those particularities in the legal system which constituted a definite status law were more significant both quantitatively and qualitatively. Besides, even the vocational special jurisdictions, so far as their jurisdictions did not depend upon the litigants' membership in a certain corporate body, have usually depended upon mere formal criteria such as acquisition of a license or a privilege. For example, under the new German Commercial Code, a person is characterized as a merchant by the mere fact that he is listed in the register of commercial firms. The personal scope of application of the commercial law is thus determined by a purely formal test, while in other respects its sphere is delimited by the economic purpose which a given transaction purports to achieve. The spheres of the special laws applicable to other occupational groups are also predominantly defined along substantive or functional criteria, and it is only under certain circumstances that applicability is governed by formal tests. Many of these modern special laws are also combined with special courts and procedures of their own.[3]

Mainly two causes are responsible for the emergence of these particularistic laws. In the first place, they have been a result of the occupational differentiation and the increasing attention which commercial and industrial pressure groups have obtained for themselves. What they expect from these particularistic arrangements is that their legal affairs will be handled by specialized experts.[4] The second cause, which has played an increasingly important role in most recent times, has been the desire to eliminate the formalities of normal legal procedure for the sake of a settlement that would be both expeditious and better adapted to the concrete case.[5] In practice, this trend signifies a weakening of legal formalism out of considerations of substantive expediency and thus constitutes but one instance among a whole series of similar contemporary phenomena.

The Anti-Formalistic Tendencies of Modern Legal Development. From a theoretical point of view, the general development of law and procedure may be viewed as passing through the following stages: first, charismatic legal revelation through "law prophets";

second, empirical creation and finding of law by legal honoratiores, i.e., law creation through cautelous jurisprudence and adherence to precedent; third, imposition of law by secular or theocratic powers; fourth and finally, systematic elaboration of law and professionalized administration of justice by persons who have received their legal training in a learned and formally logical manner. From this perspective, the formal qualities of the law emerge as follows: arising in primitive legal procedure from a combination of magically conditioned formalism and irrationality conditioned by revelation, they proceed to increasingly specialized juridical and logical rationality and systematization, passing through a stage of theocratically or patrimonially conditioned substantive and informal expediency. Finally, they assume, at least from an external viewpoint, an increasingly logical sublimation and deductive rigor and develop an increasingly rational technique in procedure.

Since we are here only concerned with the most general lines of development, we shall ignore the fact that in historical reality the theoretically constructed stages of rationalization have not everywhere followed in the sequence which we have just outlined, even if we ignore the world outside the Occident. We shall not be troubled either by the multiplicity of causes of the particular type and degree of rationalization that a given law has actually assumed. As our brief sketch has already shown, we shall only recall that the great differences in the line of development have been essentially influenced, first, by the diversity of political power relationships, which, for reasons to be discussed later, have resulted in very different degrees of power of the imperium vis-à-vis the powers of the kinship groups, the folk community, and the estates; second, by the relations between the theocratic and the secular powers; and, third, by the differences in the structure of those legal honoratiores who were significant for the development of a given law and which, too, were largely dependent upon political factors.

Only the Occident has witnessed the fully-developed administration of justice of the folk-community *(Dinggenossenschaft)* and the status group stereotyped form of patrimonialism; and only the Occident has witnessed the rise of the rational economic system, whose agents first allied themselves with the princely powers to overcome the estates and then turned against them in revolution; and only the West has known "natural law," and with it the complete elimination of the system of personal laws and of the ancient maxim that special law prevails over general law. Nowhere else, finally, has there occurred any phenomenon resembling Roman law and anything like its reception. All these events have to a very large extent been caused by concrete political factors, which have only the remotest analogies elsewhere in the world. For this reason, the stage of decisively shaping law by trained legal specialists has not been fully reached anywhere outside of the Occident. Economic conditions have, as we have seen, everywhere played an important role, but they have nowhere been decisive alone and by themselves. To the extent that they contributed to the formation of the specifically modern features of present-day occidental law, the direction in which they worked has been by and large the following: To those who had interests in the commodity market, the rationalization and systematization of the law in general and, with certain reservations to be stated later, the increasing calculability of the functioning of the legal process in particular, constituted one of the most important conditions for the existence of economic enterprise intended to function with stability and, especially, of capitalistic enterprise, which cannot do without legal security. Special forms of transactions and special procedures, like the bill of exchange and the special procedure for its speedy collection, serve this need for the purely formal certainty of the guaranty of legal enforcement.

On the other hand, the modern and, to a certain extent, the ancient Roman, legal developments have contained tendencies favorable to the dilution of legal formalism. At a first glance, the displacement of the formally bound law of evidence by the "free evaluation of proof" appears to be of a merely technical character.[6] We have seen that the primitive system of magically bound proof was exploded through the rationalism of either the theocratic or the patrimonial kind, both of which postulated procedures for the disclosure of the real truth. Thus the new system clearly appears as a product of substantive rationalization. Today, however, the scope and limits of the free evaluation of proof are determined primarily by commercial interests, i.e., by economic factors. It is clear that, through the system of free evaluation of proof, a very considerable domain which was once subject to formal juristic thought is being increasingly withdrawn therefrom.[7] But we are here more concerned with the corresponding trends in the sphere of substantive law. One such trend lies in the intrinsic necessities of legal thought. Its growing logical sublimation has meant everywhere the substitution for a dependence on externally tangible formal characteristics of an increasingly logical interpretation of meaning in relation to the legal norms themselves, as well as in relation to legal transactions. In the doctrine of the continental "common law" this interpretation claimed that it would give effect to the "real" intentions of the parties; in precisely this manner it introduced an individualizing and relatively substantive factor into legal formalism. This kind of interpretation seeks to construct the relations of the parties to one another from the point of view of the "inner" kernel of their behavior, from the point of view of their mental "attitudes" (such as good faith or malice). Thus it relates legal consequences to informal elements of the situation and this treatment provides a telling parallel to that systematization of religious ethics which we have already considered previously. Much of the system of commodity exchange, in primitive as well as in technically differentiated patterns of trade, is possible only on the basis of far-reaching personal confidence and trust in the loyalty of others. Moreover, as commodity exchange increases in importance, the need in legal practice to guarantee or secure such trustworthy conduct becomes proportionally greater. But in the very nature of the case, we cannot, of course, define with formal certainty the legal tests according to which the new relations of trust and confidence are to be governed. Hence, through such ethical rationalization the courts have been helpful to powerful interests. Also, outside of the sphere of commodity exchange, the rationalization of the law has substituted attitude-evaluation as the significant element for assessment of events according to external criteria. In criminal law, legal rationalization has replaced the purely mechanistic remedy of vengeance by rational "ends of punishment" of an either ethical or utilitarian character, and has thereby introduced increasingly non-formal elements into legal practice. In the sphere of private law the concern for a party's mental attitude has quite generally entailed evaluation by the judge. "Good faith and fair dealing" or the "good" usage of trade or, in other words, ethical categories have become the test of what the parties are entitled to mean by their "intention."[8] Yet, the reference to the "good" usage of trade implies in substance the recognition of such attitudes which are held by the average party concerned with the case, i.e., a general and purely business criterion of an essentially factual nature, such as the average expectation of the parties in a given transaction. It is this standard which the law has consequently to accept.[9]

Now we have already seen that the expectations of parties will often be disappointed by the results of a strictly professional legal logic.[10] Such disappointments are inevitable indeed where the facts of life are juridically "construed" in order to make them fit the abstract propositions of law and in accordance with the maxim that nothing can exist in the realm of law unless it can be "conceived" by the jurist in conformity with those "principles" which are revealed to him by juristic science. The expectations of the parties are oriented towards the economic and utilitarian meaning of a legal proposition. However, from the point of view of legal logic, this meaning is an "irrational" one. For example, the layman will never understand why it should be impossible under the traditional definition of larceny to commit a larceny of electric power.[11] It is by no means the peculiar foolishness of modern jurisprudence which leads to such conflicts. To a large extent such conflicts rather are the inevitable consequence of the incompatibility that exists between the intrinsic necessities of logically consistent formal legal thinking and the fact that the legally relevant agreements and activities of private parties are aimed at economic results and oriented toward economically determined expectations. It is for this reason that we find the ever-recurrent protests against the professional legal method of thought as such, which are finding support even in the lawyers' own reflections on their work. But a "lawyers' law" has never been and never will be brought into conformity with lay expectation unless it totally renounces that formal character which is immanent in it. This is just as true of the English law which we glorify so much today,[12] as it has been of the ancient Roman jurists or of the methods of modern continental legal thought. Any attempt, like that of Erich Jung,[13] to replace the antiquated "law of nature"[14] by a new "natural law"[15] aiming at "dispute settlement" *(Streitschlichtung)* in accordance with the average expectations of average parties would thus come up against certain immanent limitations. But, nevertheless, this idea does have some validity in relation to the realities of legal history. The Roman law of the later Republic and the Empire developed a type of commercial ethics that was in fact oriented toward that which is to be expected on the average. Such a view means, of course, that only a small group of clearly corrupt or fraudulent practices would be outlawed, and the law would not go beyond what is regarded as the "ethical minimum."[16] In spite of the bona fides (which a seller had to display), the maxim of caveat emptor remained valid.

New demands for a "social law" to be based upon such emotionally colored ethical postulates as justice or human dignity, and thus directed against the very dominance of a mere business morality have arisen in modern times with the emergence of the modern class problem. They are advocated not only by labor and other interested groups but also by legal ideologists.[17] By these demands legal formalism itself has been challenged. Such a concept as economic duress,[18] or the attempt to treat as immoral, and thus as invalid, a contract because of a gross disproportion between promise and consideration,[19] are derived from norms which, from the legal standpoint, are entirely amorphous and which are neither juristic nor conventional nor traditional in character but ethical and which claim as their legitimation substantive justice rather than formal legality.

Internal professional ideologies of the lawyers themselves have been operative in legal theory and practice along with those influences which have been engendered by both the social demands of democracy and the welfare ideology of monarchical bureaucracy. The status of being confined to the interpretation of statutes and contracts, like a slot machine into which one just drops the facts (plus the fee) in order to have it spew out the decision (plus opinion), appears to the modern lawyer as beneath his dignity; and the more universal the codified formal statute law has become, the more unattractive has this notion come to be. The present demand is for "judicial creativeness," at least where the statute is silent. The school of "free law" has undertaken to prove that such silence is the inevitable fate of every statute in view of the irrationality of the facts of life; that in countless instances the application of the statutes as "interpreted" is a delusion, and that the decision is, and ought to be, made in the light of concrete evaluations rather than in accordance with formal norms.[20]

For the case where the statute fails to provide a clear rule, the well-known Article I of the Swiss Civil Code orders the judge to decide according to that rule which he himself would promulgate if he were the legislator.[21] This provision, the practical import of which should not be overestimated, however,[22] corresponds formally with the Kantian formula. But in reality a judicial system which would practice such ideals would, in view of the inevitability of value-compromises, very often have to forget about abstract norms and, at least in cases of conflict, would have to admit concrete evaluations, i.e., not only nonformal but irrational lawfinding. Indeed, the doctrine of the inevitability of gaps in the legal order as well as the campaign to recognize as fiction the systematic coherence of the law has been given further impetus by the assertions that the judicial process never consisted, or, at any rate never should consist, in the "application" of general norms to a concrete case, just as no utterance in language should be regarded as an application of the rules of grammar.[23] In this view, the "legal propositions" are regarded as secondary and as being derived by abstraction from the concrete decisions which, as the products of judicial practice, are said to be the real embodiment of the law. Going still farther, one has pointed out the quantitative infrequency of those cases which ever come to trial and judicial decision as against the tremendous mass of rules by which human behavior is actually determined; from this observation one has come derogatively to call "mere rules of decision" those norms which appear in the judicial process, to contrast them with those norms which are factually valid in the course of everyday life and independently of their reaffirmation or declaration in legal procedure, and, ultimately, to establish the postulate that the true foundation of the law is entirely "sociological."[24]

Use has also been made of the historical fact that for long periods, including our own, private parties have to a large extent been advised by professional lawyers and judges who have had technical legal training or that, in other words, all customary law is in reality lawyers' law. This fact has been associated with the incontrovertible observation that entirely new legal principles are being established not only *praeter legem* but also *contra legem*[25] by judicial practice; for instance, that of the German Supreme Court after the entry into force of the Civil Code. From all these facts the idea was derived that case law is superior to the rational establishment of objective norms and that the expediential balancing of concrete interests is superior to the creation and recognition of "norms" in general.[26] The modern theory of legal sources has thus disintegrated both the half-mystical concept of "customary law," as it had been created by historicism, as well as the equally historicist concept of the "will of the legislator" that could be discovered through the study of the legislative history of an enactment as revealed in committee reports and similar sources. The statute rather than the legislator has been thus proclaimed to be the jurists' main concern. Thus isolated from its background, the "law" is then turned over for elaboration and application to the jurists, among whom the predominant influence is ascribed at one time to the practitioners and at others, for instance, in the reports accompanying certain of the modern codes, to the scholars.[27] In this manner the significance of the legislative determination of a legal command is, under certain circumstances, degraded to the role of a mere "symptom" of either the validity of a legal proposition or even of the mere desire of such validity which, however, until it has been accepted in legal practice, is to remain uncertain. But the preference for a case law which remains in contact with legal reality—which means with the reality of the lawyers—to statute law is in turn subverted by the argument that no precedent should be regarded as binding beyond its concrete facts. The way is thus left open to the free balancing of values in each individual case.

In opposition to all such value-irrationalism, there have also arisen attempts to reestablish an objective standard of values. The more the impression grows that legal orders as such are no more than "technical tools," the more violently will such degradation be rejected by the lawyers. For to place on the same level such merely "technical rules" as a customs tariff and legal norms concerning marriage, parental power, or the incidents of ownership, offends the sentiment of the legal practitioners, and there emerges the nostalgic notion of a transpositive law above that merely technical positive law which is acknowledged to be subject to change. The old natural law, it is true, looks discredited by the criticisms leveled at it from the historical and positivist points of view. As a substitute there are now advanced the religiously inspired natural law of the Catholic scholars,[28] and certain efforts to deduce objective standards from the "nature" of the law itself. The latter effort has taken two forms. In the a prioristic, non-Kantian doctrines, the "right law," as the normative system of a "society of free men," is to be both a legislative standard for rational legislation and a source for judicial decisions where the law refers the judge to apparently nonformal criteria.[29] In the empiricist, Comtean, way those "expectations" which private parties are justified to have in view of the average conception existing with regard to the obligations of others, are to serve as the ultimate standard, which is to be superior even to the statute and which is to replace such concepts as equity, etc., which are felt to be too vague.[30]

At this place we cannot undertake a detailed discussion or a full criticism of these tendencies which, as our brief sketch has shown, have produced quite contradictory answers. All these movements are international in scope, but they have been most pronounced in Germany and France.[31] They are agreed only in their rejection of the once universally accepted and until recently prevalent petitio principii of the consistency and "gaplessness" of the legal order. Moreover, they have directed themselves against very diverse opponents, for instance, in France against the school of the Code-interpreters and in Germany against the methodology of the Pandectists. Depending upon who are the leaders of a particular movement, the results favor either the prestige of "science," i.e., of the legal scholars, or that of the practitioners. As a result of the continuous growth of formal statute law and, especially, of systematic codification, the academic scholars feel themselves to be painfully threatened both in their importance and in their opportunities for unencumbered intellectual activity. The rapid growth of anti-logical as well as the antihistorical movements in Germany can be historically explained by the fear that, following codification, German legal science might have to undergo the same decline which befell French jurisprudence after the enactment of the Napoleonic Code, or Prussian jurisprudence after the enactment of the Allgemeine Landrecht. Up to this point these fears are thus the result of an internal constellation of intellectual interests. However, all variants of the developments which have led to the rejection of that purely logical systematization of the law as it had been developed by Pandectist learning, including even the irrational variants, are in their turn products of a self-defeating scientific rationalization of legal thought as well as of its relentless self-criticism. To the extent that they do not themselves have a rationalistic character, they are a flight into the irrational and as such a consequence of the increasing rationalization of legal technique. In that respect they are a parallel to the irrationalization of religion. One must not overlook, however, that the same trends have also been inspired by the desire of the modern lawyers, through the pressure groups in which they are so effectively organized, to heighten their feeling of self-importance and to increase their sense of power. This is undoubtedly one of the reasons why in Germany such continuous reference is made to the "distinguished" position of the English judge who is said not to be bound to any rational law. Yet, the differences in the attribution of honorific status on the continent and in England are rather rooted in circumstances which are connected with differences in the general structure of authority.

Contemporary Anglo-American Law. The differences between continental and common-law methods of legal thought have been produced mostly by factors which are respectively connected with the internal structure and the modes of existence of the legal profession as well as by factors related to differences in political development. The economic elements, however, have been determinative only in connection with these elements. What we are concerned with here is the fact that, once everything is said and done about these differences in historical developments, modern capitalism prospers equally and manifests essentially identical economic traits under legal systems containing rules and institutions which considerably differ from each other at least from the juridical point of view. Even what is on the face of it so fundamental a concept of continental law as *dominium* still does not exist in Anglo-American law.[32] Indeed, we may say that the legal systems under which modern capitalism has been prospering differ profoundly from each other even in their ultimate principles of formal structure.

Even today, and in spite of all influences by the ever more rigorous demands for academic training, English legal thought is essentially an empirical art. Precedent still fully retains its old significance, except that it is regarded as unfair to invoke a case from too remote a past, which means older than about a century. One can also still observe the charismatic character of lawfinding, especially, although not exclusively, in the new countries, and quite particularly the United States. In practice, varying significance is given to a decided case not only, as happens everywhere, in accordance with the hierarchal position of the court by which it was decided but also in accordance with the very personal authority of an individual judge. This is true for the entire common-law sphere, as illustrated, for instance, by the prestige of Lord Mansfield. But in the American view, the judgment is the very personal creation of the concrete individual judge, to whom one is accustomed to refer by name, in contrast to the impersonal "District Court" of continental European officialese. The English judge, too, lays claim to such a position. All these circumstances are tied up with the fact that the degree of legal rationality is essentially lower than, and of a type different from, that of continental Europe. Up to the recent past, and at any rate up to the time of Austin, there was practically no English legal science which would have merited the name of "learning" in the continental sense. This fact alone would have sufficed to render any such codification as was desired by Bentham practically impossible. But it is also this feature which has been responsible for the "practical" adaptibility of English law and its "practical" character from the standpoint of the public.

The legal thinking of the layman is, on the one hand, literalistic. He tends to be a definition-monger when he believes he is arguing "legally." Closely connected with this trait is the tendency to draw conclusions from individual case to individual case; the abstractionism of the "professional" lawyer is far from the layman's mind.

In both respects, however, the art of empirical jurisprudence is cognate to him, although he may not like it. No country, indeed, has produced more bitter complaints and satires about the legal profession than England. The formularies of the conveyancers, too, may be quite unintelligible to the layman, as again is the case in England. Yet, he can understand the basic character of the English way of legal thinking, he can identify himself with it and, above all, he can make his peace with it by retaining once and for all a solicitor as his legal father confessor for all contingencies of life, as is indeed done by practically every English businessman. He simply neither demands nor expects of the law anything which could be frustrated by "logical" legal construction.

Safety valves are also provided against legal formalism. As a matter of fact, in the sphere of private law, both common law and equity are "formalistic" to a considerable extent in their practical treatment. It would hardly be otherwise under a system of stare decisis and the traditionalist spirit of the legal profession. But the institution of the civil jury imposes on rationality limits which are not merely accepted as inevitable but are actually prized because of the binding force of precedent and the fear that a precedent might thus create "bad law" in a sphere which one wishes to keep open for a concrete balancing of interests. We must forego the analysis of the way in which this division of the two spheres of stare decisis and concrete balancing of interests is actually functioning in practice. It does in any case represent a softening of rationality in the administration of justice. Alongside all this we find the still quite patriarchal, summary and highly irrational jurisdiction of the justices of the peace. They deal with the petty causes of everyday life and, as can be readily seen in Mendelssohn's description, they represent a kind of khadi-justice which is quite unknown in Germany.[33] All in all, the common law thus presents a picture of an administration of justice which in the most fundamental formal features of both substantive law and procedure differs from the structure of continental law as much as is possible within a secular system of justice, that is, a system that is free from theocratic and patrimonial powers. Quite definitely, English law-finding is not, like that of the Continent, "application" of "legal propositions" logically derived from statutory texts.

These differences have had some tangible consequences both economically and socially; but these consequences have all been isolated single phenomena rather than differences touching upon the total structure of the economic system. For the development of capitalism two features have been relevant and both have helped to support the capitalistic system. Legal training has primarily been in the hands of the lawyers from among whom also the judges are recruited; i.e., in the hands of a group which is active in the service of propertied, and particularly capitalistic, private interests and which has to gain its livelihood from them. Furthermore and in close connection with this, the concentration of the administration of justice at the central courts in London and its extreme costliness have amounted almost to a denial of access to the courts for those with inadequate means. At any rate, the essential similarity of the capitalistic development on the Continent and in England has not been able to eliminate the sharp contrasts between the two types of legal systems. Nor is there any visible tendency toward a transformation of the English legal system in the direction of the continental under the impetus of the capitalist economy. On the contrary, wherever the two kinds of administration of justice and of legal training have had the opportunity to compete with one another, as for instance in Canada, the common law way has come out on top and has overcome the continental alternative rather quickly. We may thus conclude that capitalism has not been a decisive factor in the promotion of that form of rationalization of the law which has been peculiar to the continental West ever since the rise of Romanist studies in the medieval universities.

Lay Justice and Corporative Tendencies in the Modern Legal Profession. Modern social development, aside from the already mentioned political and internal professional motives, has given rise to certain other factors by which formal legal rationalism is being weakened. Irrational khadi-justice is exercised today in criminal cases clearly and extensively in the "popular" justice of the jury.[34] It appeals to the sentiments of the layman, who feels annoyed whenever he meets with formalism in a concrete case, and it satisfies the emotional demands of those underprivileged classes which clamor for substantive justice.

Against this "popular justice" element of the jury system, attacks have been directed from two quarters. The jury has been attacked because of the strong interest orientation of the jurors as against the technical matter-of-factness of the specialist. Just as in ancient Rome the jurors' list was the object of class conflict, so today the selection of jurors is attacked, especially by the working class, as favoring class justice, upon the ground that the jurors, even though they may be "plebeians," are picked predominantly from among those who can afford the loss of time. Although such a test of selection can hardly be avoided entirely, it also depends, in part at least, on political considerations. Where, on the other hand, the jurors' bench is occupied by working-class people, it is attacked by the propertied class. Moreover, not only "classes" as such are the interested parties. In Germany, for instance, male jurors can practically never be moved to find a fellow male guilty of rape, especially where they are not absolutely convinced of the girl's chaste character.[35] But in this connection we must consider that in Germany female virtue is not held in great respect anyway.

From the standpoint of professional legal training lay justice has been criticized on the ground that the laymen's verdict is delivered as an irrational oracle without any statement of reasons and without the possibility of any substantive criticism. Thus one has come to demand that the lay judges be subjected to the control of the legal experts. In answer to this demand there was created the system of the mixed bench, which, however, experience has shown to be a system in which the laymen's influence is inferior to that of the experts. Thus their presence has practically no more significance than that of giving some compulsory publicity to the deliberation of professional judges in a way similar to that of Switzerland, where the judges must hold their deliberation in full view of the public.[36] The professional judges, in turn, are threatened, in the sphere of criminal law, by the overshadowing power of the professional psychiatrist, onto whom more and more responsibility is passed, especially in the most serious cases, and on whom rationalism is thus imposing a task which can by no means be solved by means of pure science.

Obviously all of these conflicts are caused by the course of technical and economic development only indirectly, namely insofar as it has favored intellectualism. Primarily they are rather consequences of the insoluble conflict between the formal and the substantive principles of justice, which may clash with one another even where their respective protagonists belong to one and the same social class. Moreover, it is by no means certain that those classes which are underprivileged today, especially the working class, may safely expect from an informal administration of justice those results which are claimed for it by the ideology of the jurists. A bureaucratized judiciary, which is being planfully recruited in the higher ranks from among the personnel of the career service of the prosecutor's office and which is completely dependent on the politically ruling powers for advancement, cannot be set alongside the Swiss or English judiciary, and even less the (federal) judges in the United States. If one takes away from such judges their belief in the sacredness of the purely objective legal formalism and directs them simply to balance interests, the result will be very different from those legal systems to which we have just referred. However, the problem does not belong to this discussion. There remains only the task of correcting a few historical errors.

Prophets are the only ones who have taken a really consciously "creative" attitude toward existing law; only through them has new law been consciously created. For the rest, as must be stressed again and again, even those jurists who, from the objective point of view, have been the most creative ones, have always and not only in modern times, regarded themselves to be but the mouthpiece of norms already existing, though perhaps only latently, and to be their interpreters or appliers rather than their creators. This subjective belief is held by even the most eminent jurists. It is due to the disillusionment of the intellectuals that today this belief is being confronted with objectively different facts and that one is trying to elevate this state of facts to the status of a norm for subjective judicial behavior. As the bureaucratization of formal legislation progresses, the traditional position of the English judge is also likely to be transformed permanently and profoundly. On the other hand, it may be doubted whether, in a code country, the bestowal of the "creator's" crown upon bureaucratic judges will really turn them into law prophets. In any case, the juristic precision of judicial opinions will be seriously impaired if sociological, economic, or ethical argument were to take the place of legal concepts.

Summary

All in all the movement is one of those characteristic onslaughts against the dominance of "specialization" and rationalism, which latter has in the last analysis been its very parent. Thus the development of the formal qualities of the law appears to have produced peculiar antinomies. Rigorously formalistic and dependent on what is tangibly perceivable as far as it is required for security to do business, the law has at the same time become informal for the sake of business loyalty, insofar as required by the logical interpretation of the intention of the parties or by the "good usage" of business intercourse, which is understood to be tending toward some "ethical minimum."

The law is drawn into antiformal directions, moreover, by all those powers which demand that it be more than a mere means of pacifying conflicts of interests. These forces include the demand for substantive justice by certain social class interests and ideologies; they also include the tendencies inherent in certain forms of political authority of either authoritarian or democratic character concerning the ends of law which are respectively appropriate to them; and also the demand of the "laity" for a system of justice which would be intelligible to them; finally, as we have seen, anti-formal tendencies are being promoted by the ideologically rooted power aspirations of the legal profession itself.

Whatever form law and legal practice may come to assume under the impact of these various influences, it will be inevitable that, as a result of technical and economic developments, the legal ignorance of the layman will increase. The use of jurors and similar lay judges will not suffice to stop the continuous growth of the technical element in the law and hence of its character as a specialists' domain. Inevitably the notion must expand that the law is a rational technical apparatus, which is continually transformable in the light of expediential considerations and devoid of all sacredness of content. This fate may be obscured by the tendency of acquiescence in the existing law, which is growing in many ways for several reasons, but it cannot really be stayed. All of the modern sociological and philosophical analyses, many of which are of a high scholarly value, can only contribute to strengthen this impression, regardless of the content of their theories concerning the nature of law and the judicial process.

Translated by Edward Shils and Max Rheinstein

Sociology and Science

26. Definition of Sociology

Sociology (in the sense in which this highly ambiguous word is used here) is a science which attempts the interpretive understanding of social action in order thereby to arrive at a causal explanation of its course and effects. In "action" is included all human behavior when and insofar as the acting individual attaches a subjective meaning to it. Action in this sense may be either overt or purely inward or subjective; it may consist of positive intervention in a situation, or of deliberately refraining from such intervention or passively acquiescing in the situation. Action is social insofar as, by virtue of the subjective meaning attached to it by the acting individual (or individuals), it takes account of the behavior of others and is thereby oriented in its course.[1]

Translated by A. M. Henderson and Talcott Parsons

27. The Methodological Foundations of Sociology[1]

1. "Meaning" may be of two kinds. The term may refer first to the actual existing meaning in the given concrete case of a particular actor, or to the average or approximate meaning attributable to a given plurality of actors; or secondly to the theoretically conceived pure type[2] of subjective meaning attributed to the hypothetical actor or actors in a given type of action. In no case does it refer to an objectively "correct" meaning or one which is "true" in some metaphysical sense. It is this which distinguishes the empirical sciences of action, such as sociology and history, from the dogmatic disciplines in that area, such as jurisprudence, logic, ethics, and esthetics, which seek to ascertain the "true" and "valid" meanings associated with the objects of their investigation.

2. The line between meaningful action and merely reactive behavior to which no subjective meaning is attached, cannot be sharply drawn empirically. A very considerable part of all sociologically relevant behavior, especially purely traditional behavior, is marginal between the two. In the case of many psychophysical processes, meaningful (i.e., subjectively understandable) action is not to be found at all; in others it is discernible only by the expert psychologist. Many mystical experiences which cannot be adequately communicated in words are, for a person who is not susceptible to such experiences, not fully understandable. At the same time the ability to imagine one's self performing a similar action is not a necessary prerequisite to understanding; "one need not have been Caesar in order to understand Caesar." For the verifiable accuracy[3] of interpretation of the meaning of a phenomenon, it is a great help to be able to put one's self imaginatively in the place of the actor and thus sympathetically to participate in his experiences, but this is not an essential condition of meaningful interpretation. Understandable and nonunderstandable components of a process are often intermingled and bound up together.

3. All interpretation of meaning, like all scientific observation, strives for clarity and verifiable accuracy of insight and comprehension *(Evidenz)*. The basis for certainty in understanding can be either rational, which can be further subdivided into logical and mathematical, or it can be of an emotionally empathic or artistically appreciative quality. In the sphere of action things are rationally evident chiefly when we attain a completely clear intellectual grasp of the action-elements in their intended context of meaning. Empathic or appreciative accuracy is attained when, through sympathetic participation, we can adequately grasp the emotional context in which the action took place. The highest degree of rational understanding is attained in cases involving the meanings of logically or mathematically related propositions; their meaning may be immediately and unambiguously intelligible. We have a perfectly clear understanding of what it means when somebody employs the proposition $2\times2=4$ or the Pythagorean theorem in reasoning or argument, or when someone correctly carries out a logical train of reasoning according to our accepted modes of thinking. In the same way we also understand what a person is doing when he tries to achieve certain ends by choosing appropriate means on the basis of the facts of the situation as experience has accustomed us to interpret them. Such an interpretation of this type of rationally purposeful action possesses,

for the understanding of the choice of means, the highest degree of verifiable certainty. With a lower degree of certainty, which is, however, adequate for most purposes of explanation, we are able to understand errors, including confusion of problems of the sort that we ourselves are liable to, or the origin of which we can detect by sympathetic self-analysis.

On the other hand, many ultimate ends or values toward which experience shows that human action may be oriented, often cannot be understood completely, though sometimes we are able to grasp them intellectually. The more radically they differ from our own ultimate values, however, the more difficult it is for us to make them understandable by imaginatively participating in them. Depending upon the circumstances of the particular case we must be content either with a purely intellectual understanding of such values or when even that fails, sometimes we must simply accept them as given data. Then we can try to understand the action motivated by them on the basis of whatever opportunities for approximate emotional and intellectual interpretation seem to be available at different points in its course. These difficulties apply, for instance, for people not susceptible to the relevant values, to many unusual acts of religious and charitable zeal; also certain kinds of extreme rationalistic fanaticism of the type involved in some forms of the ideology of the "rights of man" are in a similar position for people who radically repudiate such points of view.

The more we ourselves are susceptible to them the more readily can we imaginatively participate in such emotional reactions as anxiety, anger, ambition, envy, jealousy, love, enthusiasm, pride, vengefulness, loyalty, devotion, and appetites of all sorts, and thereby understand the irrational conduct which grows out of them. Such conduct is "irrational," that is, from the point of view of the rational pursuit of a given end. Even when such emotions are found in a degree of intensity of which the observer himself is completely incapable, he can still have a significant degree of emotional understanding of their meaning and can interpret intellectually their influence on the course of action and the selection of means.

For the purposes of a typological scientific analysis it is convenient to treat all irrational, affectually determined elements of behavior as factors of deviation from a conceptually pure type of rational action. For example, a panic on the stock exchange can be most conveniently analyzed by attempting to determine first what the course of action would have been if it had not been influenced by irrational affects; it is then possible to introduce the irrational components as accounting for the observed deviations from this hypothetical course. Similarly, in analyzing a political or military campaign it is convenient to determine in the first place what would have been a rational course, given the ends of the participants and adequate knowledge of all the circumstances. Only in this way is it possible to assess the causal significance of irrational factors as accounting for the deviations from this type. The construction of a purely rational course of action in such cases serves the sociologist as a type ("ideal type") which has the merit of clear understandability and lack of ambiguity. By comparison with this it is possible to understand the ways in which actual action is influenced by irrational factors of all sorts, such as affects and errors, in that they account for the deviation from the line of conduct which would be expected on the hypothesis that the action were purely rational.

Only in this respect and for these reasons of methodological convenience, is the method of sociology "rationalistic." It is naturally not legitimate to interpret this procedure as involving a "rationalistic bias" of sociology, but only as a methodological device. It certainly does not involve a belief in the actual predominance of rational elements in human life, for on the question of how far this predominance does or does not exist, nothing whatever has been said. That there is, however, a danger of rationalistic interpretations where they are out of place naturally cannot be denied. All experience unfortunately confirms the existence of this danger.

4. In all the sciences of human action, account must be taken of processes and phenomena which are devoid of subjective meaning,[4] in the role of stimuli, results, favoring or hindering circumstances. To be devoid of meaning is not identical with being lifeless or nonhuman; every artifact, such as for example a machine, can be understood only in terms of the meaning which its production and use have had or will have for human action; a meaning which may derive from a relation to exceedingly various purposes. Without reference to this meaning such an object remains wholly unintelligible. That which is intelligible or understandable about it is thus its relation to human action in the role either of means or of end; a relation of which the actor or actors can be said to have been aware and to which their action has been oriented. Only in terms of such categories is it possible to "understand" objects of this kind. On the other hand, proceesses or conditions, whether they are animate or inanimate, human or nonhuman, are in the present sense devoid of

meaning insofar as they cannot be related to an intended purpose. That is to say they are devoid of meaning if they cannot be related to action in the role of means or ends but constitute only the stimulus, the favoring or hindering circumstances.[5] It may be that the incursion of the Dollart at the beginning of the twelfth century[6] had historical significance as a stimulus to the beginning of certain migrations of considerable importance. Human mortality, indeed the organic life cycle generally from the helplessness of infancy to that of old age, is naturally of the very greatest sociological importance through the various ways in which human action has been oriented to these facts. To still another category of facts devoid of meaning belong certain psychic or psycho-physical phenomena such as fatigue, habituation, memory, etc.; also certain typical states of euphoria under some conditions of ascetic mortification; finally, typical variations in the reactions of individuals according to reaction-time, precision, and other modes. But in the last analysis the same principle applies to these as to other phenomena which are devoid of meaning. Both the actor and the sociologist must accept them as data to be taken into account.

It is altogether possible that future research may be able to discover nonunderstandable uniformities underlying what has appeared to be specifically meaningful action, though little has been accomplished in this direction thus far. Thus, for example, differences in hereditary biological constitution, as of "races," would have to be treated by sociology as given data in the same way as the physiological facts of the need of nutrition or the effect of senescence on action. This would be the case if, and insofar as, we had statistically conclusive proof of their influence on sociologically relevant behavior. The recognition of the causal significance of such factors would naturally not in the least alter the specific task of sociological analysis or of that of the other sciences of action, which is the interpretation of action in terms of its subjective meaning. The effect would be only to introduce certain nonunderstandable data of the same order as others which, it has been noted above, are already present, into the complex of subjectively understandable motivation at certain points. Thus it may come to be known that there are typical relations between the frequency of certain types of teleological orientation of action or of the degree of certain kinds of rationality and the cephalic index or skin color or any other biologically inherited characteristic.

5. Understanding may be of two kinds: the first is the direct observational understanding[7] of the subjective meaning of a given act

as such, including verbal utterances. We thus understand by direct observation, in this sense, the meaning of the proposition $2 \times 2 = 4$ when we hear or read it. This is a case of the direct rational understanding of ideas. We also understand an outbreak of anger as manifested by facial expression, exclamations or irrational movements. This is direct observational understanding of irrational emotional reactions. We can understand in a similar observational way the action of a woodcutter or of somebody who reaches for the knob to shut a door or who aims a gun at an animal. This is rational observational understanding of actions.

Understanding may, however, be of another sort, namely explanatory understanding. Thus we understand in terms of *motive* the meaning an actor attaches to the proposition twice two equals four, when he states it or writes it down, in that we understand what makes him do this at precisely this moment and in these circumstances. Understanding in this sense is attained if we know that he is engaged in balancing a ledger or in making a scientific demonstration, or is engaged in some other task of which this particular act would be an appropriate part. This is rational understanding of motivation, which consists in placing the act in an intelligible and more inclusive context of meaning.[8] Thus we understand the chopping of wood or aiming of a gun in terms of motive in addition to direct observation if we know that the woodchopper is working for a wage, or is chopping a supply of firewood for his own use, or possibly is doing it for recreation. But he might also be "working off" a fit of rage, an irrational case. Similarly we understand the motive of a person aiming a gun if we know that he has been commanded to shoot as a member of a firing squad, that he is fighting against an enemy, or that he is doing it for revenge. The last is affectually determined and thus in a certain sense irrational. Finally we have a motivational understanding of the outburst of anger if we know that it has been provoked by jealousy, injured pride, or an insult. The last examples are all affectually determined and hence derived from irrational motives. In all the above cases the particular act has been placed in an understandable sequence of motivation, the understanding of which can be treated as an explanation of the actual course of behavior. Thus for a science which is concerned with the subjective meaning of action, explanation requires a grasp of the complex of meaning in which an actual course of understandable action thus interpreted belongs.[9] In all such cases, even where the processes are largely affectual, the subjective meaning of the action, including that also of the relevant meaning complexes, will be called the "intended" meaning.[10] This involves a departure from ordinary usage, which speaks of intention in this sense only in the case of rationally purposive action.

6. In all these cases understanding involves the interpretive grasp of the meaning present in one of the following contexts: (a) as in the historical approach, the actually intended meaning for concrete individual action; or (b) as in cases of sociological mass phenomena the average of, or an approximation to, the actually intended meaning; or (c) the meaning appropriate to a scientifically formulated pure type (an ideal type) of a common phenomenon. The concepts and "laws" of pure economic theory are examples of this kind of ideal type. They state what course a given type of human action would take if it were strictly rational, unaffected by errors or emotional factors and if, furthermore, it were completely and unequivocally directed to a single end, the maximization of economic advantage. In reality, action takes exactly this course only in unusual cases, as sometimes on the stock exchange; and even then there is usually only an approximation to the ideal type.[11]

Every interpretation attempts to attain clarity and certainty, but no matter how clear an interpretation as such appears to be from the point of view of meaning, it cannot on this account alone claim to be the causally valid interpretation. On this level it must remain only a peculiarly plausible hypothesis. In the first place the "conscious motives" may well, even to the actor himself, conceal the various "motives" and "repressions" which constitute the real driving force of his action. Thus in such cases even subjectively honest self-analysis has only a relative value. Then it is the task of the sociologist to be aware of this motivational situation and to describe and analyze it, even though it has not actually been concretely part of the conscious "intention" of the actor; possibly not at all, at least not fully. This is a borderline case of the interpretation of meaning. Secondly, processes of action which seem to an observer to be the same or similar may fit into exceedingly various complexes of motive in the case of the actual actor. Then even though the situations appear superficially to be very similar we must actually understand them or interpret them as very different; perhaps, in terms of meaning, directly opposed.[12] Third, the actors in any given situation are often subject to opposing and conflicting impulses, all of which we are able to understand. In a large number of cases we know from experience it is not possible to arrive at even an approximate estimate of the relative strength of conflicting motives and very often we cannot be certain of our interpretation. Only the actual outcome of the conflict gives a solid basis of judgment.

More generally, verification of subjective interpretation by comparison with the concrete course of events is, as in the case of all hypotheses, indispensable. Unfortunately this type of verification is feasible with relative accuracy only in the few very special cases susceptible of psychological experimentation. The approach to a satisfactory degree of accuracy is exceedingly various, even in the limited number of cases of mass phenomena which can be statistically described and unambiguously interpreted. For the rest there remains only the possibility of comparing the largest possible number of historical or contemporary processes which, while otherwise similar, differ in the one decisive point of their relation to the particular motive or factor the role of which is being investigated. This is a fundamental task of comparative sociology. Often, unfortunately, there is available only the dangerous and uncertain procedure of the "imaginary experiment" which consists in thinking away certain elements of a chain of motivation and working out the course of action which would then probably ensue, thus arriving at a causal judgment.[13]

For example, the generalization called Gresham's Law is a rationally clear interpretation of human action under certain conditions and under the assumption that it will follow a purely rational course. How far any actual course of action corresponds to this can be verified only by the available statistical evidence for the actual disappearance of undervalued monetary units from circulation. In this case our information serves to demonstrate a high degree of accuracy. The facts of experience were known before the generalization, which was formulated afterward; but without this successful interpretation our need for causal understanding would evidently be left unsatisfied. On the other hand, without the demonstration that what can here be assumed to be a theoretically adequate interpretation also is in some degree relevant to an actual course of action, a "law," no matter how fully demonstrated theoretically, would be worthless for the understanding of action in the real world. In this case the correspondence between the theoretical interpretation of motivation and its empirical verification is entirely satisfactory and the cases are numerous enough so that verification can be considered established. But to take another example, Eduard Meyer has advanced an ingenious theory of the causal significance of the battles of Marathon, Salamis, and Platea for the development of the cultural peculiarities of Greek, and hence, more generally, Western, civilization.[14] This is derived from a meaningful interpretation of certain symptomatic facts having to do with the attitudes of the Greek oracles and prophets toward the Persians. It can only be directly verified by reference to the examples of the conduct of the Persians in cases where they were victorious, as in Jerusalem, Egypt, and Asia Minor, and even this verification must necessarily remain unsatisfactory in certain respects. The striking rational plausibility of the hypothesis must here necessarily be relied on as a support. In very many cases of historical interpretation which seem highly plausible, however, there is not even a possibility of the order of verification which was feasible in this case. Where this is true the interpretation must necessarily remain a hypothesis.

7. A motive is a complex of subjective meaning which seems to the actor himself or to the observer an adequate ground for the conduct in question. We apply the term "adequacy on the level of meaning"[15] to the subjective interpretation of a coherent course of conduct when and insofar as, according to our habitual modes of thought and feeling, its component parts taken in their mutual relation are recognized to constitute a "typical" complex of meaning. It is more common to say "correct." The interpretation of a sequence of events will on the other hand be called causally adequate insofar as, according to established generalizations from experience, there is a probability that it will always actually occur in the same way. An example of adequacy on the level of meaning in this sense is what is, according to our current norms of calculation or thinking, the correct solution of an arithmetical problem. On the other hand, a causally adequate interpretation of the same phenomenon would concern the statistical probability that, according to verified generalizations from experience, there would be a correct or an erroneous solution of the same problem. This also refers to currently accepted norms but includes taking account of typical errors or of typical confusions. Thus causal explanation depends on being able to determine that there is a probability, which in the rare ideal case can be numerically stated, but is always in some sense calculable, that a given observable event (overt or subjective) will be followed or accompanied by another event.

A correct causal interpretation of a concrete course of action is arrived at when the overt action and the motives have both been correctly apprehended and at the same time their relation has become meaningfully comprehensible. A correct causal interpretation of typical action means that the process which is claimed to be typical is shown to be both adequately grasped on the level of meaning and at the same time the interpretation is to some degree causally adequate. If adequacy in respect to meaning is lacking, then no matter how high the degree of uniformity and how precisely its probability can be numerically determined, it is still an incomprehensible statistical probability, whether dealing with overt or subjective processes. On the other hand, even the most perfect adequacy on the level of meaning has causal significance from a sociological point of view only insofar as there is some kind of proof for the existence of a probability[16] that action in fact normally takes the course which has been held to be meaningful. For this there must be some degree of determinable frequency of approximation to an average or a pure type.

Statistical uniformities constitute understandable types of action in the sense of this discussion, and thus constitute "sociological generalizations," only when they can be regarded as manifestations of the understandable subjective meaning of a course of social action. Conversely, formulations of a rational course of subjectively understandable action constitute sociological types of empirical process only when they can be empirically observed with a significant degree of approximation. It is unfortunately by no means the case that the actual likelihood of the occurrence of a given course of overt action is always directly proportional to the clarity of subjective interpretation. There are statistics of processes devoid of meaning such as death rates, phenomena of fatigue, the production rate of machines, the amount of rainfall, in exactly the same sense as there are statistics of meaningful phenomena. But only when the phenomena are meaningful is it convenient to speak of sociological statistics. Examples are such cases as crime rates, occupational distributions, price statistics, and statistics of crop acreage. Naturally there are many cases where both components are involved, as in crop statistics.

8. Processes and uniformities which it has here seemed convenient not to designate as (in the present case) sociological phenomena or uniformities because they are not "understandable," are naturally not on that account any the less important. This is true even for sociology in the present sense which restricts it to subjectively understandable phenomena—a usage which there is no intention of attempting to impose on anyone else. Such phenomena, however important, are simply treated by a different method from the others;

they become conditions, stimuli, furthering or hindering circumstances of action.

9. Action in the sense of a subjectively understandable orientation of behavior exists only as the behavior of one or more individual human beings. For other cognitive purposes it may be convenient or necessary to consider the individual, for instance, as a collection of cells, as a complex of biochemical reactions, or to conceive his "psychic" life as made up of a variety of different elements, however these may be defined. Undoubtedly such procedures yield valuable knowledge of causal relationships. But the behavior of these elements, as expressed in such uniformities, is not subjectively understandable. This is true even of psychic elements because the more precisely they are formulated from a point of view of natural science, the less they are accessible to subjective understanding. This is never the road to interpretation in terms of subjective meaning. On the contrary, both for sociology in the present sense, and for history, the object of cognition is the subjective meaning-complex of action. The behavior of physiological entities such as cells, or of any sort of psychic elements may at least in principle be observed and an attempt made to derive uniformities from such observations. It is further possible to attempt, with their help, to obtain a causal explanation of individual phenomena; that is, to subsume them under uniformities. But the subjective understanding of action takes the same account of this type of fact and uniformity as of any others not capable of subjective interpretation. This is true, for example, of physical, astronomical, geological, meteorological, geographical, botanical, zoological, and anatomical facts and of such facts as those aspects of psychopathology which are devoid of subjective meaning or the facts of the natural conditions of technological processes.

For still other cognitive purposes as, for instance, juristic, or for practical ends, it may on the other hand be convenient or even indispensable to treat social collectivities, such as states, associations, business corporations, foundations, as if they were individual persons. Thus they may be treated as the subjects of rights and duties or as the performers of legally significant actions. But for the subjective interpretation of action in sociological work these collectivities must be treated as solely the resultants and modes of organization of the particular acts of individual persons, since these alone can be treated as agents in a course of subjectively understandable action. Nevertheless, the sociologist cannot for his purposes afford to ignore these collective concepts derived from other disciplines. For the subjective interpretation of action has at least two important relations to these concepts. In the first place it is often necessary to employ very similar collective concepts, indeed often using the same terms, in order to obtain an understandable terminology. Thus both in legal terminology and in everyday speech the term "state" is used both for the legal concept of the state and for the phenomena of social action to which its legal rules are relevant. For sociological purposes, however, the phenomenon "the state" does not consist necessarily or even primarily of the elements which are relevant to legal analysis; and for sociological purposes there is no such thing as a collective personality which "acts." When reference is made in a sociological context to a "state," a "nation," a "corporation," a "family," or an "army corps," or to similar collectivities, what is meant is, on the contrary, only a certain kind of development of actual or possible social actions of individual persons. Both because of its precision and because it is established in general usage the juristic concept is taken over, but is used in an entirely different meaning.

Secondly, the subjective interpretation of action must take account of a fundamentally important fact. These concepts of collective entities which are found both in common sense and in juristic and other technical forms of thought, have a meaning in the minds of individual persons, partly as of something actually existing, partly as something with normative authority. This is true not only of judges and officials, but of ordinary private individuals as well. Actors thus in part orient their action to them, and in this role such ideas have a powerful, often a decisive, causal influence on the course of action of real individuals. This is above all true where the ideas concern a recognized positive or negative normative pattern.[17] Thus, for instance, one of the important aspects of the "existence" of a modern state, precisely as a complex of social interaction of individual persons, consists in the fact that the action of various individuals is oriented to the belief that it exists or should exist, thus that its acts and laws are valid in the legal sense. This will be further discussed below. Though extremely pedantic and cumbersome it would be possible, if purposes of sociological terminology alone were involved, to eliminate such terms entirely, and substitute newly-coined words. This would be possible even though the word "state" is used ordinarily not only to designate the legal concept but also the real process of action. But in the above important connection, at least, this would naturally be impossible.

Thirdly, it is the method of the so-called "organic" school of sociology[18] to attempt to understand social interaction by using as a point of departure the "whole" within which the individual acts. His action and behavior are then interpreted somewhat in the way that a physiologist would treat the role of an organ of the body in the "economy" of the organism, that is from the point of view of the survival of the latter.[19] How far in other disciplines this type of functional analysis of the relation of "parts" to a "whole" can be regarded as definitive, cannot be discussed here; but it is well known that the biochemical and biophysical modes of analysis of the organism are in principle opposed to stopping there. For purposes of sociological analysis two things can be said. First, this functional frame of reference is convenient for purposes of practical illustration and for provisional orientation. In these respects it is not only useful but indispensable. But at the same time if its cognitive value is overestimated and its concepts illegitimately "reified,"[20] it can be highly dangerous. Secondly, in certain circumstances this is the only available way of determining just what processes of social action it is important to understand in order to explain a given phenomenon.[21] But this is only the beginning of sociological analysis as here understood. In the case of social collectivities, precisely as distinguished from organisms, we are in a position to go beyond merely demonstrating functional relationships and uniformities. We can accomplish something which is never attainable in the natural sciences, namely the subjective understanding of the action of the component individuals. The natural sciences on the other hand cannot do this, being limited to the formulation of causal uniformities in objects and events, and the explanation of individual facts by applying them. We do not "understand" the behavior of cells, but can only observe the relevant functional relationships and generalize on the basis of these observations. This additional achievement of explanation by interpretive understanding, as distinguished from external observation, is of course attained only at a price—the more hypothetical and fragmentary character of its results. Nevertheless, subjective understanding is the specific characteristic of sociological knowledge.

It would lead too far afield even to attempt to discuss how far the behavior of animals is subjectively understandable to us and vice versa; in both cases the meaning of the term understanding and its extent of application would be highly problematical. But insofar as such understanding existed it would be theoretically possible to formulate a sociology of the relations of men to animals, both domestic and wild. Thus many animals "understand" commands, anger, love, hostility, and react to them in ways which are evidently often by no means purely instinctive and mechanical and in some sense both consciously meaningful and affected by experience. There is no a priori reason to suppose that our ability to share the feelings of primitive men is very much greater.[22] Unfortunately we either do not have any reliable means of determining the subjective state of mind of an animal or what we have is at best very unsatisfactory. It is well known that the problems of animal psychology, however interesting, are very thorny ones. There are in particular various forms of social organization among animals: "monogamous and polygamous families," herds, flocks, and finally "state," with a functional division of labor. The extent of functional differentiation found in these animal societies is by no means, however, entirely a matter of the degree of organic or morphological differentiation of the individual members of the species. Thus, the functional differentiation found among the termites, and in consequence that of the products of their social activities, is much more advanced than in the case of the bees and ants. In this field it goes without saying that a purely functional point of view is often the best that can, at least for the present, be attained, and the investigator must be content with it. Thus it is possible to study the ways in which the species provides for its survival; that is, for nutrition, defense, reproduction, and reconstruction of the social units. As the principal bearers of these functions, differentiated types of individuals can be identified: "kings," "queens," "workers," "soldiers," "drones," "propagators," "queen's substitutes," and so on. Anything more than that was for a long time merely a matter of speculation or of an attempt to determine the extent to which heredity on the one hand and environment on the other would be involved in the development of these "social" proclivities. This was particularly true of the controversies between Götte and Weisman. The latter's conception of the omnipotence of natural selection was largely based on wholly nonempirical deductions. But all serious authorities are naturally fully agreed that the limitation of analysis to the functional level is only a necessity imposed by our present ignorance which it is hoped will only be temporary.

It is relatively easy to grasp the significance of the functions of these various differentiated types for survival. It is also not difficult to work out the bearing of the hypothesis of the inheritance of acquired characteristics or its reverse on the problem of explaining how these differentiations have come about, and further, what is the bearing of different variants of the theory of heredity. But this is not enough. We would like especially to know first what factors account for the original differentiation of specialized types from the still neutral undifferentiated species-type. Secondly, it would be important to know what leads the differentiated individual in the typical case to behave in a way which actually serves the survival value of the organized group. Wherever research has made any progress in the solution of these problems it has been through the experimental demonstration of the probability or possibility of the role of chemical stimuli or physiological processes, such as nutritional states, the effects of parasitic castration, etc., in the case of the individual organism. How far there is even a hope that the existence of "subjective" or "meaningful" orientation could be made experimentally probable, even the specialist to-day would hardly be in a position to say. A verifiable conception of the state of mind of these social animals, accessible to meaningful understanding, would seem to be attainable even as an ideal goal only within narrow limits. However that may be, a contribution to the understanding of human social action is hardly to be expected from this quarter. On the contrary, in the field of animal psychology, human analogies are and must be continually employed. The most that can be hoped for is, then, that these biological analogies may someday be useful in suggesting significant problems. For instance they may throw light on the question of the relative role in the early stages of human social differentiation of mechanical and instinctive factors, as compared with that of the factors which are accessible to subjective interpretation generally, and more particularly to the role of consciously rational action. It is necessary for the sociologist to be thoroughly aware of the fact that in the early stages even of human development, the first set of factors is completely predominant. Even in the later stages he must take account of their continual interaction with the others in a role which is often of decisive importance. This is particularly true of all "traditional" action and of many aspects of charisma.[23] In the latter field of phenomena lie the seeds of certain types of psychic "contagion" and it is thus the bearer of many dynamic tendencies of social processes. These types of action are very closely related to phenomena which are understandable either only in biological terms or are subject to interpretation in terms of subjective motives only in fragments and with an almost imperceptible transition to the biological. But all these facts do not discharge sociology from the obligation, in full awareness of the narrow limits to which it is confined, to accomplish what it alone can do.

The various works of Othmar Spann are often full of suggestive ideas, though at the same time he is guilty of occasional misunderstandings, and above all, of arguing on the basis of pure value judgments which have no place in an empirical investigation. But he is undoubtedly correct in doing something to which, however, no one seriously objects, namely, emphasizing the sociological significance of the functional point of view for preliminary orientation to problems. This is what he calls the "universalistic method." We certainly need to know what kind of action is functionally necessary for "survival," but further and above all for the maintenance of a cultural type and the continuity of the corresponding modes of social action, before it is possible even to inquire how this action has come about and what motives determine it. It is necessary to know what a "king," an "official," an "entrepreneur," a "procurer," or a "magician" does; that is, what kind of typical action, which justifies classifying an individual in one of these categories, is important and relevant for an analysis, before it is possible to undertake the analysis itself. But it is only this analysis itself which can achieve the sociological understanding of the actions of typically differentiated human (and only human) individuals, and which hence constitutes the specific function of sociology. It is a monstrous misunderstanding to think that an "individualistic" method should involve what is in any conceivable sense an individualistic system of values. It is as important to avoid this error as the related one which confuses the unavoidable tendency of sociological concepts to assume a rationalistic character with a belief in the predominance of rational motives, or even a positive valuation of "rationalism." Even a socialistic economy would have to be understood sociologically in exactly the same kind of "individualistic" terms; that is, in terms of the action of individuals, the types of "officials" found in it, as would be the case with a system of free exchange analyzed in terms of the theory of marginal utility. It might be possible to find a better method, but in this respect it would be similar. The real empirical sociological investigation begins with the question: What motives determine and lead the individual members and participants in this socialistic community to behave in such a way that the community came into being in the first place, and that it continues to exist? Any form of functional analysis which proceeds from the whole to the parts can accomplish only a preliminary preparation for this investigation—a preparation, the utility and indispensability of which, if properly carried out, is naturally beyond question.

10. It is customary to designate various sociological generalizations, as for example "Gresham's Law," as scientific "laws." These are in fact typical probabilities confirmed by observation to the effect that under certain given conditions an expected course of social action will occur, which is understandable in terms of the typical motives and typical subjective intentions of the actors.[24] These generalizations are both understandable and define in the highest degree insofar as the typically observed course of action can be understood in terms of the purely rational pursuit of an end, or where for reasons of methodological convenience such a theoretical type can be heuristically employed. In such cases the relations of means and end will be clearly understandable on grounds of experience, particularly where the choice of means was "inevitable." In such cases it is legitimate to assert that insofar as the action was rigorously rational it could not have taken any other course because for technical reasons, given their clearly defined ends, no other means were available to the actors. This very case demonstrates how erroneous it is to regard any kind of "psychology" as the ultimate foundation of the sociological interpretation of action. The term "psychology," to be sure, is today understood in a wide variety of senses. For certain quite specific methodological purposes the type of treatment which attempts to follow the procedures of the natural sciences employs a distinction between "physical" and "psychic" phenomena which is entirely foreign to the disciplines concerned with human action, at least in the present sense. The results of a type of psychological investigation which employs the methods of the natural sciences in any one of various possible ways may naturally, like the results of any other science, have, in specific contexts, outstanding significance for sociological problems; indeed this has often happened. But this use of the results of psychology is something quite different from the investigation of human behavior in terms of its subjective meaning. Hence sociology has no closer logical relationship on a general analytical level to this type of psychology than to any other science. The source of error lies in the concept of the "psychic." It is held that everything which is not physical is *ipso facto* psychic, but that the meaning of a train of mathematical reasoning which a person carries out is not in the relevant sense "psychic." Similarly the rational deliberation of an actor as to whether the results of a given proposed course of action will or will not promote certain specific

interests, and the corresponding decision, do not become one bit more understandable by taking "psychological" considerations into account. But it is precisely on the basis of such rational assumptions that most of the laws of sociology, including those of economics, are built up. On the other hand, in explaining the irrationalities of action sociologically, that form of psychology which employs the method of subjective understanding undoubtedly can make decisively important contributions. But this does not alter the fundamental methodological situation.

11. It has continually been assumed as obvious that the science of sociology seeks to formulate type concepts and generalized uniformities of empirical process. This distinguishes it from history, which is oriented to the causal analysis and explanation of individual actions, structures, and personalities possessing cultural significance. The empirical material which underlies the concepts of sociology consists to a very large extent, though by no means exclusively, of the same concrete processes of action which are dealt with by historians. Among the various bases on which its concepts are formulated and its generalizations worked out, is an attempt to justify its important claim to be able to make a contribution to the causal explanation of some historically and culturally important phenomenon.[25] As in the case of every generalizing science, the abstract character of the concepts of sociology is responsible for the fact that, compared with actual historical reality, they are relatively lacking in fullness of concrete content. To compensate for this disadvantage, sociological analysis can offer a greater precision of concepts. This precision is obtained by striving for the highest possible degree of adequacy on the level of meaning in accordance with the definition of that concept put forward above. It has already been repeatedly stressed that this aim can be realized in a particularly high degree in the case of concepts and generalizations which formulate rational processes. But sociological investigation attempts to include in its scope various irrational phenomena, as well as prophetic, mystic, and affectual modes of action, formulated in terms of theoretical concepts which are adequate on the level of meaning. In all cases, rational or irrational, sociological analysis both abstracts from reality and at the same time helps us to understand it, in that it shows with what degree of approximation a concrete historical phenomenon can be subsumed under one or more of these concepts. For example, the same historical phenomenon may be in one aspect "feudal," in another "patrimonial," in another "bureaucratic," and in still another "char-

ismatic." In order to give a precise meaning to these terms, it is necessary for the sociologist to formulate pure ideal types of the corresponding forms of action which in each case involve the highest possible degree of logical integration by virtue of their complete adequacy on the level of meaning. But precisely because this is true, it is probably seldom if ever that a real phenomenon can be found which corresponds exactly to one of these ideally constructed pure types. The case is similar to a physical reaction which has been calculated on the assumption of an absolute vacuum. Theoretical analysis in the field of sociology is possible only in terms of such pure types. It goes without saying that in addition it is convenient for the sociologist from time to time to employ average types of an empirical statistical character. These are concepts which do not require methodological discussion at this point. But when reference is made to "typical" cases, the term should always be understood, unless otherwise stated, as meaning ideal-types, which may in turn be rational or irrational as the case may be (thus in economic theory they are always rational), but in any case are always constructed with a view to adequacy on the level of meaning.

It is important to realize that in the sociological field as elsewhere, averages, and hence average types, can be formulated with a relative degree of precision only where they are concerned with differences of degree in respect to action which remains qualitatively the same. Such cases do occur, but in the majority of cases of action important to history or sociology the motives which determine it are qualitatively heterogeneous. Then it is quite impossible to speak of an "average" in the true sense. The ideal-types of social action which for instance are used in economic theory are thus "unrealistic" or abstract in that they always ask what course of action would take place if it were purely rational and oriented to economic ends alone. But this construction can be used to aid in the understanding of action not purely economically determined but which involves deviations arising from traditional restraints, affects, errors, and the intrusion of other than economic purposes or considerations. This can take place in two ways. First, in analyzing the extent to which in the concrete case, or on the average for a class of cases, the action was in part economically determined along with the other factors. Secondly, by throwing the discrepancy between the actual course of events and the ideal-type into relief, the analysis of the noneconomic motives actually involved is facilitated. The procedure would be very similar in employing an ideal-type of mystical orientation with its appropriate attitude of indifference to worldly things, as a tool for analyzing its consequences for the actor's relation to ordinary life; for instance, to political or economic affairs. The more sharply and precisely the ideal-type has been constructed, thus the more abstract and unrealistic in this sense it is, the better it is able to perform its methodological functions in formulating the clarification of terminology, and in the formulation of classifications, and of hypotheses. In working out a concrete causal explanation of individual events, the procedure of the historian is essentially the same. Thus in attempting to explain the campaign of 1866, it is indispensable both in the case of Moltke and of Benedek to attempt to construct imaginatively how each, given fully adequate knowledge both of his own situation and of that of his opponent, would have acted. Then it is possible to compare with this the actual course of action and to arrive at a causal explanation of the observed deviations, which will be attributed to such factors as misinformation, strategical errors, logical fallacies, personal temperament, or considerations outside the realm of strategy. Here, too, an ideal-typical construction of rational action is actually employed even though it is not made explicit.

The theoretical concepts of sociology are ideal-types not only from the objective point of view, but also in their application to subjective processes. In the great majority of cases actual action goes on in a state of inarticulate half-consciousness or actual unconsciousness of its subjective meaning. The actor is more likely to "be aware" of it in a vague sense than he is to "know" what he is doing or be explicitly self-conscious about it. In most cases his action is governed by impulse or habit. Only occasionally and, in the uniform action of large numbers often only in the case of a few individuals, is the subjective meaning of the action, whether rational or irrational, brought clearly into consciousness. The ideal-type of meaningful action where the meaning is fully conscious and explicit is a marginal case. Every sociological or historical investigation, in applying its analysis to the empirical facts, must take this fact into account. But the difficulty need not prevent the sociologist from systematizing his concepts by the classification of possible types of subjective meaning. That is, he may reason as if action actually proceeded on the basis of clearly self-conscious meaning. The resulting deviation from the concrete facts must continually be kept in mind whenever it is a question of this level of concreteness, and must be carefully studied with reference both to degree and kind. It is often necessary to choose between terms which are either clear or unclear. Those which are clear will, to be sure, have the abstractness of ideal types, but they are nonetheless preferable for scientific purposes.

Translated by A. M. Henderson and Talcott Parsons

28. "Objectivity" in Social Science

There is no absolutely "objective" scientific analysis of culture—or put perhaps more narrowly but certainly not essentially differently for our purposes—of "social phenomena" independent of special and "one-sided" viewpoints according to which—expressly or tacitly, consciously or unconsciously—they are selected, analyzed and organized for expository purposes. The reasons for this lie in the character of the cognitive goal of all research in social science which seeks to transcend the purely *formal* treatment of the legal or conventional norms regulating social life.

The type of social science in which we are interested is an empirical science of concrete reality *(Wirklichkeitswissenschaft)*. Our aim is the understanding of the characteristic uniqueness of the reality in which we move. We wish to understand on the one hand the relationships and the cultural significance of individual events in their contemporary manifestations and on the other the causes of their being historically so and not otherwise. Now, as soon as we attempt to reflect about the way in which life confronts us in immediate concrete situations, it presents an infinite multiplicity of successively and coexistently emerging and disappearing events, both "within" and "outside" ourselves. The absolute infinitude of this multiplicity is seen to remain undiminished even when our attention is focused on a single "object," for instance, a concrete act of exchange, as soon as we seriously attempt an exhaustive description of *all* the individual components of this "individual phenomenon," to say nothing of explaining it causally. All the analysis of infinite reality which the finite human mind can conduct rests on the tacit assumption that only a finite portion of this reality constitutes the object of scientific investigation, and that only it is "important" in the sense of being "worthy of being known." But what are the criteria by which this segment is selected? It has often been thought that the decisive criterion in the cultural sciences, too, was in the last analysis, the "regular" recurrence of certain causal relationships. The "laws" which we are able to perceive in the infinitely manifold stream of events must—according to this conception—contain the scientifically "essential" aspect of reality. As soon as we have shown some causal relationship to be a "law," (i.e., if we have shown it to be universally valid by means of comprehensive historical induction, or have made it immediately and tangibly plausible according to our subjective experience), a great number of similar cases order themselves under the formula thus attained. Those elements in each individual event which are left unaccounted for by the selection of their elements subsumable under the "law" are considered as scientifically unintegrated residues which will be taken care of in the further perfection of the system of "laws." Alternatively they will be viewed as "accidental" and therefore scientifically unimportant because they do not fit into the structure of the "law;" in other words, they are not typical of the event and hence can only be the objects of "idle curiosity." Accordingly, even among the followers of the Historical School we continually find the attitude which declares that the ideal, which all the sciences, including the cultural sciences, serve and toward which they should strive even in the remote future, is a system of propositions from which reality can be "deduced." As is well known, a leading natural scientist believed that he could designate the (factually unattainable) ideal goal of such a treatment of cultural reality as a sort of "astronomical" knowledge.

Let us not, for our part, spare ourselves the trouble of examining these matters more closely—however often they have already been discussed. The first thing that impresses one is that the "astronomical" knowledge which was referred to is not a system of laws at all. On the contrary, the laws which it presupposes have been taken from other disciplines like mechanics. But it too concerns itself with the question of the individual consequence which the working of these laws in a unique configuration produces, since it is these individual configurations which are significant for us. Every individual constellation which it "explains" or predicts is causally explicable only as the consequence of another equally individual constellation which has preceded it. As far back as we may go into the grey mist of the far-off past, the reality to which the laws apply always remains equally individual, equally undeducible from laws. A cosmic "primeval state" which had no individual character or less individual character than the cosmic reality of the present would naturally be a meaningless notion. But is there not some trace of similar ideas in our field in those propositions sometimes derived from natural law and sometimes verified by the observation of "primitives," concerning an economic-social "primeval state" free from historical "accidents," and characterized by phenomena such as "primitive agrarian communism," sexual "promiscuity," etc., from which individual historical development emerges by a sort of fall from grace into concreteness?

The social-scientific interest has its point of departure, of course, in the real, i.e., concrete, individually-structured configuration of our cultural life in its universal relationships which are themselves no less individually structured, and in its development out of other social cultural conditions, which themselves are obviously likewise individually structured. It is clear here that the situation which we illustrated by reference to astronomy as a limiting case (which is regularly drawn on by logicians for the same purpose) appears in a more accentuated form. Whereas in astronomy, the heavenly bodies are of interest to us only in their quantitative and exact aspects, the qualitative aspect of phenomena concerns us in the social sciences. To this should be added that in the social sciences we are concerned with psychological and intellectual *(geistig)* phenomena the empathic understanding of which is naturally a problem of a specifically different type from those which the schemes of the exact natural sciences in general can or seek to solve. Despite that, this distinction in itself is not a distinction in principle, as it seems at first glance. Aside from pure mechanics, even the exact natural sciences do not proceed without qualitative categories. Furthermore, in our own field we encounter the idea (which is obviously distorted) that at least the phenomena characteristic of a money-economy—which are basic to our culture—are quantifiable and on that account subject to formulation as "laws." Finally it depends on the breadth or narrowness of one's definition of "law" as to whether one will also include regularities which because they are not quantifiable are not subject to numerical analysis. Especially insofar as the influence of psychological and intellectual factors is concerned, it does not in any case exclude the establishment of rules governing rational conduct. Above all, the point of view still persists which claims that the task of psychology is to play a role comparable to mathematics for the *Geisteswissenschaften* in the sense that it analyzes the complicated phenomena of social life into their psychic conditions and effects, reduces them to their most elementary possible psychic factors and then analyzes their functional interdependences. Thereby a sort of "chemistry," if not "mechanics," of the psychic foundations of social life would be created. Whether such investigations can produce valuable and—what is something else—useful results for the cultural sciences, we cannot decide here. But this would be irrelevant to the question as to whether the aim of social-economic knowledge in our sense, i.e., knowledge of reality with respect to its cultural significance and its causal relationships, can be attained through the quest for recurrent sequences. Let us assume that we have succeeded by means of psychology or otherwise in analyzing all the observed and imaginable relationships, of social phenomena into some ultimate elementary "factors," that we have made an exhaustive analysis and classification of them and then formulated rigorously exact laws covering their behavior.—What would be the significance of these results for our knowledge of the historically given culture or any individual phase thereof, such as capitalism, in its development and cultural significance? As an analytical tool, it would be as useful as a textbook of organic chemical combinations would be for our knowledge of the biogenetic aspect of the animal and plant world. In each case, certainly an important and useful preliminary step would have been taken. In neither case can concrete reality be deduced from "laws" and "factors." This is not because some higher mysterious powers reside in living phenomena (such as "dominants," "entelechies," or whatever they might be called). This, however, presents a problem in its own right. The real reason is that the analysis of reality is concerned with the configuration into which those (hypothetical!) "factors" are arranged to form a cultural phenomenon which is historically significant to us. Furthermore, if we wish to "explain" this individual configuration "causally" we must invoke other equally individual configurations on the basis of which we will explain it with the aid of those (hypothetical!) "laws."

The determination of those (hypothetical) "laws" and "factors" would in any case only be the first of the many operations which would lead us to the desired type of knowledge. The analysis of the historically given individual configuration of those "factors" and their significant concrete interaction, conditioned by their historical context and especially the rendering intelligible of the basis and type of this significance would be the next task to be achieved. This task must be achieved, it is true, by the utilization of the preliminary analysis, but it is nonetheless an entirely new and distinct task. The tracing as far into the past as possible of the individual features of these historically evolved configurations which are contemporaneously significant, and their historical explanation by antecedent and equally individual configurations would be the third task. Finally the prediction of possible future constellations would be a conceivable fourth task.

For all these purposes, clear concepts and the knowledge of those (hypothetical) "laws" are obviously of great value as heuristic means—but only as such. Indeed they are quite indispensable for this purpose. But even in this function their limitations become evident at a decisive point. In stating this, we arrive at the decisive feature of the method of the cultural sciences. We have designated as "cultural sciences" those disciplines which analyze the phenomena of life in terms of their cultural significance. The significance of a configuration of cultural phenomena and the basis of this significance cannot however be derived and rendered intelligible by a system of analytical laws *(Gesetzesbegriffen)*, however perfect it may be, since the significance of cultural events presupposes a value-orientation toward these events. The concept of culture is a value-concept. Empirical reality becomes "culture" to us because and insofar as we relate it to value ideas. It includes those segments and only those segments of reality which have become significant to us because of this value-relevance. Only a small portion of existing concrete reality is colored by our value-conditioned interest and it alone is significant to us. It is significant because it reveals relationships which are important to us due to their connection with our values. Only because and to the extent that this is the case is it worthwhile for us to know it in its individual features. We cannot discover, however, what is meaningful to us by means of a "presuppositionless" investigation of empirical data. Rather, perception of its meaningfulness to us is the presupposition of its becoming an object of investigation. Meaningfulness naturally does not coincide with laws as such, and the more general the law the less the coincidence. For the specific meaning which a phenomenon has for us is naturally not to be found in those relationships which it shares with many other phenomena.

The focus of attention on reality under the guidance of values which lend it significance and the selection and ordering of the phenomena which are thus affected in the light of their cultural significance is entirely different from the analysis of reality in terms of laws and general concepts. Neither of these two types of the analysis of reality has any necessary logical relationship with the other. They can coincide in individual instances but it would be most disastrous if their occasional coincidence caused us to think that they were not distinct in principle. The cultural significance of a phenomenon, e.g., the significance of exchange in a money economy, can be the fact that it exists on a mass scale as a fundamental component of modern culture. But the historical fact that it plays this role must be causally explained in order to render its cultural significance understandable. The analysis of the general aspects of exchange and the technique of the market is a—highly important and indispensable—preliminary task. For not only does this type of analysis leave unanswered the question as to how exchange historically acquired its fundamental significance in the modern world; but above all else, the fact with which we are primarily concerned, namely, the cultural significance of the money-economy—for the sake of which we are interested in the description of exchange technique, and for the sake of which alone a science exists which deals with that technique—is not derivable from any "law." The generic features of exchange, purchase, etc., interest the jurist—but we are concerned with the analysis of the cultural significance of the concrete historical fact that today exchange exists on a mass scale. When we require an explanation, when we wish to understand what distinguishes the social-economic aspects of our culture, for instance, from that of Antiquity, in which exchange showed precisely the same generic traits as it does today, and when we raise the question as to where the significance of "money economy" lies, logical principles of quite heterogenous derivation enter into the investigation. We will apply those concepts with which we are provided by the investigation of the general features of economic mass phenomena—indeed, insofar as they are relevant to the meaningful aspects of our culture, we shall use them as means of exposition. The goal of our investigation is not reached through the exposition of those laws and concepts, precise as it may be. The question as to what should be the object of universal conceptualization cannot be decided "presuppositionlessly" but only with reference to the significance which certain segments of that infinite multiplicity which we call "commerce" have for culture. We seek knowledge of an historical phenomenon, meaning by historical: significant in its individuality *(Eigenart)*. And the decisive element in this is that only through the presupposition that a finite part alone of the infinite variety of phenomena is significant, does the knowledge of an individual phenomenon become logically meaningful. Even with the widest imaginable knowledge of "laws," we are helpless in the face of the question: how is the causal explanation of an individual fact possible—since a description of even the smallest slice of reality can never be exhaustive? The number and type of causes which have influenced any given event are always infinite and there is nothing in the things themselves to set some of them apart as alone meriting attention. A chaos of "existential judgments" about countless individual events would be the only result of a serious attempt to analyze reality "without presuppositions." And even this result is only seemingly possible, since every single perception discloses on closer examination an infinite number of constituent perceptions which can never be exhaustively expressed in a judgment. Order is brought into this chaos only on the condition that in every case only a part of concrete reality is interesting and significant to us, because only it is related to the cultural values with which we approach reality. Only certain sides of the infinitely complex concrete phenomenon, namely those to which we attribute a general cultural significance, are therefore worthwhile knowing. They alone are objects of causal explanation. And even this causal explanation evinces the same character; an exhaustive causal investigation of any concrete phenomena in its full reality is not only practically impossible—it is simply nonsense. We select only those causes to which are to be imputed in the individual case, the "essential" feature of an event. Where the *individuality* of a phenomenon is concerned, the question of causality is not a question of laws but of concrete causal relationships; it is not a question of the subsumption of the event under some general rubric as a representative case but of its imputation as a consequence of some constellation. It is in brief a question of imputation. Wherever the causal explanation of a "cultural phenomenon"—a "historical individual"[1]—is under consideration, the knowledge of causal laws is not the end of the investigation but only a means. It facilitates and renders possible the causal imputation to their concrete causes of those components of a phenomenon the individuality of which is culturally significant. So far and only so far as it achieves this, is it valuable for our knowledge of concrete relationships. And the more "general" (i.e., the more abstract) the laws, the less they can contribute to the causal imputation of individual phenomena and, more indirectly, to the understanding of the significance of cultural events.

What is the consequence of all this?

Naturally, it does not imply that the knowledge of universal propositions, the construction of abstract concepts, the knowledge of regularities and the attempt to formulate "laws" have no scientific justification in the cultural sciences. Quite the contrary, if the causal knowledge of the historians consists of the imputation of concrete effects to concrete causes, a valid imputation of any individual effect without the application of "nomological" knowledge—i.e., the knowledge of recurrent causal sequences—would in general be impossible. Whether a single individual component of a relationship is, in a concrete case, to be assigned causal responsibility for an effect, the causal explanation of which is at issue, can in doubtful cases be determined only by estimating the effects which we generally expect from it and from the other components of the same complex which are relevant to the explanation. In other words, the "adequate" effects of the causal elements involved must be considered in arriving at any such conclusion. The extent to which the historian (in the widest sense of the word) can perform this imputation in a reasonably certain manner, with his imagination sharpened by personal experience and trained in analytic methods, and the extent to which he must have recourse to the aid of special disciplines which make it possible, varies with the individual case. Everywhere, however, and hence also in the sphere of complicated economic processes, the more certain and the more comprehensive our general knowledge the greater is the certainty of imputation. This proposition is not in the least affected by the fact that even in the case of all so-called "economic laws" without exception, we are concerned here not with "laws" in the narrower exact natural-science sense, but with adequate causal relationships expressed in rules and with the application of the category of "objective possibility." The establishment of such regularities is not the end but rather the means of knowledge. It is entirely a question of expediency, to be settled separately for each individual case, whether a regularly recurrent causal relationship of everyday experience should be formulated into a "law." Laws are important and valuable in the exact natural sciences, in the measure that those sciences are universally valid. For the knowledge of historical phenomena in their concreteness, the most general laws, because they are most devoid of content, are also the least valuable. The more comprehensive the validity—or scope—of a term, the more it leads us away from the richness of reality since in order to include the common elements of the largest possible number of phenomena, it must necessarily be as abstract as possible and hence devoid of content. In the cultural sciences, the knowledge of the universal or general is never valuable in itself.

The conclusion which follows from the above is that an "objective" analysis of cultural events, which proceeds according to the thesis that the ideal of science is the reduction of empirical reality to "laws," is meaningless. It is not meaningless, as is often maintained, because cultural or psychic events for instance are "objectively" less governed by laws. It is meaningless for a number of other reasons. Firstly, because the knowledge of social laws is not knowledge of social reality but is rather one of the various aids used by our minds for attaining this end; secondly, because knowledge of cultural events is inconceivable except on a basis of the significance which the concrete constellations of reality have for us in certain individual concrete situations. In which sense and in which situations this is the case is not revealed to us by any law; it is decided according to the value-ideas in the light of which we view "culture" in each individual case. "Culture" is a finite segment of the meaningless infinity of the world process, a segment on which human beings confer meaning and significance. This is true even for the human being who views a particular culture as a mortal enemy and who seeks to "return to nature." He can attain this point of view only after viewing the culture in which he lives from the standpoint of his values, and finding it "too soft." This is the purely logical-formal fact which is involved when we speak of the logically necessary rootedness of all historical entities *(historische Individuen)* in "evaluative ideas." The transcendental presupposition of every cultural science lies not in our finding a certain culture or any "culture" in general to be valuable but rather in the fact that we are cultural beings, endowed with the capacity and the will to take a deliberate attitude toward the world and to lend it significance. Whatever this significance may be, it will lead us to judge certain phenomena of human existence in its light and to respond to them as being (positively or negatively) meaningful. Whatever may be the content of this attitude, these phenomena have cultural significance for us and on this significance alone rests its scientific interest. Thus when we speak here of the conditioning of cultural knowledge through evaluative ideas *(Wertideen)* (following the terminology of modern logic), it is done in the hope that we will not be subject to crude misunderstandings such as the opinion that cultural significance should be attributed only to valuable phenomena. Prostitution is a cultural phenomenon just as much as religion or money. All three are cultural phenomena only because, and only insofar as, their existence and the form which they historically assume touch directly or indirectly on our cultural interests and arouse our striving for knowledge concerning problems brought into focus by the evaluative ideas which give significance to the fragment of reality analyzed by those concepts.

All knowledge of cultural reality, as may be seen, is always knowledge from particular points of view. When we require from the historian and social research worker as an elementary presupposition that they distinguish the important from the trivial and that they should have the necessary "point of view" for this distinction, we mean that they must understand how to relate the events of the real world consciously or unconsciously to universal "cultural values," and to select out those relationships which are significant for us. If the notion that those standpoints can be derived from the "facts themselves" continually recurs, it is due to the naive self-deception of the specialist, who is unaware that it is due to the evaluative ideas with which he unconsciously approaches his subject matter, that he has selected from an absolute infinity a tiny portion with the study of which he concerns himself. In connection with this selection of individual special "aspects" of the event, which always and everywhere occurs, consciously or unconsciously, there also occurs that element of cultural-scientific work which is referred to by the often-heard assertion that the "personal" element of a scientific work is what is really valuable in it, and that personality must be expressed in every work if its existence is to be justified. To be sure, without the investigator's evaluative ideas, there would be no principle of selection of subject-matter and no meaningful knowledge of the concrete reality. Just as without the investigator's conviction regarding the significance of particular cultural facts, every attempt to analyze concrete reality is absolutely meaningless, so the direction of his personal belief, the refraction of values in the prism of his mind, gives direction to his work. And the values to which the scientific genius relates the object of his inquiry may determine (i.e., decide) the "conception" of a whole epoch, not only concerning what is regarded as "valuable," but also concerning what is significant or insignificant, "important" or "unimportant" in the phenomena.

Accordingly, cultural science in our sense involves "subjective" presuppositions insofar as it concerns itself only with those components of reality which have some relationship, however indirect, to events to which we attach cultural significance. Nonetheless, it is entirely causal knowledge exactly in the same sense as the knowledge of significant concrete *(individueller)* natural events which have a qualitative character. Among the many confusions which the overreaching tendency of a formal-juristic outlook has brought about in the cultural sciences, there has recently appeared the attempt to "refute" the "materialistic conception of history" by a series of clever but fallacious arguments which state that since all economic life must take place in legally or conventionally regulated forms, all economic "development" must take the form of striving for the creation of new legal forms. Hence it is said to be intelligible only through ethical maxims, and is on this account essentially different from every type of "natural" development. Accordingly the knowledge of economic development is said to be "teleological" in character. Without wishing to discuss the meaning of the ambiguous term "development," or the logically no-less-ambiguous term "teleology" in the social sciences, it should be stated that such knowledge need not be "teleological" in the sense assumed by this point of view. The cultural significance of normatively regulated legal relations and even norms themselves can undergo fundamental revolutionary changes even under conditions of the formal identity of the prevailing legal norms. Indeed, if one wishes to lose one's self for a moment in fantasies about the future, one might theoretically imagine, let us say, the "socialization of the means of production" unaccompanied by any conscious "striving" toward this result, and without even the disappearance or addition of a single paragraph of our legal code; the statistical frequency of certain legally regulated relationships might be changed fundamentally, and in many cases, even disappear entirely; a great number of legal norms might become practically meaningless and their whole cultural significance changed beyond identification. *De lege ferenda* discussions may be justifiably disregarded by the "materialistic conception of history," since its central proposition is the indeed inevitable change in the significance of legal institutions. Those who view the painstaking labor of causally understanding historical reality as of secondary importance can disregard it, but it is impossible to supplant it by any type of "teleology." From our viewpoint, "purpose" is the conception of an effect which becomes a cause of an action. Since we take into account every cause which produces or can produce a significant effect, we also consider this one. Its specific significance consists only in the fact that we not only observe human conduct but can and desire to understand it.

Undoubtedly, all evaluative ideas are "subjective." Between the "historical" interest in a family chronicle and that in the development of the greatest conceivable cultural phenomena which were and are common to a nation or to mankind over long epochs, there exists an infinite gradation of "significance" arranged into an order which differs for each of us. And they are, naturally, historically variable in accordance with the character of the culture and the ideas which rule men's minds. But it obviously does not follow from this that research in the cultural sciences can only have results which are "subjective" in the sense that they are valid for one person and not for others. Only the degree to which they interest different persons varies. In other words, the choice of the object of investigation and the extent or depth to which this investigation attempts to penetrate into the infinite causal web, are determined by the evaluative ideas which dominate the investigator and his age. In the method of investigation, the guiding "point of view" is of great importance for the construction of the conceptual scheme which will be used in the investigation. In the mode of their use, however, the investigator is obviously bound by the norms of our thought just as much here as elsewhere. For scientific truth is precisely what is valid for all who seek the truth.

Translated by Edward A. Shils
and Henry A. Finch

29. The Tension between Science and Policy-Making

It may be asserted without the possibility of a doubt that as soon as one seeks to derive concrete directives from practical political (particularly economic and social-political) evaluations; (1) the indispensable means, and (2) the inevitable repercussions, and (3) the thus-conditioned competition of numerous possible evaluations in their practical consequences, are all that an empirical discipline can demonstrate with the means at its disposal. Philosophical disciplines can go further and lay bare the "meaning" of evaluations (i.e., their ultimate meaningful structure and their meaningful consequences); in other words, they can indicate their "place" within the totality of all the possible "ultimate" evaluations and delimit their spheres of meaningful validity. Even such simple questions as the extent to which an end should sanction unavoidable means, or the extent to which undesired repercussions should be taken into consideration, or how conflicts between several concretely conflicting ends are to be arbitrated, are entirely matters of choice or compromise. There is no (rational or empirical) scientific procedure of any kind whatsoever which can provide us with a decision here. The social sciences, which are strictly empirical sciences, are the least fitted to presume to save the individual the difficulty of making a choice, and they should therefore not create the impression that they can do so.

Finally it should be explicitly noted that the recognition of the existence of this situation is, as far as our disciplines are concerned, completely independent of the attitude one takes toward the very brief remarks made above regarding the theory of value. For there is, in general, no logically tenable standpoint from which it could be denied except a hierarchical ordering of values unequivocally prescribed by ecclesiastical dogmas. I need not consider whether there really are persons who assert that such problems as (*a*) does a concrete event occur thus and so or otherwise, or (*b*) why do the concrete events in question occur thus and so and not otherwise, or (*c*) does a given event ordinarily succeed another one according to a certain law and with what degree of probability—are not basically different from the problems: (a^1) what should one do in a concrete situation, or (b^2) from which standpoints may those situations be satisfactory or unsatisfactory, or (c^3) whether they are—whatever their form—generally formulatable propositions (axioms) to which these standpoints can be reduced. There are many who insist further that there is no logical disjunction between such enquiries as, (*a*) in which direction will a concrete situation (or generally, a situation of a certain type) develop and with what greater degree of probability in which particular direction than in any other and (*b*) a problem which investigates whether one should attempt to influence the development of a certain situation in a given direction—regardless of whether it be the one in which it would also move if left alone, or the opposite direction or one which is different from either. There are those who assert that (*a*) the problem as to which attitudes toward any given problem specified persons or an unspecified number of persons under specified conditions will probably or even certainly take and (*b*) the problem as to whether the attitude which emerged in the situation referred to above is right—are in no way different from one another. The proponents of such views will resist any statement to the effect that the problems in the above-cited juxtapositions do not have even the slightest connection with one another and that they really are "to be separated from one another." These persons will insist furthermore that their position is not in contradiction with the requirements of scientific thinking. Such an attitude is by no means the same as that of an author who, conceding the absolute heterogeneity of both types of problems, nevertheless, in one and the same book, on one and the same page—indeed in a principal and subordinate clause of one and the same sentence—makes statements bearing on each of the two heterogeneous problems referred to above. Such a procedure is strictly a matter of choice. All that can be demanded of him is that he does not unwittingly (or just to be clever) deceive his readers concerning the absolute heterogeneity of the problems. Personally I am of the opinion that nothing is too "pedantic" if it is useful for the avoidance of confusions.

Thus, the discussion of value judgments can have only the following functions:

(*a*) The elaboration and explication of the ultimate, internally "consistent" value axioms, from which the divergent attitudes are derived. People are often in error, not only about their opponent's evaluations, but also about their own. This procedure is essentially an operation which begins with concrete particular evaluations and analyzes their meanings and then moves to the more general level of irreducible evaluations. It does not use the techniques of an empirical discipline and it produces no new knowledge of facts. Its "validity" is similar to that of logic.

(*b*) The deduction of "implications" (for those accepting certain value judgments) which follow from certain irreducible value axioms, when the practical evaluation of factual situations is based on these axioms alone. This deduction depends, on one hand, on logic, and on the other, on empirical observations for the completest possible casuistic analyses of all such empirical situations as are in principle subject to practical evaluation.

(*c*) The determination of the factual consequences which the realization of a certain practical evaluation must have: (1) in consequence of being bound to certain indispensable means, (2) in consequence of the inevitability of certain not directly desired repercussions. These purely empirical observations may lead us to the conclusion that (a) it is absolutely impossible to realize the object of the preference, even in a remotely approximate way, because no means of carrying it out can be discovered; (b) the more or less considerable improbability of its complete or even approximate realization, either for the same reason or because of the probable appearance of undesired repercussions which might directly or indirectly render the realization undesirable; (c) the necessity of taking into account such means or such repercussions as the proponent of the practical postulate in question did not consider, so that his evaluation of end, means, and repercussions becomes a new problem for him. Finally: (d) the uncovering of new axioms (and the postulates to be drawn from them) which the proponent of a practical postulate did not take into consideration. Since he was unaware of those axioms, he did not formulate an attitude toward them although the execution of his own postulate conflicts with the others either (1) in principle or (2) as a result of the practical consequences, (i.e., logically or actually). In (1) it is a matter of further discussion of problems of type (a); in (2), of type (c).

Far from being meaningless, value-discussions of this type can be of the greatest utility as long as their potentialities are correctly understood.

The utility of a discussion of practical evaluations at the right place and in the correct sense is, however, by no means exhausted with such direct "results." When correctly conducted, it can be extremely valuable for empirical research in the sense that it provides it with problems for investigation.

The problems of the empirical disciplines are, of course, to be solved "nonevaluatively." They are not problems of evaluation. But the problems of the social sciences are selected by the value-relevance of the phenomena treated. Concerning the significance of the expression "relevance to values" I refer to my earlier writings and above all to the works of Heinrich Rickert and will forbear to enter upon that question here. It should only be recalled that the expression "relevance to values" refers simply to the philosophical interpretation of that specifically scientific "interest" which determines the selection of a given subject matter and the problems of an empirical analysis.

In empirical investigation, no "practical evaluations" are legitimated by this strictly logical fact. But together with historical experience, it shows that cultural (i.e., evaluative) interests give purely empirical scientific work its direction. It is now clear that these evaluative interests can be made more explicit and differentiated by the analysis of value judgments. These considerably reduce, or at any rate lighten, the task of "value interpretation"—an extremely important preparation for empirical work—for the scientific investigator and especially the historian.[1]

Translated by Edward A. Shils
and Henry A. Finch

30. Ideal-Type Constructs

In the establishment of the propositions of abstract theory, it is only apparently a matter of "deductions" from fundamental psychological motives. Actually, the former are a special case of a kind of concept-construction which is peculiar and, to a certain extent, indispensable to the cultural sciences. It is worthwhile at this point to describe it in further detail since we can thereby approach more closely the fundamental question of the significance of theory in the social sciences. Therewith we leave undiscussed, once and for all, whether *the* particular analytical concepts which we cite or to which we allude as illustrations, correspond to the purposes they are to serve, i.e., whether in fact they were well-adapted. The question as to how far, for example, contemporary "abstract theory" should be further elaborated, is ultimately also a question of the strategy of science, which must, however, concern itself with other problems as well. Even the "theory of marginal utility" is subsumable under a "law of marginal utility."

We have in abstract economic theory an illustration of those synthetic constructs which have been designated as "ideas" of historical phenomena. It offers us an ideal picture of events on the commodity-market under conditions of a society organized on the principles of an exchange economy, free competition, and rigorously rational conduct. This conceptual pattern brings together certain relationships and events of historical life into a complex, which is conceived as an internally consistent system. Substantively, this construct in itself is like a utopia which has been arrived at by the analytical accentuation of certain elements of reality. Its relationship to the empirical data consists solely in the fact that where market-conditioned relationships of the type referred to by the abstract construct are discovered or suspected to exist in reality to some extent, we can make the characteristic features of this relationship pragmatically clear and understandable by reference to an ideal-type. This procedure can be indispensable for heuristic as well as expository purposes. The ideal-typical concept will help to develop our skill in imputation in research: it is no "hypothesis" but it offers guidance to the construction of hypotheses. It is not a description of reality but it aims to give unambiguous means of expression to such a description. It is thus the "idea" of the historically given modern society, based on an exchange economy, which is developed for us by quite the same logical principles as are used in constructing the idea of the medieval "city economy" as a "genetic" concept. When we do this, we construct the concept "city-economy" not as an average of the economic structures actually existing in all the cities observed, but as an ideal-type. An ideal type is formed by the one-sided accentuation of one or more points of view and by the synthesis of a great many diffuse, discrete, more or less present, and occasionally absent concrete individual phenomena, which are arranged according to those one-sidedly emphasized viewpoints into a unified analytical construct *(Gedankenbild)*. In its conceptual purity, this mental construct *(Gedankenbild)* cannot be found empirically anywhere in reality. It is a utopia. Historical research faces the task of determining, in each individual case, the extent to which this ideal-construct approximates to or diverges from reality; to what extent for example, the economic structure of a certain city is to be classified as a "city-economy." When carefully applied, those concepts are particularly useful in research and exposition. In very much the same way one can work the "idea" of "handicraft" into a utopia by arranging certain traits, actually found in an unclear, confused state in the industrial enterprises of the most diverse epochs and countries, into a consistent ideal-construct by an accentuation of their essential tendencies. This ideal-type is then related to the idea *(Gedankenausdruck)* which one finds expressed there. One can further delineate a society in which all branches of economic and even intellectual activity are governed by maxims which appear to be applications of the same principle which characterizes the ideal-typical "handicraft" system. Furthermore, one can juxtapose alongside the ideal-typical "handicraft" system the antithesis of a correspondingly ideal-typical capitalistic productive system, which has been abstracted out of certain features of modern large-scale industry. On the basis of this, one can delineate the utopia of a "capitalistic" culture, i.e., one in which the governing principle is the investment of private capital. This procedure would accentuate certain individual concretely diverse traits of modern material and intellectual culture in its unique aspects into an ideal construct which from our point of view would be completely self-consistent. This would then be the delineation of an "idea" of capitalistic culture. We must disregard for the moment whether and how this procedure could be carried out. It is possible, or rather, it must be accepted as certain that numerous, indeed a very great many, utopias of this sort can be worked out, of which none is like another, and none of which can be observed in empirical reality as an actually existing economic system, but each of which claims that it is a representation of the "idea" of capitalistic culture. Each of these can claim to be a representation of the "idea" of capitalistic culture to the extent that it has really taken certain traits, meaningful in their essential features, from the empirical reality of our culture and brought them together into a unified ideal-construct. For those phenomena which interest us as cultural phenomena are interesting to us with respect to very different kinds of evaluative ideas to which we relate them. Inasmuch as the "points of view" from which they can become significant for us are very diverse, the most varied criteria can be applied to the selection of the traits which are to enter into the construction of an ideal-typical view of a particular culture.

What is the significance of such ideal-typical constructs for an empirical science, as we wish to constitute it? Before going any further, we should emphasize that the idea of an ethical imperative, of a "model" of what "ought" to exist is to be carefully distinguished from the analytical construct, which is "ideal" in the strictly logical sense of the term. It is a matter here of constructing relationships which our imagination accepts as plausibly motivated and hence as "objectively possible" and which appear as adequate from the nomological standpoint.

Whoever accepts the proposition that the knowledge of historical reality can or should be a "presuppositionless" copy of "objective" facts, will deny the value of the ideal-type. Even those who recognize that there is no "presuppositionlessness" in the logical sense, and that even the simplest excerpt from a statute or from a documentary source can have scientific meaning only with reference to "significance" and ultimately to evaluative ideas, will more or less regard the construction of any such historical "utopias" as an expository device which endangers the autonomy of historical research and which is, in any case, a vain sport. And, in fact, whether we are dealing simply with a conceptual game or with a scientifically fruitful method of conceptualization and theory-construction can never be decided *a priori*. Here, too, there is only one criterion, namely, that of success in revealing concrete cultural phenomena in their interdependence, their causal conditions and their significance. The construction of abstract ideal-types recommends itself not as an end but as a means. Every conscientious examination of the conceptual elements of historical exposition shows, however, that the historian, as soon as he attempts to go beyond the bare establishment of concrete relationships and to determine the cultural significance of even the simplest individual event in order to "characterize" it, must use concepts which are precisely and unambiguously definable only in the form of ideal types. Or are concepts such as "individualism," "imperialism," "feudalism," "mercantilism," "conventional," etc., and innumerable concepts of like character (by means of which we seek analytically and empathically to understand reality) constructed substantively by the "presuppositionless" description of some concrete phenomenon, or through the abstract synthesis of those traits which are common to numerous concrete phenomena? Hundreds of words in the historian's vocabulary are ambiguous constructs created to meet the unconsciously felt need for adequate expression; the meaning of which is only concretely felt but not clearly thought out. In a great many cases, particularly in the field of descriptive political history, their ambiguity has not been prejudicial to the clarity of the presentation. It is sufficient that in each case the reader should feel what the historian had in mind; or, one can content one's self with the idea that the author used a particular meaning of the concept with special reference to the concrete case at hand. The greater the need, however, for a sharp appreciation of the significance of a cultural phenomenon, the more imperative is the need to operate with unambiguous concepts which are not only particularly but also systematically defined. A "definition" of such synthetic historical terms according to the scheme of *genus proximum* and *differentia specifica* is naturally nonsense. But let us consider it. Such a form of the establishment of the meanings of words is to be found only in axiomatic disciplines which use syllogisms. A simple "descriptive analysis" of these concepts into their components either does not exist or else exists only illusorily, for the question arises as to which of these components should be regarded as essential. When a genetic definition of the content of the concept is sought, there remains only the ideal-type in the sense explained above. It is a conceptual construct *(Gedankenbild)* which is neither historical reality nor even the "true" reality. It is even less fitted to serve as a schema under which a real situation or action is to be subsumed as one instance. It has the significance of a purely ideal limiting concept with which the real situation or action is compared and surveyed for the explication of certain of its significant components. Such concepts are constructs in terms of which we formulate relationships by the application of the category of objective possibility. By means of this category, the adequacy of our imagination, oriented and disciplined by reality, is judged.

In this function especially, the ideal-type is an attempt to analyze historically unique configurations or their individual components by means of genetic concepts. Let us take for instance the concepts "church" and "sect." They may be broken down purely classificatorily into complexes of characteristics whereby not only the distinction between them but also the content of the concept must constantly remain fluid. If, however, I wish to formulate the concept of "sect" genetically, e.g., with reference to certain important cultural significances which the "sectarian spirit" has had for modern culture, certain characteristics of both become essential because they stand in an adequate causal relationship to those influences. However, the concepts thereupon become ideal-typical in the sense that they appear in full conceptual integrity either not at all or only in individual instances. Here as elsewhere every concept which is not purely classificatory diverges from reality. But the discursive nature of our knowledge (i.e., the fact that we comprehend reality only through a chain of intellectual modifications) postulates such a conceptual shorthand. Our imagination can often dispense with explicit conceptual formulations as a means of investigation. But as regards exposition, to the extent that it wishes to be unambiguous, the use of precise formulations in the sphere of cultural analysis is in many cases absolutely necessary. Whoever disregards it entirely must confine himself to the formal aspect of cultural phenomena, e.g., to legal history. The universe of legal norms is naturally clearly definable and is valid (in the legal sense!) for historical reality. But social science in our sense is concerned with practical significance. This significance however can very often be brought unambiguously to mind only by relating the empirical data to an ideal limiting case. If the historian (in the widest sense of the word) rejects an attempt to construct such ideal-types as a "theoretical construction" (i.e., as useless or dispensable for his concrete heuristic purposes), the inevitable consequence is either that he consciously or unconsciously uses other similar concepts without formulating them verbally and elaborating them logically or that he remains stuck in the realm of the vaguely "felt."

Nothing, however, is more dangerous than the confusion of theory and history stemming from naturalistic prejudices. This confusion expresses itself firstly in the belief that the "true" content and the essence of historical reality is portrayed in such theoretical constructs, or secondly, in the use of these contructs as a procrustean bed into which history is to be forced, or thirdly, in the hypostatization of such "ideas" as real "forces" and as a "true" reality which operates behind the passage of events and which works itself out in history.

This latter danger is especially great since we are also, indeed primarily, accustomed to understand by the "ideas" of an epoch the thoughts or ideals which dominated the mass or at least an historically decisive number of the persons living in that epoch itself, and who were therefore significant as components of its culture. Now there are two aspects to this: in the first place, there are certain relationships between the "idea" in the sense of a tendency of practical or theoretical thought and the "idea" in the sense of the ideal-typical portrayal of an epoch constructed as a heuristic device. An ideal-type of certain situations, which can be abstracted from certain characteristic social phenomena of an epoch, might—and this is indeed quite often the case—have also been present in the minds of the persons living in that epoch as an ideal to be striven for in practical life or as a maxim for the regulation of certain social relationships. This is true of the "idea" of "provision" *(Nahrungsschutz)* and many other Canonist doctrines, especially those of Thomas Aquinas, in relationship to the modern ideal type of medieval "city-economy" which we discussed above. The same is also true of the much-talked-of "basic concept" of economics: economic "value." From Scholasticism to Marxism, the idea of an objectively "valid" value (i.e., of an ethical imperative) was amalgamated with an abstraction drawn from the empirical process of price formation. The notion that the "value" of commodities should be regulated by certain principles of natural law, has had and still has immeasurable significance for the development of culture—and not merely the culture of the Middle Ages. It has also influenced actual price formation very markedly. But what was meant and what can be meant by that theoretical concept can be made unambiguously clear only through precise, ideal-typical constructs. Those who are so contemptuous of the "Robinsonades" of classical theory should restrain themselves if they are unable to replace them with better concepts, which in this context means clearer concepts.

Thus the causal relationship between the historically determinable idea which governs the conduct of men and those components of historical reality from which their corresponding ideal-type may be abstracted, can naturally take on a considerable number of different forms. The main point to be observed is that in principle they are both fundamentally different things. There is still another aspect: those "ideas" which govern the behavior of the population of a certain epoch (i.e., which are concretely influential in determining their conduct) can, if a somewhat complicated construct is involved, be formulated precisely only in the form of an ideal-type, since empirically it exists in the minds of an indefinite and constantly changing mass of individuals and assumes in their minds the most multifarious nuances of form and content, clarity and meaning. Those elements of the spiritual life of the individuals living in a certain epoch of the Middle Ages, for example, which we may designate as the "Christianity" of those individuals, would, if they could be completely portrayed, naturally constitute a chaos of infinitely differentiated and highly contradictory complexes of ideas and feelings. This is true despite the fact that the medieval church was certainly able to bring about a unity of belief and conduct to a particularly high degree. If we raise the question as to what in this chaos was the "Christianity" of the Middle Ages (which we must nonetheless use as a stable concept) and wherein lay those "Christian" elements which we find in the institutions of the Middle Ages, we see that here too in every individual case, we are applying a purely analytical construct created by ourselves. It is a combination of articles of faith, norms from church law and custom, maxims of conduct, and countless concrete interrelationships which we have fused into an "idea." It is a synthesis which we could not succeed in attaining with consistency without the application of ideal-type concepts.

The relationship between the logical structure of the conceptual system in which we present such "ideas" and what is immediately given in empirical reality naturally varies considerably. It is relatively simple in cases in which one or a few easily formulated theoretical main principles (as for instance, Calvin's doctrine of predestination) or clearly definable ethical postulates govern human conduct and produce historical effects, so that we can analyze the "idea" into a hierarchy of ideas which can be logically derived from those theses. It is of course easily overlooked that however important the significance even of the purely logically persuasive force of ideas—Marxism is an outstanding example of this type of force—nonetheless empirical-historical events occurring in men's minds must be understood as primarily psychologically and not logically conditioned. The ideal-typical character of such syntheses of historically effective ideas is revealed still more clearly when those fundamental main principles and postulates no longer survive in the minds of those individuals who are still dominated by ideas which were logically or associatively derived from them because the "idea" which was historically and originally fundamental has either died out or has in general achieved wide diffusion only for its broadest implications. The basic fact that the synthesis is an "idea" which we have created emerges even more markedly when those fundamental main principles have either only very imperfectly or not at all been raised to the level of explicit consciousness or at least have not taken the form of explicitly elaborated complexes of ideas. When we adopt this procedure, as it very often happens and must happen, we are concerned in these ideas (e.g., the "liberalism" of a certain period, or "Methodism," or some intellectually unelaborated variety of "socialism") with a *pure* ideal type of much the same character as the synthetic "principles" of economic epochs in which we had our point of departure. The more inclusive the relationships to be presented, and the more many-sided their cultural significance has been, the *more* their comprehensive systematic exposition in a conceptual system approximates the character of an ideal type, and the less is it possible to operate with one such concept. In such situations the frequently repeated attempts to discover ever new aspects of significance by the construction of new ideal-typical concepts is all the more natural and unavoidable. All expositions, for example, of the "essence" of Christianity are ideal-types enjoying only a necessarily very relative and problematic validity when they are intended to be regarded as the historical portrayal of empirically existing facts. On the other hand, such presentations are of great value for research and of high systematic value for expository purposes when they are used as conceptual instruments for comparison with and the measurement of reality. They are indispensable for this purpose.

There is still another even more complicated significance implicit in such ideal-typical presentations. They regularly seek to be, or are unconsciously, ideal-types not only in the logical sense but also in the practical sense, i.e., they are model types which—in our illustration—contain what, from the point of view of the expositor, should be and what to him is "essential" in Christianity because it is enduringly valuable. If this is consciously or—as it is more frequently—unconsciously the case, they contain ideals to which the expositor evaluatively relates Christianity. These ideals are tasks and ends toward which he orients his "idea" of Christianity and which naturally can and indeed doubtless always will differ greatly from the values which other persons, for instance, the early Christians, connected with Christianity. In this sense, however, the "ideas" are naturally no longer purely logical auxiliary devices, no longer concepts with which reality is compared, but ideals by which it is evaluatively judged. Here it is no longer a matter of the purely theoretical procedure of treating empirical reality with respect to values but of value-judgments which are integrated into the concept of "Christianity." Because the ideal type claims empirical validity here, it penetrates into the realm of the evaluative interpretation of Christianity. The sphere of empirical science has been left behind and we are confronted with a profession of faith, not an ideal-typical construct. As fundamental as this distinction is in principle, the confusion of these two basically different meanings of the term "idea" appears with extraordinary frequency in historical writings. It is always close at hand whenever the descriptive historian begins to develop his "conception" of a personality or an epoch. In contrast with the fixed ethical standards which Schlosser applied in the spirit of rationalism, the modern relativistically educated historian who on the one hand seeks to "understand" the epoch of which he speaks "in its own terms," and on the other still seeks to "judge" it, feels the need to derive the standards for his judgment from the subject-matter itself, i.e., to allow the "idea" in the sense of the ideal to emerge from the "idea" in the sense of the "ideal-type." The esthetic satisfaction produced by such a procedure constantly tempts him to disregard the line where these two ideal types diverge—an error which on the one hand hampers the value-judgment and on the other, strives to free itself from the responsibility for its own judgment. In contrast with this, the elementary duty of scientific self-control and the only way to avoid serious and foolish blunders requires a sharp, precise distinction between the logically comparative analysis of reality by ideal-types in the logical sense and the value judgment of reality on the basis of ideals. An "ideal-type" in our sense, to repeat once more, has no connection at all with value judgments, and it has nothing to do with any type of perfection other than a purely logical one. There are ideal-types of brothels as well as of religions; there are also ideal-types of those kinds of brothels which are technically "expedient" from the point of view of police ethics as well as those of which the exact opposite is the case.

It is necessary for us to forego here a detailed discussion of the case which is by far the most complicated and most interesting; namely, the problem of the logical structure of the concept of the state. The following however should be noted: when we inquire as to what corresponds to the idea of the "state" in empirical reality, we find an infinity of diffuse and discrete human actions, both active and passive, factually and legally regulated relationships, partly unique and partly recurrent in character, all bound together by an idea, namely, the belief in the actual or normative validity of rules and of the authority-relationships of some human beings toward others. This belief is in part consciously, in part dimly felt, and in part passively accepted by persons who, should they think about the "idea" in a really clearly defined manner, would not first need a "general theory of the state" which aims to articulate the idea. The scientific conception of the state, however it is formulated, is naturally always a synthesis which we construct for certain heuristic purposes. But on the other hand, it is also abstracted from the unclear syntheses which are found in the minds of human beings. The concrete content, however, which the historical "state" assumes in those syntheses in the minds of those who make up the state, can in its turn only be made explicit through the use of ideal-typical concepts. Nor, furthermore, can there be the least doubt that the manner in which those syntheses are made (always in a logically imperfect form) by the members of a state, or in other words, the "ideas" which they construct for themselves about the state (as for example, the German "organic" metaphysics of the state in contrast with the American "business" conception) are of great practical significance. In other words, here too the practical idea which should be valid or is believed to be valid and the heuristically intended, theoretical ideal-type approach each other very closely and constantly tend to merge with each other.

We have purposely considered the ideal-type essentially—if not exclusively—as a mental construct for the scrutiny and systematic characterization of individual concrete patterns which are significant in their uniqueness, such as Christianity, capitalism, etc. We did this in order to avoid the common notion that in the sphere of cultural phenomena, the abstract type is identical with the abstract kind *(Gattungsmässigen)*. This is not the case. Without being able to make here a full logical analysis of the widely discussed concept of the "typical" which has been discredited through misuse, we can state on the basis of our previous discussion that the construction of type-concepts in the sense of the exclusion of the "accidental" also has a place in the analysis of historically individual phenomena. Naturally, however, those generic concepts which we constantly encountered as elements of historical analysis and of concrete historical concepts, can also be formed as ideal-types by abstracting and accentuating certain conceptually essential elements. Practically, this is indeed a particularly frequent and important instance of the application of ideal-typical concepts. Every individual ideal-type comprises both generic and ideal-typically constructed conceptual elements. In this case too, we see the specifically logical function of ideal-typical concepts. The concept of "exchange" is, for instance, a simple class concept *(Gattungsbegriff)* in the sense of a complex of traits which are common to many phenomena, as long as we disregard the meaning of the component parts of the concept, and simply analyze the term in its everyday usage. If however we relate this concept to the concept of "marginal utility" for instance, and construct the concept of "economic exchange" as an economically rational event, this then contains (as does every concept of "economic exchange" which is fully elaborated logically) a judgment concerning the "typical" conditions of exchange. It assumes a genetic character and becomes therewith ideal-typical in the logical sense; i.e., it removes itself from empirical reality which can only be compared or related to it. The same is true of all the so-called "fundamental concepts" of economics: they can be developed in genetic form only as ideal-types. The distinction between simple class or generic concepts *(Gattungsbegriffe)* which merely summarize the common features of certain empirical phenomena and the quasi-generic *(Gattungsmässigen)* ideal-type—as for instance an ideal-typical concept of the "nature" of "handicraft"—varies naturally with each concrete case. But no class or generic concept as such has a "typical" character and there is no purely generic "average" type. Wherever we speak of typical magnitudes—as for example, in statistics—we speak of something more than a mere average. The more it is a matter of the simple classification of events which appear in reality as mass phenomena, the more it is a matter of class concepts. On the other hand, the greater the event to which we conceptualize complicated historical patterns with respect to those components in which their specific cultural significance is contained, the greater the extent to which the concept—or system of concepts—will be ideal-typical in character. The goal of ideal-typical concept-construction is always to make clearly explicit not the class or average character, but rather the unique individual character of cultural phenomena.

The fact that ideal-types, even classificatory ones, can be and are applied, first acquires methodological significance in connection with another fact.

Thus far we have been dealing with ideal-types only as abstract concepts of relationships which are conceived by us as stable in the flux of events, as historically individual complexes in which developments are realized. There emerges however a complication, which reintroduces, with the aid of the concept of "type," the naturalistic prejudice that the goal of the social sciences must be the reduction of reality to "laws." Developmental sequences, too, can be constructed into ideal-types and these constructs can have quite considerable heuristic value. But this quite particularly gives rise to the danger that the ideal-type and reality will be confused with one another. One can, for example, arrive at the theoretical conclusion that in a society which is organized on strict "handicraft" principles, the only source of capital accumulation can be ground rent. From this perhaps, one can—for the correctness of the construct is not in question here—construct a pure ideal picture of the shift, conditioned by certain specific factors—e.g., limited land, increasing population, influx of precious metals, rationalization of the conduct of life—from a handicraft to a capitalistic economic organization. Whether the empirical-historical course of development was actually identical with the constructed one can be investigated only by using this construct as a heuristic device for the comparison of the ideal-type and the "facts." If the ideal-type were "correctly" constructed and the actual course of events did not correspond to that predicted by the ideal-type, the hypothesis that medieval society was not in certain respects a strictly "handicraft" type of society would be proved. And if the ideal-type were constructed in a heuristically "ideal" way—whether and in what way this could occur in our example will be entirely disregarded here—it will guide the investigation into a path leading to a more precise understanding of the nonhandicraft components of medieval society in their peculiar characteristics and their historical significance. If it leads to this result, it fulfils its logical purpose, even though, in doing so, it demonstrates its divergence from reality. It was—in this case—the test of a hypothesis. This procedure gives rise to no methodological doubts so long as we clearly keep in mind that ideal-typical developmental constructs and history are to be sharply distinguished from each other, and that the construct here is no more than the means for explicitly and validly imputing an historical event to its real causes while eliminating those which on the basis of our present knowledge seem possible.

The maintenance of this distinction in all its rigor often becomes uncommonly difficult in practice due to a certain circumstance. In the interest of the concrete demonstration of an ideal-type or of an ideal-typical developmental sequence, one seeks to make it clear by the use of concrete illustrative material drawn from empirical-historical reality. The danger of this procedure, which in itself is entirely legitimate, lies in the fact that historical knowledge here appears as a servant of theory instead of the opposite role. It is a great temptation for the theorist to regard this relationship either as the normal one or, far worse, to mix theory with history and indeed to confuse them with each other. This occurs in an extreme way when an ideal construct of a developmental sequence and a conceptual classification of the ideal-types of certain cultural structures (e.g., the forms of industrial production deriving from the "closed domestic economy" or the religious concepts beginning with the "gods of the moment") are integrated into a genetic classification. The series of types which results from the selected conceptual criteria appears then as a historical sequence unrolling with the necessity of a law. The logical classification of analytical concepts, on the one hand, and the empirical arrangements of the events thus conceptualized in space, time, and causal relationship, on the other, appear to be so bound up together that there is an almost irresistible temptation to do violence to reality in order to prove the real validity of the construct.

We have intentionally avoided a demonstration with respect to that ideal-typical construct which is the most important one from our point of view; namely, the Marxian theory. This was done in order not to complicate the exposition any further through the introduction of an interpretation of Marx and in order not to anticipate the discussions in our journal which will make a regular practice of presenting critical analyses of the literature concerning and following the great thinker. We will only point out here that naturally all specifically Marxian "laws" and developmental constructs—insofar as they are theoretically sound—are ideal types. The eminent, indeed unique, heuristic significance of these ideal types when they are used for the assessment of reality is known to everyone who has ever employed Marxian concepts and hypotheses. Similarly, their perniciousness, as soon as they are thought of as empirically valid or as real (*i.e.*, truly metaphysical) "effective forces," "tendencies," etc., is likewise known to those who have used them.

Class or generic concepts *(Gattungsbegriffe)*—ideal-types—ideal-typical generic concepts—ideas in the sense of thought-patterns which actually exist in the minds of human beings—ideal-types of such ideals—ideals which govern human beings—ideal-types of such ideals—ideals with which the historian approaches historical facts—

theoretical constructs using empirical data illustratively—historical investigations which utilize theoretical concepts as ideal limiting cases—the various possible combinations of these which could only be hinted at here; they are pure mental constructs, the relationships of which to the empirical reality of the immediately given is problematical in every individual case. This list of possibilities only reveals the infinite ramifications of the conceptual-methodological problems which face us in the sphere of the cultural sciences. We must renounce the serious discussion of the practical methodological issues the problems of which were only to be exhibited, as well as the detailed treatment of the relationships of ideal-types to "laws," of ideal-typical concepts to collective concepts, etc. . . .

Translated by Edward A. Shils and Henry A. Finch

31. Science as a Vocation

You wish me to speak about "Science as a Vocation." Now, we political economists have a pedantic custom, which I should like to follow, of always beginning with the external conditions. In this case, we begin with the question: What are the conditions of science as a vocation in the material sense of the term? Today this question means, practically and essentially: What are the prospects of a graduate student who is resolved to dedicate himself professionally to science in university life? In order to understand the peculiarity of German conditions it is expedient to proceed by comparison and to realize the conditions abroad. In this respect, the United States stands in the sharpest contrast with Germany, so we shall focus upon that country.

Everybody knows that in Germany the career of the young man who is dedicated to science normally begins with the position of *Privatdozent*. After having conversed with and received the consent of the respective specialists, he takes up residence on the basis of a book and, usually, a rather formal examination before the faculty of the university. Then he gives a course of lectures without receiving any salary other than the lecture fees of his students. It is up to him to determine, within his *venia legendi*, the topics upon which he lectures.

In the United States the academic career usually begins in quite a different manner, namely, by employment as an "assistant." This is similar to the great institutes of the natural science and medical faculties in Germany, where usually only a fraction of the assistants try to habilitate themselves as *Privatdozenten* and often only later in their career.

Practically, this contrast means that the career of the academic man in Germany is generally based upon plutocratic prerequisites. For it is extremely hazardous for a young scholar without funds to expose himself to the conditions of the academic career. He must be able to endure this condition for at least a number of years without knowing whether he will have the opportunity to move into a position which pays well enough for maintenance.

In the United States, where the bureaucratic system exists, the young academic man is paid from the very beginning. To be sure, his salary is modest; usually it is hardly as much as the wages of a semi-skilled laborer. Yet he begins with a seemingly secure position, for he draws a fixed salary. As a rule, however, notice may be given to him just as with German assistants, and frequently he definitely has to face this should he not come up to expectations.

These expectations are such that the young academic in America must draw large crowds of students. This cannot happen to a German docent; once one has him, one cannot get rid of him. To be sure, he cannot raise any "claims." But he has the understandable notion that after years of work he has a sort of moral right to expect some consideration. He also expects—and this is often quite important—that one have some regard for him when the question of the possible habilitation of other *Privatdozenten* comes up.

Whether, in principle, one should habilitate every scholar who is qualified or whether one should consider enrollments, and hence give the existing staff a monopoly to teach—that is an awkward dilemma. It is associated with the dual aspect of the academic profession, which we shall discuss presently. In general, one decides in favor of the second alternative. But this increases the danger that the respective full professor, however conscientious he is, will prefer his own disciples. If I may speak of my personal attitude, I must say I have followed the principle that a scholar promoted by me must legitimize and habilitate himself with somebody else at another university. But the result has been that one of my best disciples has been turned down at another university because nobody there believed this to be the reason.

A further difference between Germany and the United States is that in Germany the *Privatdozent* generally teaches fewer courses than he wishes. According to his formal right, he can give any course in his field. But to do so would be considered an improper lack of consideration for the older docents. As a rule, the full professor gives the "big" courses and the docent confines himself to secondary ones. The advantage of these arrangements is that during his youth the academic man is free to do scientific work, although this restriction of the opportunity to teach is somewhat involuntary.

In America, the arrangement is different in principle. Precisely during the early years of his career the assistant is absolutely overburdened just because he is paid. In a department of German, for instance, the full professor will give a three-hour course on Goethe and that is enough, whereas the young assistant is happy if, besides the drill in the German language, his twelve weekly teaching hours include assignments of, say, Uhland. The officials prescribe the curriculum, and in this the assistant is just as dependent as the institute assistant in Germany.

Of late we can observe distinctly that the German universities in the broad fields of science develop in the direction of the American system. The large institutes of medicine or natural science are "state capitalist" enterprises, which cannot be managed without very considerable funds. Here we encounter the same condition that is found wherever capitalist enterprise comes into operation: the "separation of the worker from his means of production." The worker, that is, the assistant, is dependent upon the implements that the state puts at his disposal; hence he is just as dependent upon the head of the institute as is the employee in a factory upon the management. For, subjectively and in good faith, the director believes that this institute is "his," and he manages its affairs. Thus the assistant's position is often as precarious as is that of any "quasi-proletarian" existence and just as precarious as the position of the assistant in the American university.

In very important respects German university life is being Americanized, as is German life in general. This development, I am convinced, will engulf those disciplines in which the craftsman personally owns the tools, essentially the library, as is still the case to a large extent in my own field. This development corresponds entirely to what happened to the artisan of the past and it is now fully under way.

As with all capitalist and at the same time bureaucratized enterprises, there are indubitable advantages in all this. But the "spirit" that rules in these affairs is different from the historical atmosphere of the German university. An extraordinarily wide gulf, externally and internally, exists between the chief of these large, capitalist, university enterprises and the usual full professor of the old style. This contrast also holds for the inner attitude, a matter that I shall not go into here. Inwardly as well as externally, the old university constitution has become fictitious. What has remained and what has been essentially increased is a factor peculiar to the university career: the question whether or not such a *Privatdozent,* and still more an assistant, will ever succeed in moving into the position of a full professor or even become the head of an institute. That is simply a hazard. Certainly, chance does not rule alone, but it rules to an unusually high degree. I know of hardly any career on earth where chance plays such a role. I may say so all the more since I personally owe it to some mere accidents that during my very early years I was appointed to a full professorship in a discipline in which men of my generation undoubtedly had achieved more than I had. And, indeed, I fancy, on the basis of this experience, that I have a sharp eye for the undeserved fate of the many whom accident has cast in the opposite direction and who within this selective apparatus in spite of all their ability do not attain the positions that are due them.

The fact that hazard rather than ability plays so large a role is not alone or even predominantly owing to the "human, all too human" factors, which naturally occur in the process of academic selection as in any other selection. It would be unfair to hold the personal inferiority of faculty members or educational ministries responsible for the fact that so many mediocrities undoubtedly play an eminent role at the universities. The predominance of mediocrity is rather due to the laws of human cooperation, especially of the cooperation of several bodies, and, in this case, cooperation of the faculties who recommend and of the ministries of education.

A counterpart are the events at the papal elections, which can be traced over many centuries and which are the most important controllable examples of a selection of the same nature as the academic selection. The cardinal who is said to be the "favorite" only rarely has a chance to win out. The rule is rather that the Number Two cardinal or the Number Three wins out. The same holds for the President of the United States. Only exceptionally does the first-rate and more prominent man get the nomination of the convention. Mostly the Number Two and often the Number Three men are nominated and later run for election. The Americans have already formed technical sociological terms for these categories, and it would be quite interesting to enquire into the laws of selection by a collective will by studying these examples, but we shall not do so here. Yet these laws also hold for the collegiate bodies of German universities, and one must not be surprised at the frequent mistakes that are made, but rather at the number of correct appointments, the proportion of which, in spite of all, is very considerable. Only where parliaments, as in some countries, or monarchs, as in Germany thus far (both work out in the same way), or revolutionary power-holders, as in Germany now, intervene for political reasons in academic selections, can one be certain that convenient mediocrities or strainers will have the opportunities all to themselves.

No university teacher likes to be reminded of discussions of appointments, for they are seldom agreeable. And yet I may say that in the numerous cases known to me there was, without exception, the good will to allow purely objective reasons to be decisive.

One must be clear about another thing: that the decision over academic fates is so largely a "hazard" is not merely because of the insufficiency of the selection by the collective formation of will. Every young man who feels called to scholarship has to realize clearly that the task before him has a double aspect. He must qualify not only as a scholar but also as a teacher. And the two do not at all coincide. One can be a preeminent scholar and at the same time an abominably poor teacher. May I remind you of the teaching of men like Helmholtz or Ranke; and they are not by any chance rare exceptions.

Now, matters are such that German universities, especially the small universities, are engaged in a most ridiculous competition for enrollments. The landlords of rooming houses in university cities celebrate the advent of the thousandth student by a festival, and they would love to celebrate Number Two Thousand by a torchlight procession. The interest in fees—and one should openly admit it—is affected by appointments in the neighboring fields that "draw crowds." And quite apart from this, the number of students enrolled is a test of qualification, which may be grasped in terms of numbers, whereas the qualification for scholarship is imponderable and, precisely with audacious innovators, often debatable—that is only natural. Almost everybody thus is affected by the suggestion of the immeasurable blessing and value of large enrollments. To say of a docent that he is a poor teacher is usually to pronounce an academic sentence of death, even if he is the foremost scholar in the world. And the question whether he is a good or a poor teacher is answered by the enrollments with which the students condescendingly honor him.

It is a fact that whether or not the students flock to a teacher is determined in large measure, larger than one would believe possible, by purely external things: temperament and even the inflection of his voice. After rather extensive experience and sober reflection, I have a deep distrust of courses that draw crowds, however unavoidable they may be. Democracy should be used only where it is in place. Scientific training, as we are held to practice it in accordance with the tradition of German universities, is the affair of an intellectual aristocracy, and we should not hide this from ourselves. To be sure, it is true that to present scientific problems in such a manner that an untutored but receptive mind can understand them and—what for us is alone decisive—can come to think about them independently is perhaps the most difficult pedagogical task of all. But whether this task is or is not realized is not decided by enrollment figures. And—to return to our theme—this very art is a personal gift and by no means coincides with the scientific qualifications of the scholar.

In contrast to France, Germany has no corporate body of "immortals" in science. According to German tradition, the universities shall do justice to the demands both of research and of instruction. Whether the abilities for both are found together in a man is a matter of absolute chance. Hence academic life is a mad hazard. If the young scholar asks for my advice with regard to habilitation, the responsibility of encouraging him can hardly be borne. If he is a Jew, of course one says *lasciate ogni speranza*. But one must ask every other man: Do you in all conscience believe that you can stand seeing mediocrity after mediocrity, year after year, climb beyond you, without becoming embittered and without coming to grief? Naturally, one always receives the answer: "Of course, I live only for my 'calling.'" Yet, I have found that only a few men could endure this situation without coming to grief.

This much I deem necessary to say about the external conditions of the academic man's vocation. But I believe that actually you wish to hear of something else, namely, of the inward calling for science. In our time, the internal situation, in contrast to the organization of science as a vocation, is first of all conditioned by the facts that science has entered a phase of specialization previously unknown and that this will forever remain the case. Not only externally, but inwardly, matters stand at a point where the individual can acquire the sure consciousness of achieving something truly perfect in the field of science only in case he is a strict specialist.

All work that overlaps neighboring fields, such as we occasionally undertake and which the sociologists must necessarily undertake again and again, is burdened with the resigned realization that at best one provides the specialist with useful questions which he would not so easily hit upon from his own specialized point of view. One's own work must inevitably remain highly imperfect. Only by strict specialization can the scientific worker become fully conscious, for once and perhaps never again in his lifetime, that he has achieved something that will endure. A really definitive and good accomplishment is today always a specialized accomplishment. And whoever lacks the capacity to put on blinders, so to speak, and to come up to the idea that the fate of his soul depends upon whether or not he makes the correct conjecture at this passage of this manuscript may as well stay away from science. He will never have what one may call the "personal experience" of science. Without this strange intoxication, ridiculed by every outsider; without this passion, this "thousands of years must pass before you enter into life and thousands more wait in silence"—according to whether or not you succeed in making this conjecture; without this, you have *no* calling for science and you should do something else. For nothing is worthy of man as man unless he can pursue it with passionate devotion.

Yet it is a fact that no amount of such enthusiasm, however sincere and profound it may be, can compel a problem to yield scientific results. Certainly enthusiasm is a prerequisite of the "inspiration" which is decisive. Nowadays in circles of youth there is a widespread notion that science has become a problem in calculation, fabricated in laboratories or statistical filing systems just as "in a factory," a calculation involving only the cool intellect and not one's "heart and soul." First of all one must say that such comments lack all clarity about what goes on in a factory or in a laboratory. In both, some idea has to occur to someone's mind, and it has to be a correct idea, if one is to accomplish anything worthwhile. And such intuition cannot be forced. It has nothing to do with any cold calculation. Certainly calculation is also an indispensable prerequisite. No sociologist, for instance, should think himself too good, even in his old age, to make tens of thousands of quite trivial computations in his head, and perhaps for months at a time. One cannot with impunity try to transfer this task entirely to mechanical assistants if one wishes to figure something, even though the final result is often small indeed. But if no "idea" occurs to his mind about the direction of his computations and, during his computations, about the bearing of the emergent single results, then even this small result will not be yielded.

Normally such an "idea" is prepared only on the soil of very hard work, but certainly this is not always the case. Scientifically, a dilettante's idea may have the very same or even a greater bearing for science than that of a specialist. Many of our very best hypotheses and insights are due precisely to dilettantes. The dilettante differs from the expert, as Helmholtz has said of Robert Mayer, only in that he lacks a firm and reliable work procedure. Consequently he is usually not in the position to control, to estimate, or to exploit the idea in its bearings. The idea is not a substitute for work; and work, in turn, cannot substitute for or compel an idea, just as little as enthusiasm can. Both, enthusiasm and work, and above all both of them jointly, can entice the idea.

Ideas occur to us when they please, not when it pleases us. The best ideas do indeed occur to one's mind in the way in which Ihering describes it: when smoking a cigar on the sofa; or as Helmholtz states of himself with scientific exactitude: when taking a walk on a slowly ascending street; or in a similar way. In any case, ideas come when we do not expect them, and not when we are brooding and searching at our desks. Yet ideas would certainly not come to mind had we not brooded at our desks and searched for answers with passionate devotion.

However this may be, the scientific worker has to take into his bargain the risk that enters into all scientific work: Does an "idea" occur or does it not? He may be an excellent worker and yet never have had any valuable idea of his own. It is a grave error to believe that this is so only in science, and that things, for instance, in a business office are different from a laboratory. A merchant or a big industrialist without "business imagination," that is, without ideas or ideal intuitions, will for all his life remain a man who would better have remained a clerk or a technical official. He will never be truly creative in organization. Inspiration in the field of science by no means plays any greater role, as academic conceit fancies, than it does in the field of mastering problems of practical life by a modern entrepreneur. On the other hand, and this also is often misconstrued, inspiration plays no less a role in science than it does in the realm of art. It is a childish notion to think that a mathematician attains any scientifically valuable results by sitting at his desk with the ruler, calculating machines, or other mechanical means. The mathematical imagination of a Weierstrass is naturally quite differently oriented in meaning and result than is the imagination of an artist, and differs basically in quality. But the psychological processes do not differ. Both are frenzy (in the sense of Plato's "mania") and "inspiration."

Now, whether we have scientific inspiration depends upon destinies that are hidden from us, and besides upon "gifts." Last but not least, because of this indubitable truth, a very understandable attitude has become popular, especially among youth, and has put them in the service of idols whose cult today occupies a broad place on all street corners and in all periodicals. These idols are "personality" and "personal experience." Both are intimately connected; the notion prevails that the latter constitutes the former and belongs to it. People belabor themselves in trying to "experience" life—for that befits a personality, conscious of its rank and station. And if we do not succeed in "experiencing" life, we must at least pretend to have this gift of grace. Formerly we called this "experience," in plain German, "sensation"; and I believe that we then had a more adequate idea of what personality is and what it signifies.

Ladies and gentlemen. In the field of science only he who is devoted solely to the work at hand has "personality." And this holds not only for the field of science; we know of no great artist who has ever done anything but serve his work and only his work. As far as his art is concerned, even with a personality of Goethe's rank, it has been detrimental to take the liberty of trying to make his "life" into a work of art. And even if one doubts this, one has to be a Goethe in order to dare permit oneself such liberty. Everybody will admit at least this much: that even with a man like Goethe, who appears once in a thousand years, this liberty did not go unpaid for. In politics, matters are not different; but we shall not discuss that today. In the field of science, however, the man who makes himself the impresario of the subject to which he should be devoted, and steps upon the stage and seeks to legitimate himself through "experience," asking: How can I prove that I am something other than a mere "specialist" and how can I manage to say something in form or in content that nobody else has ever said?—such a man is no "personality." Today such conduct is a crowd phenomenon, and it always makes a petty impression and debases the one who is thus concerned. Instead of this, an inner devotion to the task, and that alone, should lift the scientist to the height and dignity of the subject he pretends to serve. And in this it is not different with the artist.

In contrast with these preconditions which scientific work shares with art, science has a fate that profoundly distinguishes it from artistic work. Scientific work is chained to the course of progress; whereas in the realm of art there is no progress in the same sense. It is not true that the work of art of a period that has worked out new technical means, or, for instance, the laws of perspective, stands therefore artistically higher than a work of art devoid of all knowledge of those means and laws—if its form does justice to the material, that is, if its object has been chosen and formed so that it could be artistically mastered without applying those conditions and means. A work of art which is genuine "fulfilment" is never surpassed; it will never be antiquated. Individuals may differ in appreciating the personal significance of works of art, but no one will ever be able to say of such a work that it is outstripped by another work which is also "fulfilment."

In science, each of us knows that what he has accomplished will be antiquated in ten, twenty, fifty years. That is the fate to which science is subjected; it is the very meaning of scientific work, to which it is devoted in a quite specific sense, as compared with other spheres of culture for which in general the same holds. Every scientific "fulfilment" raises new "questions"; it asks to be "surpassed" and outdated. Whoever wishes to serve science has to resign himself to this fact. Scientific works certainly can last as "gratifications" because of their artistic quality, or they may remain important as a means of training. Yet they will be surpassed scientifically—let that be repeated—for it is our common fate and, more, our common goal. We cannot work without hoping that others will advance further than we have. In principle, this progress goes on *ad infinitum*. And with this we come to inquire into the meaning of science. For, after all, it is not self-evident that something subordinate to such a law is sensible and meaningful in itself. Why does one engage in doing something that in reality never comes, and never can come, to an end?

One does it, first, for purely practical—in the broader sense of the word, for technical—purposes: in order to be able to orient our practical activities to the expectations that scientific experience places at our disposal. Good. Yet this has meaning only to practitioners. What is the attitude of the academic man toward his vocation—that is, if he is at all in quest of such a personal attitude? He maintains that he engages in "science for science's sake" and not merely because others, by exploiting science, bring about commercial or technical success and can better feed, dress, illuminate, and govern. But what does he who allows himself to be integrated into this specialized organization, running on *ad infinitum*, hope to accomplish that is significant in these productions that are always destined to be outdated? This question requires a few general considerations.

Scientific progress is a fraction, the most important fraction, of the process of intellectualization which we have been undergoing for thousands of years and which nowadays is usually judged in such an extremely negative way. Let us first clarify what this intellectualist rationalization, created by science and by scientifically oriented technology, means practically.

Does it mean that we, today, for instance, everyone sitting in this hall, have a greater knowledge of the conditions of life under which we exist than has an American Indian or a Hottentot? Hardly. Unless he is a physicist, one who rides on the streetcar has no idea how the car happened to get into motion. And he does not need to know. He is satisfied that he may "count" on the behavior of the streetcar, and he orients his conduct according to this expectation; but he knows nothing about what it takes to produce such a car so that it can move. The savage knows incomparably more about his tools. When we spend money today I bet that even if there are colleagues of political economy here in the hall, almost every one of them will hold a different answer in readiness to the question: How does it happen that one can buy something for money—sometimes more and sometimes less? The savage knows what he does in order to get his daily food and which institutions serve him in this pursuit. The increasing intellectualization and rationalization do not, therefore, indicate an increased and general knowledge of the conditions under which one lives.

It means something else, namely, the knowledge or belief that if one but wished one could learn at any time. Hence, it means that principally there are no mysterious incalculable forces that come into play, but rather that one can, in principle, master all things by calculation. This means that the world is disenchanted. One need no longer have recourse to magical means in order to master or implore the spirits, as did the savage, for whom such mysterious powers existed. Technical means and calculations perform the service. This above all is what intellectualization means.

Now, this process of disenchantment, which has continued to exist in Occidental culture for millennia, and, in general, this "process," to which science belongs as a link and motive force, do they have any meanings that go beyond the purely practical and technical?

You will find this question raised in the most principled form in the works of Leo Tolstoi. He came to raise the question in a peculiar way. All his broodings increasingly revolved around the problem of whether or not death is a meaningful phenomenon. And his answer was: for civilized man death has no meaning. It has none because the individual life of civilized man, placed into an infinite "progress," according to its own imminent meaning should never come to an end; for there is always a further step ahead of one who stands in the march of progress. And no man who comes to die stands upon the peak which lies in infinity. Abraham, or some peasant of the past, died "old and satiated with life" because he stood in the organic cycle of life; because his life, in terms of its meaning and on the eve of his days, had given to him what life had to offer; because for him there remained no puzzles he might wish to solve; and therefore he could have had "enough" of life. Whereas civilized man, placed in the midst of the continuous enrichment of culture by ideas, knowledge, and problems, may become "tired of life" but not "satiated with life." He catches only the most minute part of what the life of the spirit brings forth ever anew, and what he seizes is always something provisional and not definitive, and therefore death for him is a meaningless occurrence. And because death is meaningless, civilized life as such is meaningless; by its very "progressiveness" it gives death the imprint of meaninglessness. Throughout his late novels one meets with this thought as the keynote of the Tolstoyan art.

What stand should one take? Has "progress" as such a recognizable meaning that goes beyond the technical, so that to serve it is a meaningful vocation? The question must be raised. But this is no longer merely the question of man's calling *for* science; hence the problem of what science as a vocation means to its devoted disciples. To raise this question is to ask for the vocation of science within the total life of humanity. What is the value of science?

Here the contrast between the past and the present is tremendous. You will recall the wonderful image at the beginning of the seventh book of Plato's *Republic:* those enchained cavemen whose faces are turned toward the stone wall before them. Behind them lies the source of the light which they cannot see. They are concerned only with the shadowy images that this light throws upon the wall, and they seek to fathom their interrelations. Finally one of them succeeds in shattering his fetters, turns around, and sees the sun. Blinded, he gropes about and stammers of what he saw. The others say he is raving. But gradually he learns to behold the light, and then his task is to descend to the cavemen and to lead them to the light. He is the philosopher; the sun, however, is the truth of science, which alone seizes not upon illusions and shadows but upon the true being.

Well, who today views science in such a manner? Today youth feels rather the reverse: the intellectual constructions of science constitute an unreal realm of artificial abstractions, which with their bony hands seek to grasp the blood-and-the-sap of true life without ever catching up with it. But here in life, in what for Plato was the play of shadows on the walls of the cave, genuine reality is pulsating; and the rest are derivatives of life, lifeless ghosts, and nothing else. How did this change come about?

Plato's passionate enthusiasm in *The Republic* must, in the last analysis, be explained by the fact that for the first time the concept, one of the great tools of all scientific knowledge, had been consciously discovered. Socrates had discovered it in his bearing. He was not the only man in the world to discover it. In India one finds the beginnings of a logic that is quite similar to that of Aristotle. But nowhere else do we find this realization of the significance of the concept. In Greece, for the first time, appeared a handy means by which one could put the logical screws upon somebody so that he could not come out without admitting either that he knew nothing or that this and nothing else was truth, the eternal truth that never would vanish as the doings of the blind men vanish. That was the tremendous experience which dawned upon the disciples of Socrates. And from this it seemed to follow that if one only found the right concept of the beautiful, the good, or, for instance, of bravery, of the soul—or whatever—that then one could also grasp its true being. And this, in turn, seemed to open the way for knowing and for teaching how to act rightly in life and, above all, how to act as a citizen of the state; for this question was everything to the Hellenic man, whose thinking was political throughout. And for these reasons one engaged in science.

The second great tool of scientific work, the rational experiment, made its appearance at the side of this discovery of the Hellenic spirit during the Renaissance period. The experiment is a means of reliably controlling experience. Without it, present-day empirical science would be impossible. There were experiments earlier; for instance, in India physiological experiments were made in the service of ascetic yoga technique; in Hellenic antiquity, mathematical experiments were made for purposes of war technology; and in the Middle Ages, for purposes of mining. But to raise the experiment to a principle of research was the achievement of the Renaissance. They were the great innovators in art, who were the pioneers of experiment. Leonardo and his like and, above all, the sixteenth-century experimenters in music with their experimental pianos were characteristic. From these circles the experiment entered science, especially through Galileo, and it entered theory through Bacon; and then it was taken over by the various exact disciplines of the continental universities, first of all those of Italy and then those of the Netherlands.

What did science mean to these men who stood at the threshold of modern times? To artistic experimenters of the type of Leonardo and the musical innovators, science meant the path to true art, and that meant for them the path to true nature. Art was to be raised to the rank of a science, and this meant at the same time and above all to raise the artist to the rank of the doctor, socially and with reference to the meaning of his life. This is the ambition on which, for instance, Leonardo's sketch book was based. And today? "Science as the way to nature" would sound like blasphemy to youth. Today, youth proclaims the opposite: redemption from the intellectualism of science in order to return to one's own nature and therewith to nature in general. Science as a way to art? Here no criticism is even needed.

But during the period of the rise of the exact sciences one expected a great deal more. If you recall Swammerdam's statement, "Here I bring you the proof of God's providence in the anatomy of a louse," you will see what the scientific worker, influenced (indirectly) by Protestantism and Puritanism, conceived to be his task: to show the path to God. People no longer found this path among the philosophers, with their concepts and deductions. All pietist theology of the time, above all Spener, knew that God was not to be found along the road by which the Middle Ages had sought him. God is hidden; His ways are not our ways, His thoughts are not our thoughts. In the exact sciences, however, where one could physically grasp His works, one hoped to come upon the traces of what He planned for the world. And today? Who—aside from certain big children who are indeed found in the natural sciences—still believes that the findings of astronomy, biology, physics, or chemistry could teach us anything about the meaning of the world? If there is any such "meaning," along what road could one come upon its tracks? If these natural sciences lead to anything in this way, they are apt to make the belief that there is such a thing as the "meaning" of the universe die out at its very roots.

And finally, science as a way "to God"? Science, this specifically irreligious power? That science today is irreligious no one will doubt in his innermost being, even if he will not admit it to himself. Redemption from the rationalism and intellectualism of science is the fundamental presupposition of living in union with the divine. This, or something similar in meaning, is one of the fundamental watchwords one hears among German youth, whose feelings are attuned to religion or who crave religious experiences. They crave not only religious experience but experience as such. The only thing that is strange is the method that is now followed: the spheres of the irrational, the only spheres that intellectualism has not yet touched, are now raised into consciousness and put under its lens. For in practice this is where the modern intellectualist form of romantic irrationalism leads. This method of emancipation from intellectualism may well bring about the very opposite of what those who take to it conceive as its goal.

After Nietzsche's devastating criticism of those "last men" who "invented happiness," I may leave aside altogether the naive optimism in which science—that is, the technique of mastering life which rests upon science—has been celebrated as the way to happiness. Who believes in this?—aside from a few big children in university chairs or editorial offices. Let us resume our argument.

Under these internal presuppositions, what is the meaning of science as a vocation, now after all these former illusions—the "way to true being," the "way to true art," the "way to true nature," the "way to true God," the "way to true happiness"—have been dispelled? Tolstoi has given the simplest answer, with the words: "Science is meaningless because it gives no answer to our question, the only question important for us: 'What shall we do and how shall we live?'" That science does not give an answer to this is indisputable. The only question that remains is the sense in which science gives "no" answer, and whether or not science might yet be of some use to the one who puts the question correctly.

Today one usually speaks of science as "free from presuppositions." Is there such a thing? It depends upon what one understands thereby. All scientific work presupposes that the rules of logic and method are valid; these are the general foundations of our orientation in the world; and, at least for our special question, these presuppositions are the least problematic aspect of science. Science further presupposes that what is yielded by scientific work is important in the sense that it is "worth being known." In this, obviously, are contained all our problems. For this presupposition cannot be proved by scientific means. It can only be interpreted with reference to its ultimate meaning, which we must reject or accept according to our ultimate position toward life.

Furthermore, the nature of the relationship of scientific work and its presuppositions varies widely according to their structure. The natural sciences, for instance, physics, chemistry, and astronomy, presuppose as self-evident that it is worthwhile to know the ultimate laws of cosmic events as far as science can construe them. This is the case not only because with such knowledge one can attain technical results, but for its own sake, if the quest for such knowledge is to be a "vocation." Yet this presupposition can by no means be proved. And still less can it be proved that the existence of the world which these sciences describe is worthwhile, that it has any "meaning," or that it makes sense to live in such a world. Science does not ask for the answers to such questions.

Consider modern medicine, a practical technology which is highly developed scientifically. The general "presupposition" of the medical enterprise is stated trivially in the assertion that medical science has the task of maintaining life as such and of diminishing suffering as such to the greatest possible degree. Yet this is problematical. By his means the medical man preserves the life of the mortally ill man, even if the patient implores us to relieve him of life, even if his relatives, to whom his life is worthless and to whom the costs of maintaining his worthless life grow unbearable, grant his redemption from suffering. Perhaps a poor lunatic is involved, whose relatives, whether they admit it or not, wish and must wish for his death. Yet the presuppositions of medicine, and the penal code, prevent the physician from relinquishing his therapeutic efforts. Whether life is worthwhile living and when—this question is not asked by medicine. Natural science gives us an answer to the question of what we must do if we wish to master life technically. It leaves quite aside, or assumes for its purposes, whether we should and do wish to master life technically and whether it ultimately makes sense to do so.

Consider a discipline such as aesthetics. The fact that there are works of art is given for aesthetics. It seeks to find out under what conditions this fact exists, but it does not raise the question whether or not the realm of art is perhaps a realm of diabolical grandeur, a realm of this world, and therefore, in its core, hostile to God and, in its innermost and aristocratic spirit, hostile to the brotherhood of man. Hence, aesthetics does not ask whether there should be works of art.

Consider jurisprudence. It establishes what is valid according to the rules of juristic thought, which is partly bound by logically compelling and partly by conventionally given schemata. Juridical thought holds when certain legal rules and certain methods of interpretations are recognized as binding. Whether there should be law and whether one should establish just these rules—such questions jurisprudence does not answer. It can only state: If one wishes this result, according to the norms of our legal thought, this legal rule is the appropriate means of attaining it.

Consider the historical and cultural sciences. They teach us how to understand and interpret political, artistic, literary, and social phenomena in terms of their origins. But they give us no answer to the question whether the existence of these cultural phenomena have been and are worthwhile. And they do not answer the further question whether it is worth the effort required to know them. They presuppose that there is an interest in partaking, through this procedure, of the community of "civilized men." But they cannot prove "scientifically" that this is the case; and that they presuppose this interest by no means proves that it goes without saying. In fact it is not at all self-evident.

Finally, let us consider the disciplines close to me: sociology, history, economics, political science, and those types of cultural philosophy that make it their task to interpret these sciences. It is said, and I agree, that politics is out of place in the lecture-room. It does not belong there on the part of the students. If, for instance, in the lecture-room of my former colleague Dietrich Schäfer in Berlin, pacifist students were to surround his desk and make an uproar, I should deplore it just as much as I should deplore the uproar which anti-pacifist students are said to have made against Professor Förster, whose views in many ways are as remote as could be from mine. Neither does politics, however, belong in the lecture-room on the part of the docents, and when the docent is scientifically concerned with politics, it belongs there least of all.

To take a practical political stand is one thing, and to analyze political structures and party positions is another. When speaking in a political meeting about democracy, one does not hide one's personal standpoint; indeed, to come out clearly and take a stand is one's damned duty. The words one uses in such a meeting are not means of scientific analysis but means of canvassing votes and winning over others. They are not plowshares to loosen the soil of contemplative thought; they are swords against the enemies: such words are weapons. It would be an outrage, however, to use words in this fashion in a lecture or in the lecture-room. If, for instance, "democracy" is under discussion, one considers its various forms, analyzes them in the way they function, determines what results for the conditions of life the one form has as compared with the other. Then one confronts the forms of democracy with nondemocratic forms of political order and endeavors to come to a position where the student may find the point from which, in terms of his ultimate ideals, he can take a stand. But the true teacher will beware of imposing from the platform any political position upon the student, whether it is expressed or suggested. "To let the facts speak for themselves" is the most unfair way of putting over a political position to the student.

Why should we abstain from doing this? I state in advance that some highly esteemed colleagues are of the opinion that it is not possible to carry through this self-restraint and that, even if it were possible, it would be a whim to avoid declaring oneself. Now one cannot demonstrate scientifically what the duty of an academic teacher is. One can only demand of the teacher that he have the intellectual integrity to see that it is one thing to state facts, to determine mathematical or logical relations or the internal structure of cultural values, while it is another thing to answer questions of the value of culture and its individual contents and the question of how one should act in the cultural community and in political associations. These are quite heterogeneous problems. If he asks further why he should not deal with both types of problems in the lecture-room, the answer is: because the prophet and the demagogue do not belong on the academic platform.

To the prophet and the demagogue, it is said: "Go your ways out into the streets and speak openly to the world," that is, speak where criticism is possible. In the lecture-room we stand opposite our audience, and it has to remain silent. I deem it irresponsible to exploit the circumstance that for the sake of their career the students have to attend a teacher's course while there is nobody present to oppose him with criticism. The task of the teacher is to serve the students with his knowledge and scientific experience and not to imprint upon them his personal political views. It is certainly possible that the individual teacher will not entirely succeed in eliminating his personal sympathies. He is then exposed to the sharpest criticism in the forum of his own conscience. And this deficiency does not prove anything; other errors are also possible, for instance, erroneous statements of fact, and yet they prove nothing against the duty of searching for the truth. I also reject this in the very interest of science. I am ready to prove from the works of our historians that whenever the man of science introduces his personal value judgment, a full understanding of the facts ceases. But this goes beyond tonight's topic and would require lengthy elucidation.

I ask only: How should a devout Catholic, on the one hand, and a Freemason, on the other, in a course on the forms of church and state or on religious history ever be brought to evaluate these subjects alike? This is out of the question. And yet the academic teacher must desire and must demand of himself to serve the one as well as the other by his knowledge and methods. Now you will rightly say that the devout Catholic will never accept the view of the factors operative in bringing about Christianity which a teacher who is free of his dogmatic presuppositions presents to him. Certainly! The difference, however, lies in the following: Science "free from presuppositions," in the sense of a rejection of religious bonds, does not know of the "miracle" and the "revelation." If it did, science would be unfaithful to its own "presuppositions." The believer knows both, miracle and revelation. And science "free from presuppositions" expects from him no less—and no more—than acknowledgment that *if* the process can be explained without those supernatural interventions, which an empirical explanation has to eliminate as causal factors, the process has to be explained the way science attempts to do. And the believer can do this without being disloyal to his faith.

But has the contribution of science no meaning at all for a man who does not care to know facts as such and to whom only the practical standpoint matters? Perhaps science nevertheless contributes something.

The primary task of a useful teacher is to teach his students to recognize "inconvenient" facts—I mean facts that are inconvenient for their party opinions. And for every party opinion there are facts that are extremely inconvenient, for my own opinion no less than for others. I believe the teacher accomplishes more than a mere intellectual task if he compels his audience to accustom itself to the existence of such facts. I would be so immodest as even to apply the expression "moral achievement," though perhaps this may sound too grandiose for something that should go without saying.

Thus far I have spoken only of practical reasons for avoiding the imposition of a personal point of view. But these are not the only reasons. The impossibility of "scientifically" pleading for practical and interested stands—except in discussing the means for a firmly given and presupposed end—rests upon reasons that lie far deeper.

"Scientific" pleading is meaningless in principle because the various value spheres of the world stand in irreconcilable conflict with each other. The elder Mill, whose philosophy I will not praise otherwise, was on this point right when he said: If one proceeds from pure experience, one arrives at polytheism. This is shallow in formulation and sounds paradoxical, and yet there is truth in it. If anything, we realize again today that something can be sacred not only in spite of its not being beautiful, but rather because and insofar as it is not beautiful. You will find this documented in the fifty-third chapter of the Book of Isaiah and in the Twenty-first Psalm. And, since Nietzsche, we realize that something can be beautiful, not only in spite of the aspect in which it is not good, but rather in that very aspect. You will find this expressed earlier in the *Fleurs du mal,* as Baudelaire named his volume of poems. It is commonplace to observe that something may be true although it is not beautiful and not holy and not good. Indeed it may be true in precisely those aspects. But all these are only the most elementary cases of the struggle that the gods of the various orders and values are engaged in. I do not know how one might wish to decide "scientifically" the value of French and German culture; for here, too, different gods struggle with one another, now and for all times to come.

We live as did the ancients when their world was not yet disenchanted of its gods and demons, only we live in a different sense. As Hellenic man at times sacrificed to Aphrodite and at other times to Apollo, and, above all, as everybody sacrificed to the gods of his city, so do we still nowadays, only the bearing of man has been disenchanted and denuded of its mystical but inwardly genuine plasticity. Fate, and certainly not "science," holds sway over these gods and their struggles. One can only understand what the godhead is for the one order or for the other, or better, what godhead is in the one or in the other order. With this understanding, however, the matter has reached its limit so far as it can be discussed in a lecture-room and by a professor. Yet the great and vital problem that is contained therein is, of course, very far from being concluded. But forces other than university chairs have their say in this matter.

What man will take upon himself the attempt to "refute scientifically" the ethic of the Sermon on the Mount? For instance, the sentence, "resist no evil," or the image of turning the other cheek? And yet it is clear, in mundane perspective, that this is an ethic of undignified conduct; one has to choose between the religious dignity which this ethic confers and the dignity of manly conduct which preaches something quite different; "resist evil—lest you be co-responsible for an overpowering evil." According to our ultimate standpoint, the one is the devil and the other the God, and the individual has to decide which is God for him and which is the devil. And so it goes throughout all the orders of life.

The grandiose rationalism of an ethical and methodical conduct of life which flows from every religious prophecy has dethroned this polytheism in favor of the "one thing that is needful." Faced with the realities of outer and inner life, Christianity has deemed it necessary to make those compromises and relative judgments, which we all know from its history. Today the routines of everyday life challenge religion. Many old gods ascend from their graves; they are disenchanted and hence take the form of impersonal forces. They strive to gain power over our lives and again they resume their eternal struggle with one another. What is hard for modern man, and especially for the younger generation, is to measure up to workaday existence. The ubiquitous chase for "experience" stems from this weakness; for it is weakness not to be able to countenance the stern seriousness of our fateful times.

Our civilization destines us to realize more clearly these struggles again, after our eyes have been blinded for a thousand years—blinded by the allegedly or presumably exclusive orientation toward the grandiose moral fervor of Christian ethics.

But enough of these questions which lead far away. Those of our youth are in error who react to all this by saying, "Yes, but we happen to come to lectures in order to experience something more than mere analyses and statements of fact." The error is that they seek in the professor something different from what stands before them. They crave a leader and not a teacher. But we are placed upon the platform solely as teachers. And these are two different things, as one can readily see. Permit me to take you once more to America, because there one can often observe such matters in their most massive and original shape.

The American boy learns unspeakably less than the German boy. In spite of an incredible number of examinations, his school life has not had the significance of turning him into an absolute creature of examinations, such as the German. For in America, bureaucracy, which presupposes the examination diploma as a ticket of admission to the realm of office prebends, is only in its beginnings. The young American has no respect for anything or anybody, for tradition or for public office—unless it is for the personal achievement of individual men. This is what the American calls "democracy." This is the meaning of democracy, however distorted its intent may in reality be, and this intent is what matters here. The American's conception of the teacher who faces him is: he sells me his knowledge and his methods for my father's money, just as the greengrocer sells my mother cabbage. And that is all. To be sure, if the teacher happens to be a football coach, then, in this field, he is a leader. But if he is not this (or something similar in a different field of sports), he is simply a teacher and nothing more. And no young American would think of having the teacher sell him a *Weltanschauung* or a code of conduct. Now, when formulated in this manner, we should reject this. But the question is whether there is not a grain of salt contained in this feeling, which I have deliberately stated in extreme with some exaggeration.

Fellow students! You come to our lectures and demand from us the qualities of leadership, and you fail to realize in advance that of a hundred professors at least ninety-nine do not and must not claim to be football masters in the vital problems of life, or even to be "leaders" in matters of conduct. Please, consider that a man's value does not depend on whether or not he has leadership qualities. And in any case, the qualities that make a man an excellent scholar and academic teacher are not the qualities that make him a leader to give directions in practical life or, more specifically, in politics. It is pure accident if a teacher also possesses this quality, and it is a critical situation if every teacher on the platform feels himself confronted with the students' expectation that the teacher should claim this quality. It is still more critical if it is left to every academic teacher to set himself up as a leader in the lecture-room. For those who most frequently think of themselves as leaders often qualify least as leaders. But irrespective of whether they are or are not, the platform situation simply offers no possibility of proving themselves to be leaders. The professor who feels called upon to act as a counselor of youth and enjoys their trust may prove himself a man in personal human relations with them. And if he feels called upon to intervene in the struggles of world views and party opinions, he may do so outside, in the market place, in the press, in meetings, in associations, wherever he wishes. But after all, it is somewhat too convenient to demonstrate one's courage in taking a stand where the audience and possible opponents are condemned to silence.

Finally, you will put the question: "If this is so, what then does science actually and positively contribute to practical and personal 'life'?" Therewith we are back again at the problem of science as a "vocation."

First, of course, science contributes to the technology of controlling life by calculating external objects as well as man's activities. Well, you will say, that, after all, amounts to no more than the greengrocer of the American boy. I fully agree.

Second, science can contribute something that the greengrocer cannot: methods of thinking, the tools and the training for thought. Perhaps you will say: well, that is no vegetable, but it amounts to no more than the means for procuring vegetables. Well and good, let us leave it at that for today.

Fortunately, however, the contribution of science does not reach its limit with this. We are in a position to help you to a third objective: to gain clarity. Of course, it is presupposed that we ourselves possess clarity. As far as this is the case, we can make clear to you the following:

In practice, you can take this or that position when concerned with a problem of value—for simplicity's sake, please think of social phenomena as examples. If you take such and such a stand, then, according to scientific experience, you have to use such and such a means in order to carry out your conviction practically. Now, these means are perhaps such that you believe you must reject them. Then you simply must choose between the end and the inevitable means. Does the end "justify" the means? Or does it not? The teacher can confront you with the necessity of this choice. He cannot do more, so long as he wishes to remain a teacher and not to become a demagogue. He can, of course, also tell you that if you want such and such an end, then you must take into the bargain the subsidiary consequences which according to all experience will occur. Again we find ourselves in the same situation as before. These are still problems that can also emerge for the technician, who in numerous instances has to make decisions according to the principle of the lesser evil or of the relatively best. Only to him one thing, the main thing, is usually given; namely, the end. But as soon as truly "ultimate" problems are at stake for us this is not the case. With this, at long last, we come to the final service that science as such can render to the aim of clarity, and at the same time we come to the limits of science.

Besides we can and we should state: In terms of its meaning, such and such a practical stand can be derived with inner consistency, and hence integrity, from this or that ultimate *weltanschauliche* position. Perhaps it can only be derived from one such fundamental position, or maybe from several, but it cannot be derived from these or those other positions. Figuratively speaking, you serve this god and you offend the other god when you decide to adhere to this position. And if you remain faithful to yourself, you will necessarily come to certain final conclusions that subjectively make sense. This much, in principle at least, can be accomplished. Philosophy, as a special discipline, and the essentially philosophical discussions of principles in the other sciences attempt to achieve this. Thus, if we are competent in our pursuit (which must be presupposed here) we can force the individual, or at least we can help him, to give himself an account of the ultimate meaning of his own conduct. This appears to me as not so trifling a thing to do, even for one's own personal life. Again, I am tempted to say of a teacher who succeeds in this: he stands in the service of "moral" forces; he fulfils the duty of bringing about self-clarification and a sense of responsibility. And I believe he will be the more able to accomplish this, the more conscientiously he avoids the desire personally to impose upon or suggest to his audience his own stand.

This proposition, which I present here, always takes its point of departure from the one fundamental fact, that so long as life remains immanent and is interpreted in its own terms, it knows only of an unceasing struggle of these gods with one another. Or speaking directly, the ultimately possible attitudes toward life are irreconcilable, and hence their struggle can never be brought to a final conclusion. Thus it is necessary to make a decisive choice. Whether, under such conditions, science is a worthwhile "vocation" for somebody, and whether science itself has an objectively valuable "vocation" are again value judgments about which nothing can be said in the lecture-room. To affirm the value of science is a presupposition for teaching there. I personally by my very work answer in the affirmative, and I also do so from precisely the standpoint that hates intellectualism as the worst devil, as youth does today, or usually only fancies it does. In that case the word holds for these youths: "Mind you, the devil is old; grow old to understand him." This does not mean age in the sense of the birth certificate. It means that if one wishes to settle with this devil, one must not take to flight before him as so many like to do nowadays. First of all, one has to see the devil's ways to the end in order to realize his power and his limitations.

Science today is a "vocation" organized in special disciplines in the service of self-clarification and knowledge of interrelated facts. It is not the gift of grace of seers and prophets dispensing sacred values and revelations, nor does it partake of the contemplation of sages and philosophers about the meaning of the universe. This, to be sure, is the inescapable condition of our historical situation. We cannot evade it so long as we remain true to ourselves. And if Tolstoi's question recurs to you: as science does not, who is to answer the question: "What shall we do, and, how shall we arrange our lives?" or, in the words used here tonight: "Which of the warring gods should we serve? Or should we serve perhaps an entirely different god, and who is he?" then one can say that only a prophet or a savior can give the answers. If there is no such man, or if his message is no longer believed in, then you will certainly not compel him to appear on this earth by having thousands of professors, as privileged hirelings of the state, attempt as petty prophets in their lecture-rooms to take over his role. All they will accomplish is to show that they are unaware of the decisive state of affairs: the prophet for whom so many of our younger generation yearn simply does not exist. But this knowledge in its forceful significance has never become vital for them. The inward interest of a truly religiously "musical" man can never be served by veiling to him and to others the fundamental fact that he is destined to live in a godless and prophetless time by giving him the *ersatz* of armchair prophecy. The integrity of his religious organ, it seems to me, must rebel against this.

Now you will be inclined to say: Which stand does one take toward the factual existence of "theology" and its claims to be a "science"? Let us not flinch and evade the answer. To be sure, "theology" and "dogmas" do not exist universally, but neither do they exist for Christianity alone. Rather (going backward in time), they exist in highly developed form also in Islam, in Manicheanism, in Gnosticism, in Orphism, in Parsism, in Buddhism, in the Hindu sects, in Taoism, and in the Upanishads, and, of course, in Judaism. To be sure their systematic development varies greatly. It is no accident that Occidental Christianity—in contrast to the theological possessions of Jewry—has expanded and elaborated theology more systematically, or strives to do so. In the Occident the development of theology has had by far the greatest historical significance. This is the product of the Hellenic spirit, and all theology of the West goes back to it, as (obviously) all theology of the East goes back to Indian thought. All theology represents an intellectual rationalization of the possession of sacred values. No science is absolutely free from presuppositions, and no science can prove its fundamental value to the man who rejects these presuppositions. Every theology, however, adds a few specific presuppositions for its work and thus for the justification of its existence. Their meaning and scope vary. Every theology, including for instance Hinduist theology, presupposes that the world must have a meaning, and the question is how to interpret this meaning so that it is intellectually conceivable.

It is the same as with Kant's epistemology. He took for his point of departure the presupposition: "Scientific truth exists and it is valid," and then asked: "Under which presuppositions of thought is truth possible and meaningful?" The modern aestheticians (actually or expressly, as for instance, G. v. Lukacs) proceed from the presupposition that "works of art exist," and then ask: "How is their existence meaningful and possible?"

As a rule, theologies, however, do not content themselves with this (essentially religious and philosophical) presupposition. They regularly proceed from the further presupposition that certain "revelations" are facts relevant for salvation and as such make possible a meaningful conduct of life. Hence, these revelations must be believed in. Moreover, theologies presuppose that certain subjective states and acts possess the quality of holiness, that is, they constitute a way of life, or at least elements of one, that is religiously meaningful. Then the question of theology is: How can these presuppositions, which must simply be accepted, be meaningfully interpreted in a view of the universe? For theology, these presuppositions as such lie beyond the limits of "science." They do not represent "knowledge," in the usual sense, but rather a "possession." Whoever does not "possess" faith, or the other holy states, cannot have theology as a substitute for them, least of all any other science. On the contrary, in every "positive" theology, the devout reaches the point where the Augustinian sentence holds: *credo non quod, sed quia absurdum est.*

The capacity for the accomplishment of religious virtuosos—the "intellectual sacrifice"—is the decisive characteristic of the positively religious man. That this is so is shown by the fact that in spite (or rather in consequence) of theology (which unveils it) the tension between the valuespheres of "science" and the sphere of "the holy" is unbridgeable. Legitimately, only the disciple offers the "intellectual sacrifice" to the prophet, the believer to the church. Never as yet has a new prophecy emerged (and I repeat here deliberately this image which has offended some) by way of the need of some modern intellectuals to furnish their souls with, so to speak, guaranteed genuine antiques. In doing so, they happen to remember that religion has belonged among such antiques, and of all things religion is what they do not possess. By way of substitute, however, they play at decorating a sort of domestic chapel with small sacred images from all over the world, or they produce surrogates through all sorts of psychic experiences to which they ascribe the dignity of mystic holiness, which they peddle in the book market. This is plain humbug or self-deception. It is, however, no humbug but rather something very sincere and genuine if some of the youth groups who during recent years have quietly grown together give their human community the interpretation of a religious, cosmic, or mystical relation, although occasionally perhaps such interpretation rests on misunderstanding of self. True as it is that every act of genuine brotherliness may be linked with the awareness that it contributes something imperishable to a super-personal realm, it seems to me dubious whether the dignity of purely human and communal relations is enhanced by these religious interpretations. But that is no longer our theme.

The fate of our times is characterized by rationalization and intellectualization and, above all, by the "disenchantment of the world." Precisely the ultimate and most sublime values have retreated from public life either into the transcendental realm of mystic life or into the brotherliness of direct and personal human relations. It is not accidental that our greatest art is intimate and not monumental, nor is it accidental that today only within the smallest and intimate circles, in personal human situations, in *pianissimo*, that something is pulsating that corresponds to the prophetic *pneuma*, which in former times swept through the great communities like a firebrand, welding them together. If we attempt to force and to "invent" a monumental style in art, such miserable monstrosities are produced as the many monuments of the last twenty years. If one tries intellectually to construe new religions without a new and genuine prophecy, then, in an inner sense, something similar will result, but with still worse effects. An academic prophecy, finally, will create only fanatical sects but never a genuine community.

To the person who cannot bear the fate of the times like a man, one must say: may he rather return silently, without the usual publicity build-up of renegades, but simply and plainly. The arms of the old churches are opened widely and compassionately for him. After all, they do not make it hard for him. One way or another he has to bring his "intellectual sacrifice"—that is inevitable. If he can really do it, we shall not rebuke him. For such an intellectual sacrifice in favor of an unconditional religious devotion is ethically quite a different matter than the evasion of the plain duty of intellectual integrity, which sets in if one lacks the courage to clarify one's own ultimate standpoint and rather facilitates this duty by feeble relative judgments. In my eyes, such religious return stands higher than the academic prophecy, which does not clearly realize that in the lecture-rooms of the university no other virtue holds but plain intellectual integrity. Integrity, however, compels us to state that for the many who today tarry for new prophets and saviors, the situation is the same as resounds in the beautiful Edomite watchman's song of the period of exile that has been included among Isaiah's oracles:

> He calleth to me out of Seir, Watchman, what of the night? The watchman said, The morning cometh, and also the night: if ye will enquire, enquire ye: return, come.

The people to whom this was said has enquired and tarried for more than two millennia, and we are shaken when we realize its fate. From this we want to draw the lesson that nothing is gained by yearning and tarrying alone, and we shall act differently. We shall set to work and meet the "demands of the day," in human relations as well as in our vocation. This, however, is plain and simple, if each finds and obeys the demon who holds the fibers of his very life.

Translated by Hans H. Gerth
and C. Wright Mills

Notes

Chapter 1: The Concept of Social Action

1. A definition of social action is given below, Ch. 26.

Chapter 2: The Types of Social Action

1. The two terms *zweckrational* and *wertrational* are of central significance to Weber's theory, but at the same time present one of the most difficult problems to the translator. Perhaps the keynote of the distinction lies in the absoluteness with which the values involved in *Wertrationalität* are held. The sole important consideration to the actor becomes the realization of the value. Insofar as it involves ends, rational considerations, such as those of efficiency, are involved in the choice of means. But there is no question either of rational weighing of this end against others, nor is there a question of "counting the cost" in the sense of taking account of possible results other than the attainment of the absolute end. In the case of *Zweckrationalität,* on the other hand, Weber conceives action as motivated by a plurality of relatively independent ends, none of which is absolute. Hence, rationality involves on the one hand the weighing of the relative importance of their realization, on the other hand, consideration of whether undesirable consequences would outweigh the benefits to be derived from the projected course of action. It has not seemed possible to find English terms which would express this distinction succinctly. Hence the attempt has been made to express the ideas as clearly as possible without specific terms.

It should also be pointed out that, as Weber's analysis proceeds, there is a tendency of the meaning of these terms to shift, so that *Wertrationalität* comes to refer to a system of ultimate ends, regardless of the degree of their absoluteness, while *Zweckrationalität* refers primarily to considerations respecting the choice of means and ends which are in turn means to further ends, such as money. What seems to have happened is that Weber shifted from a classification of ideal types of action to one of elements in the structure of action. In the latter context "expediency" is often an adequate rendering of *Zweckrationalität.*

The other two terms *affektuell* and *traditional* do not present any difficulty of translation. The term affectual has come into English psychological usage from the German largely through the influence of psychoanalysis.

Chapter 4: The Concept of Legitimate Order

1. The term *Gelten* has already been dealt with. From the very use of the term in this context it is clear that by 'order' *(Ordnung)* Weber here means a *normative*

system. The pattern for the concept of 'order' is not, as in the law of gravitation, the 'order of nature,' but the order involved in a system of law.

2. When this was written (probably about 1913), duelling was still a relatively common practice in Germany and, in certain circles, was regarded as a definite obligation of honor in the face of some kinds of provocation. It was, however, at the same time an explicitly punishable offense under the criminal law.

3. Those familiar with the literature of this subject will recall the part played by the concept of "order" in the brilliant book of Rudolf Stammler, which was cited in the prefatory note; a book which, like all his works is very able, but is nevertheless fundamentally misleading and confuses the issues in a catastrophic fashion. The reader may compare the author's critical discussion of it which was also cited in the same place; a discussion which, because of the author's annoyance at Stammler's confusion, was unfortunately written in somewhat too acrimonious a tone.

Stammler fails to distinguish the normative meaning of "validity" from the empirical. He further fails to recognize that social action is oriented to other things besides systems of order. Above all, however, in a way which is wholly indefensible from a logical point of view, he treats order as a "form" of social action and then attempts to bring it into a type of relation to "content," which is analogous to that of form and content in the theory of knowledge. Other errors in his argument will be left aside. But actually, action which is, for instance, primarily economic, is oriented to knowledge of the relative scarcity of certain available means to satisfaction of want, in relation to the actor's state of needs and to the present and probable action of others, insofar as the latter affects the same resources. But at the same time, of course, the actor in his choice of economic procedures naturally orients himself *in addition* to the conventional and legal rules which he recognizes as valid, or of which he knows that a violation on his part would call forth a given reaction of other persons. Stammler succeeds in introducing a state of hopeless confusion into this very simple empirical situation, particularly in that he maintains that a causal relationship between an order and actual empirical action involves a contradiction in terms. It is true, of course, that there is no causal relationship between the *normative* validity of an order in the legal sense and any empirical process. In that context there is only the question of whether the order as correctly interpreted in the legal sense "applies" to the empirical situation. The question is whether in a *normative* sense it *should* be treated as valid and, if so, what the content of its normative prescriptions for this situation should be. But for sociological purposes, as distinguished from legal, it is only the probability of orientation to the subjective *belief* in the validity of an order which constitutes the valid order itself. It is undeniable that, in the ordinary sense of the word "causal," there is a causal relationship between this probability and the relevant course of economic action.

Chapter 5: The Bases of Legitimacy of an Order

1. *Wertrational.*

Chapter 7: Types of Solidary Social Relationships

1. The two types of relationship which Weber distinguishes in this section he himself calls *Vergemeinschaftung* and *Vergesellschaftung.* His own usage here is an adaptation of the well-known terms of Tönnies, *Gemeinschaft* and *Gesellschaft,* and has been directly influenced by Tönnies' work. Though there has been much discussion of them in English, it is safe to say that no satisfactory equivalents of Tönnies' terms have been found. In particular, "community" and either "society" or "association" are unsatisfactory, since these terms have quite different connotations in English. In the context, however, in which Weber uses his slightly altered terms, that

of action within a social relationship, the adjective forms "communal" and "associative" do not seem to be objectionable. Their exact meanings should become clear from Weber's definitions and comments.

2. Weber's emphasis on the importance of these communal elements even within functionally specific formal organizations like industrial plants has been strongly confirmed by the findings of research since this was written. One important study which shows the importance of informal social organization on this level among the workers of an industrial plant is reported in Roethlisberger and Dickson, *Management and the Worker.*

Chapter 8: Open and Closed Relationships

1. This is a reference to the *Betriebsräte* which were formed in German industrial plants during the Revolution of 1918–19 and were recognized in the Weimar Constitution as entitled to representation in the Federal Economic Council. The standard work in English is W. C. Guillebaud: *The German Works Councils.*

Chapter 9: Power, Authority, and Imperative Control

1. As has already been noted, the term *Herrschaft* has no satisfactory English equivalent. The term 'imperative control,' however, as used by N. S. Timasheff in his *Introduction to the Sociology of Law* is close to Weber's meaning and has been borrowed for the most general purposes. In a majority of instances, however, Weber is concerned with *legitime Herrschaft,* and in these cases "authority" is both an accurate and a far less awkward translation. *Macht,* as Weber uses it, seems to be quite adequately rendered by "power."

2. In this case imperative control is confined to the legitimate type, but it is not possible in English to speak here of an "authoritarian" group. The citizens of any state, no matter how "democratic," are "imperatively controlled" because they are subject to law.

Chapter 10: Political and Religious Corporate Groups

1. The German is *Devisenpolitik.* Translation in this context is made more difficult by the fact that the German language does not distinguish between 'politics' and 'policy,' *Politik* having both meanings. The remarks which Weber makes about various kinds of policy would have been unnecessary, had he written originally in English.

2. See below.

Chapter 17: The Chinese Literati

1. Yu tsiuan tung kian kang mu, *Geschichte der Ming-Dynastie des Kaisers Kian Lung,* trans. by Delamarre (Paris, 1865), p. 417.

2. As eminent an authority as von Rosthorn disputes this point in his "The Burning of the Books," *Journal of the Peking Oriental Society,* vol. iv, Peking, 1898, pp. 1 ff. He believes that the sacred texts were orally transmitted until the Han period, and hence that they are in the same tradition that prevailed exclusively in early India. The outsider is not entitled to pass judgment, but perhaps the following may be said. The annalistic scriptures at least cannot rest on oral tradition and, as the calculation of the eclipses of the sun shows, they go back into the second millennium. Very much of what elsewhere is (according to the usual assumption, reliably) reported of the archives of the princes and the importance of script and the written communication of the literati could just as little be reconciled with the above, if one were to extend the view of the eminent expert beyond the ritual literature (that is, literature which

has been brought into poetic form). Here, of course, only expert sinologists have the last word, and a "criticism" on the part of a nonexpert would be presumptuous. The principle of strictly oral tradition has almost everywhere applied only to charismatic revelations and to charismatic commentaries of these, and not to poetry and didactics. The great age of script as such comes out in its pictorial form and also in its arrangement of the pictorial characters: at a late period the vertical columns divided by lines still referred back to the origin from scored disks of bamboo sticks which were placed side by side. The oldest "contracts" were bamboo scores or knotted cords. The fact that all contracts and documents were made out in duplicate form is probably rightly considered a survival of this technique (Conrady).

3. This explains also the stereotyping of script in such an extraordinarily early stage of development, and hence it produces an aftereffect even today.

4. E. de Chavannes, *Journal of the Peking Oriental Society,* vol. III, 1, 1890, p. iv, translates *Tai che ling* by "grand astrologer," instead of "court annalist," as it is usually rendered. Yet, the later, and especially the modern period knows the representatives of literary education to be sharp opponents of the astrologers. Cf. below.

5. P. A. Tschepe (S.J.), "Histoire du Royaume de Han," *Variétés Sinologiques,* 31 (Shanghai, 1910), p. 48.

6. During the fourth century the representatives of the feudal order, foremost among them the interested princely sibs, argued against the intended bureaucratization of the state of *Tsin* by pointing out "that the forbears had improved the people by education, not by administrative changes" (this harmonizes fully with the later theories of Confucian orthodoxy). Thereupon the new minister Yang, belonging to the literati, comments in highly un-Confucian manner: "the ordinary person lives according to tradition; the higher minds, however, create tradition, and for extraordinary things the rites give no precepts. The weal of the people is the highest law," and the prince accedes to his opinion. (Cf. the passages in Tschepe's "Histoire du Royaume de Tsin," *Variétés Sinologiques,* 27, p. 118.) It is quite probable that when Confucian orthodoxy articulated and purified the *Annals* it very strongly erased and retouched these features in favor of the traditionalism which was later considered correct. On the other hand, one must beware of simply taking at face value all the reports referred to below which testify to the astonishing deference paid to the early literati!

7. Although the princely heir of Wei alights from the chariot he receives no response to his repeated salutations from the king's courtier and literary man, who is a parvenu. To the question "whether the rich or the poor may be proud" the *literatus* replies "the poor," and he motivates this by saying that he might find employment any day at another court. (Tschepe, "Histoire du Royaume de Han," op. cit. p. 43.) One of the literati is seized by a great rage about a brother of the prince being preferred over him for the post of a minister. (Cf. ibid.)

8. The prince of Wei listens only in standing to the report of the court *literatus,* a disciple of Confucius (loc. cit.; cf. preceding note).

9. Cf. the statements of Tschepe, "Histoire du Royaume de Tsin," p. 77.

10. The hereditary transmission of the ministerial position is considered ritually objectionable by the literati (Tschepe, loc. cit.). When the prince of Chao orders his minister to scrutinize and find some land suitable as fiefs for several worthy literati the minister thrice declares after having thrice been warned, that he has as yet not found any land worthy of them. Thereupon the prince finally understands and makes them officials. (Tschepe, "Histoire du Royaume de Han," pp. 54–5.)

11. Cf. the passage concerning the respective question by the King of U in Tschepe, "Histoire du Royaume de U," *Variétés Sinologiques* 10, Shanghai, 1891.

12. That income also was an end sought goes without saying, as the *Annals* show.

13. Once when a prince's concubine laughed at one of the literati, all the prince's literati went on strike until she was executed (Tschepe, "Histoire du Royaume de Han," loc. cit. p. 128).

14. The event reminds one of the "finding" of the sacred law under Josiah with the Jews. The contemporary great annalist, Se ma tsien, does not mention the find.

15. Tschepe, "Histoire du Royaume de Tsin," loc. cit. p. 53.

16. Individual concealments are confirmed (for instance, the attack of the state U upon its own state Lu). For the rest, in view of the scantiness of the material, one may seriously raise the question as to whether one should not rather consider the great, strongly moralizing commentary to the *Annals* as his work.

17. In 1900 the Empress-Dowager still took very unfavorable notice of a censor's request to abolish them. Cf. the rescripts in the *Peking Gazette* concerning the "orthodox army" (10 January 1899), concerning the "review" during the Japanese war (21 December 1894), concerning the importance of military ranks (1 and 10 November 1898), and from an earlier period, e.g. (23 May 1878).

18. Concerning this practice cf. Etienne Zi (S.J.), "Pratique des Examens Militaires en Chine," *Variétés Sinologiques,* no. 9. Subjects for examination were archery and certain gymnastic feats of strength; and, formerly, the writing of a dissertation; since 1807, however, the writing of a section of one hundred characters from the U-King (theory of war), allegedly dated from the time of the Chou dynasty, was required. A great many officers did not acquire degrees and the Manchus were freed from taking them altogether.

19. A *Taotai* (prefect) for his military merits had been taken over from the officers' ranks into the civil administration. In response to a complaint an Imperial rescript (*Peking Gazette,* 17 September 1894) comments as follows: although the officer's conduct in the matter in question has substantively been found free from fault, he nevertheless has shown his "rough soldierly manners" by his conduct, "and we have to ask ourselves whether he possesses the cultivated manners which for a person of his rank and position must appear indispensable." Therefore it is recommended that he resume a military position.

The abolition of age-old archery and of other very old sports as elements of "military" training was made almost impossible by the rites, which in their beginnings probably were still connected with the "bachelor house." Thus the Empress, when rejecting the reform proposals, makes reference to these rites.

20. The French authors for the most part designate *seng yuen, siu tsai* by "baccalaureate" [bachelor's degree], *kiu jin* by "licentiate" [master's degree], *tien se* by "doctorate." The lowest degree gave a claim to a stipend only to the top graduates. The bachelors who had received a stipend were called *lin cheng* (magazine prebendaries), bachelors selected by the director and sent to Peking were called *pao kong,* those among them who were admitted to the college *yu kong,* and those who had acquired the bachelor degree by purchase were called *kien cheng.*

21. The charismatic qualities of the descendant simply were proof for those of his sib, hence of the forebears. At the time, Chi Hwang-Ti had abolished this custom, as the son was not to judge the father. But since then almost every founder of a new dynasty has bestowed ranks to his ancestors.

22. By the way, this is a rather certain symptom of its recent origin!

23. Cf. for this: Biot, *Essai sur l'histoire de l'instruction publique en Chine et de la corporation des Lettres* (Paris, 1847). (It is still useful.)

24. Complaints at Ma Tuan Lin, translated in Biot, p. 481.

25. Themes for them are given by Williams, cf. Zi, loc. cit.

26. This held especially for the examinations for the master's degree, where the theme of the dissertation often called for an erudite, philological, literary, and historical analysis of the respective classical text. Cf. the example given by Zi, loc. cit. p. 144.

27. This held especially for the highest degree ("doctorate") for which the emperor, often in person, gave the themes and for which he classified the graduates. Questions of administrative expediency, preferably connected with one of the "six questions"

of Emperor Tang, were customary topics. (Cf. Biot, p. 209, note 1, and Zi, loc. cit. p. 209, note 1.)

28. *Siao Hio*, ed. de Harlez, v, 11, 1, 29, 40. Cf. the quotation from Chu Tse, ibid. p. 46. Concerning the question of generations, cf. 1, 13.

29. Loc. cit. 1, 25, furthermore 2. Introduction No.5f.

30. There were literary prescriptions also for this.

31. It need hardly be mentioned that what is here said about language and script reproduces exclusively what such eminent sinologists, as especially the late W. Grube, teach the layman. It does not result from the author's own studies.

32. J. Edkins, 'Local Values in Chinese Arithmetical Notation,' *Journal of the Peking Oriental Society*, 1, no. 4, pp. 161f. The Chinese abacus used the (decimal) positional value. The older positional system which has fallen into oblivion seems to be of Babylonian origin.

33. de Harlez, *Siao Hio*, p. 42, note 3.

34. Also, Timkovski, *Reise durch China* (1820–21), *German by Schmid* (Leipzig, 1825), emphasizes this.

35. For such a self-impeachment of a frontier officer who had been inattentive, see No. 567 of Aurel Stein's documents, edited by E. de Chavannes. It dates from the Han period, hence long before the introduction of examinations.

36. The beginnings of the present *Peking Gazette* go back to the time of the second ruler of the Tang dynasty (618–907).

37. Actually one finds in the *Peking Gazette*, with reference to the reports partly of censors, partly of superiors, laudations and promotions (or the promise of such) for deserving officials, demotions of insufficiently qualified officials for other offices ("that he may gather experiences," loc. cit. 31 December, 1897 and many other issues), suspension from office with half pay, expulsion of totally unqualified officials, or the statement that the good services of an official are balanced by faults which he would have to remedy before further promotion. Almost always detailed reasons are given. Such announcements were especially frequent at the end of the year but there was also a great volume at other times. There are also to be found posthumous sentences to be whipped for (obviously) posthumously demoted officials. (*Peking Gazette*, 26 May 1895.)

38. Cf. A. H. Smith, *Village Life in China* (Edinburgh, 1899), p. 78.

39. For the following see Kun Yu, *Discours des Royaumes, Annales Nationales des Etats Chinoises de X au V siècles*, ed. de Harlez [London, 1895], pp. 54, 75, 89, 159, 189, and elsewhere.

40. Tschepe, *Variétés Sinologiques*, 27, p. 38. He *begs* to be punished. Similarly in A. Stein's documents, loc. cit. no. 567.

41. See, however, the rescript in the *Peking Gazette* of 10 April 1895, by which promotions were posthumously given to officers who chose death after the surrender of Wei-hai-wei (obviously because they took the guilt upon themselves and thus prevented the compromise of the Emperor's charisma by the disgrace).

42. There was, however, at least in one district, also a temple of *Tai Ki*, the primary matter (chaos), from which the two substances are said to have developed by division ('Schih Luh Kuoh Kiang Yuh Tschi,' translated by Michels, p. 39).

43. According to de Groot.

44. Cf. the excerpts translated from his memoirs by Gräfin Hagen (Berlin, 1915), pp. 27, 29, 33.

45. Cf. the elegant and ingenious, though quite shallow, notes of Cheng Ki Tong, which were intended for Europeans. (*China und die Chinesen*, German by A. Schultze [Dresden und Leipzig, 1896], p. 158.) Concerning Chinese conversation, there are some observations which well agree with what has been said above in Hermann A. Keyserling, *The Travel Diary of a Philosopher*, trans. by J. Holroyd Reece (New York, 1925).

46. *Siao Hioe* (trans. by de Harlez, *Annales du Musée, Guimet* xv, 1889) is the work of Chou Hi (twelfth century A.D.). His most essential achievement was the definitive canonization of Confucianism in the systematic form he gave to it. For Chou Hi cf. Gall, 'Le Philosophe Tchou Hi, sa doctrine etc.,' *Variétés Sinologiques,* 6 (Shanghai, 1894). It is essentially a popular commentary to the *Li Ki,* making use of historical examples. In China every grade school pupil was familiar with it.

47. The number of "masters" was allocated to the provinces. If an emergency loan was issued—even after the Taiping rebellion—higher quotas were promised occasionally to the provinces for the raising of certain minimum sums. At every examination only ten "doctors" were allowed to graduate, the first three of whom enjoyed an especially high prestige.

48. The paramount position of personal patronage is illustrated by the comparison between the extraction of the three highest graduates and that of the highest mandarins as given by Zi, loc. cit. Appendix II, p. 221, note 1. Disregarding the fact that of the 748 high official positions, occupied from 1646 to 1914, 398 were occupied by Manchus although but three of them were among the highest graduates (the three *tien she* put in the first place by the Emperor), the province of Honan procured 58, that is, one sixth of all high officials, solely by virtue of the powerful position of the Tseng family, whereas almost two thirds of the highest graduates stemmed from other provinces which altogether had a share of only 30 percent in these offices.

49. This means was first systematically used by the Ming Emperors in 1453. (But, as a financial measure, it is to be found even under Chi Hwang-Ti.) The lowest degree originally cost 108 piasters, equal to the capitalized value of the study prebends, then it cost 60 taëls. After an inundation of the Hoang-ho, the price had been reduced to about 20 to 30 taëls in order to expand the market and thereby procure ample funds. Since 1693 the purchasers of the bachelor's degree were also admitted to the higher examinations. A *Taotai* position with all secondary expenses cost about 40,000 taëls.

50. That is why the emperors under certain conditions when placing the candidates took into consideration whether or not the candidate belonged to a province which as yet had no graduate who had been put in first place.

51. Se Ma Tsien's treatise on the balance of trade *(ping shoan)* (no. 8, chap. 30, in vol. III of Chavannes' edition) represents a rather good example of Chinese camerialism. It is also the oldest document of Chinese economics that has been preserved. Topics which in our view do not belong to the "balance of trade" are: big trading profits during the period of the Warring States, degradation of the merchants in the unified empire, exclusion from office, fixation of salaries and, in accordance with them, fixation of land taxes, taxes of commerce, forest, water (appropriated by the "great families"), the question of private monetization, the danger of too large an enrichment of private persons (but: where there is wealth there is *virtue,* which is quite Confucian in thought), costs of transport, purchases of titles, monopolies of salt and iron, registering of merchants, internal tariffs, policies of price stabilization, struggles against commissions being given to wholesale purveyors to the state instead of direct commissions being given the artisans. The objective of this cameralist financial policy was internal order through stability, and not a favorable balance of foreign trade.

52. The Ko Hong merchants' monopoly of the trade of Canton harbor, the only one opened to foreigners, existed until 1892 and had been set up in order to choke any intercourse of the Barbarians with the Chinese. The enormous profits which this monopoly yielded caused the concerned office prebendaries to be disinclined to any voluntary change in this condition.

53. Not only the official Ming history (cf. the following note) is full of this but so is the "Chi li kuo kiang yu chi" (*Histoire géographique des XVI Royaumes,* ed. Michels, [Paris, 1891]). Thus, in 1368 the harem is excluded from affairs of state at the request of the Hanlin Academy (p. 7); in 1498 representation of the Hanlin

Academy at the occasion of the palace fire and the demand (typical for accidents) to "speak freely" against the favorite eunuch (cf. following note).

54. Numerous cases illustrating this struggle are to be found, for instance in the "Yu tsiuan tung kien kang mu" [*Ming History of Emperor Kien Lung*], trans. by Delamarre (Paris, 1865). Consider the fifteenth century: in 1404 a eunuch is at the head of the army (p. 155). Since then this occurs repeatedly; thus, in 1428 (p. 223). Hence, the intrusion of palace officials into the administration in 1409 (p. 168). In 1443 a Hanlin doctor demands the abolition of cabinet rule, a reduction of the *corvée,* and above all, council meetings of the Emperor, with the literati. A eunuch kills him (p. 254). In 1449 the favorite eunuch is killed at the request of the literati (p. 273), in 1457, however, temples are established in his honor.

In 1471 the counselors have to communicate with the Emperor through the eunuch (p. 374). The very same is reported by Hiao Kong (361–28 B.C.). In 1472 we meet eunuchs as secret policemen (p. 273), which in 1481 is abolished at the request of the censors (p. 289). In 1488 the old ritual is restored (the same occurs in numerous instances).

The removal of a eunuch in 1418 took an awkward course for the literati when the list was found on the eunuch of the literati who had bribed him. The literati were successful in having the list secreted and in seeing to it that a different pretext was found for the removal of the literati who had done the bribing (ibid. p. 422).

55. Cf. E. Backhouse and J. O. P. Bland, *China under the Empress Dowager* (Heinemann, 1910) and, against this, the famous memorial of Tao Mo from the year 1901.

56. When in 1441 a sun eclipse predicted by the astrologers failed to occur, the Board of Rites congratulated him—but the Emperor rejected this.

57. See the (previously cited) memorial, 1878, of the Hanlin Academy to the Empress.

58. Loc. cit. chap. 9, pp. 130 f.

59. See the decree of the Empress of February 1901.

60. Loc. cit. p. 457.

61. For instance, "Yu tsiuan kien kang mu" of Emperor Kien Lung (loc. cit. pp. 167, 223), 1409 and 1428. An edict forbidding in a similar manner interference in the administration was given the military even in 1388 (ibid.).

Chapter 18: The Origins of Modern Capitalism

1. The principal supporters of the slave trade were originally the Arabs, who have maintained their position to the present in Africa. In the middle ages the Jews and the Genoese divided the business; they were followed by the Portuguese, the French, and finally the English.

Chapter 20: The Dualism of In-Group and Out-Group Morality

1. Jud. 13:4 appears to suggest that the prohibition of eating "unclean things" originally held for laymen only by virtue of a vow.

2. Correct Jews in general did not, due to dietary rules, hesitate to extend hospitality to non-Jews, but on their part declined that of the pagans and Christians. The Frankish Synods declaimed against this as against a humiliation of the Christians and in their turn exhort the Christians to decline Jewish hospitality.

Chapter 24: Formal and Substantive Rationalization in Law

1. *Ius honorarium*—The law created by the praetor in addition to, or in modification of, the *ius civile* as contained in the formal *leges* or in ancient tradition.

2. Legal procedure, civil or criminal, is said to be inquisitorial when the ascertainment of the facts is regarded primarily as the task of the judge, while in the so-called adversary procedure the true facts are expected to emerge from the allegations and proofs of the parties without the active cooperation of the judge. A shift from the predominantly adversary procedure of the Germanic laws was initiated in the later Middle Ages by the Church, whose model became influential for procedural development through Western Europe.

3. On the Roman distinction between *ius* and *fas* see Jolowicz, *op. cit.* 86 *et seq.*; Mitteis 22–30 and literature there listed. For a baroque use of the terms, see Blackstone III, 2.

4. Namely, of continental Europe, i.e., the procedure which was common on the Continent before the reforms introduced by the codification of the nineteenth and twentieth centuries. In this and the following sentences Weber speaks also, however, of the continental procedure of the present day, which, as will appear, is not basically different from Anglo-American procedure.

5. Weber has anticipated the procedural reforms of the modern totalitarian states which have shown marked tendencies to strengthen the inquisitorial at the expense of the adversary principle. Cf. M. Ploscowe, *Purging Italian Criminal Justice of Fascism* (1945), 45 Col. L. Rev. 240; Berman, Justice in Russia 207; Eberhard Schmidt, *Einführrung in die Geschichte der Deutschen Strafrechtspflege* (1947) 406; also Schoenke, *Zivilprozessrecht* (6th ed. 1949) 25; H. Schroeder, *Die Herrschaft der Parteien im Zivilprozess* (1943), 16 *Annuario di Diritto Comparato* 168.

6. Apparently, Weber is thinking here of the democracy of the Athenian rather than of the modern Western type.

7. Famous case in which Frederick tried to intervene in a private lawsuit.

In 1779, upon suit by his landlord, a baron, Arnold, a humble miller, was ejected because of nonpayment of rent. Arnold turned to the king who ordered the court to vacate its judgment and restore Arnold to the possession of the mill. The judges refused to render a decision "which would be against the law." When they continued in their "obstinate" refusal to obey the king's angrily repeated command, he ordered the supreme court to sentence them to jail. When the supreme court judges declared that the law would not permit such a step, they, together with the judges of the lower court, were ordered to be arrested by the king and were sentenced by him to one year's imprisonment, loss of office, and payment of damages to Arnold. It was one of the first acts of government of Frederick's successor, Frederick William II, to comply with the demand of the public to rehabilitate the judges and to indemnify them out of the public treasury. See W. Jellinek, *Verwaltungsrecht* 85 and literature cited there; for an account in English, see the translation by I. Husik of R. *Stammler, The Theory of Justice* (1925) 243 *et seq.*

8. Cf. A. Mendelssohn-Bartholdy, *Imperium des Richters* (1908). The allusion points to the early period when Rome was dominated by the patricians, who entirely dominated the administration of justice, until their power was broken in the long struggle of the plebeians. Cf. Mommsen, *History of Rome* (Dickson's tr. 1900) 341–369; Jolowicz 7–12.

9. In their struggle against patrician domination the plebeians achieved one of their most important successes when they compelled the patricians to consent to the appointment of a commission to write down the laws and thus to make their knowledge generally accessible. The product of the commission's work was the law of the Twelve Tables, which is reported by Livy (III, 9 *et seq.*) to have been promulgated in 450/449 B.C. and which for centuries was taken as the basis of the Roman *ius civile.*

10. In the fifteenth and sixteenth centuries the laws were collected and "reformed" in numerous German cities. On these "Stadtrechte," see Gierke, *Privatrecht* 63; Stobbe I, 488; II, 3; also Brunner, *Grundzüge der deutschen Rechtsgeschichte* (5th ed. 1912) 270. On one of the most important city laws of this kind, the Frankfurter

Reformation, see Coing, *Die Rezeption des römischen Rechts in Frankfurt am Main* (1939) 141.

Chapter 25: The Formal Qualities of Modern Law

1. These transactions, which are enumerated in Sec. 1 of the German Commercial Code of 1861/97, are the following:

(a) purchase and resale of commodities or securities such as bonds; (b) enterprise by an independent contractor to do work on materials or goods supplied by the other party; (c) underwriting of insurance; (d) banking; (e) transportation of goods or passengers, on land, at sea, and on inland waterways; (f) transactions of factors, brokers, forwarding agents, and warehousemen; (g) transactions of commercial brokers, jobbers, and agents; (h) transactions of publishers, book and art dealers; (i) transactions of printers.

2. The German Commercial Code, in Sec. 2, has the following definition: "Any enterprise which requires an established business because of its size or because of the manner in which it is carried on, is a commercial enterprise, even though it does not fall within any of the categories stated in Sec. 1." Similarly, the French Commercial Code of 1807 states in Art. I: "Merchants are all those who carry on commercial transactions and make this activity their habit and profession."

3. The most important special law of this kind is the labor law with its special hierarchy of labor courts. There are, furthermore, the administrative tribunals of general administrative jurisdiction and a set of special tribunals dealing respectively with claims arising under the social security laws or the war pensions laws, with tax matters, with certain matters of agricultural administration, etc.

4. Both the commercial and the labor courts are usually organized in panels chosen from those lines of business or industry whose affairs are dealt with by the particular division of the court. Cf. Arbeitsgerichtsgesetz of 23 December, 1926 (R.G. Bl. 1, 507), Sec. 17.

5. In the labor courts representation by attorneys is, as a general rule, not permitted at the trial stage (Arbeitsgerichtsgesetz of 23 December, 1926 [R.G. Bl. 1, 507], Sec. 11).

6. Roman-canonical procedure, as it had come to be adopted generally in the continental courts, was characterized by its system of "formal proof," which was in many respects similar to the law of evidence of Anglo-American procedure. There were rules about exclusion of certain kinds of evidence and, quite particularly, detailed rules about corroboration and about the mechanical ways in which the judge had to evaluate conflicting evidence. The testimony of two credible witnesses constituted full proof *(probatio plena);* one credible witness made half proof *(probatio semiplena),* but one doubtful witness *(testis suspectus)* made less than half proof *(probatio semiplena minor),* etc.

This entire system of formal proof was swept away by the procedural reforms of the nineteenth century and replaced by the system of free or rational proof, which did away with most of the exclusionary rules, released the judge from his arithmetical shackles, and authorized him to evaluate the evidence in the light of experience and reason. Cf. Engelmann-Millar 39.

7. Together with the rule of stare decisis and, to some extent, the jury system, the fact that the Common Law has preserved a much more formalistic law of evidence is the principal cause why in such fields as torts, damages, interpretation and construction of legal instruments, English and American law have developed so much more numerous and detailed rules of law than the systems of the Civil Law. The comparison, for instance, of the 951 sections of the Restatement of Torts and the 31 sections dealing with torts in the German Civil Code (Secs. 823–853) or the 5 sections of the French Code (Arts. 1382–86) is revealing in this respect, just as is the comparison of

the few sections of the German Code dealing with the interpretation of wills (Secs. 2087 *et seq.*) with the elaborate treatment of the topic in American law.

As to the law of evidence itself, compare the ten volumes of Wigmore's treatise (3rd ed. 1940) with the complete absence of books on evidence in Germany or the brief treatment of a few evidentiary problems in the French treatises on private law, for instance, in Josserand's *Cours de Droit Civil Positif Français* (1939), where the chapter on "preuves" covers 43 pages.

8. For illustrations of this judicial attitude see the case surveys given in connection with Sec. 242 of the German Civil Code (good faith and fair dealing) or Sec. 346 of the Commercial Code ("good" custom of trade) in the annotated editions of these Codes. The dangers of excessive judicial resort to legal provisions referring the judge to such indefinite standards have been pointed out by Hedemann, *Die Flucht in die Generalklauseln, Eine Gefahr für Recht und Staat* (1933).

9. The German Supreme Court has consistently maintained, however, that a usage is not to be considered when it is unfair, and especially when it constitutes a gross abuse of a position of economic power; see, for instance, 114 *Entscheidungen des Reichsgerichts in Zivilsachen* 97; [1922] *Juristische Wochenschrift* 488; [1932] o.c. 586.

10. The possibilities of such discrepancies have been pointed out especially in the writings of Heck and other advocates of the "jurisprudence of interests." See in this respect *The Jurisprudence of Interests,* vol. 2 of this 20th Century Legal Philosophy Series.

11. Such was the decision of the German Supreme Court in 29 *Entscheidungen des Reichsgerichts in Strafsachen* 111 and 32 o.c. 165. In Sec. 242 of the German Criminal Code larceny is defined as the unlawful taking of a chattel. Electric power is not a chattel; hence it cannot be the subject matter of larceny. The gap in the law was filled by the enactment of a Special Law Concerning the Unlawful Taking of Electric Power, of 9 April 1900 (R.G. Bl. 1900, 228). The decisions just mentioned have become the stock "horrible" in modern German excoriations of conceptual jurisprudence.

12. In the years preceding the First World War, the English administration of justice and, particularly, the creative role and prominent position of the English "judicial kings" *(Richterkönige)* were highly praised and advocated for adoption, particularly by A. Mendelssohn-Bartholdy, *Imperium des Richters* (1908), and F. Adickes, *Grundlinien einer durchgreifenden Justizreform* (1906).

13. *Das Problem des Natürlichen Rechts* (1912).

14. *Naturrecht.* [Weber's note.]

15. *Natürliches Recht.* [Weber's note.]

16. Expression of G. *Jellinek, in Die sozial-ethische Bedeutung von Recht, Unrecht und Strafe* (2nd ed. 1908).

17. On Gierke as the leading legal scholar in the movement for law as an expression of "social justice," see G. Böhmer, *Grundlagen der Bürgerlichen Rechtsordnung* (1951) II, 155; see, especially, Gierke's lecture on *The Social Task of Private Law* (*Die soziale Aufgabe des Privatrechts,* 1899), repr. E. Wolf, *Deutsches Rechtsdenken* (1948).

18. On the development of the doctrine of economic duress in positive German law, see J. Dawson, *Economic Duress and the Fair Exchange in French and German Law* (1937), 12 *Tulane L. Rev.* 42.

19. In Sec. 138 the German Civil Code provides as follows:

"A legal transaction which violates good morals is void.

"Void, in particular, is any transaction in which one party, by exploiting the emergency situation, the imprudence, or the inexperience of another causes such other person to promise or to give to him or to a third person a pecuniary benefit which so transcends the value of his own performance that under the circumstances of the case the relationship between them appears as manifestly disproportionate."

20. The School of Free Law *(Freirecht)* constitutes the German counterpart of American and Scandinavian "realism." The basic theoretical idea of these three schools, viz., that law is not "found" by the judges but "made" by them, was anticipated in 1885 by Oskar Bülow in his *Gesetz und Richteramt.* The first attack upon the Pandectist "Konstruktionsjurisprudenz" (conceptual jurisprudence) or, in Weber's terminology, rational formalism, was made in 1848 by v. Kirchmann in his sensational pamphlet *Über die Wertlosigkeit der Jurisprudenz als Wissenschaft.* The attack was later joined by no less a scholar than Jhering, who until then had been one of the most prominent expounders of the traditional method, but who now came to emphasize the role of the law as a means to obtain utilitarian ends in a way which would now be called "social engineering" or, in Weber's terms, "substantive rationality" (*Der Zweck im Recht,* 1877/83; Husik's tr. s.t. *Law as a Means to an End,* 1913) and to ridicule legal conceptualism in his *Scherz und Ernst in der Jurisprudenz* (1855; on Jhering see Stone 299). At the turn of the century the attack was intensified and combined with the postulates that the courts should shake off the technique of conceptual jurisprudence (i.e., in Weber's terminology, the technique of rational formalism), should give up the fiction of the gaplessness of the legal order, should thus treat statutes and codes as ordaining nothing beyond the narrowest meaning of the words of the text, and should fill in the gaps thus created, i.e., in the great mass of problems, in a process of free, "kingly" creativeness. The leaders of this movement were E. Fuchs, a practicing attorney (principal works: *Die Gemeinschädlichkeit der Konstruktiven Jurisprudenz* ["The Dangers of the Conceptual Jurisprudence to the Common Weal," 1909]; *Was Will die Freirechtsschule?* ["What Are the Aims of the School of Free Law?" 1929]). Professor H. Kantorowicz (writing under the pen name of Gnaeus Flavius: *Der Kampf um die Rechtswissenschaft* [1908]; *Aus der Vorgeschichte der Freirechtslehre* [1925]; see also the article by him and E. Patterson, *Legal Science—a Summary of its Methodology* [1928], 28 Col. L. Rev. 679, and *Some Rationalizations about Realism* [1934], 43 Yale L.J., 1240, where Kantorowicz recedes from some of his earlier theses), and the judge J. G. Gmelin (*Quousque? Beitrag zur soziologischen Rechtsfindung* [1910, Bruncken's transl. in Modern Legal Philosophy Series, IX, *Science of Legal Method* (1917)]). These passionate radicals were joined by E. Ehrlich, who provided for the new movement a broad historical and sociological basis (*Freie Rechtsfindung und freie Rechtswissenschaft* [1903, Bruncken's transl. in Modern Legal Philosophy Series, IX, *Science of Legal Method* (1917), 47]; *Die juristische Logik* [1918], 115 *Archiv für die civilistische Praxis,* nos. 2 and 3, repr. as a book in 1925; and his *Grundlegung der Soziologie des Rechts* [1913], Moll's transl. s.t. *Fundamental Principles of the Sociology of Law* [1936]).

The movement stirred up violent discussion (see especially H. Reichel, Gesetz und Richterspruch [1915]; G. Böhmer, *Grundlagen der bürgerlichen Rechtsordnung* [1951], II, 158) and also found some attention in the United States. (See the translations listed above in this note.) Its exaggerations were generally repudiated, however, and actual developments came to be more effectively influenced by the ideas of the so-called school of jurisprudence of interests, whose principal writings are collected in vol. II of this 20th Century Legal Philosophy Series, entitled *The Jurisprudence of Interests* (1948). The method was elaborated primarily by M. Rümelin, P. Heck, and their companions at Tübingen, and by R. Müller-Erzbach, who has been working at the elaboration of social and concrete bases for that "balancing of interests" which the method requires (see especially *Das private Recht der Mitgliedschaft als Prüfstein eines kausalen Rechtsdenkens* [1948] and *Die Rechtswissenschaft im Umbau* [1950]). The Jurisprudence of Interests is close to Roscoe Pound's sociological jurisprudence. It aims at replacing the system of formally rational with one of substantively rational concepts, and it has come to establish itself firmly in German legal practice (for a concise survey and evaluation see Böhmer, *op. cit.* 190, and, very brief, W. Friedmann, *Legal Theory* [2nd ed. 1949] 225; no complete survey is as yet available in English).

21. The following passages in Weber's text are concerned with the School of Free Law.

"The law must be applied in all cases which come within the letter or the spirit of its provisions.

"Where no provision is applicable, the judge shall decide according to the existing customary law and, in default thereof, according to the rule which he would lay down if he had himself to act as legislator.

"Herein he must be guided by tested doctrine and tradition."

22. Cf. I. Williams, *The Sources of Law in the Swiss Civil Code* (1923) 34; see also the discussion of this provision and the similarly worded Sec. 1 of the Civil Code of the Russian Federal Soviet Socialist Republic by V. E. Greaves, *Social-economic Purpose of Private Rights* (1934/5, 12 N.Y.U.L.Q. Rev. 165, 430).

23. Cf. H. Isay, *Rechtsnorm und Entscheidung* (1929).

24. Cf. Ehrlich, esp. chapters 5 and 6.

25. *Praeter legem*—alongside the (statute) law; *contra legem*—in contradiction to the (statute) law.

26. So especially Lambert, *op. cit.* (1903); Ehrlich.

27. In the last two sentences of the text three different phenomena are brought together in a way which indicates the possibility that some connecting part has been omitted. The postulate that in statutory interpretation the judge has to look upon the text "objectively" as a self-sufficient entity and that he should not, or that he is not even allowed to, inquire into the intentions of the legislature has not been confined to Germany. It has long been the established method of statutory interpretation in England and for a considerable time it was dominant in the United States. In Germany its principal representatives were A. Wach (*Handbuch des Zivilprozesses* [1885]) and K. Binding (*Handbuch des Strafrechts* [1885]); see also J. Kohler, *Über die Interpretation von Gesetzen* (1886), 13 *Grünhut's Zeitschrift 1*. The Theory has had some influence on the German courts but could not prevent them in the long run from paying careful attention to parliamentary hearings and other legislative materials.

The idea that statutes ought to be interpreted narrowly so as to leave free reign to free judicial law creation in the interstices constituted one of the postulates of the School of Free Law (see *supra* n. 20).

The phrase that the solution of certain problems be left to "legal science and doctrine" recurs constantly in the report *(Motive)* accompanying the Draft of the German Civil Code. The draftsmen used it whenever they felt that too much detail would be detrimental to the purposes of the codification. It is difficult to see what it might have to do with the Free Law tenet stated in the following sentence of the text.

28. Especially Victor Cathrein, Recht, Naturrecht und positives Recht (2nd ed. 1909); v. Hertling, *Recht, Staat und Gesellschaft* (4th ed. 1917); Mausbache, *Naturrecht und Völkerrecht* (1918); more recently H. Rommen, *Die ewige Wiederkehr des Naturrechts* (1936; Hanley's transl. s.t. *The Natural Law,* 1948), and the survey of the latest Catholic literature by I. Zeiger in (1952) 149 *Stimmen der Zeit* 468.

29. On Neo-Kantianism, see Friedmann, *op. cit.* 91; the principal representative is R. Stammler, whose *Lehre von dem richtigen Recht* (1902) has been translated by Husik s.t. *The Theory of Justice* (1925). For a trenchant criticism, see E. Kaufmann, *Kritik der neukantischen Rechtsphilosophie* (1921).

30. The reference is to the continuation and elaboration of Jhering's ideas through the school of jurisprudence of interests; see *supra,* n. 20.

31. On French legal theory, see vol. 7 of the Modern Legal Philosophy Series: *Modern French Legal Philosophy* (1916) containing writings by A. Fouillée, J. Charmont, L. Duguit, and R. Demogue. A comprehensive, critical history is presented by J. Bonnecase, *La pensée juridique française de 1804 à l'heure présente* (1933). Cf.

also in the 20th Century Legal Philosophy Series, vol. 4, *The Legal Philosophies of Lask, Radbruch, and Dabin* (1950) 227; and, for latest trends, B. Horváth, *Social Value and Reality in Current French Legal Thought* (1952), 1 *Am. J. of Compar. Law* 243.

The principal representatives of the trends mentioned by Weber are François Gény, the founder of the French counterpart to the jurisprudence of interests (*Methode d'interprétation* [1899]; cf. his article in Modern Legal Philosophy Series, vol. IX, *Science of Legal Method* [1917] 498); the sociological jurists Edouard Lambert *(op. cit.)*, Léon Duguit (*Le droit social, le droit individuel, et la transformation de l'état* [1910]; *L'etat, le droit objectif et la loi positive* [1901]; *Les transformations générales du droit privé* [1912], trans.l. in Continental Legal History Series, vol. XI, s.t. *The Progress of Continental Law in the 19th Century* [1918]; *Les transformations du droit public* [1913], transl. by Laski s.t. *Law in the Modern State* [1919]), and Raymond Saleilles (*Methode et codification* [1903]; *Le code civil et la méthode historique* in *Livre du centenaire du code civil* [1904]).

32. Apparently Weber was not conversant with recent common law use of the concept of title. In the classical form of the law of real property, it is true, the various ways in which one might be entitled to the use and disposition of a piece of land were defined by the various tenures, estates, and other rights in land which had come to be recognized in the royal courts of law and equity. There did not exist, however, any term which comprehensively covered, like the Roman term *dominium*, the fullness of all rights, privileges, powers, and immunities, which can possibly exist in a piece of land. But in modern usage the terms title, fee, or fee title, are generally used in exactly this sense, especially in the United States.

33. *Das Imperium des Richters* (1908).

34. Written before the abolition of the jury in Germany by the Law of 1924.

35. This passage was written before the Revolution of 1918, which resulted in the admission of women both to professional judicial office and to membership in the lay part of the mixed bench of the criminal, labor, commercial, and administrative courts. At present the percentage of women in the German judiciary, including the Supreme Court, is probably higher than in any other Western country.

36. Weber's judgment on the inferior role of the lay members of the mixed bench is by no means shared generally in Germany, Sweden, the U.S.S.R., or those other countries in which the system has been adopted. For an objective effort at evaluating the merit of the system of the mixed bench, see R. C. K. Ensor, *Courts and Judges in France, Germany, and England* (1933) 68.

Chapter 26: Definition of Sociology

1. In this series of definitions Weber employs several important terms which need discussion. In addition to *Verstehen*, which has already been commented upon, there are four important ones: *Deuten, Sinn, Handeln,* and *Verhalten*. *Deuten* has generally been translated as 'interpret.' As used by Weber in this context it refers to the interpretation of subjective states of mind and the meanings which can be imputed as intended by an actor. Any other meaning of the word "interpretation" is irrelevant to Weber's discussion. The term *Sinn* has generally been translated as "meaning"; and its variations, particularly the corresponding adjectives, *sinnhaft, sinnvoll, sinnfremd,* have been dealt with by appropriately modifying the term meaning. The reference here again is always to features of the content of subjective states of mind or of symbolic systems which are ultimately referable to such states of mind.

The terms *Handeln* and *Verhalten* are directly related. *Verhalten* is the broader term referring to any mode of behavior of human individuals, regardless of the frame of reference in terms of which it is analysed. "Behavior" has seemed to be the most appropriate English equivalent. *Handeln*, on the other hand, refers to the concrete phenomenon of human behavior only insofar as it is capable of "understanding," in Weber's technical sense, in terms of subjective categories. The most appropriate English equivalent has seemed to be "action." This corresponds to the editor's usage in *The Structure of Social Action* and would seem to be fairly well established. "Conduct" is also closely similar and has sometimes been used. *Deuten, Verstehen,* and *Sinn* are thus applicable to human behavior only insofar as it constitutes action or conduct in this specific sense.

Chapter 27: The Methodological Foundations of Sociology

1. Weber's text is organized in a somewhat unusual manner. He lays down certain fundamental definitions and then proceeds to comment upon them. The definitions themselves are in the original printed in large type, the subsidiary comments in smaller type. For the purposes of this translation it has not seemed best to make a distinction in type form, but the reader should be aware that the numbered paragraphs which follow a definition or group of them are in the nature of comments, rather than the continuous development of a general line of argument. This fact accounts for what is sometimes a relatively fragmentary character of the development and for the abrupt transition from one subject to another. Weber apparently did not intend this material to be "read" in the ordinary sense, but rather to serve as a reference work for the clarification and systematization of theoretical concepts and their implications. While the comments under most of the definitions are relatively brief, under the definitions of Sociology and of Social Action, Weber wrote what is essentially a methodological essay. This makes sec. 1 out of proportion to the other sections of this and the following chapters. It has, however, seemed best to retain Weber's own plan for the subdivision of the material.

2. Weber means by "pure type" what he himself generally called and what has come to be known in the literature about his methodology as the "ideal type." The reader may be referred for general orientation to Weber's own Essay (to which he himself refers below), *Die Objektivität sozialwissenschaftlicher Erkenntnis;* to two works of Dr. Alexander von Schelting, "Die logische Theorie der historischen Kulturwissenschaften von Max Weber" (*Archiv fuer Sozialwissenschaft,* vol. xlix), and *Max Webers Wissenschaftslehre;* and to the editor's *Structure of Social Action,* chap. xvi. A somewhat different interpretation is given in Theodore Abel, *Systematic Sociology in Germany,* chap. iv.

3. This is an imperfect rendering of the German term *Evidenz,* for which, unfortunately, there is no good English equivalent. It has hence been rendered in a number of different ways, varying with the particular context in which it occurs. The primary meaning refers to the basis on which a scientist or thinker becomes satisfied of the certainty or acceptability of a proposition. As Weber himself points out, there are two primary aspects of this. On the one hand a conclusion can be "seen" to follow from given premises by virtue of logical, mathematical, or possibly other modes of meaningful relation. In this sense one "sees" the solution of an arithmetical problem or the correctness of the proof of a geometrical theorem. The other aspect is concerned with empirical observation. If an act of observation is competently performed, in a similar sense one "sees" the truth of the relevant descriptive proposition. The term *Evidenz* does not refer to the process of observing, but to the quality of its result, by virtue of which the observer feels justified in affirming a given statement. Hence "certainty" has seemed a suitable translation in some contexts, "clarity" in others, "accuracy" in still others. The term "intuition" is not usable because it refers to the process rather than to the result.

4. The German term is *sinnfremd.* This should not be translated by "meaningless," but interpreted in the technical context of Weber's use of *Verstehen* and *Sinndeutung.* The essential criterion is the impossibility of placing the object in question in a complex of relations on the meaningful level.

5. Surely this passage states too narrow a conception of the scope of meaningful interpretation. It is certainly not *only* in terms such as those of the rational means-end schema, that it is possible to make action understandable in terms of subjective categories. This probably can actually be called a source of rationalistic bias in Weber's work. In practice he does not adhere at all rigorously to this methodological position.

6. A gulf of the North Sea which broke through the Netherlands coast, flooding an area.

7. Weber here uses the term *aktuelles Verstehen,* which he contrasts with *erklärendes Verstehen.* The latter he also refers to as *motivationsmaessig.* "Aktuell" in this context has been translated as "observational." It is clear from Weber's discussion that the primary criterion is the possibility of deriving the meaning of an act or symbolic expression from immediate observation without reference to any broader context. In *erklärendes Verstehen,* on the other hand, the particular act must be placed in a broader context of meaning involving facts which cannot be derived from immediate observation of a particular act or expression.

8. The German term is *Sinnzusammenhang.* It refers to a plurality of elements which form a coherent whole on the level of meaning. There are several possible modes of meaningful relation between such elements, such as logical consistency, the esthetic harmony of a style, or the appropriateness of means to an end. In any case, however, a *Sinnzusammenhang* must be distinguished from a system of elements which are causally interdependent. There seems to be no single English term or phrase which is always adequate. According to variations in the context, "context of meaning," "complex of meaning," and sometimes "meaningful system" have been employed.

9. On the significance of this type of explanation for causal relationship. See para. 6, below in the present section.

10. The German is *gemeinter Sinn.* Weber departs from ordinary usage not only in broadening the meaning of this conception. As he states at the end of the present methodological discussion, he does not restrict the use of this concept to cases where a clear self-conscious awareness of such meaning can be reasonably attributed to every individual actor. Essentially, what Weber is doing is to formulate an operational concept. The question is not whether in a sense obvious to the ordinary person such an intended meaning "really exists," but whether the concept is capable of providing a logical framework within which scientifically important observations can be made. The test of validity of the observations is not whether their object is immediately clear to common sense, but whether the results of these technical observations can be satisfactorily organized and related to those of others in a systematic body of knowledge.

11. The scientific functions of such construction have been discussed in the author's article in the *Archiv für Sozialwissenschaft,* vol. xix, pp. 64 ff.

12. Simmel, in his *Probleme der Geschichtsphilosophie,* gives a number of examples.

13. The above passage is an exceedingly compact statement of Weber's theory of the logical conditions of proof of causal relationship. He developed this most fully in his essay *Die Objektivität sozialwissenschaftlicher Erkenntnis,* Ch. 28, below. It is also discussed in certain of the other essays that have been collected in the volume, *Gesammelte Aufsätze zur Wissenschaftslehre.* The best and fullest secondary discussion is to be found in Von Schelting's book, *Max Webers Wissenschaftslehre.*

14. See Eduard Meyer, *Geschichte des Altertums,* Stuttgart, 1901, vol. iii, pp. 420, 444 ff.

15. The expression *sinnhafte Adäquanz* is one of the most difficult of Weber's technical terms to translate. In most places the cumbersome phrase "adequacy on the level of meaning" has had to be employed. It should be clear from the progress

of the discussion that what Weber refers to is a satisfying level of knowledge for the particular purposes of the subjective state of mind of the actor or actors. He is, however, careful to point out that *causal* adequacy involves in addition to this a satisfactory correspondence between the results of observations from the subjective point of view and from the objective; that is, observations of the overt course of action which can be described without reference to the state of mind of the actor.

16. This is the first occurrence in Weber's text of the term *Chance* which he uses very frequently. It is here translated by "probability," because he uses it as interchangeable with *Wahrscheinlichkeit*. As the term "probability" is used in a technical mathematical and statistical sense, however, it implies the possibility of numerical statement. In most of the cases where Weber uses *Chance* this is out of the question. It is, however, possible to speak in terms of higher and lower degrees of probability. To avoid confusion with the technical mathematical concept, the term "likelihood" will often be used in the translation. It is by means of this concept that Weber, in a highly ingenious way, has bridged the gap between the interpretation of meaning and the inevitably more complex facts of overt action.

17. By a negative normative pattern, Weber means one which prohibits certain possible modes of action.

18. A classical example is Schäffle's brilliant work, *Bau und Leben des sozialen Körpers*.

19. One of the most illuminating treatments of physiological problems from such a functional point of view, which is readily understandable to the layman, is W. B. Cannon: *The Wisdom of the Body*, second edition, 1938. The point of reference on this physiological level is not primarily survival value to the species in the sense of the Darwinian theory of evolution, but rather the maintenance of the individual organism as a "going concern" in carrying through its typical life cycle. What is the life cycle, is to the physiologist essentially a matter of empirical observation.

20. The term "reification" as used by Professor Morris Cohen in his book, *Reason and Nature*, seems to fit Weber's meaning exactly. A concept or system of concepts, which critical analysis can show to be abstract, is "reified" when it is used naively as though it provided an adequate total description of the concrete phenomenon in question. The fallacy of "reification" is virtually another name for what Professor Whitehead has called "the fallacy of misplaced concreteness." See his *Science and the Modern World*.

21. Compare the famous dictum of a well-known physiologist: "Sec. 10. The spleen. Of the spleen, gentlemen, we know nothing. So much for the spleen." Actually, of course, he "knew" a good deal about the spleen—its position, size, shape, etc.; but he could say nothing about its function, and it was his inability to do this that he called "ignorance."

22. The present state of anthropological research, which has advanced enormously since Weber wrote, would seem to throw considerable doubt on the validity of this statement. In making it, Weber apparently does not adequately take account of the fundamental fact that no nonhuman species has even a primitive form of language; whereas no human group is known without a "fully-developed" one. The ability to use language is on the one hand a fundamental index of the state of development of the individual himself, so far as it is relevant to the theory of action. On the other hand, language is perhaps the most crucially important source of evidence for subjective phenomena. What has seemed to so many "civilized" men to be the strangeness and incomprehensibility of the behavior and thought of primitive peoples, is apparently primarily a matter of the former's failure to submit the latter to an adequately thorough and rigorous investigation. It can be said with considerable confidence that a competently trained anthropological field worker is in a position to obtain a level of insight into the states of mind of a people whom he has carefully studied, which

is quite comparable, if not superior, to that of the historian of a civilization at all widely different from his own.

23. Since the term "charisma" was, in its sociological usage, introduced by Weber himself from a different field, no attempt has been made to find an English equivalent and it will be used directly throughout. Weber took it from the corresponding Greek which was used in the literature of early Christianity and means "the gift of grace." For further discussion of the concept, see above, Ch. 12.

24. It is desirable at this point to call attention to Weber's usage of the term "law" in a scientific sense. In conformity with his strong emphasis upon the role of ideal types among possible kinds of generalized concepts in the social sciences, by "law," or a German expression he frequently uses, *generelle Erfahrungsregel*, he usually means what is perhaps most conveniently called a "type generalization." It is not an empirical generalization in the ordinary sense in that it does not adequately describe any particular concrete course of events but is abstract in the same sense as the ideal type. Where it is possible on the basis of ideal type analysis to construct not merely a structural form, but, under certain conditions, a course of events which can be predicted if certain conditions are given, it is possible to formulate such generalizations. These generalizations are, however, not methodologically equivalent to most of the laws of physics, especially of analytical mechanics. The latter do not generally formulate a concrete course of events, but rather a uniform relationship between the values of two or more variables. Weber does not even consider the possibility of formulating laws of this latter type, essentially because he does not develop social theory explicitly in the direction of setting up a system of interdependent variables, but confines it to the ideal type level.

25. This is one of the most important problems with which Weber was concerned in his methodological studies. He insisted on the very great importance of the cultural significance of a problem for the values of the time in determining the direction of interest of the investigator. He formulated this relation in his important concept of the *Wertbeziehung* of social science concepts. But he went so far as to deny the legitimacy of the formulation of a generalized theoretical system as an aim of theoretical analysis in social science. This denial seems to rest on a failure on Weber's part to carry his criticism of certain aspects of German idealistic social thought through to its logical conclusion. For Weber's position, see below, Ch. 28 and the original text "Die Objektivitaet sozialwissenschaftlicher Erkenntnis"; also A. v. Schelting, *Max Weber's Wissenschaftslehre*. For a criticism of Weber's position, see T. Parsons, *The Structure of Social Action*.

Chapter 28: "Objectivity" in Social Science

1. We will use the term that is already occasionally used in the methodology of our discipline and that is now becoming widespread in a more precise formulation in logic.

Chapter 29: The Tension between Science and Policy-Making

1. Since not only the distinction between evaluation and value-relations but also the distinction between evaluation and value-interpretation (i.e., the elaboration of the various possible meaningful attitudes towards a given phenomena) is very often not clearly made and since the consequent ambiguities impede the analysis of the logical nature of history, I will refer the reader to the remarks in "Critical Studies in the Logic of the Cultural Sciences." These remarks are not, however, to be regarded as in any way conclusive.

ACKNOWLEDGMENTS

Every reasonable effort has been made to locate the owners of rights to previously published translations printed here. We gratefully acknowledge permission to reprint the following material:

From *Ancient Judaism,* translated by Hans Gerth and Don Martindale. Reprinted with the permission of The Free Press, a Division of Macmillan, Inc. Copyright © 1952 by The Free Press.

From *General Economic History,* translated by Frank H. Knight. Reprinted with the permission of The Free Press, a Division of Macmillan, Inc. Copyright © 1927 by The Free Press; reprinted 1950.

From *The Methodology of the Social Sciences,* translated and edited by Edward A. Shils and Henry A. Finch. Reprinted with the permission of The Free Press, a Division of Macmillan, Inc. Copyright © 1949 by The Free Press. renewed 1977 by Edward A. Shils.

From *The Theory of Social and Economic Organization,* translated by A. M. Henderson and Talcott Parsons. Reprinted with the permission of The Free Press, a Division of Macmillan, Inc. Copyright © 1947, renewed 1975 by Talcott Parsons.

From *From Max Weber: Essays in Sociology,* edited and translated by H. H. Gerth and C. Wright Mills. Copyright 1946 by Oxford University Press, Inc.; renewed 1973 by Hans H. Gerth. Reprinted by permission.

Reprinted by permission of the publishers from *Max Weber on Law in Economy and Society,* edited by Max Rheinstein, translated by Edward Shils and Max Rheinstein, Cambridge, Mass.: Harvard University Press, Copyright © 1954 by the President and Fellows of Harvard College, © 1982 by Edward Shils.

From *Sociology and Religion.* Copyright © 1963. English translation by Beacon Press. Reprinted by permission of Beacon Press.